# FIX-IT
*and*
# FORGET-IT™
## COOKBOOK
### Feasting with your Slow Cooker

# FIX-IT and FORGET-IT™

## COOKBOOK

### Feasting with your slow cooker

Dawn J. Ranck
Phyllis Pellman Good

Good Books

Intercourse, PA 17534

800/762-7171 • www.goodbks.com

Cover design and illustrations by Cheryl Benner
Design by Dawn J. Ranck

**FIX-IT AND FORGET-IT™ COOKBOOK: FEASTING WITH YOUR SLOW COOKER**
Copyright © 2000 by Good Books, Intercourse, PA 17534

Publishing History
Original Paperback Edition published 2000.
Hardcover Gift Edition published 2001.
Comb-bound Paperback Edition published 2001.

International Standard Book Number: 1-56148-317-6 (paperback edition)
International Standard Book Number: 1-56148-338-9 (hardcover gift edition)
International Standard Book Number: 1-56148-339-7 (comb-bound paperback edition)
Library of Congress Catalog Card Number: 00-052110

All rights reserved. Printed in the United States of America.
No part of this book may be reproduced in any manner,
except for brief quotations in critical articles or reviews, without permission.

**Library of Congress Cataloging-in-Publication Data**
Ranck, Dawn J.
    Fix-it and forget-it cookbook : feasting with your slow cooker / Dawn J. Ranck,
Phyllis Pellman Good.
    p.cm.
    Includes index.
    1. Electric cookery, Slow. I. Good, Phyllis Pellman II. Title.
TX827.R35 2000
641.5'884--dc21
                                            00-052110

# Table of Contents

# About This Cookbook

Slow Cookers have long ago proven to be the efficient friend of those cooks who are gone all day, but want to offer substantial home-cooked food to their households.

Slow Cookers have aged, but they haven't faded. Instead, they've shown themselves to be first-rate adaptable appliances. They handle dried beans famously well, pleasing the growing numbers of vegetarians. They do their job whatever their size—1-quart, 3-quart, 6-quart, or in between. Little ones work well for singles or doubles—or cook the vegetables while the beef stew burbles away in a bigger Cooker, sharing the counter-space.

And Slow Cookers are mobile tools. You can prepare a dish one evening, store the filled "lift-out" vessel in the frig overnight, and then place it into its electric holder in the morning as you do your dash to the door. Or you can tote the whole works to a buffet or carry-in meal, doing no damage to the quality of its contents.

Slow Cookers prefer cheap cuts of meat. Tell that to your favorite graduate student, or newly independent young adult, or to the parents of a growing brood.

The recipes in this collection are tried and true favorites from heavy-duty Cooker-users. We've weeded out a lot of duplicates and still have 800 plus for you to try. There's tempting variety among the recipes, and many that differ only by a tantalizing ingredient or two.

What's more, you'll find helpful Tips spread among the recipes—the kind of pointers that you usually learn only after a long acquaintance with a Slow Cooker. These Tips tell you how to maximize the usefulness of your Cooker, plus how to realize top flavor from the food you prepare in it.

May the *Fix-It and Forget-It Cookbook* help make your meal preparations less harried and your dinners more satisfying!

— *Dawn J. Ranck and Phyllis Pellman Good*

# Appetizers, Snacks, and Spreads

## Quick and Easy Nacho Dip

**Kristina Shull**
Timberville, VA

---

*Makes 10-15 servings*

1 lb. ground beef
dash of salt
dash of pepper
dash of onion powder
2 garlic cloves, minced,
  optional
2 16-oz. jars salsa (as hot
  *or* mild as you like)
15-oz. can refried beans
1½ cups sour cream
3 cups shredded cheddar
  cheese, divided
tortilla chips

1. Brown ground beef.
Drain. Add salt, pepper,
onion powder, and minced
garlic.
2. Combine beef, salsa,
beans, sour cream, and 2
cups cheese in slow cooker.

3. Cover. Heat on Low 2
hours. Just before serving
sprinkle with 1 cup cheese.
4. Serve with tortilla chips.

## Southwest Hot Chip Dip

**Annabelle Unternahrer**
Shipshewana, IN

---

*Makes 15-20 servings*

1 lb. ground beef,
  browned, crumbled fine,
  and drained
2 15-oz. cans refried beans
2 10-oz. cans diced
  tomatoes and chilies
1 pkg. taco seasoning
1 lb. Velveeta cheese,
  cubed
tortilla chips

1. Combine ground beef,
beans, tomatoes, and taco seasoning in slow cooker.

2. Cover. Cook on Low 3-4
hours, or on High 1½ hours.
3. Add cheese. Stir occa-
sionally. Heat until cheese is
melted.
4. Serve with tortilla chips.

**Note:**
Serve as a main dish alongside a soup.

# Hot Refried Bean Dip

**Sharon Anders**
Alburtis, PA

*Makes 1½ quarts,
or 12-20 servings*

15-oz. can refried beans,
    drained and mashed
½ lb. ground beef
3 Tbsp. bacon drippings
1 lb. American cheese,
    cubed
1-3 Tbsp. taco sauce
1 Tbsp. taco seasoning
dash garlic salt
tortilla chips

1. In skillet, brown beans
and ground beef in bacon
drippings. Pour into slow
cooker.
2. Stir in cheese, taco
sauce, taco seasoning, and
garlic salt.
3. Cover. Cook on High 45
minutes, or until cheese is
melted, stirring occasionally.
Turn to Low until ready to
serve, up to 6 hours.

# Chili-Cheese Taco Dip

**Kim Stoltzfus**
New Holland, PA

*Makes 10-12 servings*

1 lb. ground beef
1 can chili, without beans
1 lb. mild Mexican
    Velveeta cheese, cubed
taco *or* tortilla chips

1. Brown beef, crumble
into small pieces, and drain.
2. Combine beef, chili, and
cheese in slow cooker.
3. Cover. Cook on Low 1-
1½ hours, or until cheese is
melted, stirring occasionally
to blend ingredients.
4. Serve warm with taco or
tortilla chips.

# Hamburger Cheese Dip

**Julia Lapp**
New Holland, PA

*Makes 8-10 servings*

1 lb. ground beef, browned
    and crumbled into small
    pieces
½ tsp. salt
½ cup chopped green
    peppers
¾ cup chopped onion
8-oz. can tomato sauce
4-oz. can green chilies,
    chopped
1 Tbsp. Worcestershire
    sauce
1 Tbsp. brown sugar
1 lb. Velveeta cheese,
    cubed
1 Tbsp. paprika
red pepper to taste
tortilla chips

1. Combine beef, salt,
green peppers, onion, tomato
sauce, green chilies,
Worcestershire sauce, and
brown sugar in slow cooker.
2. Cover. Cook on Low 2-3
hours. During the last hour
stir in cheese, paprika, and
red pepper.
3. Serve with tortilla chips.

**Variation:**
Prepare recipe using only
⅓-½ lb. ground beef.

Leave the lid on while the slow cooker cooks. The steam
that condenses on the lid helps cook the food from the top.
Every time you take the lid off, the cooker loses steam. After
you put the lid back on, it takes one to 20 minutes to regain
the lost steam and temperature. That means it takes longer
for the food to cook.

**Pam Hochstedler**
Kalona, IA

## Chili-Cheese Dip

**Ruth Hofstetter**
Versailles, Missouri
**Paula King**
Harrisonburg, VA

*Makes 10 servings*

1 lb. ground beef,
    browned, crumbled fine,
    and drained.
2 lbs. Velveeta cheese,
    cubed
10-oz. can tomatoes with
    chilies
1 tsp. Worcestershire sauce
½ tsp. chili powder
tortilla *or* corn chips

1. Combine all ingredients
except chips in slow cooker.
Mix well.
2. Cover. Cook on High 1
hour, stirring occasionally
until cheese is fully melted.
3. Serve immediately, or
turn to Low for serving up to
6 hours later.
4. Serve with tortilla or
corn chips.

**Variation:**
    For a thicker dip, make a
smooth paste of 2 Tbsp. flour
mixed with 3 Tbsp. cold
water. Stir into hot dip.

## Michelle's Taco Dip

**Michelle Strite**
Harrisonburg, VA

*Makes 6-8 servings*

1½ lbs. ground beef,
    browned, crumbled fine,
    and drained
1 pkg. taco seasoning mix
10-oz. jar salsa
1 lb. Velveeta cheese,
    cubed
¼ cup chopped onion
tortilla chips

1. Combine all ingredients
except chips in slow cooker.
2. Cover. Heat on Low for
2-3 hours.
3. Serve with tortilla chips.

**Variation:**
    The recipe can be made
with half the amount of meat
called for, if you prefer.

## Karen's Nacho Dip

**Karen Stoltzfus**
Alto, MI

*Makes 10-12 servings*

1 lb. ground beef
2 lbs. American cheese,
    cubed
16-oz. jar salsa (mild,
    medium, *or* hot,
    whichever you prefer)
1 Tbsp. Worcestershire
    sauce
tortilla *or* corn chips

1. Brown beef, crumble
into small pieces, and drain.
2. Combine beef, cheese,
salsa, and Worcestershire
sauce in slow cooker.
3. Cover. Cook on High 1
hour, stirring occasionally
until cheese is fully melted.
4. Serve immediately, or
turn to Low for serving up to
6 hours later.

# Mexican Chip Dip Ole'

**Joy Sutter**
Iowa City, IA

*Makes 10-12 servings*

2 lbs. ground turkey
1 large onion, chopped
15-oz. can tomato sauce
4-oz. can green chilies, chopped
3-oz. can jalapeno peppers, chopped
2 lbs. Velveeta cheese, cubed
tortilla chips

1. Brown turkey and onion. Drain.
2. Add tomato sauce, chilies, jalapeno peppers, and cheese. Pour into slow cooker.
3. Cover. Cook on Low 4 hours, or High 2 hours.
4. Serve warm with tortilla chips.

# Barbara's Chili Cheese Dip

**Barbara Shie**
Colorado Springs, CO

*Makes 8-10 servings*

1 lb. ground beef
1 lb. Velveeta cheese, cubed
8-oz. can green chilies and tomato sauce
2 tsp. Worcestershire sauce
1/2 tsp., or more, chili powder
1/4 cup salsa with jalapeno peppers
tortilla *or* corn chips

1. Brown ground beef, crumble fine, and drain.
2. Combine all ingredients except chips in slow cooker. Stir well.
3. Cover. Cook on High 1 hour, stirring until cheese is melted. Serve immediately, or turn on Low for serving up to 6 hours later.
4. Serve with tortilla or corn chips.

**Note:**
Serve over rice, noodles, or baked potatoes as a main dish, making 4-5 servings.

# Pizza Fondue

**Lisa Warren**
Parkesburg, PA

*Makes 8-12 servings*

1 lb. ground beef
2 cans pizza sauce with cheese
8 oz. grated cheddar cheese
8 oz. grated mozzarella cheese
1 tsp. dried oregano
1/2 tsp. fennel seed, optional
1 Tbsp. cornstarch
tortilla chips

1. Brown beef, crumble fine, and drain.
2. Combine all ingredients except tortilla chips in slow cooker.
3. Cover. Heat on Low 2-3 hours.
4. Serve with tortilla chips.

# Super Bowl Super Dip

**Colleen Heatwole**
Burton, MI

*Makes 4-5 cups,
or approximately 12 servings*

1 lb. ground beef
1 lb. Mexican Velveeta
   cheese spread
8-oz. salsa (mild, medium,
   *or* hot)
tortilla chips

1. Brown ground beef, crumble into fine pieces, and drain. Place in slow cooker. Add cheese.
2. Cover. Cook on High for 45 minutes, stirring occasionally until cheese melts.
3. Add salsa. Reduce heat to Low and cook until heated through.
4. Serve warm with tortilla chips.

# Hamburger Hot Dip

**Janice Martins**
Fairbank, IA

*Makes 6 cups dip*

1 lb. ground beef
1 medium onion, chopped
   fine
1/2 tsp. salt
1/4 tsp. pepper
8-oz. jar salsa
14-oz. can nacho cheese
   soup
8 slices Velveeta cheese
nacho chips

1. Brown ground beef and onions in saucepan. Drain. Season with salt and pepper.
2. Combine all ingredients in slow cooker.
3. Cover. Cook on Low 4 hours. Stir occasionally.
4. Serve with nacho chips.

# Chili Con Queso Cheese Dip

**Melanie Thrower**
McPherson, KS

*Makes 8 servings*

1 lb. ground beef
1/2 cup chopped onion
1 cup Velveeta cheese,
   cubed
10-oz. can diced tomatoes
   and green chilies
1 can evaporated milk
2 Tbsp. chili powder
tortilla chips

1. Brown ground beef and onion. Crumble beef into fine pieces. Drain.
2. Combine all ingredients except tortilla chips in slow cookers.
3. Cover. Heat on Low 1-2 hours, until cheese is melted.
4. Serve with tortilla chips.

# Good 'n' Hot Dip

**Joyce B. Suiter**
Garysburg, NC

*Makes 30-50 servings*

1 lb. ground beef
1 lb. bulk sausage
10¾-oz. can cream of
   chicken soup
10¾-oz. can cream of
   celery soup
24-oz. jar salsa (use hot for
   some zing)
1 lb. Velveeta cheese,
   cubed
chips

1. Brown beef and
sausage, crumbling into small
pieces. Drain.
2. Combine meat, soups,
salsa, and cheese in slow
cooker.
3. Cover. Cook on High 1
hour. Stir. Cook on Low until
ready to serve.
4. Serve with chips.

# Cheese Queso Dip

**Janie Steele**
Moore, OK

*Makes about 2 quarts dip*

2-lbs. Velveeta cheese,
   cubed
10-oz. can diced tomatoes
   and chilies
1 lb. bulk sausage,
   browned, crumbled fine,
   and drained
tortilla chips

1. Combine cheese, toma-
toes, and sausage in slow
cooker.
2. Cover. Heat on Low 1-2
hours.
3. Serve with tortilla chips.

# Hot Cheese and Bacon Dip

**Lee Ann Hazlett**
Freeport, IL

*Makes 6-8 servings*

16 slices bacon, diced
2 8-oz. pkgs. cream cheese,
   cubed and softened
4 cups shredded mild
   cheddar cheese
1 cup half-and-half
2 tsp. Worcestershire sauce
1 tsp. dried minced onion
½ tsp. dry mustard
½ tsp. salt
2-3 drops Tabasco

1. Brown and drain bacon.
Set aside.
2. Mix remaining ingredi-
ents in slow cooker.
3. Cover. Cook on Low 1
hour, stirring occasionally
until cheese melts.
4. Stir in bacon.
5. Serve with fruit slices or
French bread slices. (Dip fruit
in lemon juice to prevent
browning.)

# Championship Bean Dip

**Renee Shirk**
Mt. Joy, PA
**Ada Miller**
Sugarcreek, OH

*Makes 4½ cups dip*

15-oz. can refried beans
1 cup picante sauce
1 cup (4 oz.) shredded
  Monterey Jack cheese
1 cup (4 oz.) shredded
  cheddar cheese
¾ cup sour cream
3-oz. pkg. cream cheese,
  softened
1 Tbsp. chili powder
¼ tsp. ground cumin
tortilla chips
salsa

1. In a bowl, combine all ingredients except chips and salsa. Transfer to slow cooker.
2. Cover. Cook on High 2 hours, or until heated through, stirring once or twice.
3. Serve with tortilla chips and salsa.

# Refried Bean Dip

**Maryann Markano**
Wilmington, DE

*Makes 6 servings*

20-oz. can refried beans
1 cup shredded cheddar
  cheese
½ cup chopped green
  onions
¼ tsp. salt
2-4 Tbsp. bottled taco
  sauce (depending upon
  how spicy a dip you
  like)
tortilla chips

1. Combine beans, cheese, onions, salt, and taco sauce in slow cooker.
2. Cover. Cook on Low 2-2½ hours, or cook on High 30 minutes and then on Low 30 minutes.
3. Serve with tortilla chips.

# Jeanne's Chile Con Queso

**Jeanne Allen**
Rye, CO

*Makes 15-20 servings*

40-oz. can chili without
  beans
2-lbs. Velveeta cheese,
  cubed
16-oz. jar picante sauce
  (mild, medium, *or* hot,
  whichever you prefer)
tortilla chips

1. Combine all ingredients except chips in slow cooker.
2. Cover. Cook on Low 1-2 hours, until cheese is melted. Stir.
3. Serve with tortilla chips.

A slow cooker is great for taking food to a potluck supper, even if you didn't prepare it in the cooker.
**Irma H. Schoen**
Windsor, CT

# Maryann's Chili Cheese Dip

**Maryann Westerberg**
Rosamond, CA

*Makes about 10 servings*

2 lbs. Velveeta cheese,
 cubed
16-oz. can chili without
 beans
10-oz. can diced tomatoes
 with chilies, drained
10¾-oz. can cream of
 mushroom soup
tortilla chips

1. Combine cheese and
chili in slow cooker. Heat on
Low until cheese melts, stirring occasionally.
 2. Add tomatoes and soup.
 3. Cover. Cook on Low 2
hours. Stir before serving.
 4. Serve with tortilla chips.

# Tina's Cheese Dip

**Tina Houk**
Clinton, MO

*Makes 12 servings*

2 8-oz. pkgs. cream cheese,
 softened
3 15½-oz. cans chili
2 cups shredded cheddar
 *or* mozzarella cheese
tortilla chips

1. Spread cream cheese in
bottom of slow cooker.
 2. Spread chili on top of
cream cheese.
 3. Top with shredded
cheese.
 4. Cover. Cook on Low
1-1½ hours, until shredded
cheese is melted. Stir.
 5. Serve with tortilla chips.

# Cheese Spread

**Barbara Kuhns**
Millersburg, OH

*Makes approximately
12-15 servings*

1 lb. white American
 cheese, cubed
1½ cups milk
crackers

1. Combine cheese and
milk in slow cooker.
 2. Cover. Cook on Low
about 2 hours, or until cheese
is melted, stirring occasionally.
 3. Serve on crackers.

# Mexicana Dip

**Julia B. Boyd**
Memphis, TN
**Sue Williams**
Gulfport, MS

*Makes 10-12 servings*

2 lbs. American, *or*
 Velveeta cheese, cubed
10-oz. can tomatoes with
 green chilies
tortilla chips, corn chips,
 *or* potato chips

1. Combine cheese and
tomatoes in slow cooker.
 2. Cover. Cook on Low
2-3 hours, stirring until
cheese is melted. If mixture is
too thick, add a little milk.
 3. Serve as a dip, or pour
over platter of favorite chips.

**Variation:**
 Stir in ½ lb. browned bulk
sausage, crumbled into small
pieces.

**Jane Steele**
Moore, OK

# Marilyn's Chili Con Queso

**Marilyn Mowry**
Irving, TX

*Makes 2 cups dip*

1 Tbsp. chopped green peppers
1 Tbsp. chopped celery
1 Tbsp. chopped onions
2 Tbsp. diced tomatoes
2 tsp. chopped jalapeno pepper
1/2 cup water
3/4 cup heavy cream
8 oz. Velveeta cheese, cubed
2 oz. cheddar cheese, shredded
tortilla chips

1. Place first 5 ingredients in slow cooker. Add water.
2. Cover. Cook on High 1 hour, or until vegetables are tender.
3. Stir in cream and cheeses.
4. Reduce heat to Low. Cook until cheese is melted. Serve immediately, or keep warm on Low for hours.
5. Serve with tortilla chips.

# Chili Con Queso Dip

**Jenny R. Unternahrer**
Wayland, IA

*Makes approximately 12 servings*

1 lb. Velveeta cheese, cubed
1 cup salsa (mild, medium, *or* hot, whichever you prefer)
1 cup sour cream
tortilla chips

1. Combine cheese, salsa, and sour cream in slow cooker.
2. Cover. Heat on Low, stirring occasionally until cheese melts and dip is well blended, about 1-1 1/2 hours.
3. Serve with tortilla chips.

# Short-Cut Fondue Dip

**Jean Butzer**
Batavia, NY

*Makes 8-10 servings*

2 10 3/4-oz. cans condensed cheese soup
2 cups grated sharp cheddar cheese
1 Tbsp. Worcestershire sauce
1 tsp. lemon juice
2 Tbsp. dried chopped chives
celery sticks
cauliflower florets
corn chips

1. Combine soup, cheese, Worcestershire sauce, lemon juice, and chives in slow cooker.
2. Cover. Heat on Low 2-2 1/2 hours. Stir until smooth and well blended.
3. Serve warm dip with celery sticks, cauliflower, and corn chips.

13

# Chili Verde con Queso Dip

Bonita Ensenberger
Albuquerque, NM

*Makes 1 quart (8-10 servings)*

2 10¾-oz. cans cheddar
cheese soup
7-oz. can chopped green
chilies
1 garlic clove, minced
½ tsp. dried cilantro leaves
½ tsp. ground cumin
corn chips

1. Mix together all ingredients except corn chips in slow cooker.
2. Cover. Cook on Low 1-1½ hours. Stir well. Cook an additional 1½ hours.
3. Serve with corn chips.

**Variation:**
Make this a main dish by serving over baked potatoes.

# Lilli's Nacho Dip

Lilli Peters
Dodge City, KS

*Makes 10 servings*

3-lbs. Velveeta cheese, cubed
10¾-oz. can cream of chicken soup
2 4-oz. cans chopped green chilies and juice
tortilla chips

1. Place cheese in slow cooker. Cook on Low until cheese melts, stirring occasionally.
2. Add soup and chilies. Stir. Heat on Low 1 hour.
3. Pour over tortilla chips just before serving.

**Note:**
If you want to speed up the process, melt the cheese in the microwave. Heat on High for 1½ minutes, stir, and continue heating at 1½-minute intervals as long as needed.

**Variations:**
1. Instead of using 2 4-oz. cans chilies, use 10-oz. can tomatoes and chilies.
2. For a heartier dip, add ½-1 lb. bulk sausage, browned, crumbled into small pieces, and drained.

# Reuben Spread

Clarice Williams
Fairbank, IA
Julie McKenzie
Punxsutawney, PA

*Makes 5 cups spread*

½ lb. corned beef, shredded *or* chopped
16-oz. can sauerkraut, well drained
1-2 cups shredded Swiss cheese
1-2 cups shredded cheddar cheese
1 cup mayonnaise
snack rye bread
Thousand Island dressing, optional

1. Combine all ingredients except bread and Thousnd Island dressing in slow cooker. Mix well.
2. Cover. Cook on High 1-2 hours until heated through, stirring occasionally.
3. Turn to Low and keep warm in cooker while serving. Put spread on bread slices. Top individual servings with Thousand Island dressing, if desired.

**Note:**
Low-fat cheese and mayonnaise are not recommended for this spread.

**Variation:**
Use dried beef instead of corned beef.

# Cheesy New Orleans Shrimp Dip

**Kelly Evenson**
Pittsboro, NC

*Makes 3-4 cups dip*

1 slice bacon
3 medium onions, chopped
1 garlic clove, minced
4 jumbo shrimp, peeled
  and deveined
1 medium tomato, peeled
  and chopped
3 cups Monterey Jack
  cheese, shredded
4 drops Tabasco sauce
1/8 tsp. cayenne pepper
dash of black pepper
chips

1. Cook bacon until crisp. Drain on paper towel. Crumble.
2. Saute onion and garlic in bacon drippings. Drain on paper towel.
3. Coarsely chop shrimp.
4. Combine all ingredients except chips in slow cooker.
5. Cover. Cook on Low 1 hour, or until cheese is melted. Thin with milk if too thick. Serve with chips.

# Broccoli Cheese Dip

**Carla Koslowsky**
Hillsboro, KS

*Makes 6 cups dip*

1 cup chopped celery
1/2 cup chopped onion
10-oz. pkg. frozen chopped
  broccoli, cooked
1 cup cooked rice
10 3/4-oz. can cream of
  mushroom soup
16-oz. jar cheese spread, *or*
  15 slices American
  cheese, melted and
  mixed with 2/3 cup milk
snack breads or crackers

1. Combine all ingredients in slow cooker.
2. Cover. Heat on Low 2 hours.
3. Serve with snack breads or crackers.

# Roasted Pepper and Artichoke Spread

**Sherril Bieberly**
Salina, KS

*Makes 3 cups,
or about 12 servings*

1 cup grated Parmesan
  cheese
1/2 cup mayonnaise
8-oz. pkg. cream cheese,
  softened
1 garlic clove, minced
14-oz. can artichoke
  hearts, drained and
  chopped finely
1/3 cup finely chopped
  roasted red bell peppers
  (from 7 1/4-oz. jar)
crackers, cut-up fresh
  vegetables, *or* snack-
  bread slices

1. Combine Parmesan cheese, mayonnaise, cream cheese, and garlic in food processor. Process until smooth. Place mixture in slow cooker.
2. Add artichoke hearts and red bell pepper. Stir well.
3. Cover. Cook on Low 1 hour. Stir again.
4. Use as spread for crackers, cut-up fresh vegetables, or snack-bread slices.

The great thing about using a slow cooker in hot weather is that it doesn't heat up your kitchen like an oven does.
**Carol Peachey**
Lancaster, PA

# Baked Brie with Cranberry Chutney

**Amymarlene Jensen**
Fountain, CO

*Makes 8-10 servings*

1 cup fresh, *or* dried, cranberries
1/2 cup brown sugar
1/3 cup cider vinegar
2 Tbsp. water, *or* orange juice
2 tsp. minced crystallized ginger
1/4 tsp. cinnamon
1/8 tsp. ground cloves
oil
8-oz. round of Brie cheese
1 Tbsp. sliced almonds, toasted
crackers

1. Mix together cranberries, brown sugar, vinegar, water or juice, ginger, cinnamon, and cloves in slow cooker.

2. Cover. Cook on Low 4 hours. Stir once near the end to see if it is thickening. If not, remove top, turn heat to High and cook 30 minutes without lid.

3. Put cranberry chutney in covered container and chill for up to 2 weeks. When ready to serve, bring to room temperature.

4. Brush ovenproof plate with vegetable oil, place unpeeled Brie on plate, and bake uncovered at 350° for 9 minutes, until cheese is soft and partially melted. Remove from oven.

5. Top with at least half the chutney and garnish with almonds. Serve with crackers.

# Artichokes

**Susan Yoder Graber**
Eureka, IL

*Makes 4 servings*

4 artichokes
1 tsp. salt
2 Tbsp. lemon juice
melted butter

1. Wash and trim artichokes by cutting off the stems flush with the bottoms of the artichokes and by cutting 3/4-1 inch off the tops. Stand upright in slow cooker.

2. Mix together salt and lemon juice and pour over artichokes. Pour in water to cover 3/4 of artichokes.

3. Cover. Cook on Low 8-10 hours, or High 2-4 hours.

4. Serve with melted butter. Pull off individual leaves and dip bottom of each into butter. Using your teeth, strip the individual leaf of the meaty portion at the bottom of each leaf.

# Curried Almonds

**Barbara Aston**
Ashdown, AR

*Makes 4 cups nuts*

2 Tbsp. melted butter
1 Tbsp. curry powder
1/2 tsp. seasoned salt
1 lb. blanched almonds

1. Combine butter with curry powder and seasoned salt.

2. Pour over almonds in slow cooker. Mix to coat well.

3. Cover. Cook on Low 2-3 hours. Turn to High. Uncover cooker and cook 1-1 1/2 hours.

4. Serve hot or cold.

# Chili Nuts

**Barbara Aston**
Ashdown, AR

*Makes 5 cups nuts*

1/4 cup melted butter
2 12-oz. cans cocktail peanuts
1 5/8-oz. pkg. chili seasoning mix

1. Pour butter over nuts in slow cooker. Sprinkle in dry chili mix. Toss together.

2. Cover. Heat on Low 2-2 1/2 hours. Turn to High. Remove lid and cook 10-15 minutes.

3. Serve warm or cool.

# All-American Snack

**Doris M. Coyle-Zipp**
South Ozone Park, NY
**Melissa Raber,** Millersburg, OH
**Ada Miller,** Sugarcreek, OH
**Nanci Keatley,** Salem, OR

*Makes 3 quarts snack mix*

3 cups thin pretzel sticks
4 cups Wheat Chex
4 cups Cheerios
12-oz. can salted peanuts
¼ cup melted butter, *or*
    margarine
1 tsp. garlic powder
1 tsp. celery salt
½ tsp. seasoned salt
2 Tbsp. grated Parmesan
    cheese

1. Combine pretzels, cereal, and peanuts in large bowl.
2. Melt butter. Stir in garlic powder, celery salt, seasoned salt, and Parmesan cheese. Pour over pretzels and cereal. Toss until well mixed.
3. Pour into large slow cooker. Cover. Cook on Low 2½ hours, stirring every 30 minutes. Remove lid and cook another 30 minutes on Low.
4. Serve warm or at room temperature. Store in tightly covered container.

**Variations:**
1. Use 3 cups Wheat Chex (instead of 4 cups) and 3 cups Cheerios (instead of 4 cups). Add 3 cups Corn Chex.
    **Marcia S. Myer**
    Manheim, PA

2. Alter the amounts of pretzels, cereal, and peanuts to reflect your preferences.

# Hot Caramel Dip

**Marilyn Yoder**
Archbold, OH

*Makes about 3 cups dip*

½ cup butter
½ cup light corn syrup
1 cup brown sugar
1 can sweetened
    condensed milk
apple slices

1. Mix together all ingredients except apples in saucepan. Bring to boil.
2. Pour into crockpot. Set on Low.
3. Dip fresh apple slices into hot caramel.

**Variation:**
Add ½ cup peanut butter to dip.

# Rhonda's Apple Butter

**Rhonda Burgoon**
Collingswood, NJ

*Makes about 2 pints apple butter*

4 lbs. apples
2 tsp. cinnamon
½ tsp. ground cloves

1. Peel, core, and slice apples. Place in slow cooker.
2. Cover. Cook on High 2-3 hours. Reduce to Low and cook 8 hours. Apples should be a rich brown and be cooked down by half.
3. Stir in spices. Cook on High 2-3 hours with lid off. Stir until smooth.
4. Pour into freezer containers and freeze, or into sterilized jars and seal.

# Shirley's Apple Butter

**Shirley Sears**
Tiskilwa, IL

*Makes 6-10 pints apple butter*

4 qts. finely chopped tart
   apples
2¾ cups sugar
2¾ tsp. cinnamon
¼ tsp. ground cloves
⅛ tsp. salt

1. Pour apples into slow
cooker.
2. Combine remaining
ingredients. Drizzle over
apples.
3. Cover. Cook on High 3
hours, stirring well with a
large spoon every hour.
Reduce heat to Low and cook
10-12 hours, until butter
becomes thick and dark in
color. Stir occasionally with
strong wire whisk for smooth
butter.
4. Freeze or pour into sterilized jars and seal.

# Kelly's Apple Butter

**Kelly Evenson**
Pittsboro, NC

*Makes 4-5 pints apple butter*

4 lbs. cooking apples
2 cups cider
3 cups sugar
2 tsp. cinnamon
1 tsp. ground cloves,
   optional
⅛ tsp. allspice

1. Stem, core, and quarter
apples. Do not peel.
2. Combine apples and
cider in large slow cooker.
3. Cover. Cook on Low 10
hours.
4. Stir in sugar and spices.
Continue cooking 1 hour.
Remove from heat and cool
thoroughly. Blend to mix in
skins.
5. Freeze in pint containers, or pour into hot sterilized
jars and seal.

# Charlotte's Apple Butter

**Charlotte Fry**
St. Charles, MO

*Makes 5 pints apple butter*

3 quarts Jonathan, *or*
   Winesap, apples
2 cups apple cider
2½ cups sugar
1 tsp. star anise, optional
2 Tbsp. lemon juice
2 sticks cinnamon

1. Peel, core, and chop
apples. Combine with apple
cider in large slow cooker.
2. Cover. Cook on Low 10-
12 hours.
3. Stir in sugar, star anise,
lemon juice, and stick cinnamon.
4. Cover. Cook on High 2
hours. Stir. Remove lid and
cook on High 2-4 hours more,
until thickened.
5. Pour into sterilized jars
and seal.

# Dolores' Apple Butter

**Dolores Metzler**
Mechanicsburg, PA

*Makes 3 quarts apple butter*

3 quarts unsweetened applesauce
3 cups sugar (or sweeten to taste)
2 tsp. cinnamon
1 tsp., *or* less, ground cloves

1. Combine all ingredients in large slow cooker.
2. Cover. Cook on High 8-10 hours. Remove lid during last 4 hours. Stir occasionally.

# Ann's Apple Butter

**Ann Bender**
Ft. Defiance, VA

*Makes 2 pints apple butter*

7 cups unsweetened applesauce
2-3 cups sugar, depending upon the sweetness of the applesauce and your own preference
2 tsp. cinnamon
1 tsp. ground nutmeg
¼ tsp. allspice

1. Combine all ingredients in slow cooker.
2. Put a layer of paper towels under lid to prevent condensation from dripping into apple butter. Cook on High 8-10 hours. Remove lid during last hour. Stir occasionally.

**Variation:**
Use canned peaches, pears, or apricots in place of applesauce.

# Anna's Slow-Cooker Apple Butter

**Anna Musser**
Manheim, PA

*Makes 6 pints apple butter*

1 cup cider, *or* apple juice
2 ½ quarts unsweetened applesauce
2-3 cups sugar, depending upon the sweetness of the applesauce and your own preference
1 tsp. vinegar
1 tsp. cinnamon
½ tsp. allspice

1. Boil cider until ½ cup remains.
2. Combine all ingredients in slow cooker.
3. Cover. Cook on High 12-16 hours, until apple butter has cooked down to half the original amount. Put in containers and freeze.

# Marilyn's Slow-Cooker Apple Butter

**Marilyn Yoder**
Archbold, OH

*Makes 80 servings*

2 qts. unsweetened applesauce
2-4 cups sugar, depending upon sweetness of applesauce and your preference
½ tsp. ground cloves
2 Tbsp. lemon juice
¼ heaping cup red hot candies

1. Combine all ingredients in slow cooker.
2. Vent lid. Cook on Low 8-10 hours, stirring about every hour. Apple butter thickens as it cooks, so cook longer to make it thicker.

# Dianna's Apple Butter

**Dianna Milhizer**
Springfield, VA

*Makes 6 pints apple butter*

1 bushel red tart apples
  (Winesap, Rome, *or*
  Macintosh)
1 quart "raw" honey *or*
  least-processed honey
  available
1/2 cup cinnamon sticks
1 Tbsp. salt

1. Peel, core, and slice apples.
2. Combine all ingredients in large slow cooker. If apples don't fit, continue to add them as butter cooks down.
3. Cover. Cook on High 8 hours. Stir. Remove lid and let butter cook down on Low 8 additional hours. Consistency should be thick and creamy.
4. Freeze, or pack into sterilized jars and seal.

# Lilli's Apple Butter

**Lilli Peters**
Dodge City, KS

*Makes about 2 pints apple butter*

7 cups unsweetened
  applesauce
2 cups apple cider
1 1/2 cups honey
1 tsp. cinnamon
1/2 tsp. ground cloves
1/2 tsp. allspice

1. Combine all ingredients in slow cooker. Mix well with whisk.
2. Cook on Low 14-15 hours.

# Peach or Apricot Butter

**Charlotte Shaffer**
East Earl. PA

*Makes 6 8-oz. jars butter*

4 1-lb. 13-oz. cans peaches,
  *or* apricots
2 3/4-3 cups sugar
2 tsp. cinnamon
1 tsp. ground cloves

1. Drain fruit. Remove pits. Puree in blender. Pour into slow cooker.
2. Stir in remaining ingredients.

3. Cover. Cook on High 8-10 hours. Remove cover during last half of cooking. Stir occasionally.

**Note:**
  Spread on bread, or use as a topping for ice cream or toasted pound cake.

# Pear Butter

**Dorothy Miller**
Gulfport, MI

*Makes 6 pints pear butter*

8 cups pear sauce
3 cups brown sugar
1 Tbsp. lemon juice
1 Tbsp. cinnamon

1. Combine all ingredients in slow cooker.
2. Cover. Cook on High 10-12 hours.

**Note:**
  To make pear sauce, peel, core, and slice 12 large pears. Place in slow cooker with 3/4 cup water. Cover and cook on Low 8-10 hours, or until very soft. Stir to blend.

# Breakfast Foods

## Welsh Rarebit

**Sharon Timpe**
Mequon, WI

*Makes 6-8 servings*

12-oz. can beer
1 Tbsp. dry mustard
1 tsp. Worcestershire sauce
1/2 tsp. salt
1/8 tsp. black, *or* white, pepper
1 lb. American cheese, cubed
1 lb. sharp cheddar cheese, cubed
English muffins, *or* toast
bacon, cooked until crisp
tomato slices

1. In slow cooker, combine beer, mustard, Worcestershire sauce, salt, and pepper.
2. Cover and cook on High 1-2 hours, until mixture boils.
3. Add cheese, a little at a time, stirring constantly until all the cheese melts.
4. Heat on High 20-30 minutes with cover off, stirring frequently.
5. Serve hot over toasted English muffins or over toasted bread cut into triangles. Garnish with strips of crisp bacon and tomato slices.

**Note:**
This is a good dish for brunch with fresh fruit, juice, and coffee. Also makes a great lunch or late-night light supper. Serve with a tossed green salad, especially fresh spinach and orange slices with a vinaigrette dressing.

One hour on High equals about 2 to 2½ hours on Low.
**Rachel Kauffman**
Alto, MI

# Cheese Souffle Casserole

**Iva Schmidt**
Fergus Falls, MN

*Makes 6 servings*

8 slices bread (crusts removed), cubed *or* torn into squares
2 cups (8 oz.) grated cheddar, Swiss, *or* American, cheese
1 cup cooked, chopped ham
4 eggs
1 cup light cream, *or* milk
1 cup evaporated milk
1/4 tsp. salt
1 Tbsp. parsley
paprika

1. Lightly grease slow cooker. Alternate layers of bread and cheese and ham.
2. Beat together eggs, milk, salt, and parsley. Pour over bread in slow cooker.
3. Sprinkle with paprika.
4. Cover and cook on Low 3-4 hours. (The longer cooking time yields a firmer, dryer dish.)

# Breakfast Casserole

**Shirley Hinh**
Wayland, IA

*Makes 8-10 servings*

6 eggs, beaten
1 lb. little smokies (cocktail wieners), *or* 1 1/2 lbs. bulk sausage, browned and drained
1 1/2 cups milk
1 cup shredded cheddar cheese
8 slices bread, torn into pieces
1 tsp. salt
1/2 tsp. dry mustard
1 cup shredded mozzarella cheese

1. Mix together all ingredients except cheese. Pour into greased slow cooker.
2. Sprinkle mozzarella cheese over top.
3. Cover and cook 2 hours on High, and then 1 hour on Low.

# Egg and Cheese Bake

**Evie Hershey**
Atglen, PA

*Makes 6 servings*

3 cups toasted bread cubes
1 1/2 cups shredded cheese
fried, crumbled bacon, *or* ham chunks, optional
6 eggs, beaten
3 cups milk
3/4 tsp. salt
1/4 tsp. pepper

1. Combine bread cubes, cheese, and meat in greased slow cooker.
2. Mix together eggs, milk, salt, and pepper. Pour over bread.
3. Cook on Low 4-6 hours.

# Egg and Broccoli Casserole

**Joette Droz**
Kalona, IA

*Makes 6 servings*

24-oz. carton small-curd
cottage cheese
10-oz. pkg. frozen chopped
broccoli, thawed and
drained
2 cups (8 oz.)shredded
cheddar cheese
6 eggs, beaten
1/3 cup flour
1/4 cup melted butter, *or*
margarine
3 Tbsp. finely chopped
onion
1/2 tsp. salt
shredded cheese, optional

1. Combine first 8 ingredients. Pour into greased slow cooker.
2. Cover and cook on High 1 hour. Stir. Reduce heat to Low. Cover and cook 2 1/2-3 hours, or until temperature reaches 160° and eggs are set.
3. Sprinkle with cheese and serve.

# Creamy Old-Fashioned Oatmeal

**Mary Wheatley**
Mashpee, MA

*Makes 4 servings*

1 1/3 cups dry old-fashioned
rolled oats
2 1/2 cups, plus 1 Tbsp.,
water
dash of salt

1. Mix together cereal, water, and salt in slow cooker.
2. Cook on Low 6 hours.

**Note:**
The formula is this: for one serving, use 1/3 cup dry oats and 2/3 cup water, plus a few grains salt. Multiply by the number of servings you need.

**Variation:**
Before cooking, stir in a few chopped dates or raisins for each serving, if you wish.
**Cathy Boshart**
Lebanon, PA

# Baked Oatmeal

**Ellen Ranck**
Gap, PA

*Makes 4-6 servings*

1/3 cup oil
1/2 cup sugar
1 large egg, beaten
2 cups dry quick oats
1 1/2 tsp. baking powder
1/2 tsp. salt
3/4 cup milk

1. Pour the oil into the slow cooker to grease bottom and sides.
2. Add remaining ingredients. Mix well.
3. Bake on Low 2 1/2-3 hours.

# Apple Oatmeal

**Frances B. Musser**
Newmanstown, PA

*Makes 4-5 servings*

2 cups milk
2 Tbsp. honey
1 Tbsp. butter (no
   substitute!)
1/4 tsp. salt
1/2 tsp. cinnamon
1 cup dry old-fashioned
   oats
1 cup chopped apples
1/2 cup chopped walnuts
2 Tbsp. brown sugar

1. Mix together all ingredients in greased slow cooker.
2. Cover. Cook on Low 5-6 hours.
3. Serve with milk or ice cream.

**Variation:**
Add 1/2 cup light or dark raisins to mixture.
**Jeanette Oberholtzer**
Manheim, PA

Don't peek. It takes 15-20 minutes for the cooker to regain lost steam and return to the right temperature.
**Janet V. Yocum**
Elizabethtown, PA

# Breads

## Healthy Whole Wheat Bread

**Esther Becker**
Gordonville, PA

*Makes 8 servings*

2 cups warm reconstituted
   powdered milk
2 Tbsp. vegetable oil
1/4 cup honey, *or* brown
   sugar
3/4 tsp. salt
1 pkg. yeast
2 1/2 cups whole wheat
   flour
1 1/4 cups white flour

1. Mix together milk, oil,
honey or brown sugar, salt,
yeast, and half the flour in
electric mixer bowl. Beat
with mixer for 2 minutes.
Add remaining flour. Mix
well.

2. Place dough in well-
greased bread or cake pan
that will fit into your cooker.

Cover with greased tin foil.
Let stand for 5 minutes. Place
in slow cooker.

3. Cover cooker and bake
on High 2 1/2-3 hours. Remove
pan and uncover. Let stand
for 5 minutes. Serve warm.

## Corn Bread From Scratch

**Dorothy M. Van Deest**
Memphis, TN

*Makes 6 servings*

1 1/4 cups flour
3/4 cup yellow cornmeal
1/4 cup sugar
4 1/2 tsp. baking powder
1 tsp. salt
1 egg, slightly beaten
1 cup milk
1/3 cup melted butter, *or* oil

1. In mixing bowl sift
together flour, cornmeal,
sugar, baking powder, and
salt. Make a well in the center.

2. Pour egg, milk, and butter into well. Mix into the dry
mixture until just moistened.

3. Pour mixture into a
greased 2-quart mold. Cover
with a plate. Place on a trivet
or rack in the bottom of slow
cooker.

4. Cover. Cook on High 2-3
hours.

# Broccoli Corn Bread

**Winifred Ewy**
Newton, KS

*Makes 8 servings*

1 stick margarine, melted
10-oz. pkg. chopped
　broccoli, cooked and
　drained
1 onion, chopped
1 box corn bread mix
4 eggs, well beaten
8 oz. cottage cheese
1¼ tsp. salt

1. Combine all ingredients.
Mix well.
2. Pour into greased slow
cooker. Cook on Low 6 hours,
or until toothpick inserted in
center comes out clean.
3. Serve like spoon bread,
or invert the pot, remove
bread, and cut into wedges.

# Lemon Bread

**Ruth Ann Gingrich**
New Holland, PA

*Makes 6 servings*

½ cup shortening
¾ cup sugar
2 eggs, beaten
1⅔ cups flour
1⅔ tsp. baking powder
½ tsp. salt
½ cup milk
½ cup chopped nuts
grated peel from 1 lemon

Glaze:
¼ cup powdered sugar
juice of 1 lemon

1. Cream together shortening and sugar. Add eggs. Mix
well.
2. Sift together flour, baking powder, and salt. Add
flour mixture and milk alternately to shortening mixture.
3. Stir in nuts and lemon
peel.
4. Spoon batter into well-
greased 2-pound coffee can
and cover with well-greased
tin foil. Place in cooker set on
High for 2-2¼ hours, or until
done. Remove bread from
coffee can.
5. Mix together powdered
sugar and lemon juice. Pour
over loaf.
6. Serve plain or with
cream cheese.

# Old-Fashioned Gingerbread

**Mary Ann Westerberg**
Rosamond, CA

*Makes 6-8 servings*

½ cup butter, softened
½ cup sugar
1 egg
1 cup light molasses
2½ cups flour
1½ tsp. baking soda
1 tsp. ground cinnamon
2 tsp. ground ginger
½ tsp. ground cloves
½ tsp. salt
1 cup hot water
warm applesauce, optional
whipped cream, optional
nutmeg, optional

1. Cream together butter
and sugar. Add egg and
molasses. Mix well.
2. Stir in flour, baking
soda, cinnamon, ginger,
cloves, and salt. Mix well.
3. Add hot water. Beat
well.
4. Pour batter into greased
and floured 2-pound coffee
can.
5. Place can in cooker.
Cover top of can with 8 paper
towels. Cover cooker and
bake on High 2½-3 hours.
6. Serve with applesauce.
Top with whipped cream and
sprinkle with nutmeg.

A slow cooker provides enough warmth to a raise dough.
**Donna Barnitz**
Jenks, OK

# Soups, Stews, and Chilis

## Nancy's Vegetable Beef Soup

**Nancy Graves**
Manhattan, KS

*Makes 6-8 servings*

2-lb. roast cut into bite-sized pieces, *or* 2 lbs. stewing meat
15-oz. can corn
15-oz. can green beans
1-lb. bag frozen peas
40-oz. can stewed tomatoes
5 beef bouillon cubes
Tabasco to taste
2 tsp. salt

1. Combine all ingredients in slow cooker. Do not drain vegetables.
2. Add water to fill slow cooker to within 3 inches of top
3. Cover. Cook on Low 8 hours, or until meat is tender and vegetables are soft.

**Variation:**
Add 1 large onion, sliced, 2 cups sliced carrots, and ¾ cup pearl barley to mixture before cooking.

## Frances' Hearty Vegetable Soup

**Frances Schrag**
Newton, KS

*Makes 10 servings*

1 lb. round steak, cut into ½-inch pieces
14½-oz. can diced tomatoes
3 cups water
2 potatoes, peeled and cubed
2 onions, sliced
3 celery ribs, sliced
2 carrots, sliced
3 beef bouillon cubes
½ tsp. dried basil
½ tsp. dried oregano
1 tsp. salt
¼ tsp. pepper
1½ cups frozen mixed vegetables, *or* your choice of frozen vegetables

1. Combine first 3 ingredients in slow cooker.
2. Cover. Cook on High 6 hours.
3. Add remaining ingredients. Cover and cook on High 2 hours more, or until meat and vegetables are tender.

**Variation:**
Cut salt back to ½ tsp. Increase dried basil to 1 tsp. and dried oregano to 1 tsp.
**Tracy Clark**
Mt. Crawford, VA

# Anona's Beef Vegetable Soup

Anona M. Teel
Bangor, PA

*Makes 6 servings*

1-1½-lb. soup bone
1 lb. stewing beef cubes
1½ qts. cold water
1 Tbsp. salt
¾ cup diced celery
¾ cup diced carrots
¾ cup diced potatoes
¾ cup diced onion
1 cup frozen mixed
   vegetables of your
   choice
1-lb. can tomatoes
⅛ tsp. pepper
1 Tbsp. chopped dried
   parsley

1. Put all ingredients in slow cooker.
2. Cover. Cook on Low 8-10 hours. Remove bone before serving.

# "Absent Cook" Stew

Kathy Hertzler
Lancaster, PA

*Makes 5-6 servings*

2 lbs. stewing beef, cubed
2-3 carrots, sliced
1 onion, chopped
3 large potatoes, cubed
3 ribs celery, sliced
10¾-oz. can tomato soup
1 soup can water
1 tsp. salt
dash of pepper
2 Tbsp. vinegar

1. Combine all ingredients in slow cooker.
2. Cover. Cook on Low 10-12 hours.

# Kim's Vegetable Beef Soup

Kim McEuen
Lincoln University, PA

*Makes 8-10 servings*

1-2 lbs. beef shanks, *or*
   short ribs
1-lb. can tomatoes
2 carrots, sliced
3 ribs celery, sliced
2 medium onions, chopped
2 medium potatoes,
   chopped
3 cups water
1 tsp. salt
4-6 whole peppercorns
5 beef bouillon cubes
10-oz. pkg. frozen mixed
   vegetables, *or* its
   equivalent of your
   favorite frozen, fresh, *or*
   canned vegetables

1. Combine all ingredients in slow cooker. Mix well.
2. Cover. Cook on Low 12-14 hours, or High 4-6 hours.

**Note:**
   I have a scrap vegetable container which I keep in the freezer. When I have too much of a fresh vegetable I throw it in this container and freeze it. When the container gets full, I make soup.

**Variation:**
   To increase the proportion of vegetables, add another 10-oz. pkg. of vegetables.

---

You may want to revise herb amounts when using a slow cooker. Whole herb and spices increase their flavoring power, while ground spices tend to lose some flavor. It's a good idea to season to taste before serving.
**Irma H. Schoen**
Windsor, CT

# Lilli's Vegetable Beef Soup

**Lilli Peters**
Dodge City, KS

*Makes 10-12 servings*

3 lbs. stewing meat, cut in
  1-inch pieces
2 Tbsp. oil
4 potatoes, cubed
4 carrots, sliced
3 ribs celery, sliced
14-oz. can diced tomatoes
14-oz. can Italian
  tomatoes, crushed
2 medium onions, chopped
2 wedges cabbage, sliced
  thinly
2 beef bouillon cubes
2 Tbsp. fresh parsley
1 tsp. seasoned salt
1 tsp. garlic salt
1/2 tsp. pepper
water

1. Brown meat in oil in
skillet. Drain.
2. Combine all ingredients
except water in large slow
cooker. Cover with water.
3. Cover. Cook on Low 8-
10 hours.

# Ruby's Vegetable Beef Soup

**Ruby Stoltzfus**
Mount Joy, PA

*Makes 8-10 servings*

1 lb. beef cubes
1 cup beef broth
1 1/2 cups chopped cabbage
1 1/2 cups stewed tomatoes,
  undrained
1 1/2 cups frozen, *or* canned,
  corn
1 1/2 cups frozen peas
1 1/2 cups frozen green
  beans
1 1/2 cups sliced carrots
3/4 tsp. salt
1/4-1/2 tsp. pepper

1. Combine all ingredients
in slow cooker.
2. Cover. Cook on Low 6-8
hours, or High 3-4 hours.

# Jeanne's Vegetable Beef Borscht

**Jeanne Heyerly**
Chenoa, IL

*Makes 8 servings*

1 lb. beef roast, cooked
  and cubed
half a head of cabbage,
  sliced thin
3 medium potatoes, diced
4 carrots, sliced
1 large onion, diced
1 cup tomatoes, diced
1 cup corn
1 cup green beans
2 cups beef broth
2 cups tomato juice
1/4 tsp. garlic powder
1/4 tsp. dill seed
2 tsp. salt
1/2 tsp. pepper
water
sour cream

1. Mix together all ingredients except water and sour
cream. Add water to fill slow
cooker three-quarters full.
2. Cover. Cook on Low
8-10 hours.
3. Top individual servings
with sour cream.

**Variation:**
Add 1 cup diced cooked
red beets during the last half
hour of cooking.

# Sharon's Vegetable Soup

**Sharon Wantland**
Menomonee Falls, WI

*Makes 6-8 servings*

46-oz. can tomato juice
5 beef bouillon cubes
4 celery ribs, sliced
4 large carrots, sliced
1 onion, chopped
one-quarter head of cabbage, chopped
1-lb. can green beans
2 cups water
1 lb. beef stewing meat, browned
4-oz. can sliced mushrooms

1. Combine all ingredients in slow cooker.
2. Cover. Cook on Low 8 hours, or until meat and vegetables are tender.

# Winter's Night Beef Soup

**Kimberly Jensen**
Bailey, CO

*Makes 8-12 servings*

1 lb. boneless chuck, cut in 1/2-inch cubes
1-2 Tbsp. oil
28-oz. can tomatoes
2 tsp. garlic powder
2 carrots, sliced
2 ribs celery, sliced
4 cups water
1/2 cup red wine
1 small onion, coarsely chopped
4 beef bouillon cubes
1 tsp. pepper
1 tsp. dry oregano
1/2 tsp. dry thyme
1 bay leaf
1/4-1/2 cup couscous

1. Brown beef cubes in oil in skillet.
2. Place vegetables in bottom of slow cooker. Add beef.
3. Combine all other ingredients in separate bowl except couscous. Pour over ingredients in slow cooker.
4. Cover. Cook on Low 6 hours. Stir in couscous. Cover and cook 30 minutes.

**Variation:**
Add zucchini or mushrooms to the rest of the vegetables before cooking.

# Old-Fashioned Vegetable Beef Soup

**Pam Hochstedler**
Kalona, IA

*Makes 8-10 servings*

1-2 lbs. beef short ribs
2 qts. water
1 tsp. salt
1 tsp. celery salt
1 small onion, chopped
1 cup diced carrots
1/2 cup diced celery
2 cups diced potatoes
1-lb. can whole kernel corn, undrained
1-lb. can diced tomatoes and juice

1. Combine meat, water, salt, celery salt, onion, carrots, and celery in slow cooker.
2. Cover. Cook on Low 4-6 hours.
3. Debone meat, cut into bite-sized pieces, and return to pot.
4. Add potatoes, corn, and tomatoes.
5. Cover and cook on High 2-3 hours.

# Texican Chili
**Becky Oswald**
Broadway, VA

*Makes 15 servings*

8 bacon strips, diced
2½ lbs. beef stewing meat, cubed
28-oz. can stewed tomatoes
14½-oz. can stewed tomatoes
2 8-oz. cans tomato sauce
16-oz. can kidney beans, rinsed and drained
2 cups sliced carrots
1 medium onion, chopped
1 cup chopped celery
½ cup chopped green pepper
¼ cup minced fresh parsley
1 Tbsp. chili powder
1 tsp. salt
½ tsp. ground cumin
¼ tsp. pepper

1. Cook bacon in skillet until crisp. Drain on paper towel.
2. Brown beef in bacon drippings in skillet.
3. Combine all ingredients in slow cooker.
4. Cover. Cook on Low 9-10 hours, or until meat is tender. Stir occasionally.

# Forgotten Minestrone
**Phyllis Attig**
Reynolds, IL

*Makes 8 servings*

1 lb. beef stewing meat
6 cups water
28-oz. can tomatoes, diced, undrained
1 beef bouillon cube
1 medium onion, chopped
2 Tbsp. minced dried parsley
1½ tsp. salt
1½ tsp. dried thyme
½ tsp. pepper
1 medium zucchini, thinly sliced
2 cups finely chopped cabbage
16-oz. can garbanzo beans, drained
1 cup uncooked small elbow, *or* shell, macaroni
¼ cup grated Parmesan cheese

1. Combine beef, water, tomatoes, bouillon, onion, parsley, salt, thyme, and pepper.
2. Cover. Cook on Low 7-9 hours, or until meat is tender.
3. Stir in zucchini, cabbage, beans, and macaroni. Cover and cook on High 30-45 minutes, or until vegetables are tender.
4. Sprinkle individual servings with Parmesan cheese.

# Slow-Cooker Minestrone
**Dorothy Shank**
Sterling, IL

*Makes 8 servings*

3 cups water
1½ lbs. stewing meat, cut into bite-sized pieces
1 medium onion, diced
4 carrots, diced
14½-oz. can tomatoes
2 tsp. salt
10-oz. pkg. frozen mixed vegetables, *or* your choice of frozen vegetables
1 Tbsp. dried basil
½ cup dry vermicelli
1 tsp. dried oregano
grated Parmesan cheese

1. Combine all ingredients except cheese in slow cooker. Stir well.
2. Cover. Cook on Low 10-12 hours, or on High 4-5 hours.
3. Top individual servings with Parmesan cheese.

# Hearty Alphabet Soup

Maryann Markano
Wilmington, DE

*Makes 5-6 servings*

1/2 lb. beef stewing meat,
  *or* round steak, cubed
14 1/2-oz. can stewed
  tomatoes
8-oz. can tomato sauce
1 cup water
1 envelope dry onion soup
  mix
10-oz. pkg. frozen
  vegetables, partially
  thawed
1/2 cup uncooked alphabet
  noodles

1. Combine meat, tomatoes, tomato sauce, water, and soup mix in slow cooker.
2. Cover. Cook on Low 6-8 hours. Turn to High.
3. Stir in vegetables and noodles. Add more water if mixture is too dry and thick.
4. Cover. Cook on High 30 minutes, or until vegetables are tender.

# Hamburger Vegetable Soup

Donna Conto
Saylorsburg, PA

*Makes 6-8 servings*

1/2 lb. ground beef,
  browned
6 beef bouillon cubes,
  crushed
16-oz. can tomatoes
1 large onion, diced
3/4 cup sliced celery
1 medium carrot, diced
1 garlic clove, minced
1 bay leaf
1/2 tsp. salt
1/8 tsp. pepper
10-oz. pkg. frozen peas
3 Tbsp. chopped parsley

1. Combine all ingredients except peas and parsley in slow cooker.
2. Cover. Cook on Low 5 hours.
3. Stir in peas during last hour.
4. Garnish with parsley before serving.

# Vegetable Beef Soup

Ruth Ann Swartzendruber
Hydro, OK

*Makes 4-5 servings*

1 lb. ground beef, browned
  and drained
2 cups tomato juice
2 cups beef broth
1 lb. frozen mixed
  vegetables, *or* your
  choice of vegetables

1. Combine all ingredients in slow cooker.
2. Cover. Cook on High 3 hours, and then on Low 3-4 hours.

# Quick and Easy Italian Vegetable Beef Soup

**Lisa Warren**
Parkesburg, PA

*Makes 8-10 servings*

1 lb. ground beef, *or*
  turkey, browned and
  drained
3 carrots, sliced
4 potatoes, peeled and
  cubed
1 small onion, diced
1 tsp. garlic powder
1 tsp. Italian seasoning
3/4 tsp. salt
1/4 tsp. pepper
15-oz. can diced Italian
  tomatoes, *or* 2 fresh
  tomatoes, chopped
6-oz. can Italian-flavored
  tomato paste
4 1/2 cups water
1 quart beef broth

1. Combine all ingredients
in slow cooker.
2. Cover. Cook on High 6-8
hours, or until potatoes and
carrots are tender.

# Spicy Beef Vegetable Stew

**Melissa Raber**
Millersburg, OH

*Makes 12 servings*

1 lb. ground beef
1 cup chopped onions
30-oz. jar meatless
  spaghetti sauce
3 1/2 cups water
1 lb. frozen mixed
  vegetables
10-oz. can diced tomatoes
  with green chilies
1 cup sliced celery
1 tsp. beef bouillon
  granules
1 tsp. pepper

1. Cook beef and onion in
skillet until meat is no longer
pink. Drain. Transfer to slow
cooker.
2. Stir in remaining ingredients.
3. Cover. Cook on Low 8
hours.

# Hearty Beef and Cabbage Soup

**Carolyn Mathias**
Williamsville, NY

*Makes 8 servings*

1 lb. ground beef
1 medium onion, chopped
40-oz. can tomatoes
2 cups water
15-oz. can kidney beans
1 tsp. salt
1/2 tsp. pepper
1 Tbsp. chili powder
1/2 cup chopped celery
2 cups thinly sliced
  cabbage

1. Saute beef in skillet.
Drain.
2. Combine all ingredients
except cabbage in slow
cooker.
3. Cover. Cook on Low 3
hours. Add cabbage. Cook on
High 30-60 minutes longer.

I find that adding 1/4-1/2 cup of a burgundy or Chablis
wine to most soup and stew recipes brings out the flavor of
the other seasonings.

**Joyce Kant**
Rochester, NY

# Hamburger Soup with Barley

Becky Oswald
Broadway, VA

*Makes 10 servings*

1 lb. ground beef
1 medium onion, chopped
3 14½-oz. cans beef
   consomme
28-oz. can diced, *or*
   crushed, tomatoes
3 carrots, sliced
3 celery ribs, sliced
8 Tbsp. barley
1 bay leaf
1 tsp. dried thyme
1 Tbsp. dried parsley
1 tsp. salt
½ tsp. pepper

1. Brown beef and onion
in skillet. Drain.
2. Combine all ingredients
in slow cooker.
3. Cover. Cook on High 3
hours, or Low 6-8 hours.

# Vegetable Soup with Potatoes

Annabelle Unternahrer
Shipshewana, IN

*Makes 6-8 servings*

1 lb. hamburger, browned
   and drained
2 15-oz. cans diced
   tomatoes
2 carrots, sliced *or* cubed
2 onions, sliced *or* cubed
2 potatoes, diced
1-2 garlic cloves, minced
12-oz. can V-8 vegetable
   juice
1½-2 cups sliced celery
2 tsp. beef stock
   concentrate, *or* 2 beef
   bouillon cubes
2-3 cups vegetables
   (cauliflower, peas, corn,
   limas, *or* your choice of
   leftovers from your
   freezer)

1. Combine all ingredients
in slow cooker.
2. Cover. Cook on Low 12
hours, or High 4-6 hours.

**Note:**
   If using leftover vegetables
that are precooked, add during last hour if cooking on
Low, or during last half hour
if cooking on High.

**Variation:**
   Use 3 cups pre-cooked
dried beans or lentils instead
of hamburger.

# Vegetable Potato Beef Soup

Beth Shank
Wellman, IA

*Makes 6-8 servings*

1½ cups sliced carrots
1½ cups cubed potatoes
1 cup sliced celery
½ cup chopped onion
2 cups water
1¼ lbs. ground beef,
   browned and drained
2 tsp. salt
5 cups tomato juice
1 Tbsp. brown sugar

1. Combine vegetables and
water in microwave-safe container. Cover and microwave
on High 18-20 minutes. Do
not drain. Place vegetables in
slow cooker.
2. Combine all ingredients
in slow cooker.
3. Cover. Cook on Low 6-8
hours, or until vegetables are
done.

**Variation:**
   Add 15-oz. can green
beans, drained, *or* 15-oz. can
lima beans, drained.

# Hamburger Lentil Soup

**Juanita Marner**
Shipshewana, IN

*Makes 8 servings*

1 lb. ground beef
1/2 cup chopped onions
4 carrots, diced
3 ribs celery, diced
1 garlic clove, minced, *or* 1
   tsp. garlic powder
1 qt. tomato juice
1 Tbsp. salt
2 cups dry lentils, washed
   with stones removed
1 qt. water
1/2 tsp. dried marjoram
1 Tbsp. brown sugar

1. Brown ground beef and onion in skillet. Drain.
2. Combine all ingredients in slow cooker.
3. Cover. Cook on Low 8-10 hours, or High 4-6 hours.

# Vegetable Soup with Noodles

**Glenda S. Weaver**
New Holland, PA

*Makes 6 servings*

1 pint water
2 beef bouillon cubes
1 onion, chopped
1 lb. ground beef
1/4 cup ketchup
1 tsp. salt
1/8 tsp. celery salt
1/2 cup uncooked noodles
12-16 oz. pkg. frozen
   mixed vegetables, *or*
   vegetables of your
   choice
1 pint tomato juice

1. Dissolve bouillon cubes in water.
2. Brown onion and beef in skillet. Drain.
3. Combine all ingredients in slow cooker.
4. Cover. Cook on Low 6 hours, or on High 2-3 hours, until vegetables are tender.

# Steak Soup

**Ilene Bontrager**
Arlington, KS
**Deb Unternahrer**
Wayland, IA

*Makes 10-12 servings*

2 lbs. coarsely ground
   chuck, browned and
   drained
5 cups water
1 large onion, chopped
4 ribs celery, chopped
3 carrots, sliced
2 14 1/2-oz. cans diced
   tomatoes
10-oz. pkg. frozen mixed
   vegetables
5 Tbsp. beef-based
   granules, *or* 5 beef
   bouillon cubes
1/2 tsp. pepper
1/2 cup melted butter
1/2 cup flour
2 tsp. salt

1. Combine chuck, water, onion, celery, carrots, tomatoes, mixed vegetables, beef granules, and pepper in slow cooker.
2. Cover. Cook on Low 8-12 hours, or High 4-6 hours.
3. One hour before serving, turn to High. Make a paste of melted butter and flour. Stir until smooth. Pour into slow cooker and stir until well blended. Add salt.
4. Cover. Continue cooking on High until thickened.

# Dottie's Creamy Steak Soup

**Debbie Zeida**
Mashpee, MA

*Makes 4-6 servings*

1 lb. ground beef
half a large onion, chopped
12-oz. can V-8 vegetable juice
2-3 medium potatoes, diced
10¾-oz. can cream of mushroom soup
10¾-oz. can cream of celery soup
16-oz. pkg. frozen mixed vegetables, *or* your choice of frozen vegetables
2 tsp. salt
½-¾ tsp. pepper

1. Saute beef and onions in skillet. Drain.
2. Combine all ingredients in slow cooker.
3. Cover. Cook on Low 8-10 hours.

# Taco Soup with Black Beans

**Alexa Slonin**
Harrisonburg, VA

*Makes 6-8 servings*

1 lb. ground beef, browned and drained
28-oz. can crushed tomatoes
15¼-oz. can corn, undrained
15-oz. can black beans, undrained
15½-oz. can red kidney beans, undrained
1 envelope dry Hidden Valley Ranch Dressing mix
1 envelope dry taco seasoning
1 small onion, chopped
tortilla, *or* corn, chips
shredded cheese
sour cream

1. Combine all ingredients except chips, shredded cheese, and sour cream in slow cooker.
2. Cover. Cook on Low 4-6 hours.
3. Garnish individual servings with chips, cheese, and sour cream.

# Taco Soup with Pinto Beans

**Janie Steele**
Moore, OK

*Makes 10-12 servings*

1 lb. ground beef
1 large onion, chopped
3 14-oz. cans pinto beans
14-oz. can tomatoes with chilies
14½-oz. can chopped tomatoes
15-oz. can tomato sauce
1 pkg. dry Hidden Valley Ranch Dressing mix
1 pkg. dry taco seasoning
15¼-oz. can corn, drained

1. Brown beef and onions in skillet. Drain.
2. Combine all ingredients in slow cooker.
3. Cover. Cook on Low 4 hours, or until ingredients are heated through.

# Sante Fe Soup with Melted Cheese

Carla Koslowsky
Hillsboro, KS

*Makes 8 servings*

1 lb. Velveeta cheese, cubed
1 lb. ground beef, browned and drained
15¼-oz. can corn, undrained
15-oz. can kidney beans, undrained
14½-oz. can diced tomatoes with green chilies
14½-oz. can stewed tomatoes
2 Tbsp. dry taco seasoning
corn chips, *or* soft tortillas

1. Combine all ingredients except chips or tortillas in slow cooker.
2. Cover. Cook on High 3 hours.
3. Serve with corn chips as a side, or dip soft tortillas in individual servings in soup bowls.

# Taco Soup with Whole Tomatoes

Marla Folkerts
Holland, OH

*Makes 6-8 servings*

1 lb. ground beef
½ cup chopped onions
28-oz. can whole tomatoes with juice
14-oz. can kidney beans with juice
17-oz. can corn with juice
8-oz. can tomato sauce
1 pkg. dry taco seasoning
1-2 cups water
salt to taste
pepper to taste
1 cup grated cheddar cheese
taco, *or* corn, chips

1. Brown beef and onions in skillet. Drain.
2. Combine all ingredients except cheese and chips in slow cooker.
3. Cover. Cook on Low 4-6 hours.
4. Ladle into bowls. Top with cheese and serve with chips.

# Taco Soup with Pork and Beans

Beth Shank
Wellman, IA

*Makes 6 servings*

1 lb. ground beef
half a small onion, finely diced
1 envelope dry taco seasoning
2 Tbsp. brown sugar
⅛ tsp. red cayenne pepper
15-oz. can kidney beans, drained
15-oz. can whole kernel corn, drained
15-oz. can pork and beans
46-oz. can tomato juice
taco chips, crushed
shredded cheese
sour cream

1. Brown beef and onion in skillet. Drain. Place in slow cooker.
2. Stir in taco seasoning, brown sugar, and pepper. Add beans, corn, pork and beans, and tomato juice. Mix well.
3. Cover. Cook on Low 4-6 hours.
4. Garnish individual servings with taco chips, cheese, and dollop of sour cream.

# Taco Soup with Pizza Sauce

### Barbara Kuhns
### Millersburg, OH

*Makes 8-10 servings*

2 lbs. ground beef, browned
1 small onion, chopped and sauteed in ground beef drippings
3/4 tsp. salt
1/2 tsp. pepper
1 1/2 pkgs. dry taco seasoning
1 qt. pizza sauce
1 qt. water
tortilla chips
shredded mozzarella cheese
sour cream

1. Combine ground beef, onion, salt, pepper, taco seasoning, pizza sauce, and water in 5-quart, or larger, slow cooker.
2. Cover. Cook on Low 3-4 hours.
3. Top individual servings with tortilla chips, cheese, and sour cream.

**Variation:**
Add 15-oz. can black beans and 4-oz. can chilies to mixture before cooking. (Be sure to use one very large cooker, or two medium-sized cookers.)

# Easy Chili

### Sheryl Shenk
### Harrisonburg, VA

*Makes 10-12 servings*

1 lb. ground beef
1 onion, chopped
1 green pepper, chopped
1 1/2 tsp. salt
1 Tbsp. chili powder
2 tsp. Worcestershire sauce
29-oz. can tomato sauce
3 16-oz. cans kidney beans, drained
14 1/2-oz. can crushed, *or* stewed, tomatoes
6-oz. can tomato paste
2 cups grated cheddar cheese

1. Brown meat in skillet. Add onion and green pepper halfway through browning process. Drain. Pour into slow cooker.
2. Stir in remaining ingredients except cheese.
3. Cover. Cook on High 3 hours, or Low 7-8 hours.
4. Serve in bowls topped with cheddar cheese.

**Note:**
This chili can be served over cooked rice.

# Berenice's Favorite Chili

### Berenice M. Wagner
### Dodge City, KS

*Makes 6 servings*

2 16-oz. cans red kidney beans, drained
2 14 1/2-oz. cans diced tomatoes
2 lbs. coarsely ground beef, browned and drained
2 medium onions, coarsely chopped
1 green pepper, coarsely chopped
2 garlic cloves, minced
2-3 Tbsp. chili powder
1 tsp. pepper
2 1/2 tsp. salt

1. Combine all ingredients in slow cooker in order listed. Stir once.
2. Cover. Cook on Low 10-12 hours, or High 5-6 hours.

**Variations:**
1. Top individual servings with green onion, sour cream, and cheese.
**Judy Govotsus**
Monrovia, MD

2. Increase proportion of tomatoes in chili by adding 8-oz. can tomato sauce before cooking.
**Bernice A. Esau**
North Newton, KS

# Slow-Cooker Chili

**Wanda S. Curtin**
Bradenton, FL
**Ann Sunday McDowell**
Newtown, PA

*Makes 10 servings*

2 lbs. ground beef,
  browned and drained
2 16-oz. cans red kidney
  beans, drained
2 14½-oz. cans diced
  tomatoes, drained
2 medium onions, chopped
2 garlic cloves, crushed
2-3 Tbsp. chili powder
1 tsp. ground cumin
1 tsp. black pepper
1 tsp. salt

1. Combine all ingredients in slow cooker.
2. Cover. Cook on Low 8-10 hours.

**Note:**
Use leftovers over lettuce and other fresh garden vegetables to make a taco salad.

**Variations:**
1. For more flavor, add cayenne pepper or a jalapeno pepper before cooking.
  **Dorothy Shank**
  Sterling, IL

2. Add 1 cup chopped green peppers before cooking.

  **Mary V. Warye**
  West Liberty, OH

# Trail Chili

**Jeanne Allen**
Rye, CO

*Makes 8-10 servings*

2 lbs. ground beef
1 large onion, diced
28-oz. can diced tomatoes
2 8-oz. cans tomato puree
1, *or* 2, 16-oz. cans kidney
  beans, undrained
4-oz. can diced green
  chilies
1 cup water
2 garlic cloves, minced
2 Tbsp. mild chili powder
2 tsp. salt
2 tsp. ground cumin
1 tsp. pepper

1. Brown beef and onion in skillet. Drain. Place in slow cooker on High.
2. Stir in remaining ingredients. Cook on High 30 minutes.
3. Reduce heat to Low. Cook 4-6 hours.

**Note:**
Top individual servings with shredded cheese. Serve with taco chips.

# Judy's Chili Soup

**Judy Buller**
Bluffton, OH

*Makes 6 servings*

1 lb. ground beef
1 onion, chopped
10¾-oz. can condensed
  tomato soup
16-oz. can kidney beans,
  drained
1 qt. tomato juice
⅛ tsp. garlic powder
1 Tbsp. chili powder
½ tsp. pepper
½ tsp. ground cumin
½ tsp. salt

1. Brown hamburger and onion in skillet. Drain.
2. Combine all ingredients in slow cooker. Mix well.
3. Cover. Cook on Low 7-8 hours.

**Variation:**
Use ground venison instead of ground beef.

39

## Colleen's Favorite Chili

**Colleen Heatwole**
Burton, MI

*Makes 6-8 servings*

2 medium onions, coarsely
  chopped
1-1½ lbs. ground beef,
  browned and drained
2 garlic cloves, minced
  fine, *or* ½ tsp. garlic
  powder
¾ cup finely diced green
  peppers
2 14½-oz. cans diced
  tomatoes, *or* 1 quart
  home-canned tomatoes
30-32 oz. beans—kidney, *or*
  pinto, *or* mixture of the
  two
8-oz. can tomato sauce
¼ tsp. beaumonde spice,
  optional
1 tsp. ground cumin
½ tsp. pepper
1 tsp. seasoned salt
1 Tbsp., or more, chili
  powder
1 tsp. dried basil

1. Combine all ingredients
in slow cooker.
2. Cover. Cook on Low 8-
12 hours, or High 5-6 hours.

**Variations:**
1. Add 1 Tbsp. brown
sugar to mixture before cooking.
2. Put in another 1 lb.
beans and then decrease
ground beef to 1 lb.

## Chili Con Carne

**Donna Conto**
Saylorsburg, PA

*Makes 8 servings*

1 lb. ground beef
1 cup chopped onions
¾ cup chopped green
  peppers
1 garlic clove, minced
14½-oz. can tomatoes, cut
  up
16-oz. can kidney beans,
  drained
8-oz. can tomato sauce
2 tsp. chili powder
½ tsp. dried basil

1. Brown beef, onion,
green pepper, and garlic in
saucepan. Drain.
2. Combine all ingredients
in slow cooker.
3. Cover. Cook on Low 5-6
hours.
4. Serve in bread bowl.

**Variation:**
Add 16-oz. can pinto
beans, ¼ tsp. salt, and ¼ tsp.
pepper in Step 2.
**Alexa Slonin**
Harrisonburg, VA

## Quick and Easy Chili

**Nan Decker**
Albuquerque, NM

*Makes 4 servings*

1 lb. ground beef
1 onion, chopped
16-oz. can stewed tomatoes
11½-oz. can Hot V-8 juice
2 15-oz. cans pinto beans
¼ tsp. cayenne pepper
½ tsp. salt
1 Tbsp. chili powder
sour cream
chopped green onions
grated cheese
sliced ripe olives

1. Crumble ground beef in
microwave-safe casserole.
Add onion. Microwave, covered, on High 15 minutes.
Drain. Break meat into
pieces.
2. Combine all ingredients
in slow cooker.
3. Cook on Low 4-5 hours.
4. Garnish with sour
cream, chopped green onions,
grated cheese, and sliced ripe
olives.

# Cindy's Chili

**Cindy Krestynick**
Glen Lyon, PA

*Makes 4-6 servings*

1 lb. ground beef, browned
   and drained
3 15½-oz. cans chili beans
   (hot *or* mild)
28-oz. can stewed
   tomatoes, chopped
1 rib celery, chopped
4 cups tomato juice
½ tsp. garlic salt
½ tsp. chili powder
¼ tsp. pepper
¼ tsp. Tabasco sauce

1. Combine all ingredients
in large slow cooker.
2. Cover. Cook on Low 4-6
hours.

# Ed's Chili

**Marie Miller**
Scotia, NY

*Makes 4-6 servings*

1 lb. ground beef
1 pkg. dry taco seasoning
   mix
half a 12-oz. jar salsa
16-oz. can kidney beans,
   undrained
15-oz. can black beans,
   undrained
14½-oz. can diced
   tomatoes, undrained
pinch of sugar
shredded cheese
chopped onions
sour cream
diced fresh tomatoes
guacamole
sliced black olives

1. Brown ground beef in
skillet. Drain.
2. Combine first 7 ingredients in slow cooker.
3. Cover. Heat on High
until mixture comes to boil.
Reduce heat to Low. Simmer
1½ hours.
4. To reduce liquids, continue cooking uncovered.
5. Top individual servings
with choice of shredded
cheese, onions, a dollop of
sour cream, fresh diced tomatoes, guacamole, and sliced
olives.

# Pirate Stew

**Nancy Graves**
Manhattan, KS

*Makes 4-6 servings*

¾ cup sliced onion
1 lb. ground beef
¼ cup uncooked, long
   grain rice
3 cups diced raw potatoes
1 cup diced celery
2 cups canned kidney
   beans, drained
1 tsp. salt
⅛ tsp. pepper
¼ tsp. chili powder
¼ tsp. Worcestershire
   sauce
1 cup tomato sauce
½ cup water

1. Brown onions and
ground beef in skillet. Drain.
2. Layer ingredients in
slow cooker in order given.
3. Cover. Cook on Low 6
hours, or until potatoes and
rice are cooked.

**Variation:**
Add a layer of 2 cups
sliced carrots between pota-
toes and celery.
   **Katrine Rose**
   Woodbridge, VA

# Corn Chili

**Gladys Longacre**
Susquehanna, PA

*Makes 4-6 servings*

1 lb. ground beef
1/2 cup chopped onions
1/2 cup chopped green
   peppers
1/2 tsp. salt
1/8 tsp. pepper
1/4 tsp. dried thyme
14 1/2-oz. can diced
   tomatoes with Italian
   herbs
6-oz. can tomato paste,
   diluted with 1 can water
2 cups frozen whole kernel
   corn
16-oz. can kidney beans
1 Tbsp. chili powder
sour cream
shredded cheese

1. Saute ground beef,
onions, and green peppers in
deep saucepan. Drain and
season with salt, pepper, and
thyme.
2. Stir in tomatoes, tomato
paste, and corn. Heat until
corn is thawed. Add kidney
beans and chili powder. Pour
into slow cooker.
3. Cover. Cook on Low 5-6
hours.
4. Top individual servings
with dollops of sour cream,
or sprinkle with shredded
cheese.

# White Bean Chili

**Tracey Stenger**
Gretna, LA

*Makes 10-12 servings*

1 lb. ground beef, browned
   and drained
1 lb. ground turkey,
   browned and drained
3 bell peppers, chopped
2 onions, chopped
4 garlic cloves, minced
2 14 1/2-oz. cans chicken, *or*
   vegetable, broth
15 1/2-oz. can butter beans,
   rinsed and drained
15-oz. can black-eyed peas,
   rinsed and drained
15-oz. can garbanzo beans,
   rinsed and drained
15-oz. can navy beans,
   rinsed and drained
4-oz. can chopped green
   chilies
2 Tbsp. chili powder
3 tsp. ground cumin
2 tsp. dried oregano
2 tsp. paprika
1 1/2-2 tsp. salt
1/2 tsp. pepper

1. Combine all ingredients
in slow cooker.
2. Cover. Cook on Low 8-
10 hours.

# Lotsa-Beans Chili

**Jean Weller**
State College, PA

*Makes 12-15 servings*

1 lb. ground beef
1 lb. bacon, diced
1/2 cup chopped onions
1/2 cup brown sugar
1/2 cup sugar
1/2 cup ketchup
2 tsp. dry mustard
1 tsp. salt
1/2 tsp. pepper
2 15-oz. cans green beans,
   drained
2 14 1/2-oz. cans baked
   beans
2 15-oz. cans butter beans,
   drained
2 16-oz. cans kidney beans,
   rinsed and drained

1. Brown ground beef and
bacon in slow cooker. Drain.
2. Combine all ingredients
in slow cooker.
3. Cover. Cook on High 1
hour. Reduce heat to Low
and cook 7-8 hours.

# Dorothea's Slow-Cooker Chili
**Dorothea K. Ladd**
Ballston Lake, NY

*Makes 6-8 servings*

1 lb. ground beef
1 lb. bulk pork sausage
1 large onion, chopped
1 large green pepper, chopped
2-3 ribs celery, chopped
2 15½-oz. cans kidney beans
29-oz. can tomato puree
6-oz. can tomato paste
2 cloves garlic, minced
2 Tbsp. chili powder
2 tsp. salt

1. Brown ground beef and sausage in skillet. Drain.
2. Combine all ingredients in slow cooker.
3. Cover. Cook on Low 8-10 hours.

**Variations:**
1. For extra flavor, add 1 tsp. cayenne pepper.
2. For more zest, use mild or hot Italian sausage instead of regular pork sausage.
3. Top individual servings with shredded sharp cheddar cheese.

# Chili for Twenty
**Janie Steele**
Moore, OK

*Makes 15-20 servings*

4 lbs. ground beef
3 onions, finely chopped
3 green peppers, finely chopped
2 garlic cloves, minced
4 16-oz. cans Italian-style tomatoes
4 16-oz. cans kidney beans, drained
10-oz. can diced tomatoes and chilies
2 6-oz. cans tomato paste
1 cup water
1 Tbsp. salt
1 tsp. pepper
3 whole cloves
2 bay leaves
2 Tbsp. chili powder

1. Brown meat, onions, and peppers in soup pot on top of stove. Drain.
2. Combine all ingredients in large bowl. Divide among several medium-sized slow cookers.
3. Cover. Cook on Low 3-4 hours.

# Crab Soup
**Susan Alexander**
Baltimore, MD

*Makes 10 servings*

1 lb. carrots, sliced
½ bunch celery, sliced
1 large onion, diced
2 10-oz. bags frozen mixed vegetables, *or* your choice of frozen vegetables
12-oz. can tomato juice
1 lb. ham, cubed
1 lb. beef, cubed
6 slices bacon, chopped
1 tsp. salt
¼ tsp. pepper
1 Tbsp. Old Bay seasoning
1 lb. claw crabmeat

1. Combine all ingredients except seasonings and crabmeat in large slow cooker. Pour in water until cooker is half-full.
2. Add spices. Stir in thoroughly. Put crab on top.
3. Cover. Cook on Low 8-10 hours.
4. Stir well and serve.

# Special Seafood Chowder

**Dorothea K. Ladd**
Ballston Lake, NY

*Makes 8-10 servings*

1/2 cup chopped onions
2 Tbsp. butter
1 lb. fresh *or* frozen cod, *or* haddock
4 cups diced potatoes
15-oz. can creamed corn
1/2 tsp. salt
dash pepper
2 cups water
1 pint half-and-half

1. Saute onions in butter in skillet until transparent but not brown.
2. Cut fish into 3/4-inch cubes. Combine fish, onions, potatoes, corn, seasonings, and water in slow cooker.
3. Cover. Cook on Low 6 hours, until potatoes are tender.
4. Add half-and-half during last hour.

**Variation:**
To cut milk fat, use 1 cup half-and-half and 1 cup skim milk, instead of 1 pint half-and-half.

# Manhattan Clam Chowder

**Joyce Slaymaker**
Strasburg, PA
**Louise Stackhouse**
Benton, PA

*Makes 8 servings*

1/4 lb. salt pork, *or* bacon, diced and fried
1 large onion, chopped
2 carrots, thinly sliced
3 ribs celery, sliced
1 Tbsp. dried parsley flakes
1-lb. 12-oz. can tomatoes
1/2 tsp. salt
2, *or* 3, 8-oz. cans clams with liquid
2 whole peppercorns
1 bay leaf
1 1/2 tsp. dried crushed thyme
3 medium potatoes, cubed

1. Combine all ingredients in slow cooker.
2. Cover. Cook on Low 8-10 hours.

# Rich and Easy Clam Chowder

**Rhonda Burgoon**
Collingswood, NJ

*Makes 4-5 servings*

3 10 3/4-oz. cans cream of potato soup
2 10 3/4-oz. cans New England clam chowder
1/2 cup butter
1 small onion, diced
1 pint half-and-half
2 6 1/2-oz. cans clams, chopped

1. Combine all ingredients in slow cooker.
2. Cover. Cook on Low 2-4 hours.

# Chicken Clam Chowder

Irene Klaeger
Inverness, Fl

*Makes 10-12 servings*

1 lb. bacon, diced
1/4 lb. ham, cubed
2 cups chopped onions
2 cups diced celery
1/2 tsp. salt
1/4 tsp. pepper
2 cups diced potatoes
2 cups cooked, diced
   chicken
4 cups chicken broth
2 bottles clam juice, *or*
   2 cans clams with juice
1-lb. can whole kernel corn
   with liquid
3/4 cup flour
4 cups milk
4 cups shredded cheddar,
   *or* Jack, cheese
1/2 cup whipping cream
   (not whipped)
2 Tbsp. fresh parsley

1. Saute bacon, ham, onions, and celery in skillet until bacon is crisp and onions and celery are limp. Add salt and pepper.
2. Combine all ingredients in slow cooker except flour, milk, cheese, cream, and parsley.
3. Cover. Cook on Low 6-8 hours, or on High 3-4 hours.
4. Whisk flour into milk. Stir into soup, along with cheese, whipping cream, and parsley. Cook one more hour on High.

# Chicken Broth

Ruth Conrad Liechty
Goshen IN

*Makes about 6 cups broth*

bony chicken pieces from 2
   chickens
1 onion, quartered
3 whole cloves, optional
3 ribs celery, cut up
1 carrot, quartered
1 1/2 tsp. salt
1/4 tsp. pepper
4 cups water

1. Place chicken in slow cooker.
2. Stud onion with cloves. Add to slow cooker with other ingredients.
3. Cover. Cook on High 4-5 hours.
4. Remove chicken and vegetables. Discard vegetables. Debone chicken. Cut up meat and add to broth. Use as stock for soups.

# Chicken Noodle Soup

Beth Shank
Wellman, IA

*Makes 6-8 servings*

5 cups hot water
2 Tbsp. chicken bouillon
   granules, *or* 2 chicken
   bouillon cubes
46-oz. can chicken broth
2 cups cooked chicken
1 tsp. salt
4 cups "homestyle"
   noodles, uncooked
1/3 cup thinly sliced celery,
   lightly pre-cooked in
   microwave
1/3 cup shredded, *or*
   chopped, carrots

1. Dissolve bouillon in water. Pour into slow cooker.
2. Add remaining ingredients. Mix well.
3. Cover. Cook on Low 4-6 hours.

# Brown Jug Soup
### Dorothy Shank
### Sterling, IL

*Makes 10-12 servings*

10½-oz. can chicken broth
4 chicken bouillon cubes
1 qt. water
2 cups (3-4 ribs) diced
    celery
2 cups ( 2 medium-sized)
    diced onions
4 cups (4 large) diced
    potatoes
3 cups (8 medium-sized)
    diced carrots
10-oz. pkg. frozen whole
    kernel corn
2 10¾-oz. cans cream of
    chicken soup
½ lb. Velveeta cheese,
    cubed

1. Combine all ingredients
except cheese in slow cooker.
2. Cover. Cook on Low
10-12 hours, or until vegetables are tender.
3. Just before serving, add
cheese. Stir until cheese is
melted. Serve.

# Chicken Corn Soup
### Eleanor Larson
### Glen Lyon, PA

*Makes 4-6 servings*

2 whole boneless skinless
    chicken breasts, cubed
1 onion, chopped
1 garlic clove, minced
2 carrots, sliced
2 ribs celery, chopped
2 medium potatoes, cubed
1 tsp. mixed dried herbs
⅓ cup tomato sauce
12-oz. can cream-style corn
14-oz. can whole kernel
    corn
3 cups chicken stock
¼ cup chopped Italian
    parsley
1 tsp. salt
¼ tsp. pepper

1. Combine all ingredients
except parsley, salt, and pepper in slow cooker.
2. Cover. Cook on Low 8-9
hours, or until chicken is tender.
3. Add parsley and seasonings 30 minutes before serving.

# Chili, Chicken, Corn Chowder
### Jeanne Allen
### Rye, CO

*Makes 6-8 servings*

¼ cup oil
1 large onion, diced
1 garlic clove, minced
1 rib celery, finely chopped
2 cups frozen, *or* canned,
    corn
2 cups cooked, deboned,
    diced chicken
4-oz. can diced green
    chilies
½ tsp. black pepper
2 cups chicken broth
salt to taste
1 cup half-and-half

1. In saucepan, saute
onion, garlic, and celery in oil
until limp.
2. Stir in corn, chicken,
and chilies. Saute for 2-3 minutes.
3. Combine all ingredients
except half-and-half in slow
cooker.
4. Cover. Heat on Low 4
hours.
5. Stir in half-and-half
before serving. Do not boil,
but be sure cream is heated
through.

---

Slow cookers come in a variety of sizes, from 2- to 8-
quarts. The best size for a family of four or five is a 5-6
quart-size.
**Dorothy M. Van Deest**
Memphis, TN

# White Chili

**Esther Martin**
Ephrata, PA

*Makes 8 servings*

3 15-oz. cans Great
　Northern beans, drained
8 oz. cooked and shredded
　chicken breasts
1 cup chopped onions
1 1/2 cups chopped yellow,
　red, *or* green bell
　peppers
2 jalapeno chili peppers,
　stemmed, seeded, and
　chopped (optional)
2 garlic cloves, minced
2 tsp. ground cumin
1/2 tsp. salt
1/2 tsp. dried oregano
3 1/2 cups chicken broth
sour cream
shredded cheddar cheese
tortilla chips

1. Combine all ingredients
except sour cream, cheddar
cheese, and chips in slow
cooker.
2. Cover. Cook on Low 8-
10 hours, or High 4-5 hours.
3. Ladle into bowls and
top individual servings with
sour cream, cheddar cheese,
and chips.

# White Chili Speciality

**Barbara McGinnis**
Jupiter, FL

*Makes 8-10 servings*

1 lb. large Great Northern
　beans, soaked overnight
2 lbs. boneless, skinless
　chicken breasts, cut up
1 medium onion, chopped
2 4 1/2-oz. cans chopped
　green chilies
2 tsp. cumin
1/2 tsp. salt
14 1/2-oz. can chicken broth
1 cup water

1. Put soaked beans in
medium-sized saucepan and
cover with water. Bring to
boil and simmer 20 minutes.
Discard water.
2. Brown chicken, if
desired, in 1-2 Tbsp. oil in
skillet.
3. Combine pre-cooked
and drained beans, chicken,
and all remaining ingredients
in slow cooker.
4. Cover. Cook on Low 10-
12 hours, or High 5-6 hours.

# Chicken Tortilla Soup

**Becky Harder**
Monument, CO

*Makes 6-8 servings*

4 chicken breast halves
2 15-oz. cans black beans,
　undrained
2 15-oz. cans Mexican
　stewed tomatoes, *or*
　Rotel tomatoes
1 cup salsa (mild, medium,
　or hot, whichever you
　prefer)
4-oz. can chopped green
　chilies
14 1/2-oz. can tomato sauce
tortilla chips
2 cups grated cheese

1. Combine all ingredients
except chips and cheese in
large slow cooker.
2. Cover. Cook on Low 8
hours.
3. Just before serving,
remove chicken breasts and
slice into bite-sized pieces.
Stir into soup.
4. To serve, put a handful
of chips in each individual
soup bowl. Ladle soup over
chips. Top with cheese.

# Tortilla Soup

**Joy Mintzer**
Newark, DE

---

*Makes 6 servings*

4 chicken breast halves
1 garlic clove, minced
2 Tbsp. margarine
2 14½-oz. cans chicken broth
2 14½-oz. cans chopped stewed tomatoes
1 cup salsa (mild, medium, *or* hot, whichever you prefer)
½ cup chopped cilantro
1 Tbsp., *or* more, ground cumin
8-oz. Monterey Jack cheese, cubed
sour cream
tortilla chips

1. Cook, debone, and shred chicken.
2. Add minced garlic to margarine in slow cooker. Saute.
3. Combine all ingredients except cheese, sour cream, and chips.
4. Cover. Cook on Low 8-10 hours.
5. Divide cubed cheese among 6 individual soup bowls. Ladle soup over cheese. Sprinkle with chips and top each bowl with a dollop of sour cream.

# Tex-Mex Chicken Chowder

**Janie Steele**
Moore, OK

---

*Makes 8-10 servings*

1 cup chopped onions
1 cup thinly sliced celery
2 garlic cloves, minced
1 Tbsp. oil
1½ lbs. boneless, skinless chicken breasts, cubed
32-oz. can chicken broth
1 pkg. country gravy mix
2 cups milk
16-oz. jar chunky salsa
32-oz. bag frozen hash brown potatoes
4½-oz. can chopped green chilies
8 oz. Velveeta cheese, cubed

1. Combine onions, celery, garlic, oil, chicken, and broth in 5-quart or larger slow cooker.
2. Cover. Cook on Low 2½ hours, until chicken is no longer pink.
3. In separate bowl, dissolve gravy mix in milk. Stir into chicken mixture. Add salsa, potatoes, chilies, and cheese and combine well. Cook on Low 2-4 hours, or until potatoes are fully cooked.

# Chicken and Ham Gumbo

**Barbara Tenney**
Delta, PA

---

*Makes 4 servings*

1½ lbs. boneless, skinless chicken thighs
1 Tbsp. oil
10-oz. pkg. frozen okra
½ lb. smoked ham, cut into small chunks
1½ cups coarsely chopped onions
1½ cups coarsely chopped green peppers
2 or 3 10-oz. cans cannellini beans, drained
6 cups chicken broth
2 10-oz. cans diced tomatoes with green chilies
2 Tbsp. chopped fresh cilantro

1. Cut chicken into bite-sized pieces. Cook in oil in skillet until no longer pink.
2. Run hot water over okra until pieces separate easily.
3. Combine all ingredients but cilantro in slow cooker.
4. Cover. Cook on Low 6-8 hours. Stir in cilantro before serving.

**Variations:**
1. Stir in ½ cup long grain, dry rice with rest of ingredients.
2. Add ¾ tsp. salt and ¼ tsp. pepper with other ingredients.

# Easy Southern Brunswick Stew

**Barbara Sparks**
Glen Burnie, MD

*Makes 10-12 servings*

2-3 lbs. pork butt
17-oz. can white corn
14-oz. bottle ketchup
2 cups diced, cooked poatotes
10-oz. pkg. frozen peas
2 10¾-oz. cans tomato soup
hot sauce to taste
salt to taste
pepper to taste

1. Place pork in slow cooker.
2. Cover. Cook on Low 6-8 hours. Remove meat from bone and shred.
3. Combine all ingredients in slow cooker.
4. Cover. Bring to boil on High. Reduce heat to Low and simmer 30 minutes.

# Joy's Brunswick Stew

**Joy Sutter**
Iowa City, IA

*Makes 8 servings*

1 lb. skinless, boneless chicken breasts, cut into bite-sized pieces
2 potatoes, thinly sliced
10¾-oz. can tomato soup
16-oz. can stewed tomatoes
10-oz. pkg. frozen corn
10-oz. pkg. frozen lima beans
3 Tbsp. onion flakes
¼ tsp. salt
⅛ tsp. pepper

1. Combine all ingredients in slow cooker.
2. Cover. Cook on High 2 hours. Reduce to Low and cook 2 hours.

**Variation:**

For more flavor, add 1, or 2, bay leaves during cooking.

# Brunswick Soup Mix

**Joyce B. Suiter**
Garysburg, NC

*Makes 14 servings*

1 large onion, chopped
4 cups frozen, cubed, hash browns, thawed
4 cups chopped cooked chicken, *or* 2 20-oz. cans canned chicken
14½-oz. can diced tomatoes
15-oz. can tomato sauce
15¼-oz. can corn
15¼-oz. can lima beans, drained
2 cups chicken broth
½ tsp. salt
½ tsp. pepper
¼ tsp. Worcestershire sauce
¼ cup sugar

1. Combine all ingredients in large slow cooker.
2. Cover. Cook on High 7 hours.
3. Cool and freeze in 2-cup portions.
4. To use, empty 1 frozen portion into saucepan with small amount of liquid: tomato juice, V-8 juice, or broth. Cook slowly until soup mixture thaws. Stir frequently, adding more liquid until of desired consistency.

## Oriental Turkey Chili

**Kimberly Jensen**
Bailey, CO

*Makes 6 servings*

2 cups yellow onions, diced
1 small red bell pepper, diced
1 lb. ground turkey, browned
2 Tbsp. minced gingerroot
3 cloves garlic, minced
1/4 cup dry sherry
1/4 cup hoisin sauce
2 Tbsp. chili powder
1 Tbsp. corn oil
2 Tbsp. soy sauce
1 tsp. sugar
2 cups canned whole tomatoes
16 oz. can dark red kidney beans, undrained

1. Combine all ingredients in slow cooker.
2. Cover. Cook on Low 6 hours.
3. Serve topped with chow mein noodles or over cooked white rice.

**Note:**
If you serve this chili over rice, this recipe will yield 10-12 servings.

## Joyce's Slow-Cooked Chili

**Joyce Slaymaker**
Strasburg, PA

*Makes 10 servings*

2 lbs. ground turkey
2 16-oz. cans kidney beans, rinsed and drained
2 14 1/2-oz. cans diced tomatoes, undrained
8-oz. can tomato sauce
2 medium onions, chopped
1 green pepper, chopped
2 cloves garlic, minced
2 Tbsp. chili powder
2 tsp. salt, optional
1 tsp. pepper
shredded cheddar cheese, optional

1. Brown ground turkey in skillet. Drain. Transfer to slow cooker.
2. Stir in remaining ingredients except cheese.
3. Cover. Cook on Low 8-10 hours, or on High 4 hours.
4. Garnish individual servings with cheese.

## Turkey Chili

**Dawn Day**
Westminster, CA

*Makes 6-8 servings*

1 large chopped onion
2-3 Tbsp. oil
1 lb. ground turkey
1/2 tsp. salt
3 Tbsp. chili powder
6-oz. can tomato paste
3 1-lb. cans small red beans with liquid
1 cup frozen corn

1. Saute onion in oil in skillet until transparent. Add turkey and salt and brown lightly in skillet.
2. Combine all ingredients in slow cooker. Mix well.
3. Cover. Cook on Low 8-9 hours.

**Note:**
Ground beef can be used in place of turkey.

**Variation:**
Serve over rice, topped with shredded cheddar cheese and sour cream.

# Chili Sans Cholesterol

Dolores S. Kratz
Souderton, PA

*Makes 4 servings*

1 lb. ground turkey
1/2 cup chopped celery
1/2 cup chopped onions
8-oz. can tomatoes
14-oz. can pinto beans
14 1/2-oz. can diced
    tomatoes
1/2 tsp., *or* more, chili
    powder
1/2 tsp. salt
dash pepper

1. Saute turkey in skillet until browned. Drain.
2. Combine all ingredients in slow cooker.
3. Cover. Cook on Low 6 hours.

# Leftover Turkey Soup

Janie Steele
Moore, OK

*Makes 8-10 servings*

1 small onion, chopped
1 cup chopped celery
1 Tbsp. oil
2-3 cups diced turkey
1 cup cooked rice
leftover gravy, *or*
    combination of leftover
    gravy and chicken broth

1. Saute onion and celery in oil in saucepan until translucent.
2. Combine all ingredients in slow cooker, adding gravy and/or broth until of the consistency you want.
3. Cover. Cook on Low for at least 2-3 hours, or until heated through.

# Italian Vegetable Soup

Patti Boston
Newark, OH

*Makes 4-6 servings*

3 small carrots, sliced
1 small onion, chopped
2 small potatoes, diced
2 Tbsp. chopped parsley
1 garlic clove, minced
3 tsp. beef bouillon
    granules, *or* 3 beef
    bouillon cubes
1 1/4 tsp. dried basil
1/2 tsp. salt
1/4 tsp. pepper
16-oz. can red kidney
    beans, undrained
3 cups water
14 1/2-oz. can stewed
    tomatoes, with juice
1 cup diced, cooked ham

1. Layer carrots, onions, potatoes, parsley, garlic, beef bouillon, basil, salt, pepper, and kidney beans in slow cooker. Do not stir. Add water.
2. Cover. Cook on Low 8-9 hours, or on High 4 1/2-5 1/2 hours, until vegetables are tender.
3. Stir in tomatoes and ham. Cover and cook on High 10-15 minutes.

# Chet's Trucker Stew

Janice Muller
Derwood, MD

*Makes 8 servings*

1 lb. bulk pork sausage, cooked and drained
1 lb. ground beef, cooked and drained
31-oz. can pork and beans
16-oz. can light kidney beans
16-oz. can dark kidney beans
14 1/2-oz. can waxed beans, drained
14 1/2-oz. can lima beans, drained
1 cup ketchup
1 cup brown sugar
1 Tbsp. spicy prepared mustard

1. Combine all ingredients in slow cooker.
2. Cover. Simmer on High 2-3 hours.

# Spicy Potato Soup

Sharon Kauffman
Harrisonburg, VA

*Makes 6-8 servings*

1 lb. ground beef, *or* bulk sausage, browned
4 cups cubed peeled potatoes
1 small onion, chopped
3 8-oz. cans tomato sauce
2 tsp. salt
1 1/2 tsp. pepper
1/2-1 tsp. hot pepper sauce
water

1. Combine all ingredients except water in slow cooker. Add enough water to cover ingredients.
2. Cover. Cook on Low 8-10 hours, or High 5 hours, until potatoes are tender.

# Hearty Potato Sauerkraut Soup

Kathy Hertzler
Lancaster, PA

*Makes 6-8 servings*

4 cups chicken broth
10 3/4-oz. can cream of mushroom soup
16-oz. can sauerkraut, rinsed and drained
8 oz. fresh mushrooms, sliced
1 medium potato, cubed
2 medium carrots, peeled and sliced
2 ribs celery, chopped
2 lbs. Polish kielbasa (smoked), cubed
2 1/2 cups chopped cooked chicken
2 Tbsp. vinegar
2 tsp. dried dillweed
1 1/2 tsp. pepper

1. Combine all ingredients in large slow cooker.
2. Cover. Cook on Low 10-12 hours.
3. If necessary, skim fat before serving.

# Sauerkraut Soup

**Barbara Tenny**
Delta, PA

*Makes 8 servings*

1 lb. smoked Polish sausage, cut into 1/2-inch pieces
5 medium potatoes, cubed
2 large onions, chopped
2 large carrots, cut into 1/4-inch slices
42-45-oz. can chicken broth
32-oz. can *or* bag sauerkraut, rinsed and drained
6-oz. can tomato paste

1. Combine all ingredients in large slow cooker. Stir to combine.
2. Cover. Cook on High 2 hours, and then on Low 6-8 hours.
3. Serve with rye bread.

# Kielbasa Soup

**Bernice M. Gnidovec**
Streator, IL

*Makes 8 servings*

16-oz. pkg. frozen mixed vegetables, *or* your choice of vegetables
6-oz. can tomato paste
1 medium onion, chopped
3 medium potatoes, diced
1 1/2 lbs. kielbasa, cut into 1/4-inch pieces
4 qts. water
fresh parsley

1. Combine all ingredients except parsley in large slow cooker.
2. Cover. Cook on Low 12 hours.
3. Garnish individual servings with fresh parsley.

# Curried Pork and Pea Soup

**Kathy Hertzler**
Lancaster, PA

*Makes 6-8 servings*

1 1/2-lb. boneless pork shoulder roast
1 cup yellow, *or* green, split peas, rinsed and drained
1/2 cup finely chopped carrots
1/2 cup finely chopped celery
1/2 cup finely chopped onions
49 1/2-oz. can (approximately 6 cups) chicken broth
2 tsp. curry powder
1/2 tsp. paprika
1/4 tsp. ground cumin
1/4 tsp. pepper
2 cups torn fresh spinach

1. Trim fat from pork and cut pork into 1/2-inch pieces.
2. Combine split peas, carrots, celery, and onions in slow cooker.
3. Stir in broth, curry powder, paprika, cumin, and pepper. Stir in pork.
4. Cover. Cook on Low 10-12 hours, or on High 4 hours.
5. Stir in spinach. Serve immediately.

## Ruth's Split Pea Soup

**Ruth Conrad Liechty**
Goshen, IN

*Makes 6-8 servings*

1 lb. bulk sausage,
   browned and drained
6 cups water
1 bag (2¼ cups) dry split
   peas
2 medium potatoes, diced
1 onion, chopped
½ tsp. dried marjoram, *or*
   thyme
½ tsp. pepper

1. Wash and sort dried peas, removing any stones. Then combine all ingredients in slow cooker.
2. Cover. Cook on Low 12 hours.

## Kelly's Split Pea Soup

**Kelly Evenson**
Pittsboro, NC

*Makes 8 servings*

2 cups dry split peas
2 quarts water
2 onions, chopped
2 carrots, peeled and sliced
4 slices Canadian bacon,
   chopped
2 Tbsp. chicken bouillon
   granules, *or* 2 chicken
   bouillon cubes
1 tsp. salt
¼-½ tsp. pepper

1. Combine all ingredients in slow cooker.
2. Cover. Cook on Low 8-9 hours.

**Variation:**
   For a creamier soup, remove half of soup when done and puree. Stir back into rest of soup.

## Karen's Split Pea Soup

**Karen Stoltzfus**
Alto, MI

*Makes 6 servings*

2 carrots
2 ribs celery
1 onion
1 parsnip
1 leek (keep 3 inches of
   green)
1 ripe tomato
1 ham hock
1¾ cups (1 lb.) dried split
   peas, washed, with
   stones removed
2 Tbsp. olive oil
1 bay leaf
1 tsp. dried thyme
4 cups chicken broth
4 cups water
1 tsp. salt
¼ tsp. pepper
2 tsp. chopped fresh
   parsley

1. Cut all vegetables into ¼-inch pieces and place in slow cooker. Add remaining ingredients except salt, pepper, and parsley.
2. Cover. Cook on High 7 hours.
3. Remove ham hock. Shred meat from bone and return meat to pot.
4. Season soup with salt and pepper. Stir in parsley. Serve immediately.

# Sally's Split Pea Soup

**Sally Holzem**
Schofield, WI

*Makes 8 servings*

1-lb. pkg. split peas
1 ham hock
1 carrot, diced
1 onion, diced
1 rib celery, diced
2 qts. water
1/4 tsp. pepper
1 bay leaf
2 whole allspice
3 potatoes, diced
1 tsp. sugar

1. Wash and sort split peas, removing any stones. Then combine ingredients in slow cooker.
2. Cover. Cook on Low 8-10 hours.
3. Remove ham bone. Cut meat off and dice. Return meat to soup. Stir through.
4. Remove bay leaf before serving.

# Dorothy's Split Pea Soup

**Dorothy M. Van Deest**
Memphis, TN

*Makes 6-8 servings*

2 Tbsp. butter, *or* margarine
1 cup minced onions
8 cups water
2 cups (1 lb.) green split peas, washed and stones removed
4 whole cloves
1 bay leaf
1/4 tsp. pepper
1 ham hock
1 cup finely minced celery
1 cup diced carrots
1/8 tsp. dried marjoram
1 Tbsp. salt
1/8 tsp. dried savory

1. Combine all ingredients in slow cooker.
2. Cover. Cook on Low 8-10 hours.
3. Remove ham bone and bay leaf before serving. Debone meat, cut into bite-sized pieces, and return to soup. Stir in and serve.

**Variation:**
For a thick soup, uncover soup after 8-10 hours and turn heat to High. Simmer, stirring occasionally, until the desired consistency is reached.

# Rosemarie's Pea Soup

**Rosemarie Fitzgerald**
Gibsonia, PA
**Shirley Sears**
Tiskilwa, IL

*Makes 4-6 servings*

2 cups dried split peas
4 cups water
1 rib celery, chopped
1 cup chopped potatoes
1 large carrot, chopped
1 medium onion, chopped
1/4 tsp. dried thyme, *or* marjoram
1 bay leaf
1/2 tsp. salt
1 garlic clove
1/2 tsp. dried basil

1. Combine all ingredients in slow cooker.
2. Cover. Cook on Low 8-12 hours, or on High 6 hours, until peas are tender.

**Variations:**
For increased flavor, use chicken broth instead of water. Stir in curry powder, coriander, or red pepper flakes to taste.

# French Market Soup

**Ethel Mumaw**
Berlin, OH

*Makes 2½ quarts soup*

2 cups dry bean mix,
   washed with stones
   removed
2 quarts water
1 ham hock
1 tsp. salt
¼ tsp. pepper
16-oz. can tomatoes
1 large onion, chopped
1 garlic clove, minced
1 chili pepper, chopped, *or*
   1 tsp. chili powder
¼ cup lemon juice

1. Combine all ingredients
in slow cooker.
2. Cover. Cook on Low 8
hours. Turn to High and cook
an additional 2 hours, or until
beans are tender.
3. Debone ham, cut meat
into bite-sized pieces, and stir
back into soup.

# Nine Bean Soup with Tomatoes

**Violette Harris Denney**
Carrollton, GA

*Makes 8-10 servings*

2 cups dry nine-bean soup
   mix
1 lb. ham, diced
1 large onion, chopped
1 garlic clove, minced
½-¾ tsp. salt
2 qts. water
16-oz. can tomatoes,
   undrained and chopped
10-oz. can tomatoes with
   green chilies, undrained

1. Sort and wash bean
mix. Place in slow cooker.
Cover with water 2 inches
above beans. Let soak
overnight. Drain.
2. Add ham, onion, garlic,
salt, and 2 quarts fresh water.
3. Cover. Cook on Low 7
hours.
4. Add remaining ingredi-
ents and continue cooking on
Low another hour. Stir occasionally.

**Note:**
Bean Soup mix is a mix of
barley pearls, black beans,
red beans, pinto beans, navy
beans, Great Northern beans,
lentils, split peas, and black-
eyed peas.

# Calico Ham and Bean Soup

**Esther Martin**
Ephrata, PA

*Makes 6-8 servings*

1 lb. dry bean mix, rinsed
   and drained, with
   stones removed
6 cups water
2 cups cubed cooked ham
1 cup chopped onions
1 cup chopped carrots
1 tsp. dried basil
1 tsp. dried oregano
¾ tsp. salt
¼ tsp. pepper
2 bay leaves
6 cups water
1 tsp. liquid smoke,
   optional

1. Combine beans and 6
cups water in large saucepan.
Bring to boil, reduce heat,
and simmer uncovered for 10
minutes. Drain, discarding
cooking water, and rinse
beans.
2. Combine all ingredients
in slow cooker.
3. Cover. Cook on Low 8-
10 hours, or High 4-5 hours.
Discard bay leaves before
serving.

# Bean and Herb Soup

LaVerne A. Olson
Willow Street, PA

*Makes 6-8 servings*

1 1/2 cups dry mixed beans
5 cups water
1 ham hock
1 cup chopped onions
1 cup chopped celery
1 cup chopped carrots
2-3 cups water
1 tsp. salt
1/4-1/2 tsp. pepper
1-2 tsp. fresh basil, *or*
    1/2 tsp. dried basil
1-2 tsp. fresh oregano, *or*
    1/2 tsp. dried oregano
1-2 tsp. fresh thyme, *or*
    1/2 tsp. dried thyme
2 cups fresh tomatoes,
    crushed, *or* 14 1/2-oz. can
    crushed tomatoes

1. Combine beans, water, and ham in saucepan. Bring to boil. Turn off heat and let stand 1 hour.
2. Combine onions, celery, and carrots in 2-3 cups water in another saucepan. Cook until soft. Mash slightly.
3. Combine all ingredients in slow cooker.
4. Cover. Cook on High 2 hours, and then on Low 2 hours.

# Northern Bean Soup

Patricia Howard
Albuquerque, NM

*Makes 6-8 servings*

1 lb. dry Northern beans
1 lb. ham
2 medium onions, chopped
half a green pepper,
    chopped
1 cup chopped celery
16-oz. can diced tomatoes
4 carrots, peeled and
    chopped
4-oz. can green chili
    peppers
1 tsp. garlic powder
1-2 qts. water
2-3 tsp. salt

1. Wash beans. Cover with water and soak overnight. Drain. Pour into slow cooker.
2. Dice ham into 1-inch pieces. Add to beans.
3. Stir in remaining ingredients.
4. Cover. Cook on High 2 hours, then on Low 10-12 hours, or until beans are tender.

# Easy Lima Bean Soup

Barbara Tenney
Delta, PA

*Makes 8-10 servings*

1 lb. bag large dry lima
    beans
1 large onion, chopped
6 ribs celery, chopped
3 large potatoes, cut in
    1/2-inch cubes
2 large carrots, cut in
    1/4-inch rounds
2 cups ham, sausage, *or*
    kielbasa
1 Tbsp. salt
1 tsp. pepper
2 bay leaves
3 quarts water, *or*
    combination water and
    beef broth

1. Sort beans. Soak overnight. Drain.
2. Combine all ingredients in slow cooker.
3. Cover. Cook on Low 8-10 hours.

**Variation:**
For extra flavor, add 1 tsp. dried oregano before cooking.

---

Most slow cookers perform best when more than half full.
**Dorothy M. Van Deest**
Memphis, TN

# Slow Cooked Navy Beans with Ham

Julia Lapp
New Holland, PA

*Makes 8-10 servings*

1 lb. dry navy beans (2½ cups)
5 cups water
1 garlic clove, minced
1 ham hock
1 tsp. salt

1. Soak beans in water at least 4 hours in slow cooker.
2. Add garlic and ham hock.
3. Cover. Cook on Low 7-8 hours, or High 4 hours. Add salt during last hour of cooking time.
4. Remove ham hock from cooker. Allow to cool. Cut ham from hock and stir back into bean mixture. Correct seasonings and serve in soup bowls with hot corn bread.

**Variation:**

For added flavor, stir 1 chopped onion, 2-3 chopped celery stalks, 2-3 sliced carrots, and 3-4 cups canned tomatoes into cooker with garlic and ham hock.

# Navy Bean Soup

Joyce Bowman
Lady Lake, FL

*Makes 8 servings*

1 lb. dry navy beans
8 cups water
1 onion, finely chopped
2 bay leaves
½ tsp. ground thyme
½ tsp. nutmeg
2 tsp. salt
½ tsp. lemon pepper
3 garlic cloves, minced
one ham hock, *or* 1-lb. ham pieces

1. Soak beans in water overnight. Strain out stones but reserve liquid.
2. Combine all ingredients in slow cooker.
3. Cover. Cook on Low 8-10 hours. Debone meat and cut into bite-sized pieces. Set ham aside.
4. Puree three-fourths of soup in blender in small batches. When finished blending, stir in meat.

**Variation:**

Add small chunks of cooked potatoes when stirring in ham pieces after blending.

# Overnight Bean Soup

Marie Morucci
Glen Lyon, PA

*Makes 6-8 servings*

1 lb. dry small white beans
6 cups water
2 cups boiling water
2 large carrots, diced
3 ribs celery, diced
2 tsp. chicken bouillon granules, *or* 2 chicken bouillon cubes
1 bay leaf
½ tsp. dried thyme
½ tsp. salt
¼ tsp. pepper
¼ cup chopped fresh parsley
1 envelope dry onion soup mix
crispy, crumbled bacon, optional

1. Rinse beans. Combine beans and 6 cups water in saucepan. Bring to boil. Reduce heat to low and simmer 2 minutes. Remove from heat. Cover and let stand 1 hour or overnight.
2. Place beans and soaking water in slow cooker. Add 2 cups boiling water, carrots, celery, bouillon, bay leaf, thyme, salt, and pepper.
3. Cover. Cook on High 5-5½ hours, or on Low 10-11 hours, until beans are tender.
4. Stir in parsley and soup mix. Cover. Cook on High 10-15 minutes.

5. Remove bay leaf. Garnish individual servings with bacon.

## Old-Fashioned Bean Soup

**Gladys M. High**
Ephrata, PA

*Makes 6 servings*

1 lb. dry navy beans, *or* dry green split peas
1-lb. meaty ham bone, *or* 1 lb. ham pieces
1-2 tsp. salt
1/4 tsp. ground pepper
1/2 cup chopped celery leaves
2 qts. water
1 medium onion, chopped
1 bay leaf, optional

1. Soak beans or peas overnight. Drain, discarding soaking water.
2. Combine all ingredients in slow cooker.
3. Cover. Cook on High 8-9 hours.
4. Debone ham bone, cut meat into bite-sized pieces, and stir back into soup.

## Caribbean-Style Black Bean Soup

**Sheryl Shenk**
Harrisonburg, VA

*Makes 8-10 servings*

1 lb. dried black beans, washed and stones removed
3 onions, chopped
1 green pepper, chopped
4 cloves garlic, minced
1 ham hock, *or* 3/4 cup cubed ham
1 Tbsp. oil
1 Tbsp. ground cumin
2 tsp. dried oregano
1 tsp. dried thyme
1 Tbsp. salt
1/2 tsp. pepper
3 cups water
2 Tbsp. vinegar
sour cream
fresh chopped cilantro

1. Soak beans overnight in 4 quarts water. Drain.
2. Combine beans, onions, green pepper, garlic, ham, oil, cumin, oregano, thyme, salt, pepper, and 3 cups fresh water. Stir well.
3. Cover. Cook on Low 8-10 hours, or on High 4-5 hours.
4. For a thick soup, remove half of cooked bean mixture and puree until smooth in blender or mash with potato masher. Return to cooker. If you like a soup-ier soup, leave as is.
5. Add vinegar and stir well. Debone ham, cut into

bite-sized pieces, and return to soup.
6. Serve in soup bowls with a dollop of sour cream in the middle of each individual serving, topped with fresh cilantro.

## Vegetable Bean Soup

**Kathi Rogge**
Alexandria, IN

*Makes 6-8 servings*

6 cups cooked beans: navy, pinto, Great Northern, etc.
1 meaty ham bone
1 cup cooked ham, diced
1/4 tsp. garlic powder
1 small bay leaf
1 cup cubed potatoes
1 cup chopped onions
1 cup chopped celery
1 cup chopped carrots
water

1. Combine all ingredients except water in 3 1/2-quart slow cooker. Add water to about 1 inch from top.
2. Cover. Cook on Low 5-8 hours.
3. Remove bay leaf before serving.

# Slow-Cooker Black Bean Chili

**Mary Seielstad**
Sparks, NV

*Makes 8 servings*

1 lb. pork tenderloin, cut into 1-inch chunks
16-oz. jar thick chunky salsa
3 15-oz. cans black beans, rinsed and drained
1/2 cup chicken broth
1 medium red bell pepper, chopped
1 medium onion, chopped
1 tsp. ground cumin
2-3 tsp. chili powder
1-1 1/2 tsp. dried oregano
1/4 cup sour cream

1. Combine all ingredients except sour cream in slow cooker.
2. Cover. Cook on Low 6-8 hours, or until pork is tender.
3. Garnish individual servings with sour cream.

**Note:**
This is good served over brown rice.

# Katelyn's Black Bean Soup

**Katelyn Bailey**
Mechanicsburg, PA

*Makes 4-6 servings*

1/3 cup chopped onions
1 garlic clove, minced
1-2 Tbsp. oil
2 15 1/2-oz. cans black beans, undrained
1 cup water
1 chicken bouillon cube
1/2 cup diced, cooked, smoked ham
1/2 cup diced carrots
1 dash, *or* more, cayenne pepper
1-2 drops, *or* more, Tabasco sauce
sour cream

1. Saute onion and garlic in oil in saucepan.
2. Puree or mash contents of one can of black beans. Add to sauteed ingredients.
3. Combine all ingredients except sour cream in slow cooker.
4. Cover. Cook on Low 6-8 hours.
5. Add dollop of sour cream to each individual bowl before serving.

# Baked Bean Soup

**Maryann Markano**
Wilmington, DE

*Makes 5-6 servings*

1-lb. 12-oz. can baked beans
6 slices browned bacon, chopped
2 Tbsp. bacon drippings
2 Tbsp. finely chopped onions
14 1/2-oz. can stewed tomatoes
1 Tbsp. brown sugar
1 Tbsp. vinegar
1 tsp. seasoning salt

1. Combine all ingredients in slow cooker.
2. Cover. Cook on Low 4-6 hours.

# Mjeodrah or Esau's Lentil Soup

Dianna Milhizer
Springfield, VA

*Makes 8 servings*

1 cup chopped carrots
1 cup diced celery
2 cups chopped onions
1 Tbsp. olive oil, *or* butter
2 cups brown rice
1 Tbsp. olive oil, *or* butter
6 cups water
1 lb. lentils, washed and drained
garden salad
vinaigrette

1. Saute carrots, celery, and onions in 1 Tbsp. oil in skillet. When soft and translucent place in slow cooker.
2. Brown rice in 1 Tbsp. oil until dry. Add to slow cooker.
3. Stir in water and lentils.
4. Cover. Cook on High 6-8 hours.
5. When thoroughly cooked, serve 1 cup each in individual soup bowls. Cover each with a serving of fresh garden salad (lettuce, spinach leaves, chopped tomatoes, minced onions, chopped bell peppers, sliced olives, sliced radishes). Pour favorite vinaigrette over all.

# French Onion Soup

Jenny R. Unternahrer
Wayland, IA
**Janice Yoskovich**
Carmichaels, PA

*Makes 10 servings*

8-10 large onions, sliced
1/2 cup butter *or* margarine
6 10½-oz. cans condensed beef broth
1½ tsp. Worcestershire sauce
3 bay leaves
10 slices French bread, toasted
grated Parmesan and/or shredded mozzarella cheese

1. Saute onions in butter until crisp-tender. Transfer to slow cooker.
2. Add broth, Worcestershire sauce, and bay leaves.
3. Cover. Cook on Low 5-7 hours, or until onions are tender. Discard bay leaves.
4. Ladle into bowls. Top each with a slice of bread and some cheese.

**Note:**
For a more intense beef flavor, add one beef bouillon cube, or use home-cooked beef broth instead of canned broth.

# Potato Soup

**Jeanne Hertzog**, Bethlehem, PA
**Marcia S. Myer**, Manheim, PA
**Rhonda Lee Schmidt**
Scranton, PA
**Mitzi McGlynchey**
Downingtown, PA
**Vera Schmucker**, Goshen, IN
**Kaye Schnell**, Falmouth, MA
**Elizabeth Yoder**
Millersburg, OH

*Makes 8-10 servings*

6 potatoes, peeled and cubed
2 leeks, chopped
2 onions, chopped
1 rib celery, sliced
4 chicken bouillon cubes
1 Tbsp. dried parsley flakes
5 cups water
1 Tbsp. salt
pepper to taste
1/3 cup butter
13-oz. can evaporated milk
chopped chives

1. Combine all ingredients except milk and chives in slow cooker.
2. Cover. Cook on Low 10-12 hours, or High 3-4 hours. Stir in milk during last hour.
3. If desired, mash potatoes before serving.
4. Garnish with chives.

**Variations:**
1. Add one carrot, sliced, to vegetables before cooking.
2. Instead of water and bouillon cubes, use 4-5 cups chicken stock.

# No-Fuss Potato Soup

**Lucille Amos**
Greensboro, NC
**Lavina Hochstedler**
Grand Blanc, MI
**Betty Moore**
Plano, IL

*Makes 8-10 servings*

6 cups diced, peeled
   potatoes
5 cups water
2 cups diced onions
1/2 cup diced celery
1/2 cup chopped carrots
1/4 cup margarine, *or*
   butter
4 tsp. chicken bouillon
   granules
2 tsp. salt
1/4 tsp. pepper
12-oz. can evaporated milk
3 Tbsp. chopped fresh
   parsley
8 oz. cheddar, *or* Colby,
   cheese, shredded

1. Combine all ingredients
except milk, parsley, and
cheese in slow cooker.
2. Cover. Cook on High 7-8
hours, or until vegetables are
tender.
3. Stir in milk and parsley.
Stir in cheese until it melts.
Heat thoroughly.

**Variations:**
1. For added flavor, stir in
3 slices bacon, browned until
crisp, and crumbled.
2. Top individual servings
with chopped chives.

# Baked Potato Soup

**Kristina Shull**
Timberville, VA

*Makes 6-8 servings*

4 large baked potatoes
2/3 cup butter
2/3 cup flour
6 cups milk, whole *or* 2%
3/4 tsp. salt
1/2 tsp. pepper
4 green onions, chopped
12 slices bacon, fried and
   crumbled
2 cups shredded cheddar
   cheese
1 cup (8 oz.) sour cream

1. Cut potatoes in half.
Scoop out pulp and put in
small bowl.
2. Melt butter in large kettle. Add flour. Gradually stir
in milk. Continue to stir until
smooth, thickened, and bubbly.
3. Stir in potato pulp, salt,
pepper, and three-quarters of
the onions, bacon, and
cheese. Cook until heated.
Stir in sour cream.
4. Transfer to slow cooker
set on Low. Top with remaining onions, bacon, and
cheese. Take to a potluck, or
serve on a buffet table,
straight from the cooker.

**Variation:**
Add several slices of
Velveeta cheese to make soup
extra cheesy and creamy.

# Sandy's Potato Soup

**Sandra D. Thony**
Jenks, OK

*Makes 8-10 servings*

8 large potatoes, cubed
2 medium onions, chopped
3 Tbsp. butter, *or*
   margarine
1/2-1 lb. bacon, cooked
   crisp, drained, and
   crumbled
3 chicken bouillon cubes
2 Tbsp. dried parsley
6 cups water
2 cups milk
1/2 cup flour
1/4 cup water
1 tsp. salt
1/4-1/2 tsp. pepper

1. Combine all ingredients
except flour, 1/4 cup water,
salt, and pepper in large slow
cooker.
2. Cover. Cook on High 6
hours, and then on Low 3
hours.
3. Make paste out of flour
and water. Stir into soup one
hour before serving. Season
with salt and pepper.

**Variations:**
1. Make Cheesy Potato
Soup by adding 1/4 lb. cubed
Velveeta, or your choice of
cheese, during last hour of
cooking.
2. For added richness, use
1 cup whole milk and 1 cup
evaporated milk.

# German Potato Soup

**Lee Ann Hazlett**
Freeport, IL

*Makes 6-8 servings*

1 onion, chopped
1 leek, trimmed and diced
2 carrots, diced
1 cup chopped cabbage
1/4 cup chopped fresh
    parsley
4 cups beef broth
1 lb. potatoes, diced
1 bay leaf
1-2 tsp. black pepper
1 tsp. salt, optional
1/2 tsp. caraway seeds,
    optional
1/4 tsp. nutmeg
1 lb. bacon, cooked and
    crumbled
1/2 cup sour cream

1. Combine all ingredients
except bacon and sour cream.
2. Cover. Cook on Low 8-
10 hours, or High 4-5 hours.
3. Remove bay leaf. Use a
slotted spoon to remove potatoes. Mash potatoes and mix
with sour cream. Return to
slow cooker. Stir in. Add
bacon and mix together thoroughly.

# Potato Comfort Soup

**Charlotte Bull**
Cassville, MO

*Makes 8 servings*

6 cups cubed, peeled
    potatoes
2 cups chopped onions
1/2 cup chopped celery
1 cup chopped carrots
5 cups water
1/4 cup butter, *or*
    margarine
1-2 tsp. salt, optional
1/4-1/2 tsp. pepper
2 cups milk
2 eggs
flour
1-2 Tbsp. dried parsley
butter, *or* margarine

1. Combine vegetables,
water, 1/4 cup butter or margarine, salt, and pepper in
slow cooker.
2. Cover. Cook on High 7-8
hours, or until vegetables are
tender.
3. Add milk. Stir in.
4. Make "drop noodles" by
beating eggs in a small bowl.
Add enough flour to make a
very soft, almost runny, batter. Dribble spoonfuls into
hot soup in cooker. (You may
find it easiest to use two
spoons to do this: one spoon
to dip up the "noodles"; the
other to push them into the
cooker. "Noodles" should not
be big clumps, yet they need
to be big enough to hold
together.)
5. Cover. Cook on Low
one more hour.
6. When ready to serve,
add parsley and a block of
butter or margarine to each
individual bowl.

Milk products such as cream, milk, and sour cream can
curdle and separate when cooked for a long period. Add
them during the last 10 minutes if cooking on High, or dur-
ing the last 20-30 minutes if cooking on Low.
**Mrs. J.E. Barthold**
Bethlehem, PA
**Marilyn Yoder**
Archbold, OH

# Black-Eye and Vegetable Chili

**Julie Weaver**
Reinholds, PA

*Makes 4-6 servings*

1 cup finely chopped onions
1 cup finely chopped carrots
1 cup finely chopped red *or* green pepper, *or* mixture of two
1 garlic clove, minced
4 tsp. chili powder
1 tsp. ground cumin
2 Tbsp. chopped cilantro
14½-oz. can diced tomatoes
3 cups cooked black-eyed beans, *or* 2 15-oz. cans black-eyed beans, drained
4-oz. can chopped green chilies
¾ cup orange juice
¾ cup water, *or* broth
1 Tbsp. cornstarch
2 Tbsp. water
½ cup shredded cheddar cheese
2 Tbsp. chopped cilantro

1. Combine all ingredients except cornstarch, 2 Tbsp. water, cheese, and cilantro.
2. Cover. Cook on Low 6-8 hours, or High 4 hours.
3. Dissolve cornstarch in water. Stir into soup mixture 30 minutes before serving.
4. Garnish individual servings with cheese and cilantro.

# Veggie Chili

**Wanda Roth**
Napoleon, OH

*Makes 6 servings*

2 qts. whole *or* diced tomatoes, undrained
6-oz. can tomato paste
½ cup chopped onions
½ cup chopped celery
½ cup chopped green peppers
2 garlic cloves, minced
1 tsp. salt
1½ tsp. ground cumin
1 tsp. dried oregano
¼ tsp. cayenne pepper
3 Tbsp. brown sugar
15-oz. can garbanzo beans

1. Combine all ingredients except beans in slow cooker.
2. Cook on Low 6-8 hours, or High 3-4 hours. Add beans one hour before serving.

**Variation:**
If you prefer a less tomatoey taste, substitute 2 vegetable bouillon cubes and 1 cup water for tomato paste.

# Beans and Tomato Chili

**Becky Harder**
Monument, CO

*Makes 6-8 servings*

15-oz. can black beans, undrained
15-oz. can pinto beans, undrained
16-oz. can kidney beans, undrained
15-oz. can garbanzo beans, undrained
2 14½-oz. cans stewed tomatoes and juice
1 pkg. prepared chili seasoning

1. Pour beans, including their liquid, into slow cooker.
2. Stir in tomatoes and chili seasoning.
3. Cover. Cook on Low 4-8 hours.
4. Serve with crackers, and topped with grated cheddar cheese, sliced green onions, and sour cream, if desired.

**Variation:**
Add additional cans of white beans or 1 tsp. dried onion.

# VEGETARIAN SOUPS

## Vegetarian Chili

Connie Johnson
Loudon, NH

*Makes 6 servings*

3 garlic cloves, minced
2 onions, chopped
1 cup textured vegetable protein (T.V.P.)
1-lb. can beans of your choice, drained
1 green bell pepper, chopped
1 jalapeno pepper, seeds removed, chopped
28-oz. can diced Italian tomatoes
1 bay leaf
1 Tbsp. dried oregano
1/2-1 tsp. salt
1/4 tsp. pepper

1. Combine all ingredients in slow cooker.
2. Cover. Cook on Low 6-8 hours.

## Hearty Black Bean Soup

Della Yoder
Kalona, IA

*Makes 6-8 servings*

3 medium carrots, halved and thinly sliced
2 celery ribs, thinly sliced
1 medium onion, chopped
4 cloves garlic, minced
20-oz. can black beans, drained and rinsed
2 14½-oz. cans chicken broth
15-oz. can crushed tomatoes
1½ tsp. dried basil
½ tsp. dried oregano
½ tsp. ground cumin
½ tsp. chili powder
½ tsp. hot pepper sauce

1. Combine all ingredients in slow cooker.
2. Cover. Cook on Low 9-10 hours.

**Note:**
May be served over cooked rice.

**Variation:**
If you prefer a thicker soup, use only 1 can chicken broth.

## Black Bean and Corn Soup

Joy Sutter
Iowa City, IA

*Makes 6-8 servings*

2 15-oz. cans black beans, drained and rinsed
14½-oz. can Mexican stewed tomatoes, undrained
14½-oz. can diced tomatoes, undrained
11-oz. can whole kernel corn, drained
4 green onions, sliced
2-3 Tbsp. chili powder
1 tsp. ground cumin
½ tsp. dried minced garlic

1. Combine all ingredients in slow cooker.
2. Cover. Cook on High 5-6 hours.

**Variations:**
1. Use 2 cloves fresh garlic, minced, instead of dried garlic.
2. Add 1 large rib celery, sliced thinly, and 1 small green pepper, chopped.

# Tuscan Garlicky Bean Soup

Sara Harter Fredette
Williamsburg, MA

*Makes 8-10 servings*

1 lb. dry Great Northern,
  *or* other dry white,
  beans
1 qt. water
1 qt. beef broth
3 Tbsp. olive oil
2 garlic cloves, minced
4 Tbsp. chopped parsley
olive oil
2 tsp. salt
1/2 tsp. pepper

1. Place beans in large soup pot. Cover with water and bring to boil. Cook 2 minutes. Remove from heat. Cover pot and allow to stand for 1 hour. Drain, discarding water.

2. Combine beans, 1 quart fresh water, and beef broth in slow cooker.

3. Saute garlic and parsley in olive oil in skillet. Stir into slow cooker. Add salt and pepper.

4. Cover. Cook on Low 8-10 hours, or until beans are tender.

# Bean Soup

Joyce Cox
Port Angeles, WA

*Makes 10-12 servings*

1 cup dry Great Northern
  beans
1 cup dry red beans, *or*
  pinto beans
4 cups water
28-oz. can diced tomatoes
1 medium onion, chopped
2 Tbsp. vegetable bouillon
  granules, *or* 4 bouillon
  cubes
2 garlic cloves, minced
2 tsp. Italian seasoning,
  crushed
9-oz. pkg. frozen green
  beans, thawed

1. Soak and rinse dried beans.

2. Combine all ingredients except green beans in slow cooker.

3. Cover. Cook on High 5 1/2-6 1/2 hours, or on Low 11-13 hours.

4. Stir green beans into soup during last 2 hours.

# Veggie Stew

Ernestine Schrepfer
Trenton, MO

*Makes 10-15 servings*

5-6 potatoes, cubed
3 carrots, cubed
1 onion, chopped
1/2 cup chopped celery
2 cups canned diced *or*
  stewed tomatoes
3 chicken bouillon cubes
  dissolved in 3 cups
  water
1 1/2 tsp. dried thyme
1/2 tsp. dried parsley
1/2 cup brown rice,
  uncooked
1 lb. frozen green beans
1 lb. frozen corn
15-oz. can butter beans
46-oz. can V-8 juice

1. Combine potatoes, carrots, onion, celery, tomatoes, chicken stock, thyme, parsley, and rice in 5-quart cooker, or two medium-sized cookers.

2. Cover. Cook on High 2 hours. Puree one cup of mixture and add back to slow cooker to thicken the soup.

3. Stir in beans, corn, butter beans, and juice.

4. Cover. Cook on High 1 more hour, then reduce to Low and cook 6-8 more hours.

# Southwestern Soup

Evelyn L. Ward
Greeley, CO

*Makes 4 servings*

2 14-oz. cans beef broth
1/2 cup sliced carrots
1/2 cup diced onions
1 cup diced potatoes
1 garlic clove, minced
8-oz. can, *or* 1 cup home-
    canned, crushed
    tomatoes
1 Tbsp. Worcestershire
    sauce
salsa to taste
garnishes:
    grated cheese
    diced avocados
    diced green peppers
    diced cucumbers
    2 1/4-oz. can sliced ripe
        olives
    6-oz. fresh mushrooms,
        sliced and sauteed
        in butter
    6-oz. can cooked and
        peeled tiny shrimp
    1 cup diced cooked ham
    1 cup green onion,
        sliced
    3 hard-cooked eggs,
        chopped
    1 cup diced tomatoes
    sour cream

1. Combine broth, carrots,
onions, potatoes, garlic, tomatoes, and Worcestershire
sauce in slow cooker. Cook
on Low 6-8 hours.
2. Before serving, stir in
salsa, sampling as you go to

get the right balance of fla-
vors.
3. Serve the soup in bowls,
allowing guests to add garnishes of their choice.

# Heart Happy Tomato Soup

Anne Townsend
Albuquerque, NM

*Makes 6 servings*

46-oz. can tomato juice
8-oz. can tomato sauce
1/2 cup water
1 Tbsp. bouillon granules
1 sprig celery leaves,
    chopped
half an onion, thinly sliced
1/2 tsp. dried basil
2 Tbsp. sugar
1 bay leaf
1/2 tsp. whole cloves

1. Combine all ingredients
in greased slow cooker. Stir
well.
2. Cover. Cook on Low 5-8
hours. Remove bay leaf and
cloves before serving.

**Note:**
    If you prefer a thicker
soup, add 1/4 cup instant
potato flakes. Stir well and
cook 5 minutes longer.

# Vegetarian Minestrone Soup

Connie Johnson
Loudon, NH

*Makes 6 servings*

6 cups vegetable broth
2 carrots, chopped
2 large onions, chopped
3 ribs celery, chopped
2 garlic cloves, minced
1 small zucchini, cubed
1 handful fresh kale,
    chopped
1/2 cup dry barley
1 can chickpeas, *or* white
    kidney beans, drained
1 Tbsp. parsley
1/2 tsp. dried thyme
1 tsp. dried oregano
28-oz. can crushed Italian
    tomatoes
1 tsp. salt
1/4 tsp. pepper
grated cheese

1. Combine all ingredients
except cheese in slow cooker.
2. Cover. Cook on Low 6-8
hours, or until vegetables are
tender.
3. Sprinkle individual servings with grated cheese.

# Joyce's Minestrone

**Joyce Shackelford**
Green Bay, Wisconsin

*Makes 6 servings*

3½ cups beef broth
28-oz. can crushed
    tomatoes
2 medium carrots, thinly
    sliced
½ cup chopped onion
½ cup chopped celery
2 medium potatoes, thinly
    sliced
1-2 garlic cloves, minced
16-oz. can red kidney
    beans, drained
2 oz. thin spaghetti,
    broken into 2-inch
    pieces
2 Tbsp. parsley flakes
2-3 tsp. dried basil
1-2 tsp. dried oregano
1 bay leaf

1. Combine all ingredients
in slow cooker.
2. Cover. Cook on Low 10-
16 hours, or on High 4-6
hours.
3. Remove bay leaf. Serve.

# Grace's Minestrone Soup

**Grace Ketcham**
Marietta, GA

*Makes 8 servings*

¾ cup dry elbow macaroni
2 qts. chicken stock
2 large onions, diced
2 carrots, sliced
half a head of cabbage,
    shredded
½ cup celery, diced
1-lb. can tomatoes
½ tsp. salt
½ tsp. dried oregano
1 Tbsp. minced parsley
¼ cup each frozen corn,
    peas, and lima beans
¼ tsp. pepper
grated Parmesan, *or*
    Romano, cheese

1. Cook macaroni accord-
ing to package directions. Set
aside.
2. Combine all ingredients
except macaroni and cheese
in large slow cooker.
3. Cover. Cook on Low 8
hours. Add macaroni during
last 30 minutes of cooking
time.
4. Garnish individual servings with cheese.

# Cabbage Soup

**Margaret Jarrett**
Anderson, IN

*Makes 8 servings*

half a head of cabbage,
    sliced thin
2 ribs celery, sliced thin
2-3 carrots, sliced thin
1 onion, chopped
2 chicken bouillon cubes
2 garlic cloves, minced
1 qt. tomato juice
1 tsp. salt
¼ tsp. pepper
water

1. Combine all ingredients
except water in slow cooker.
Add water to within 3 inches
of top of slow cooker.
2. Cover. Cook on High
3½-4 hours, or until vegetables are tender.

# Salsa Soup

**Sue Hamilton**
Minooka, IL

*Makes 6 servings*

3 cups (26 oz.) corn-black
    bean mild salsa
6 cups beef broth
¼ cup white long grain
    rice, uncooked

1. Combine all ingredients
in slow cooker.

2. Cover. Cook on Low 4-6 hours, or until rice is tender.

# Winter Squash and White Bean Stew

**Mary E. Herr**
Three Rivers, MI

*Makes 6 servings*

1 cup chopped onions
1 Tbsp. olive oil
1/2 tsp. ground cumin
1/4 tsp. salt
1/4 tsp. cinnamon
1 garlic clove, minced
3 cups peeled, butternut squash, cut into 3/4-inch cubes
1 1/2 cups chicken broth
19-oz. can cannellini beans, drained
14 1/2-oz. can diced tomatoes, undrained
1 Tbsp. chopped fresh cilantro

1. Combine all ingredients in slow cooker.
2. Cover. Cook on High 1 hour. Reduce heat to Low and heat 2-3 hours.

**Variations:**
1. Beans can be pureed in blender and added during the last hour.
2. Eight ounces dried beans can be soaked overnight, cooked until soft, and used in place of canned beans.

# Corn Chowder

**Charlotte Fry**
St. Charles, MO
**Jeanette Oberholtzer**
Manheim, PA

*Makes 4 servings*

6 slices bacon, diced
1/2 cup chopped onions
2 cups diced peeled potatoes
2 10-oz. pkgs. frozen corn
16-oz. can cream-style corn
1 Tbsp. sugar
1 tsp. Worcestershire sauce
1 tsp. seasoned salt
1/4 tsp. pepper
1 cup water

1. In skillet, brown bacon until crisp. Remove bacon, reserving drippings.
2. Add onions and potatoes to skillet and saute for 5 minutes. Drain.
3. Combine all ingredients in slow cooker. Mix well.
4. Cover. Cook on Low 6-7 hours.

**Variations:**
1. To make Clam Corn Chowder, drain and add 2 cans minced clams during last hour of cooking.
2. Substitute 1 quart home-frozen corn for the store-bought frozen and canned corn.

# Cheese and Corn Chowder

**Loretta Krahn**
Mt. Lake, MN

*Makes 8 servings*

3/4 cup water
1/2 cup chopped onions
1 1/2 cups sliced carrots
1 1/2 cups chopped celery
1 tsp. salt
1/2 tsp. pepper
15 1/4-oz. can whole kernel corn, drained
15-oz. can cream-style corn
3 cups milk
1 1/2 cup grated cheddar cheese

1. Combine water, onions, carrots, celery, salt, and pepper in slow cooker.
2. Cover. Cook on High 4-6 hours.
3. Add corn, milk, and cheese. Heat on High 1 hour, and then turn to Low until you are ready to eat.

# Cream of Broccoli Soup

**Barb Yoder**
Angola, IN

*Makes 6-8 servings*

1 small onion, chopped
oil
20-oz. pkg. frozen broccoli
2 10¾-oz. cans cream of
celery soup
10¾-oz. can cream of
mushroom soup
1 cup grated American
cheese
2 soup cans milk

1. Saute onion in oil in
skillet until soft.
2. Combine all ingredients
in slow cooker.
3. Cover. Cook on Low 3-4
hours.

# Broccoli-Cheese Soup

**Darla Sathre**
Baxter, MN

*Makes 8 servings*

2 16-oz. pkgs. frozen
chopped broccoli
2 10¾-oz. cans cheddar
cheese soup
2 12-oz. cans evaporated
milk
¼ cup finely chopped onions

½ tsp. seasoned salt
¼ tsp. pepper
sunflower seeds, optional
crumbled bacon, optional

1. Combine all ingredients
except sunflower seeds and
bacon in slow cooker.
2. Cover. Cook on Low 8-
10 hours.
3. Garnish with sunflower
seeds and bacon.

# Broccoli-Cheese with Noodles Soup

**Carol Sherwood**
Batavia, NY

*Makes 8 servings*

2 cups cooked noodles
10-oz. pkg. frozen chopped
broccoli, thawed
3 Tbsp. chopped onions
2 Tbsp. butter
1 Tbsp. flour
2 cups cubed processed
cheese
½ tsp. salt
5½ cups milk

1. Cook noodles just until
soft in saucepan while combining rest of ingredients in
slow cooker. Mix well.
2. Drain cooked noodles
and stir into slow cooker.
3. Cover. Cook on Low 4
hours.

# Double Cheese Cauliflower Soup

**Zona Mae Bontrager**
Kokomo, IN

*Makes 6 servings*

4 cups (1 small head)
cauliflower pieces
2 cups water
8-oz. pkg. cream cheese,
cubed
5 oz. American cheese
spread
¼ lb. dried beef, torn into
strips *or* shredded
½ cup potato flakes *or*
buds

1. Combine cauliflower
and water in saucepan. Bring
to boil. Set aside.
2. Heat slow cooker on
Low. Add cream cheese and
cheese spread. Pour in cauliflower and water. Stir to be
sure the cheese is dissolved
and mixed through the cauliflower.
3. Add dried beef and
potato flakes. Mix well.
4. Cover. Cook on Low 2-3
hours.

# Main Dishes

## Beef Stew

**Wanda S. Curtin**, Bradenton, FL
**Paula King**, Harrisonburg, VA
**Miriam Nolt**, New Holland, PA
**Jean Shaner**, York, PA
**Mary W. Stauffer**, Ephrata, PA
**Alma Z. Weaver**, Ephrata, PA

*Makes 6 servings*

2 lbs. beef chuck, cubed
1 tsp. Worcestershire sauce
1/4-1/2 cup flour
1 1/2 tsp. salt
1/2 tsp. pepper
1 tsp. paprika
1 1/2 cups beef broth
half garlic clove, minced
1 bay leaf
4 carrots, sliced
2 onions, chopped
1 rib celery, sliced
3 potatoes, diced

1. Place meat in slow cooker.
2. Combine flour, salt, pepper, and paprika. Stir into meat until coated thoroughly.
3. Add remaining ingredients. Mix well.
4. Cover. Cook on Low 10-12 hours, or High 4-6 hours. Stir before serving.

## Audrey's Beef Stew

**Audrey Romonosky**
Austin, TX

*Makes 4-6 servings*

3 carrots, sliced
3 potatoes, cubed
2 lbs. beef chuck, cubed
2 cups water
2 beef bouillon cubes
1 tsp. Worcestershire sauce
1/2 tsp. garlic powder
1 bay leaf

1/4 tsp. salt
1/2 tsp. pepper
1 tsp. paprika
3 onions, chopped
1 rib celery, sliced
1/4 cup flour
1/3 cup cold water

1. Combine all ingredients except flour and 1/3 cup cold water in slow cooker. Mix well.
2. Cover. Cook on Low 8 hours.
3. Dissolve flour in 1/3 cup water. Stir into meat mixture. Cook on High until thickened, about 10 minutes.

# Herbed Beef Stew

**Carol Findling**
Princeton, IL

*Makes 6-8 servings*

1 lb. beef round, cubed
4 Tbsp. seasoned flour *
1½ cups beef broth
1 tsp. Worcestershire sauce
1 garlic clove
1 bay leaf
4 carrots, sliced
3 potatoes, cubed
2 onions, diced
1 rounded tsp. fresh
   thyme, *or* ½ tsp. dried
   thyme
1 rounded tsp. chopped
   fresh basil, *or* ½ tsp.
   dried basil
1 Tbsp. fresh parsley, *or*
   1 tsp. dried parsley
1 rounded tsp. fresh
   marjoram, *or* 1 tsp.
   dried marjoram

1. Put meat in slow cooker.
Add seasoned flour. Toss with
meat. Stir in remaining ingredients. Mix well.
2. Cover. Cook on High 4-6
hours, or Low 10-12 hours.

* **Seasoned Flour**
  1 cup flour
  1 tsp. salt
  1 tsp. paprika
  ¼ tsp. pepper

# Beef Stew Olé

**Andrea O'Neil**
Fairfield, CT

*Makes 6-8 servings*

4 carrots, cubed
4 potatoes, peeled and
   cubed
1 onion, quartered
1½ lbs. beef stewing meat,
   cubed
8-oz. can tomato sauce
1 pkg. dry taco seasoning
   mix
2 cups water, divided
1½ Tbsp. cornstarch
2 tsp. salt
¼ tsp. pepper

1. Layer first four ingredients in slow cooker. Add
tomato sauce.
2. Combine taco seasoning
with 1½ cups water. Stir
cornstarch into remaining ½
cup water until smooth. Stir
into rest of water with taco
seasoning. Pour over ingredients in slow cooker.
3. Sprinkle with salt and
pepper.
4. Cover. Cook on Low 7-8
hours.
5. Serve over rice.

**Variation:**
   If those eating at your
table are cautious about spicy
food, choose a "mild" taco
seasoning mix and add 1 tsp.
sugar to the seasonings.

# Pot Roast

**Carole Whaling**
New Tripoli, PA

*Makes 8 servings*

4 medium potatoes, cubed
4 carrots, sliced
1 onion, sliced
3-4-lb. rump roast, *or* pot
   roast, cut into serving-
   size pieces
1 tsp. salt
½ tsp. pepper
1 bouillon cube
½ cup boiling water

1. Put vegetables and meat
in slow cooker. Stir in salt
and pepper.
2. Dissolve bouillon cube
in water, then pour over
other ingredients.
3. Cover. Cook on Low 10-
12 hours.

# Swiss Steak

**Marilyn Mowry**
Irving, TX

*Makes 4-6 servings*

3-4 Tbsp. flour
½ tsp. salt
¼ tsp. pepper
1½ tsp. dry mustard
1½-2 lbs. round steak
oil
1 cup sliced onions
1 lb. carrots

14 1/2-oz. can whole
   tomatoes
1 Tbsp. brown sugar
1 1/2 Tbsp. Worcestershire
   sauce

1. Combine flour, salt, pepper, and dry mustard.
2. Cut steak into serving pieces. Dredge in flour mixture. Brown on both sides in oil in saucepan. Place in slow cooker.
3. Add onions and carrots.
4. Combine tomatoes, brown sugar, and Worcestershire sauce. Pour into slow cooker.
5. Cover. Cook on Low 8-10 hours, or High 3-5 hours.

# Round Steak Casserole

Gladys High
Ephrata, PA

*Makes 6 servings*

2 lbs. round steak, cut
   1/2-inch thick
1 tsp. salt
1/4 tsp. pepper
1 onion, thinly sliced
3-4 potatoes, pared and
   quartered
16-oz. can French-style
   green beans, drained
1 clove garlic, minced
10 3/4-oz. can tomato soup
14 1/2-oz. can tomatoes

1. Season roast with salt and pepper. Cut into serving pieces and place in slow cooker.

2. Add onion, potatoes, green beans, and garlic. Top with soup and tomatoes.
3. Cover and cook on Low 8-10 hours, or High 4-5 hours. Remove cover during last half hour if too much liquid has collected.

# Hearty Beef Stew

Charlotte Shaffer
East Earl, PA

*Makes 4-5 servings*

2 lbs. stewing beef, cubed
5 carrots, sliced
1 large onion, cut in
   chunks
3 ribs celery, sliced
22-oz. can stewed tomatoes
1/2 tsp. ground cloves
2 bay leaves
1 1/2 tsp. salt
1/4-1/2 tsp. pepper

1. Combine all ingredients in slow cooker.
2. Cover. Cook on High 5-6 hours.

**Variations:**
1. Substitute 1 whole clove for the 1/2 tsp. ground cloves. Remove before serving.
2. Use venison instead of beef.
3. Cut back the salt to 1 tsp. and use 1 tsp. soy sauce.

**Betty B. Dennison**
Grove City, PA

# Judy's Beef Stew

Judy Koczo
Plano, IL

*Makes 4-6 servings*

2 lbs. stewing meat, cubed
5 carrots, sliced
1 onion, diced
3 ribs celery, diced
5 potatoes, cubed
28-oz. can tomatoes
1/3-1/2 cup quick-cooking
   tapioca
2 tsp. salt
1/2 tsp. pepper

1. Combine all ingredients in slow cooker.
2. Cover. Cook on Low 10-12 hours, or High 5-6 hours.

**Variation:**
Add 1 whole clove and 2 bay leaves to stew before cooking.

**L. Jean Moore**
Pendleton, IN

73

## Slow-Cooker Stew

**Trudy Kutter**
Corfu, NY

*Makes 6-8 servings*

2 lbs. boneless beef, cubed
4-6 celery ribs, sliced
6-8 carrots, sliced
6 potatoes, cubed
2 onions, sliced
28-oz. can tomatoes
¼ cup minute tapioca
1 tsp. salt
¼ tsp. pepper
½ tsp. dried basil,
   *or* oregano
1 garlic clove, pressed *or*
   minced

1. Combine all ingredients
in slow cooker.
2. Cover. Cook on Low
8-10 hours.

**Variation:**
Add 2 10½-oz. cans beef
gravy and ½ cup water in
place of the tomatoes. Reduce
tapioca to 2 Tbsp.

## Italian Stew

**Ann Gouinlock**
Alexander, NY

*Makes 6 servings*

1½ lbs. beef cubes
2-3 carrots, cut in 1-inch
   chunks
3-4 ribs celery, cut in ¾-1-
   inch pieces
1-1½ cups coarsely
   chopped onions
14½-oz. can stewed, *or*
   diced, tomatoes
⅓ cup minute tapioca
1½ tsp. salt
¼ tsp. pepper
¼ tsp. Worcestershire
   sauce
½ tsp. Italian seasoning

1. Combine all ingredients
in slow cooker.
2. Cover. Cook on Low 8-
10 hours.

## Herby Beef Stew

**Tracy Supcoe**
Barclay, MD

*Makes 6 servings*

1-2 lbs. stewing meat,
   cubed
⅔ cup flour
1½ tsp. salt
¼ tsp. pepper
oil
14½-oz. can diced
   tomatoes
8-oz. can tomato sauce
14½-oz. can beef broth
2 Tbsp. Worcestershire
   sauce
1 bay leaf
2 tsp. kitchen bouquet
2 Tbsp. dried parsley
1 tsp. Hungarian sweet
   paprika
4 celery heart ribs,
   chopped
5 mushrooms, sliced
3 potatoes, cubed
3 cloves garlic, minced
1 large onion, chopped

1. Combine flour, salt, and
pepper in bowl. Dredge meat
in seasoned flour, then brown
in oil in saucepan. Place meat
in slow cooker.
2. Combine remaining
ingredients in bowl. Pour
over meat and mix well.
3. Cover. Cook on High 5-6
hours, or Low 10-12 hours.
Stir before serving.

Liquids don't boil down in a slow cooker. At the end of
the cooking time, remove the cover, set dial on High and
allow the liquid to evaporate, if the dish is soup-ier than you
want.

**John D. Allen**
Rye, CO

## Venison or Beef Stew

**Frances B. Musser**
Newmanstown, PA

*Makes 6 servings*

1½ lbs. venison *or* beef
  cubes
2 Tbsp. oil
1 medium onion, chopped
4 carrots, peeled and cut
  into 1-inch pieces
1 rib celery, cut into 1-inch
  pieces
4 medium potatoes, peeled
  and quartered
12-oz. can whole tomatoes,
  undrained
10½-oz. can beef broth
1 Tbsp. Worcestershire
  sauce
1 Tbsp. parsley flakes
1 bay leaf
2½ tsp. salt
¼ tsp. pepper
2 Tbsp. quick-cooking
  tapioca

1. Brown meat cubes in
skillet in oil over medium
heat. Transfer to slow cooker.
2. Add remaining ingredi-
ents. Mix well.
3. Cover. Cook on Low 8-9
hours.

**Variations:**
1. Substitute 1½ tsp. garlic
salt and 1 tsp. salt for 2½ tsp.
salt.
2. For added color and flavor, add 1 cup frozen peas 5
minutes before end of cooking time.

## Layered Herby Stew

**Elizabeth L. Richards**
Rapid City, SD

*Makes 8 servings*

2½ lbs. lean beef chuck,
  cubed
1 medium to large onion,
  cut in 1-inch pieces
8-12 small red potatoes *or*
  potato chunks
4-6 carrots, cut in 1-inch
  pieces
2 large ribs celery, cut in
  1-inch pieces
2 Tbsp. Worcestershire
  sauce
¼ cup red wine, *or* water
3 Tbsp. brown sugar
1 tsp. salt
½ tsp. pepper
⅛ tsp. allspice
¼ tsp. dried marjoram
¼ tsp. dried thyme
2 bay leaves
6 Tbsp. minute tapioca
  (use only 5 Tbsp. if
  using water instead of
  red wine)
28-oz. can diced tomatoes
½ cup chopped fresh
  parsley

1. Layer all ingredients
except parsley in slow cooker
in order given.
2. Cover. Cook on High 6
hours.
3. Immediately before
serving, garnish with parsley.

## Waldorf Astoria Stew

**Mary V. Warye**
West Liberty, OH

*Makes 6-8 servings*

3 lbs. beef stewing meat,
  cubed
1 medium onion, chopped
1 cup celery, sliced
2 cups carrots, sliced
4 medium potatoes, cubed
3 Tbsp. minute tapioca
1 Tbsp. sugar
1 Tbsp. salt
½ tsp. pepper
10¾-oz. can tomato soup
⅓ cup water

1. Layer meat, onion, celery, carrots, and potatoes in
slow cooker. Sprinkle with
seasonings and tapioca. Add
soup and water.
2. Cover. Cook on Low 7-9
hours.

## Busy Day Beef Stew

Dale Peterson
Rapid City, SC

*Makes 6-8 servings*

2 lbs. stewing meat, cubed
2 medium onions, diced
1 cup chopped celery
2 cups sliced carrots
4 medium potatoes, diced
2½ Tbsp. quick-cooking
   tapioca
1 Tbsp. sugar
1 tsp. salt
½ tsp. pepper
10¾-oz. can tomato soup
1½ soup cans water

1. Layer meat and vegetables in slow cooker. Sprinkle with tapioca, sugar, salt, and pepper. Combine soup and water and pour into slow cooker. Do not stir.

2. Cover. Cook on Low 6-8 hours.

## Pungent Beef Stew

Grace Ketcham
Marietta, GA

*Makes 4-6 servings*

2 lbs. beef chuck, cubed
1 tsp. Worcestershire sauce
1 garlic clove, minced
1 medium onion, chopped
2 bay leaves
½ tsp. salt
½ tsp. paprika
¼ tsp. pepper
dash of ground cloves, *or*
   allspice
6 carrots, quartered
4 potatoes, quartered
2 ribs celery, chopped
10¾-oz. can tomato soup
½ cup water

1. Combine all ingredients in slow cooker.

2. Cover. Cook on Low 10-12 hours.

## Donna's Beef Stew

Donna Treloar
Gaston, IN

*Makes 6 servings*

2 lbs. beef, cubed
4-5 potatoes, cubed
4-5 carrots, sliced
3 ribs celery, sliced
2 onions, chopped
1 Tbsp. sugar
2 tsp. salt
¼-½ tsp. pepper
2 Tbsp. instant tapioca
3 cups V-8, *or* tomato,
   juice

1. Place meat and vegetables in slow cooker. Sprinkle with sugar, salt, pepper, and tapioca. Toss lightly. Pour juice over the top.

2. Cover. Cook on Low 8-10 hours.

**Variation:**
   Add 10-oz. pkg. frozen succotash or green beans.

---

When I want to warm rolls to go with a slow-cooker stew, I wrap them in foil and lay them on top of the stew until they're warm.
   **Donna Barnitz**
   Jenks, OK

# Venison Swiss Steak

**Dede Peterson**
Rapid City, SD

*Makes 6 servings*

2 lbs. round venison steak
flour
2 tsp. salt
1/2 tsp. pepper
oil
2 onions, sliced
2 ribs celery, diced
1 cup carrots, diced
2 cups fresh, *or* stewed,
    tomatoes
1 Tbsp. Worcestershire
    sauce

1. Combine flour, salt, and pepper. Dredge steak in flour mixture. Brown in oil in skillet. Place in slow cooker.
2. Add remaining ingredients.
3. Cover. Cook on Low 7 1/2-8 1/2 hours.

# Swiss Steak

**Wanda S. Curtin**
Bradenton, FL
**Jeanne Hertzog**
Bethlehem, PA

*Makes 6 servings*

1 1/2 lbs. round steak, about
    3/4" thick
2-4 tsp. flour
1/2-1 tsp. salt
1/4 tsp. pepper
1 medium onion, sliced
1 carrot, chopped
1 rib celery, chopped
14 1/2-oz. can diced
    tomatoes, *or* 15-oz. can
    tomato sauce

1. Cut steak into serving pieces.
2. Combine flour, salt, and pepper. Dredge meat in seasoned flour.
3. Place onions in bottom of slow cooker. Add meat. Top with carrots and celery and cover with tomatoes.
4. Cover. Cook on Low 8-10 hours, or High 3-5 hours.
5. Serve over noodles or rice.

# Jacqueline's Swiss Steak

**Jacqueline Stafl**
East Bethany, NY

*Makes 4 servings*

1 1/2 lbs. round steak
2-4 Tbsp. flour
1/2 lb. sliced carrots, *or*
    1 lb. baby carrots
1 pkg. dry onion soup mix
8-oz. can tomato sauce
1/2 cup water

1. Cut steak into serving-size pieces. Dredge in flour.
2. Place carrots in bottom of slow cooker. Top with steak.
3. Combine soup mix, tomato sauce, and water. Pour over all.
4. Cover. Cook on Low 8-10 hours.
5. Serve over mashed potatoes.

## Margaret's Swiss Steak

Margaret Rich
North Newton, KS

*Makes 6 servings*

1 cup chopped onions
1/2 cup chopped celery
2-lb. 1/2-inch thick round
  steak
1/4 cup flour
3 Tbsp. oil
1 tsp. salt
1/4 tsp. pepper
16-oz. can diced tomatoes
1/4 cup flour
1/2 cup water

1. Place onions and celery in bottom of slow cooker.

2. Cut steak in serving-size pieces. Dredge in 1/4 cup flour. Brown on both sides in oil in saucepan. Place in slow cooker.

3. Sprinkle with salt and pepper. Pour on tomatoes.

4. Cover. Cook on Low 9 hours. Remove meat from cooker and keep warm.

5. Turn heat to High. Blend together 1/4 cup flour and water. Stir into sauce in slow cooker. Cover and cook 15 minutes. Serve with steak.

## Nadine & Hazel's Swiss Steak

Nadine Martinitz, Salina, KS
Hazel L. Propst, Oxford, PA

*Makes 6-8 servings*

3-lb. round steak
1/3 cup flour
2 tsp. salt
1/2 tsp. pepper
3 Tbsp. shortening
1 large onion, *or more,*
  sliced
1 large pepper, *or more,*
  sliced
14 1/2-oz. can stewed
  tomatoes, *or* 3-4 fresh
  tomatoes, chopped
**water**

1. Sprinkle meat with flour, salt, and pepper. Pound both sides. Cut into 6 or 8 pieces. Brown meat in shortening over medium heat on top of stove, about 15 minutes. Transfer to slow cooker.

2. Brown onion and pepper. Add tomatoes and bring to boil. Pour over steak. Add water to completely cover steak.

3. Cover. Cook on Low 6-8 hours.

**Variation:**

To add some flavor, stir in your favorite dried herbs when beginning to cook the steak, or add fresh herbs in the last hour of cooking.

## Beef, Tomatoes, & Noodles

Janice Martins
Fairbank, IA

*Makes 8 servings*

1 1/2 lbs. stewing beef,
  cubed
1/4 cup flour
2 cups stewed tomatoes (if
  you like tomato chunks),
  *or* 2 cups crushed
  tomatoes (if you prefer a
  smoother gravy
1 tsp. salt
1/4-1/2 tsp. pepper
1 medium onion, chopped
water
12-oz. bag noodles

1. Combine meat and flour until cubes are coated. Place in slow cooker.

2. Add tomatoes, salt, pepper, and onion. Add water to cover.

3. Cover. Simmer on Low 6-8 hours.

4. Serve over cooked noodles.

# Big Beef Stew

**Margaret H. Moffitt**
Bartlett, TN

*Makes 6-8 servings*

3-lb. beef roast, cubed
1 large onion, sliced
1 tsp. dried parsley flakes
1 green pepper, sliced
3 ribs celery, sliced
4 carrots, sliced
28-oz. can tomatoes with
    juice, undrained
1 garlic clove, minced
2 cups water

1. Combine all ingredients.
2. Cover. Cook on High 1 hour. Reduce heat to Low and cook 8 hours.
3. Serve on rice or noodles.

**Note:**

This is a low-salt recipe. For more zest, add 2 tsp. salt and 3/4 tsp. black pepper.

# Spanish Round Steak

**Shari Jensen**
Fountain, CO

*Makes 4-6 servings*

1 small onion, sliced
1 rib celery, chopped
1 green bell pepper, sliced
    in rings
2 lbs. round steak
2 Tbsp. chopped fresh
    parsley, *or* 2 tsp. dried
    parsley
1 Tbsp. Worcestershire
    sauce
1 Tbsp. dry mustard
1 Tbsp. chili powder
2 cups canned tomatoes
2 tsp. dry minced garlic
1/2 tsp. salt
1/4 tsp. pepper

1. Put half of onion, green pepper, and celery in slow cooker.
2. Cut steak into serving-size pieces. Place steak pieces in slow cooker.
3. Put remaining onion, green pepper, and celery over steak.
4. Combine remaining ingredients. Pour over meat.
5. Cover. Cook on Low 8 hours.
6. Serve over noodles or rice.

# Slow-Cooked Pepper Steak

**Carolyn Baer**, Conrath, WI
**Ann Driscoll**
Albuquerque, NM

*Makes 6-8 servings*

1 1/2-2 lbs. beef round
    steak, cut in 3" x 1"
    strips
2 Tbsp. oil
1/4 cup soy sauce
1 garlic clove, minced
1 cup chopped onions
1 tsp. sugar
1/2 tsp. salt
1/4 tsp. pepper
1/4 tsp. ground ginger
2 large green peppers, cut
    in strips
4 tomatoes cut into
    eighths, *or* 16-oz. can
    diced tomatoes
1/2 cup cold water
1 Tbsp. cornstarch

1. Brown beef in oil in saucepan. Transfer to slow cooker.
2. Combine soy sauce, garlic, onions, sugar, salt, pepper, and ginger. Pour over meat.
3. Cover. Cook on Low 5-6 hours.
4. Add green peppers and tomatoes. Cook 1 hour longer.
5. Combine water and cornstarch to make paste. Stir into slow cooker. Cook on High until thickened, about 10 minutes.
6. Serve over rice or noodles.

# Pepper Steak Oriental

**Donna Lantgen**
Rapid City, SD

*Makes 6 servings*

1 lb. round steak, sliced thin
3 Tbsp. soy sauce
1/2 tsp. ground ginger
1 garlic clove, minced
1 green pepper, thinly sliced
4-oz. can mushrooms, drained, *or* 1 cup fresh mushrooms
1 onion, thinly sliced
1/2 tsp. crushed red pepper

1. Combine all ingredients in slow cooker.
2. Cover. Cook on Low 6-8 hours.
3. Serve as steak sandwiches topped with provolone cheese, or over rice.

**Note:**
Round steak is easier to slice into thin strips if it is partially frozen when cut.

# Powerhouse Beef Roast with Tomatoes, Onions, and Peppers

**Donna Treloar**
Gaston, IN

*Makes 5-6 servings*

3-lb. boneless chuck roast
1 garlic clove, minced
1 Tbsp. oil
2-3 onions, sliced
2-3 sweet green and red peppers, sliced
16-oz. jar salsa
2 14 1/2-oz. cans Mexican-style stewed tomatoes

1. Brown roast and garlic in oil in skillet. Place in slow cooker.
2. Add onions and peppers.
3. Combine salsa and tomatoes and pour over ingredients in slow cooker.
4. Cover. Cook on Low 8-10 hours.
5. Slice meat to serve.

**Variation:**
Make Beef Burritos with the leftovers. Shred the beef and heat with remaining peppers, onions, and 1/2 cup of the broth. Add 1 Tbsp. chili powder, 2 tsp. cumin, and salt to taste. Heat thoroughly. Fill warm flour tortillas with mixture and serve with sour cream, salsa, and guacamole.

# Steak San Morco

**Susan Tjon**
Austin, TX

*Makes 4-6 servings*

2 lbs. stewing meat, cubed
1 envelope dry onion soup mix
29-oz. can peeled, *or* crushed, tomatoes
1 tsp. dried oregano
garlic powder to taste
2 Tbsp. oil
2 Tbsp. wine vinegar

1. Layer meat evenly in bottom of slow cooker.
2. Combine soup mix, tomatoes, spices, oil, and vinegar in bowl. Blend with spoon. Pour over meat.
3. Cover. Cook on High 6 hours, or Low 8-10 hours.

## Pat's Meat Stew
**Pat Bishop**
Bedminster, PA

*Makes 4-5 servings*

1-2 lbs. beef roast, cubed
2 tsp. salt
1/4 tsp. pepper
2 cups water
2 carrots, sliced
2 small onions, sliced
4-6 small potatoes, cut up in chunks, if desired
1/4 cup quick-cooking tapioca
1 bay leaf
10-oz. pkg. frozen peas, *or* mixed vegetables

1. Brown beef in saucepan. Place in slow cooker.
2. Sprinkle with salt and pepper. Add remaining ingredients except frozen vegetables. Mix well.
3. Cover. Cook on Low 8-10 hours, or on High 4-5 hours. Add vegetables during last 1-2 hours of cooking.

## Ernestine's Beef Stew
**Ernestine Schrepfer**
Trenton, MO

*Makes 5-6 servings*

1 1/2 lbs. stewing meat, cubed
2 1/4 cups tomato juice
10 1/2-oz. can consomme
1 cup chopped celery
2 cups sliced carrots
4 Tbsp. quick-cooking tapioca
1 medium onion, chopped
3/4 tsp. salt
1/4 tsp. pepper

1. Combine all ingredients in slow cooker.
2. Cover. Cook on Low 7-8 hours. (Do not peek.)

## Beef Stew with Vegetables
**Joyce B. Suiter**
Garysburg, NC

*Makes 8 servings*

3 lbs. stewing beef, cubed
1 cup water
1 cup red wine
1.2-oz. envelope beef-mushroom soup mix
2 cups diced potatoes
1 cup thinly sliced carrots
10-oz. pkg. frozen peas and onions

1. Layer all ingredients in order in slow cooker.
2. Cover. Cook on Low 8-10 hours.

**Note:**
You may increase all vegetable quantities with good results!

## Becky's Beef Stew
**Becky Harder**
Monument, CO

*Makes 6-8 servings*

1 1/2 lbs. beef stewing meat, cubed
2 10-oz. pkgs. frozen vegetables—carrots, corn, peas
4 large potatoes, cubed
1 bay leaf
1 onion, chopped
15-oz. can stewing tomatoes of your choice—Italian, Mexican, *or* regular
8-oz. can tomato sauce
2 Tbsp. Worcestershire sauce
1 tsp. salt
1/4 tsp. pepper

1. Put meat on bottom of slow cooker. Layer frozen vegetables and potatoes over meat.
2. Mix remaining ingredients together in large bowl and pour over other ingredients.
3. Cover. Cook on Low 6-8 hours.

# Santa Fe Stew

Jeanne Allen
Rye, CO

*Makes 4-6 servings*

2 lbs. sirloin, *or* stewing
   meat, cubed
2 Tbsp. oil
1 large onion, diced
2 garlic cloves, minced
1 1/2 cups water
1 Tbsp. dried parsley
   flakes
2 beef bouillon cubes
1 tsp. ground cumin
1/2 tsp. salt
3 carrots, sliced
14 1/2-oz. can diced
   tomatoes
14 1/2-oz. can green beans,
   drained, *or* 1 lb. frozen
   green beans
14 1/2-oz. can corn, drained,
   *or* 1 lb. frozen corn
4-oz. can diced green
   chilies
3 zucchini squash, diced,
   optional

1. Brown meat, onion, and
garlic in oil in saucepan until
meat is no longer pink. Place
in slow cooker.
2. Stir in remaining ingredients.
3. Cover. Cook on High 30
minutes. Reduce heat to Low
and cook 4-6 hours.

# Gone All-Day Casserole

Beatrice Orgish
Richardson, TX

*Makes 12 servings*

1 cup uncooked wild rice,
   rinsed and drained
1 cup chopped celery
1 cup chopped carrots
2 4-oz. cans mushrooms,
   stems and pieces,
   drained
1 large onion, chopped
1 clove garlic, minced
1/2 cup slivered almonds
3 beef bouillon cubes
2 1/2 tsp. seasoned salt
2-lb. boneless round steak,
   cut into 1-inch cubes
3 cups water

1. Please ingredients in
order listed in slow cooker.
2. Cover. Cook on Low 6-8
hours or until rice is tender.
Stir before serving.

## Variations:
1. Brown beef in saucepan
in 2 Tbsp. oil before putting
in slow cooker for deeper flavor.
2. Add a bay leaf and 4-6
whole peppercorns to mix-
ture before cooking. Remove
before serving.
3. Substitute chicken legs
and thighs (skin removed) for
beef.

# Sweet-Sour Beef and Vegetables

Jo Haberkamp
Fairbank, IA

*Makes 6 servings*

2 lbs. round steak, cut in
   1-inch cubes
2 Tbsp. oil
2 8-oz. cans tomato sauce
2 tsp. chili powder
2 cups sliced carrots
2 cups small white onions
1 tsp. paprika
1/4 cup sugar
1 tsp. salt
1/3 cup vinegar
1/2 cup light molasses
1 large green pepper, cut in
   1-inch pieces

1. Brown steak in oil in
saucepan.
2. Combine all ingredients
in slow cooker.
3. Cover. Cook on High 4-6
hours.

# Irish Beef Stew

**Teena Wagner**
Waterloo, ON

---

*Makes 4-6 servings*

2 lbs. stewing beef, cubed
1 envelope dry onion soup
  mix
2 10¾-oz. cans tomato
  soup
1 soup can water
1 tsp. salt
½ tsp. pepper
2 cups diced carrots
2 cups diced potatoes
1-lb. package frozen peas
¼ cup water

1. Place beef, onion soup,
tomato soup, soup can of
water, salt, pepper, carrots,
and potatoes in slow cooker.
2. Cover. Cook on Low 8
hours.
3. Add peas and ¼ cup
water. Cover. Cook on Low 1
more hour.

# Slow Cooker Stew

**Ruth Shank**
Gridley, IL

---

*Makes 8-10 servings*

3-4-lb. beef round steak,
  *or* beef roast, cubed
⅓ cup flour
1 tsp. salt
½ tsp. pepper
3 carrots, sliced
1-2 medium onions, cut
  into wedges
4-6 medium potatoes,
  cubed
4-oz. can sliced
  mushrooms, drained
10-oz. pkg. frozen mixed
  vegetables
10½-oz. can condensed
  beef broth
½ cup water
2 tsp. brown sugar
14½-oz. can, *or* 1 pint,
  tomato wedges with
  juice
¼ cup flour
¼ cup water

1. Toss beef cubes with ⅓
cup flour, salt, and pepper in
slow cooker.
2. Combine all vegetables
except tomatoes. Add to meat.
3. Combine beef broth, ½
cup water, and brown sugar.
Pour over meat and vegetables. Add tomatoes and stir
carefully.
4. Cover. Cook on Low 10-
14 hours, or on High 4-5½
hours.
5. One hour before serving,
mix together ¼ cup flour and
¼ cup water. Stir into slow

cooker. Turn to High. Cover
and cook remaining time.

**Note:**
  For better color add half of
the frozen vegetables (partly
thawed) during the last hour.

# Full-Flavored Beef Stew

**Stacy Petersheim**
Mechanicsburg, PA

---

*Makes 6 servings*

2-lb. beef roast, cubed
2 cups sliced carrots
2 cups diced potatoes
1 medium onion, sliced
1½ cups peas
2 tsp. quick-cooking
  tapioca
1 Tbsp. salt
½ tsp. pepper
8-oz. can tomato sauce
1 cup water
1 Tbsp. brown sugar

1. Combine beef and veg-
etables in slow cooker.
Sprinkle with tapioca, salt,
and pepper.
2. Combine tomato sauce
and water. Pour over ingredients in slow cooker. Sprinkle
with brown sugar.
3. Cover. Cook on Low 8
hours.

**Variation:**
  Add peas one hour before
cooking time ends to keep
their color and flavor.

# Lazy Day Stew

**Ruth Ann Gingrich**
New Holland, PA

*Makes 8 servings*

2 lbs. stewing beef, cubed
2 cups diced carrots
2 cups diced potatoes
2 medium onions, chopped
1 cup chopped celery
10-oz. pkg. lima beans
2 tsp. quick-cooking
  tapioca
1 tsp. salt
1/2 tsp. pepper
8-oz. can tomato sauce
1 cup water
1 Tbsp. brown sugar

1. Place beef in bottom of slow cooker. Add vegetables.
2. Sprinkle tapioca, salt, and pepper over ingredients.
3. Mix together tomato sauce and water. Pour over top.
4. Sprinkle brown sugar over all.
5. Cover. Cook on Low 8 hours.

**Variation:**
Instead of lima beans, use 1 1/2 cups green beans.
**Rose M. Hoffman**
Schuylkill Haven, PA

# Beef with Mushrooms

**Doris Perkins**
Mashpee, MA

*Makes 4-6 servings*

1 1/2 lbs. stewing beef,
  cubed
4-oz. can mushroom
  pieces, drained (save
  liquid)
half a garlic clove, minced
3/4 cup sliced onions
3 Tbsp. shortening
1 beef bouillon cube
1 cup hot water
8-oz. can tomato sauce
2 tsp. sugar
2 tsp. Worcestershire sauce
1 tsp. dried basil
1 tsp. dried oregano
1/2 tsp. salt
1/8 tsp. pepper

1. Brown meat, mushrooms, garlic, and onions in shortening in skillet.
2. Dissolve bouillon cube in hot water. Add to meat mixture.
3. Stir in mushroom liquid and rest of ingredients. Mix well. Pour into slow cooker.
4. Cover. Cook on High 3 hours, or until meat is tender.
5. Serve over cooked noodles, spaghetti, or rice.

# Easy Company Beef

**Joyce B. Suiter**
Garysburg, NC

*Makes 8 servings*

3 lbs. stewing beef, cubed
10 3/4-oz. can cream of
  mushroom soup
7-oz. jar mushrooms,
  undrained
1/2 cup red wine
1 envelope dry onion soup
  mix

1. Combine all ingredients in slow cooker.
2. Cover. Cook on Low 10 hours.
3. Serve over noodles, rice, or pasta.

To get the best flavor, saute vegetables or brown meat before placing in cooker to cook.
**Connie Johnson**
Loudon, NH

# Beef Pot Roast

**Alexa Slonin**
Harrisonburg, VA

*Makes 8-10 servings*

12 oz. whole tiny new
potatoes, *or* 2 medium
potatoes, cubed, *or*
2 medium sweet
potatoes, cubed
8 small carrots, cut in
small chunks
2 small onions, cut in
wedges
2 ribs celery, cut up
2½-3 lb. beef chuck, *or* pot
roast
2 Tbsp. cooking oil
¾ cup water, dry wine, *or*
tomato juice
1 Tbsp. Worcestershire
sauce
1 tsp. instant beef bouillon
granules
1 tsp. dried basil

1. Place vegetables in bottom of slow cooker.
2. Brown roast in oil in
skillet. Place on top of vegetables.
3. Combine water,
Worcestershire sauce, bouillon, and basil. Pour over meat
and vegetables.
4. Cover. Cook on Low 10-
12 hours.

# Easy Pot Roast and Veggies

**Tina Houk,** Clinton, MO
**Arlene Wiens,** Newton, KS

*Makes 6 servings*

3-4-lb. chuck roast
4 medium-sized potatoes,
cubed
4 medium-sized carrots,
sliced, *or* 1 lb. baby
carrots
2 celery ribs, sliced thin,
optional
1 envelope dry onion soup
mix
3 cups water

1. Put roast, potatoes, carrots, and celery in slow
cooker.
2. Add onion soup mix and
water.
3. Cover. Cook on Low 6-8
hours.

**Variations:**

1. To add flavor to the
broth, stir 1 tsp. kitchen bouquet, ½ tsp. salt, ½ tsp.
black pepper, and ½ tsp. garlic powder into water before
pouring over meat and vegetables.
**Bonita Ensenberger**
Albuquerque, NM

2. Before putting roast in
cooker, sprinkle it with the
dry soup mix, patting it on so
it adheres.
**Betty Lahman**
Elkton, VA

3. Add one bay leaf and
2 cloves minced garlic to
Step 2.
**Susan Tjon**
Austin, TX

# Pot Roast

**Janet L. Roggie**
Linville, NY

*Makes 6-8 servings*

3 potatoes, thinly sliced
2 large carrots, thinly
sliced
1 onion, thinly sliced
1 tsp. salt
½ tsp. pepper
3-4-lb. pot roast
½ cup water

1. Put vegetables in bot-
tom of slow cooker. Stir in
salt and pepper. Add roast.
Pour in water.
2. Cover. Cook on Low 10-
12 hours.

**Variations:**

1. Add ½ tsp. dried dill, a
bay leaf, and ½ tsp. dried
rosemary for more flavor.
2. Brown roast on all sides
in saucepan in 2 Tbsp. oil
before placing in cooker.
**Debbie Zeida**
Mashpee, MA

**85**

# Easy Roast

**Lisa Warren**
Parkesburg, PA

*Makes 6-8 servings*

3-4-lb. beef roast
1 envelope dry onion soup
   mix
14 1/2-oz. can stewed
   tomatoes, *or* seasoned
   tomatoes

1. Place roast in slow cooker. Cover with onion soup and tomatoes.
2. Cover. Cook on Low 8 hours.

# Hearty Beef Stew

**Lovina Baer**
Conrath, WI

*Makes 4-6 servings*

2-lb. round steak
4 large potatoes, cubed
2 large carrots, sliced
2 ribs celery, sliced
1 medium onion, chopped
1 qt. tomato juice
1 Tbsp. Worcestershire
   sauce
2 tsp. salt
1/2 tsp. pepper
1/4 cup sugar
1 Tbsp. clear jel

1. Combine meat, potatoes, carrots, celery, and onion in slow cooker.
2. Combine tomato juice, Worcestershire sauce, salt, and pepper. Pour into slow cooker.
3. Mix together sugar and clear jel. Add to remaining ingredients, stirring well.
4. Cover. Cook on High 6-7 hours.

**Variation:**
Instead of clear jel, use 1/4 cup instant tapioca.

# Virginia's Beef Stew

**Virginia Bender**
Dover, DE

*Makes 6 servings*

3 lbs. boneless beef
1 envelope dry onion soup
28-oz. can diced tomatoes,
   undrained
1 Tbsp. minute tapioca
4-5 potatoes, cubed
1 onion, chopped
6 carrots, sliced
1 tsp. sugar
1 Tbsp. salt
1/2 tsp. pepper

1. Combine all ingredients in slow cooker.
2. Cover. Bake on High 5 hours.

**Variation:**
Add 2 cups frozen peas during last 10 minutes of cooking.

# Rump Roast and Vegetables

**Kimberlee Greenawalt**
Harrisonburg, VA

*Makes 6-8 servings*

1 1/2 lbs. small potatoes
   (about 10), *or* medium
   potatoes (about 4),
   halved
2 medium carrots, cubed
1 small onion, sliced
10-oz. pkg. frozen lima
   beans
1 bay leaf
2 Tbsp. quick-cooking
   tapioca
2-2 1/2-lb. boneless beef
   round rump, round tip,
   *or* pot roast
2 Tbsp. oil
10 3/4-oz. can condensed
   vegetable beef soup
1/4 cup water
1/4 tsp. pepper

1. Place potatoes, carrots, and onion in slow cooker. Add frozen beans and bay leaf. Sprinkle with tapioca.
2. Brown roast on all sides in oil in skillet. Place over vegetables in slow cooker.
3. Combine soup, water, and pepper. Pour over roast.
4. Cover. Cook on Low 10-12 hours, or High 5-6 hours.
5. Discard bay leaf before serving.

# Hearty New England Dinner

Joette Droz
Kalona, IA

*Makes 6-8 servings*

2 medium carrots, sliced
1 medium onion, sliced
1 celery rib, sliced
3-lb. boneless chuck roast
1/2 tsp. salt
1/4 tsp. pepper
1 envelope dry onion soup mix
2 cups water
1 Tbsp. vinegar
1 bay leaf
half a small head of cabbage, cut in wedges
3 Tbsp. melted margarine, *or* butter
2 Tbsp. flour
1 Tbsp. dried minced onion
2 Tbsp. prepared horseradish
1/2 tsp. salt

1. Place carrots, onion, and celery in slow cooker. Place roast on top. Sprinkle with 1/2 tsp. salt and pepper. Add soup mix, water, vinegar, and bay leaf.

2. Cover. Cook on Low 7-9 hours. Remove beef and keep warm. Just before serving, cut into pieces or thin slices.

3. Discard bay leaf. Add cabbage to juice in slow cooker.

4. Cover. Cook on High 1 hour, or until cabbage is tender.

5. Melt margarine in saucepan. Stir in flour and onion. Add 1 1/2 cups liquid from slow cooker. Stir in horseradish and 1/2 tsp. salt. Bring to boil. Cook over low heat until thick and smooth, about 2 minutes. Return to cooker and blend with remaining sauce in cooker. When blended, serve over or alongside meat and vegetables.

# Easy Beef Stew

Connie Johnson
Loudon, NH

*Makes 6 servings*

1 lb. stewing beef
1 cup cubed turnip
2 medium potatoes, cubed
1 large onion, sliced
1 garlic clove, minced
2 large carrots, sliced
1/2 cup green beans, cut up
1/2 cup peas
1 bay leaf
1/2 tsp. dried thyme
1 tsp. chopped parsley
2 Tbsp. tomato paste
2 Tbsp. celery leaves
1/2 tsp. salt
1/4 tsp. pepper
1 qt., *or* 2 14 1/2-oz. cans, beef broth

1. Place meat, vegetables, and seasonings in slow cooker. Pour broth over all.

2. Cover. Cook on Low 6-8 hours.

# Pot Roast

Julie McKenzie
Punxsutawney, PA

*Makes 8 servings*

3-lb. rump roast
1/2 envelope dry onion soup mix
1 small onion, sliced
4-oz. can mushrooms with liquid
1/3 cup dry red wine
1/3 cup water
1 garlic clove, minced
1 bay leaf
1/2 tsp. dried thyme
2 Tbsp. chopped fresh basil, *or* 1 tsp. dried basil

1. Combine all ingredients in slow cooker.

2. Cover. Cook on Low 10-12 hours.

**Variations:**

1. Add 1/2 tsp. salt, if desired.

2. Mix 3 Tbsp. cornstarch into 1/2 cup cold water. At the end of the cooking time remove bay leaf and discard. Remove meat to serving platter and keep warm. Stir dissolved cornstarch into hot liquid in slow cooker. Stir until absorbed. Cover and cook on High 10 minutes, until sauce thickens. Serve over top or alongside sliced meat.

# Pot Roast with Gravy and Vegetables

**Irene Klaeger,** Inverness, FL
**Jan Pembleton,** Arlington, TX

*Makes 4-6 servings*

3-4-lb. bottom round, rump, *or* arm roast
2-3 tsp. salt
1/2 tsp. pepper
2 Tbsp. flour
1/4 cup cold water
1 tsp. kitchen bouquet, *or* gravy browning seasoning sauce
1 garlic clove, minced
2 medium onions, cut in wedges
4-6 medium potatoes, cubed
2-4 carrots, quartered
1 green pepper, sliced

1. Place roast in slow cooker. Sprinkle with salt and pepper.
2. Make paste of flour and cold water. Stir in kitchen bouquet and spread over roast.
3. Add garlic, onions, potatoes, carrots, and green pepper.
4. Cover. Cook on Low 8-10 hours, or High 4-5 hours.
5. Taste and adjust seasonings before serving.

# Round Steak Casserole

**Cheryl Bartel,** Hillsboro, KS
**Barbara Walker,** Sturgis, SD

*Makes 4-6 servings*

2-lb. 1/2"-thick round steak
1/2 tsp. garlic salt
1 tsp. salt
1/4-1/2 tsp. pepper
1 onion, thinly sliced
3-4 potatoes, quartered
3-4 carrots, sliced
14 1/2-oz. can French-style green beans, drained, *or* 1 lb. frozen green beans
10 3/4-oz. can tomato soup
14 1/2-oz. can stewed tomatoes

1. Cut meat into serving-size pieces, place in slow cooker, stir in seasonings, and mix well.
2. Add potatoes, carrots, and green beans. Top with soup and tomatoes.
3. Cover. Cook on High 1 hour. Reduce heat to Low and cook 8 hours, or until done. Remove cover during last half hour if there is too much liquid.

# "Smothered" Steak

**Susan Yoder Graber**
Eureka, IL

*Makes 6 servings*

1 1/2-lb. chuck, *or* round, steak, cut into strips
1/3 cup flour
1/2 tsp. salt
1/4 tsp. pepper
1 large onion, sliced
1-2 green peppers, sliced
14 1/2-oz. can stewed tomatoes
4-oz. can mushrooms, drained
2 Tbsp. soy sauce
10-oz. pkg. frozen French-style green beans

1. Layer steak in bottom of slow cooker. Sprinkle with flour, salt, and pepper. Stir well to coat steak.
2. Add remaining ingredients. Mix together gently.
3. Cover. Cook on Low 8 hours.
4. Serve over rice.

**Variations:**
1. Use 8-oz. can tomato sauce instead of stewed tomatoes.
2. Substitute 1 Tbsp. Worcestershire sauce in place of soy sauce.

**Mary E. Martin**
Goshen, IN

# Veal and Peppers

**Irma H. Schoen**
Windsor, CT

*Makes 4 servings*

1½ lbs. boneless veal,
  cubed
3 green peppers, quartered
2 onions, thinly sliced
½ lb. fresh mushrooms,
  sliced
1 tsp. salt
½ tsp. dried basil
2 cloves garlic, minced
28-oz. can tomatoes

1. Combine all ingredients
in slow cooker.
2. Cover. Cook on Low 7
hours, or on High 4 hours.
3. Serve over rice or noodles.

**Variation:**
Use boneless, skinless
chicken breast, cut into
chunks, instead of veal.

# Beef and Beans

**Robin Schrock**
Millersburg, OH

*Makes 8 servings*

1 Tbsp. prepared mustard
1 Tbsp. chili powder
½ tsp. salt
¼ tsp. pepper
1½-lb. boneless round
  steak, cut into thin
  slices
2 14½-oz. cans diced
  tomatoes, undrained
1 medium onion, chopped
1 beef bouillon cube,
  crushed
16-oz. can kidney beans,
  rinsed and drained

1. Combine mustard, chili
powder, salt, and pepper. Add
beef slices and toss to coat.
Place meat in slow cooker.
2. Add tomatoes, onion,
and bouillon.
3. Cover. Cook on Low 6-8
hours.
4. Stir in beans. Cook 30
minutes longer.
5. Serve over rice.

# Roast with Veggies

**Arlene Wengerd**
Millersburg, OH

*Makes 6 servings*

2-lb. roast, partially
  thawed
1 medium onion, sliced
1 pint tomato juice
1 tsp. salt
1 tsp. black pepper
1 tsp. dried marjoram
4-5 medium potatoes, cut
  in thick slices
4-5 carrots, sliced
dash of white vinegar
10¾-oz. can golden cream
  of mushroom soup

1. Place roast in slow
cooker. Arrange onions on
top.
2. Carefully pour tomato
juice over top. Sprinkle with
spices.
3. Cover. Cook on High 5
hours.
4. Drain juice from roast
into bowl. Pull roast apart
into bite-sized pieces. Return
meat to slow cooker.
5. Partially cook potatoes
and carrots in saucepan in
boiling water with a dash of
white vinegar. (The white
vinegar gives vegetables a
bright color.) Layer veggies on
top of roast.
6. Pour soup over all.
Cover and cook on High
1 more hour.

---

Fresh vegetables take longer to cook than meats, because,
in a slow cooker, liquid simmers rather than boils.
Remember this if you've adapted range-top recipes to slow
cooking.

**Beatrice Orgish**
Richardson, TX

# Round Steak

**Janet V. Yocum**
Elizabethtown, PA

*Makes 4 servings*

2-lb. round steak, cut into
  serving-size chunks
1 onion, chopped
4 ribs celery, chopped
4 carrots, chopped
4 potatoes, cut into bite-
  sized pieces
2 tsp. salt
1 tsp. seasoning salt
1/2 tsp. pepper
10 3/4-oz. can cream of
  celery, *or* cream of
  mushroom, soup
water

1. Put steak in bottom of
slow cooker.
2. Stir vegetables, seasonings, and soup together in
large bowl. Pour over meat.
3. Add water if needed to
cover meat and vegetables.
4. Cover. Cook on Low 8
hours.

# Forget It Pot Roast

**Mary Mitchell**
Battle Creek, MI

*Makes 6 servings*

6 potatoes, quartered
6 carrots, sliced
3-3 1/2-lb. chuck roast
1 envelope dry onion soup
  mix
10 3/4-oz. can cream of
  mushroom soup
2-3 Tbsp. flour
1/4 cup cold water

1. Place potatoes and carrots in slow cooker. Add
meat. Top with soups.
2. Cover. Cook on Low 8-9
hours.
3. To make gravy, remove
meat and vegetables to serving platter and keep warm.
Pour juices into saucepan and
bring to boil. Mix 2-3 Tbsp.
flour with 1/4 cup cold water
until smooth. Stir into juices
in pan until thickened. Serve
over meat and vegetables, or
alongside as a gravy.

# Beef Stew Bourguignonne

**Jo Haberkamp**
Fairbank, IA

*Makes 6 servings*

2 lbs. stewing beef, cut in
  1-inch cubes
2 Tbsp. cooking oil
10 3/4-oz. can condensed
  golden cream of
  mushroom soup
1 tsp. Worcestershire sauce
1/3 cup dry red wine
1/2 tsp. dried oregano
2 tsp. salt
1/2 tsp. pepper
1/2 cup chopped onions
1/2 cup chopped carrots
4-oz. can mushroom
  pieces, drained
1/2 cup cold water
1/4 cup flour
noodles, cooked

1. Brown meat in oil in
saucepan. Transfer to slow
cooker.
2. Mix together soup,
Worcestershire sauce, wine,
oregano, salt and pepper,
onions, carrots, and mushrooms. Pour over meat.
3. Cover. Cook on Low 10-
12 hours.
4. Combine water and
flour. Stir into beef mixture.
Turn cooker to High.
5. Cook and stir until
thickened and bubbly.
6. Serve over noodles.

A slow cooker is perfect for less tender meats such as a
round steak. Because the meat is cooked in liquid for hours,
it turns out tender and juicy.
**Carolyn Baer**
Conrath, WI
**Barbara Sparks**
Glen Burnie, MD

# Baked Steak
**Shirley Thieszen**
Lakin, KS

*Makes 6 servings*

2½ lbs. round steak, cut
  into 10 pieces
1 Tbsp. salt
½ tsp. pepper
oil
½ cup chopped onions
½ cup chopped green
  peppers
1 cup cream of mushroom
  soup
½ cup water

1. Season the steak with
salt and pepper. Brown on
both sides in oil in saucepan.
Place in slow cooker.
2. Stir in onions, green
peppers, mushroom soup,
and water.
3. Cover. Cook on High 1
hour, and then on Low 3-4
hours.

# Creamy
# Swiss Steak
**Jo Ellen Moore**
Pendleton, IN

*Makes 6 servings*

1½-lb. ¾-inch thick round
  steak
2 Tbsp. flour
1 tsp. salt
¼ tsp. pepper
1 medium onion, sliced
10¾-oz. can cream of
  mushroom soup
1 carrot, chopped
1 small celery rib, chopped

1. Cut steak into serving-
size pieces.
2. Combine flour, salt, and
pepper. Dredge meat in flour.
3. Place onions in bottom
of slow cooker. Add meat.
4. Spread cream of mush-
room soup over meat. Top
with carrots and celery.
5. Cover. Cook on Low 8-
10 hours, or High 3-5 hours.

# Saucy Round
# Steak Supper
**Shirley Sears**
Tiskilwa, IL

*Makes 6-8 servings*

2 lbs. round steak, sliced
  diagonally into ⅛-inch
  strips (reserve meat
  bone)
½ cup chopped onions
½ cup chopped celery
8-oz. can mushrooms,
  stems and pieces,
  drained (reserve liquid)
⅓ cup French dressing
2½-oz. pkg. sour cream
  sauce mix
⅓ cup water
1 tsp. Worcestershire sauce

1. Place steak and bone in
slow cooker. Add onions, celery, and mushrooms.
2. Combine dressing, sour
cream sauce mix, water,
Worcestershire sauce, and
mushroom liquid. Pour over
mixture in slow cooker.
3. Cover. Cook on Low 8-9
hours.
4. Serve over noodles.

**Variation:**
Instead of using the sour
cream sauce mix, remove
meat from cooker at end of
cooking time and keep warm.
Stir 1 cup sour cream into
gravy, cover, and cook on
High 10 minutes. Serve over
steak.

# Succulent Steak

### Betty B. Dennison
### Grove City, PA

*Makes 4 servings*

1½-lb. round steak, cut ½-
  ¾-inch thick
¼ cup flour
½ tsp. salt
¼ tsp. pepper
¼ tsp. paprika
2 onions, sliced
4-oz. can sliced
  mushrooms, drained
½ cup beef broth
2 tsp. Worcestershire sauce
2 Tbsp. flour
3 Tbsp. water

1. Mix together ¼ cup
flour, salt, pepper, and
paprika.
2. Cut steak into 5-6
pieces. Dredge steak pieces in
seasoned flour until lightly
coated.
3. Layer half of onions,
half of steak, and half of
mushrooms into cooker.
Repeat.
4. Combine beef broth and
Worcestershire sauce. Pour
over mixture in slow cooker.
5. Cover. Cook on Low 8-
10 hours.
6. Remove steak to serving
platter and keep warm. Mix
together 2 Tbsp. flour and
water. Stir into drippings and
cook on High until thickened,
about 10 minutes. Pour over
steak and serve.

# Steak Hi-Hat

### Bonita Ensenberger
### Albuquerque, NM

*Makes 8-10 servings*

10¾-oz. can cream of
  chicken soup
10¾-oz. can cream of
  mushroom soup
1½ Tbsp. Worcestershire
  sauce
½ tsp. black pepper
1 tsp. paprika
2 cups onion, chopped
1 garlic clove, minced
1 cup fresh, small button
  mushrooms, quartered
2 lbs. round steak, cubed
1 cup sour cream
cooked noodles with
  poppy seeds
crisp bacon bits, optional

1. Combine chicken soup,
mushroom soup, Worcester-
shire sauce, pepper, paprika,
onion, garlic, and mushrooms
in slow cooker.
2. Stir in steak.
3. Cover. Cook on Low 8-9
hours.
4. Stir in sour cream during the last 20-30 minutes.
5. Serve on hot buttered
noodles sprinkled with poppy
seeds. Garnish with bacon
bits.

**Variation:**
Add 1 tsp. salt with sea-
sonings in Step 1.

# Steak Stroganoff

### Marie Morucci
### Glen Lyon, PA

*Makes 6 servings*

2 Tbsp. flour
½ tsp. garlic powder
½ tsp. pepper
¼ tsp. paprika
1¾-lb. boneless beef round
  steak
10¾-oz. can cream of
  mushroom soup
½ cup water
1 envelope dried onion
  soup mix
9-oz. jar sliced mushrooms,
  drained
½ cup sour cream
1 Tbsp. minced fresh
  parsley

1. Combine flour, garlic
powder, pepper, and paprika
in slow cooker.
2. Cut meat into 1½ x
½-inch strips. Place in flour
mixture and toss until meat is
well coated.
3. Add mushroom soup,
water, and soup mix. Stir
until well blended.
4. Cover. Cook on High
3-3½ hours, or Low 6-7
hours.
5. Stir in mushrooms, sour
cream, and parsley. Cover
and cook on High 10-15 minutes, or until heated through.
6. Serve with rice.

# Scrumptious Beef

**Julia Lapp**
New Holland, PA

*Makes 4-8 servings (depending
upon amount of beef used)*

1-2 lbs. beef, cubed
1/2 lb. mushrooms, sliced
10 1/2-oz. can beef broth, *or*
   1 cup water and
   1 cube beef bouillon
1 onion, chopped
10 3/4-oz. can cream of
   mushroom soup
3 Tbsp. dry onion soup mix

1. Combine all ingredients
in slow cooker.
2. Cover. Cook on High 3-4
hours, or on Low 7-8 hours.
3. Serve over hot cooked
rice.

# Beef Stew with Mushrooms

**Dorothy M. Pittman**
Pickens, SC

*Makes 6 servings*

2 lbs. stewing beef, cubed
10 3/4-oz. can cream of
   mushroom soup
4-oz. can mushrooms
1 envelope dry onion soup
   mix
1/2 tsp. salt
1/4 tsp. pepper
half a soup can of water

1. Sprinkle bottom of
greased slow cooker with
one-fourth of dry soup mix.
Layer in meat, mushroom
soup, canned mushrooms,
and remaining dry onion
soup mix. Pour water over.
2. Cover. Cook on Low 8
hours, or High 4 hours.
3. Serve over potatoes,
rice, or noodles.

# Good 'n Easy Beef 'n Gravy

**Janice Crist**
Quinter, KS

*Makes 8 servings*

3-lb. beef roast, cubed
1 envelope dry onion soup
   mix
1/2 cup beef broth
10 3/4-oz. can cream of
   mushroom, *or* cream of
   celery, soup
4-oz. can sliced
   mushrooms, drained

1. Combine all ingredients
in slow cooker.
2. Cover. Cook on Low 10-
12 hours.

**Variation:**
Use 1/2 cup sauterne
instead of beef broth.
   **Joyce Shackelford**
   Green Bay, WI

# Elaine's Beef Stroganoff

**Elaine Unruh**
Minneapolis, MN

*Makes 4 servings*

1-lb. round steak, cubed
1 Tbsp. shortening
1/2 cup chopped onions
1/2 cup chopped celery
10 3/4-oz. can cream of
   celery soup
4-oz. can mushroom
   pieces, drained
1 cup sour cream
1/4 tsp. garlic salt

1. Brown meat in shorten-
ing in saucepan. Add onions
and celery and saute until
just tender.
2. Combine all ingredients
in slow cooker.
3. Cover. Cook on Low 6-8
hours.
4. Serve over hot cooked
noodles.

## Easy Dinner Surprise

**Nancy Graves**
Manhattan, KS

*Makes 4-5 servings*

1-1½ lbs. stewing meat, cubed
10¾-oz. can cream of mushroom soup
10¾-oz. can cream of celery soup
1 pkg. dry onion soup mix
4-oz. can mushroom pieces

1. Combine all ingredients in slow cooker.
2. Cover. Cook on Low 8-10 hours.
3. Serve over rice or baked potatoes.

**Variation:**
Add ¼ cup finely chopped celery for color and texture.

## Delicious, Easy Chuck Roast

**Mary Jane Musser**
Manheim, PA

*Makes 4-8 servings*

2-4-lb. chuck roast
salt to taste
pepper to taste
1 onion, sliced
10¾-oz. can cream of mushroom soup

1. Season roast with salt and pepper and place in slow cooker.
2. Add onion. Pour soup over all.
3. Cover. Cook on Low 8-10 hours, or on High 6 hours.

## Creamy Swiss Steak

**Connie B. Weaver**
Bethlehem, PA

*Makes 4-6 servings*

2 lbs. round, *or* Swiss steak, cut ¾-inch thick
salt to taste
pepper to taste
1 large onion, thinly sliced
10¾-oz. can cream of mushroom soup
½ cup water

1. Cut steak into serving-size pieces. Season with salt and pepper. Place in slow cooker. Layer onion over steak.
2. Combine soup and water. Pour into slow cooker.
3. Cover. Cook on Low 8-10 hours.
4. Serve over noodles or rice.

## Dale & Shari's Beef Stroganoff

**Dale and Shari Mast**
Harrisonburg, VA

*Makes 4 servings*

4 cups beef cubes
10¾-oz. can cream of mushroom soup
1 cup sour cream

1. Place beef in slow cooker. Cover with mushroom soup.
2. Cover. Cook on Low 8 hours, or High 4-5 hours.
3. Before serving stir in sour cream.
4. Serve over cooked rice, pasta, or baked potatoes.

# Round Steak

**Dorothy Hess,** Willow Street, PA
**Betty A. Holt,** St. Charles, MO
**Betty Moore,** Plano, IL
**Michelle Strite,**
Harrisonburg, VA
**Barbara Tenney,** Delta, PA
**Sharon Timpe,** Mequon, WI

*Makes 4-5 servings*

2-lb. boneless round steak
oil
1 envelope dry onion soup
mix
10³/4-oz. can cream of
mushroom soup
½ cup water

1. Cut steak into serving-size pieces. Brown in oil in saucepan. Place in slow cooker. Sprinkle with soup mix.
2. Combine soup and water. Pour over meat.
3. Cover. Cook on Low 7-8 hours.

**Variation:**

To make a dish lower in sodium, replace the onion soup mix and mushroom soup with 1 cup diced onions, ½ lb. sliced mushrooms, 1 Tbsp. fresh parsley, ¼ tsp. pepper, ½ tsp. dried basil, all stirred gently together. Place on top of meat in cooker. Dissolve 2 Tbsp. flour in ¾ cup cold water. Pour over vegetables and meat. Mix together. Cover and cook according to directions above.
**Della Yoder**
Kalona, IA

# Pot Roast with Creamy Mushroom Sauce

**Colleen Konetzni**
Rio Rancho, NM
**Janet V. Yocum**
Elizabethtown, PA

*Makes 6-8 servings*

2-2½-lb. boneless beef
chuck roast
1 envelope dry onion soup
mix
10³/4-oz. can condensed
cream of mushroom
soup

1. Place roast in slow cooker. Sprinkle with dry soup mix. Top with mushroom soup.
2. Cover. Cook on High 1 hour, and then on Low 8 hours, or until meat is tender.
3. Slice. Serve with mashed potatoes or cooked noodles.

**Variation:**

Add cubed potatoes and sliced carrots to beef. Proceed with directions above.
**Marla Folkert**
Holland, OH

# Slow Cooker Beef

**Sara Harter Fredette**
Williamsburg, MA

*Makes 4-6 servings*

½ cup flour
2 tsp. salt
¼ tsp. pepper
2-3 lbs. stewing beef,
cubed
2 Tbsp. oil
10³/4-oz. can cream of
mushroom soup
1 envelope dry onion soup
mix
½ cup sour cream

1. Combine flour, salt, and pepper in plastic bag. Add beef in small batches. Shake to coat beef. Saute beef in oil in saucepan. Place browned beef in slow cooker.
2. Stir in mushroom soup and onion soup mix.
3. Cover. Cook on Low 6-8 hours.
4. Stir in sour cream before serving. Heat for a few minutes.
5. Serve with noodles or mashed potatoes.

> For a juicy beef roast to be ready by noon, put a roast in the slow cooker in the evening and let it on all night on Low.
> **Ruth Hershey**
> Paradise, PA

# Paul's Beef Bourguignon

Janice Muller
Derwood, MD

*Makes 4 servings*

3-lb. chuck roast, cubed
2 Tbsp. oil
2 10¾-oz. cans golden cream of mushroom soup
1 envelope dry onion soup mix
1 cup cooking sherry

1. Brown meat in oil in skillet. Drain. Place in slow cooker. Add remaining ingredients and cover.
2. Refrigerate 6-8 hours, or up to 14 hours, to marinate.
3. Remove from refrigerator, cover, and cook on Low 8-10 hours.
4. Serve over cooked egg noodles or rice.

# Beef Pot Roast

Julia B. Boyd
Memphis, TN

*Makes 6-8 servings*

3-4-lb. chuck, *or* English-cut, beef roast
1 envelope dry onion-mushroom soup mix
10¾-oz. can cream of celery soup
1 soup can water
2-3 Tbsp. flour
2-3 beef bouillon cubes
1 medium onion, chopped

1. Combine all ingredients in slow cooker.
2. Cover. Cook on Low 10-12 hours.

**Variations:**

Use leftover meat to make soup. Add one large can tomatoes and any leftover vegetables you have on hand. Add spices such as minced onion, garlic powder, basil, bay leaf, celery seed. To increase the liquid, use V-8 juice and season with 1-2 tablespoons butter for a richer soup base. Cook on Low 6-12 hours. If you wish, stir in cooked macaroni or rice just before serving.

# Chuck Roast

Hazel L. Propst
Oxford, PA

*Makes 6-8 servings*

4-5-lb. boneless chuck roast
⅓ cup flour
3 Tbsp. oil
1 envelope dry onion soup mix
water
¼ cup flour
⅓ cup cold water

1. Rub roast with flour on both sides. Brown in oil in saucepan. Place in slow cooker (cutting to fit if necessary).
2. Sprinkle dry soup mix over roast. Add water to cover roast.
3. Cover. Cook on Low 8 hours.
4. Stir flour into ⅓ cup cold water until smooth. Remove roast to serving platter and keep warm. Stir paste into hot sauce and stir until dissolved. Cover and cook on High until sauce is thickened.

For more flavorful gravy, first brown the meat in a skillet. Scrape all browned bits from the bottom of the skillet and add to the slow cooker along with the meat.
**Carolyn Baer**
Conrath, WI

# Roast Beef

**Judy Buller**
Bluffton, OH

*Makes 6 servings*

2¹/2-3-lb. bottom round
  roast
2 cups water
2 beef bouillon cubes
¹/2 tsp. cracked pepper
¹/4 cup flour
¹/2 tsp. salt
³/4 cup cold water

1. Cut roast into 6-8 pieces and place in slow cooker. Add water and bouillon cubes. Sprinkle with pepper.
2. Cover. Cook on High 2 hours. Reduce heat to Low and cook 4-5 hours, or until meat is tender.
3. Dissolve flour and salt in cold water. Remove roast from cooker and keep warm. Stir flour paste into hot broth in cooker until smooth. Cover and cook on High for 5 minutes. Serve gravy with sliced roast beef.

# Roast

**Tracey Yohn**
Harrisburg, PA

*Makes 6 servings*

2-3-lb. shoulder roast
1 tsp. salt
1 tsp. pepper
1 tsp. garlic salt
1 small onion, sliced in
  rings
1 cup boiling water
1 beef bouillon cube

1. Place roast in slow cooker. Sprinkle with salt, pepper, and garlic salt. Place onion rings on top.
2. Dissolve bouillon cube in water. Pour over roast.
3. Cover. Cook on Low 10-12 hours, or on High 5-6 hours.

# Savory Sweet Roast

**Martha Ann Auker**
Landisburg, PA

*Makes 6-8 servings*

3-4-lb. blade, *or* chuck,
  roast
oil
1 onion, chopped
10³/4-oz. can cream of
  mushroom soup
¹/2 cup water
¹/4 cup sugar
¹/4 cup vinegar
2 tsp. salt
1 tsp. prepared mustard
1 tsp. Worcestershire sauce

1. Brown meat in oil on both sides in saucepan. Put in slow cooker.
2. Blend together remaining ingredients. Pour over meat.
3. Cover. Cook on Low 12-16 hours.

# Hungarian Goulash

Kim Stoltzfus
New Holland, PA

*Makes 8 servings*

2-lb. round steak, cubed
1/2 tsp. onion powder
1/2 tsp. garlic powder
2 Tbsp. flour
1/2 tsp. salt
1/2 tsp. pepper
1 1/2 tsp. paprika
10 3/4-oz. can tomato soup
1/2 soup can water
1 cup sour cream

1. Mix meat, onion powder, garlic powder, and flour together in slow cooker until meat is well coated.
2. Add remaining ingredients, except sour cream. Stir well.
3. Cover. Cook on Low 8-10 hours, or High 4-5 hours.
4. Add sour cream 30 minutes before serving.
5. Serve over hot noodles.

# Dilled Pot Roast

C.J. Slagle
Roann, IN

*Makes 6 servings*

3-3 1/2-lb. beef pot roast
1 tsp. salt
1/4 tsp. pepper
2 tsp. dried dillweed, divided
1/4 cup water
1 Tbsp. vinegar
3 Tbsp. flour
1/2 cup water
1 cup sour cream

1. Sprinkle both sides of meat with salt, pepper, and 1 tsp. dill. Place in slow cooker. Add water and vinegar.
2. Cover. Cook on Low 7-9 hours, or until tender. Remove meat from pot. Turn to High.
3. Dissolve flour in water. Stir into meat drippings. Stir in additional 1 tsp. dill. Cook on High 5 minutes. Stir in sour cream. Cook on High another 5 minutes.
4. Slice meat and serve with sour cream sauce over top.

# Herbed Roast with Gravy

Sue Williams
Gulfport, MS

*Makes 8-10 servings*

4-lb. roast
2 tsp. salt
1/2 tsp. pepper
2 medium onions, sliced
half a can (10 3/4-oz.) condensed cheddar cheese soup
8-oz. can tomato sauce
4-oz. can mushroom pieces and stems, drained
1/4 tsp. dried basil
1/4 tsp. dried oregano

1. Season roast with salt and pepper. Place in slow cooker.
2. Combine remaining ingredients and pour over meat.
3. Cover. Cook on Low 8-10 hours, or on High 4-5 hours.
4. Serve with gravy.

# Beef Burgundy

**Jacqueline Stefl**
East Bethany, NY

*Makes 6 servings*

5 medium onions, thinly
   sliced
2 lbs. stewing meat, cubed
1½ Tbsp. flour
½ lb. fresh mushrooms,
   sliced
1 tsp. salt
¼ tsp. dried marjoram
¼ tsp. dried thyme
⅛ tsp. pepper
¾ cup beef broth
1½ cups burgundy wine

1. Place onions in slow
cooker.
2. Dredge meat in flour.
Put in slow cooker.
3. Add mushrooms, salt,
marjoram, thyme, and pep-
per.
4. Pour in broth and wine.
5. Cover. Cook 8-10 hours
on Low.
6. Serve over cooked noo-
dles.

# Goodtime
# Beef Brisket

**AmyMarlene Jensen**
Fountain, CO

*Makes 6-8 servings*

3½-4-lb. beef brisket
1 can beer
2 cups tomato sauce
2 tsp. prepared mustard
2 Tbsp. balsamic vinegar
2 Tbsp. Worcestershire
   sauce
1 tsp. garlic powder
½ tsp. ground allspice
2 Tbsp. brown sugar
1 small green, *or* red, bell
   pepper, chopped
1 medium onion, chopped
1 tsp. salt
½ tsp. pepper

1. Place brisket in slow
cooker.
2. Combine remaining
ingredients. Pour over meat.
3. Cover. Cook on Low 8-
10 hours.
4. Remove meat from
sauce. Slice very thin.
5. Serve on rolls or over
couscous.

# Pot Roast

**Judi Manos**
West Islip, NY

*Makes 8 servings*

4-lb. chuck roast *or* stewing
   meat, cubed
1 Tbsp. oil
¾ can beer
½ cup, plus 1 Tbsp.,
   ketchup
1 onion, sliced
½ cup cold water
1½ Tbsp. flour

1. Brown meat in oil in
saucepan.
2. Combine beer and
ketchup in slow cooker. Stir
in onion and browned meat.
3. Cover. Cook on Low 8
hours.
4. Remove meat and keep
warm. Blend flour into cold
water until dissolved. Stir into
hot gravy until smooth.
5. Serve gravy and meat
together.

Less tender, less expensive cuts of meat are better suited for
slow cooking than expensive cuts of meat. If desired, you can
brown meat on top of the stove first, for additional flavor.
**Beatrice Orgish**
Richardson, TX

## Italian Beef

**Joyce Bowman**
Lady Lake, FL

*Makes 10-12 servings*

3-4-lb. beef roast
1 pkg. dry Italian dressing
  mix
12-oz. can beer

1. Place roast in slow cooker. Sprinkle with dry Italian dressing mix. Pour beer over roast.
2. Cover. Cook on Low 8-10 hours, or High 3-4 hours.
3. When beef is done, shred and serve with juice on crusty rolls.

**Variations:**
In place of beef, use pork chops or chicken legs and thighs (skin removed).

## Slow-Cooker Roast Beef

**Ernestine Schrepfer**
Trenton, MO

*Makes 6 servings*

3-lb. sirloin tip roast
1/2 cup flour
1 envelope dry onion soup
  mix
1 envelope brown gravy
  mix
2 cups ginger ale

1. Coat roast with flour (reserve remaining flour). Place in slow cooker.
2. Combine soup mix, gravy mix, remaining flour, and ginger ale in bowl. Mix well. Pour over roast.
3. Cover. Cook on Low 8-10 hours.

## Pepsi Pot Roast

**Mrs. Don Martins**
Fairbank, IA

*Makes 6-8 servings*

3-4-lb. pot roast
10¾-oz. can cream of
  mushroom soup
1 envelope dry onion soup
  mix
16-oz. bottle Pepsi, *or*
  other cola

1. Place meat in slow cooker.
2. Top with mushroom soup and onion soup mix. Pour in Pepsi.
3. Cover. Cook on High 6 hours.

## Cola Roast

**Janice Yoskovich**
Carmichaels, PA

*Makes 8-10 servings*

3-lb. beef roast
1 envelope dry onion soup
  mix
2 cans cola

1. Place roast in slow cooker. Sprinkle with soup mix. Pour soda over all.
2. Cover. Cook on Low 7-8 hours.

**Note:**
Diet cola does not work with this recipe.

## Zippy Beef Tips

**Maryann Westerberg**
Rosamond, CA

*Makes 6-8 servings*

2 lbs. stewing meat, cubed
2 cups sliced fresh
  mushrooms
10¾-oz. can cream of
  mushroom soup
1 envelope dry onion soup
  mix
1 cup 7-Up, *or* other
  lemon-lime carbonated
  drink

1. Place meat and mushrooms in slow cooker.

2. Combine mushroom soup, soup mix, and soda. Pour over meat.

3. Cover. Cook on Low 8 hours.

4. Serve over rice.

# Hungarian Goulash

Audrey Romonosky
Austin, TX

*Makes 5-6 servings*

2 lbs. beef chuck, cubed
1 onion, sliced
1/2 tsp. garlic powder
1/2 cup ketchup
2 Tbsp. Worcestershire sauce
1 Tbsp. brown sugar
1/2 tsp. salt
2 tsp. paprika
1/2 tsp. dry mustard
1 cup cold water
1/4 cup flour
1/2 cup water

1. Place meat in slow cooker. Add onion.

2. Combine garlic powder, ketchup, Worcestershire sauce, brown sugar, salt, paprika, mustard, and 1 cup water. Pour over meat.

3. Cover. Cook on Low 8 hours.

4. Dissolve flour in 1/2 cup water. Stir into meat mixture. Cook on High until thickened, about 10 minutes.

5. Serve over noodles.

# Horseradish Beef

Barbara Nolan
Pleasant Valley, NY

*Makes 6-8 servings*

3-4-lb. pot roast
2 Tbsp. oil
1/2 tsp. salt
1/2 tsp. pepper
1 onion, chopped
6-oz. can tomato paste
1/3 cup horseradish sauce

1. Brown roast on all sides in oil in skillet. Place in slow cooker. Add remaining ingredients.

2. Cover. Cook on Low 8-10 hours.

# Spicy Pot Roast

Jane Talso
Albuquerque, NM

*Makes 6-8 servings*

3-4-lb. beef pot roast
salt to taste
pepper to taste
3/4-oz. pkg. brown gravy mix
1/4 cup ketchup
2 tsp. Dijon mustard
1 tsp. Worcestershire sauce
1/8 tsp. garlic powder
1 cup water

1. Sprinkle meat with salt and pepper. Place in slow cooker.

2. Combine remaining ingredients. Pour over meat.

3. Cover. Cook on Low 8-10 hours, or High 4-5 hours.

# Chinese Pot Roast

Marsha Sabus
Fallbrook, CA

*Makes 6 servings*

3-lb. boneless beef pot roast
2 Tbsp. flour
1 Tbsp. oil
2 large onions, chopped
salt to taste
pepper to taste
1/2 cup soy sauce
1 cup water
1/2 tsp. ground ginger

1. Dip roast in flour and brown on both sides in oil in saucepan. Place in slow cooker.

2. Top with onions, salt and pepper.

3. Combine soy sauce, water, and ginger. Pour over meat.

4. Cover. Cook on High 10 minutes. Reduce heat to Low and cook 8-10 hours.

5. Slice and serve with rice.

# Peppery Roast

**Lovina Baer**
Conrath, WI

*Makes 8-10 servings*

4-lb. beef, *or* venison, roast
1 tsp. garlic salt
1 tsp. onion salt
2 tsp. celery salt
1½ tsp. salt
2 tsp. Worcestershire sauce
2 tsp. pepper
½ cup ketchup
1 Tbsp. liquid smoke
3 Tbsp. brown sugar
1 Tbsp. dry mustard
dash of nutmeg
1 Tbsp. soy sauce
1 Tbsp. lemon juice
3 drops hot pepper sauce

1. Place roast in slow cooker.
2. Combine remaining ingredients and pour over roast.
3. Cover. Cook on High 6-8 hours.

# Mexican Pot Roast

**Bernice A. Esau**
North Newton, KS

*Makes 6-8 servings*

3 lbs. beef brisket, cubed
2 Tbsp. oil
½ cup slivered almonds
2 cups mild picante sauce, *or* hot, if you prefer
2 Tbsp. vinegar
1 tsp. garlic powder
½ tsp. salt
¼ tsp. cinnamon
¼ tsp. dried thyme
¼ tsp. dried oregano
⅛ tsp. ground cloves
⅛ tsp. pepper
½-¾ cup water, as needed

1. Brown beef in oil in skillet. Place in slow cooker.
2. Combine remaining ingredients. Pour over meat.
3. Cover. Cook on Low 10-12 hours. Add water as needed.
4. Serve with potatoes, noodles, or rice.

# Chuck Wagon Beef

**Charlotte Bull**
Cassville, MO

*Makes 8 servings*

4-lb. boneless chuck roast
1 tsp. garlic salt
¼ tsp. black pepper
2 Tbsp. oil
6-8 garlic cloves, minced
1 large onion, sliced
1 cup water
1 bouillon cube
2-3 tsp. instant coffee
1 bay leaf, *or* 1 Tbsp. mixed Italian herbs
3 Tbsp. cold water
2 Tbsp. cornstarch

1. Sprinkle roast with garlic salt and pepper. Brown on all sides in oil in saucepan. Place in slow cooker.
2. Saute garlic and onion in meat drippings in saucepan. Add water, bouillon cube, and coffee. Cook over low heat for several minutes, stirring until drippings loosen. Pour over meat in cooker.
3. Add bay leaf or herbs.
4. Cover. Cook on Low 8-10 hours, or until very tender. Remove bay leaf and discard. Remove meat to serving platter and keep warm.
5. Mix water and cornstarch together until paste forms. Stir into hot liquid and onions in cooker. Cover. Cook 10 minutes on High, or until thickened.
6. Slice meat and serve with gravy over top or on the side.

## French Dip

**Barbara Walker**
Sturgis, SD

*Makes 6-8 servings*

3-lb. rump roast
1/2 cup soy sauce
1 beef bouillon cube
1 bay leaf
1 tsp. dried thyme
3-4 peppercorns
1 tsp. garlic powder

1. Combine all ingredients in slow cooker. Add water to almost cover meat.
2. Cover. Cook on Low 10-12 hours.

## French Dip Roast

**Patti Boston**
Newark, OH

*Makes 8-10 servings*

1 large onion, sliced
3-lb. beef bottom roast
1/2 cup dry white wine, *or* water
1 pkg. dry au jus gravy mix
2 cups beef broth

1. Place onion in slow cooker. Add roast.
2. Combine wine and gravy mix. Pour over roast.
3. Add enough broth to cover roast.

4. Cover. Cook on High 5-6 hours, or Low 10-12 hours.
5. Remove meat from liquid. Let stand 5 minutes before slicing thinly across grain.

## Beef Au Jus

**Jean Weller**
State College, PA

*Makes 6-8 servings*

3-lb. eye, *or* rump, roast
1 pkg. dry au jus gravy mix
1 tsp. garlic powder
1 tsp. onion powder
1/2 tsp. salt
1/4-1/2 tsp. pepper

1. Place roast in slow cooker.
2. Prepare gravy according to package directions. Pour over roast.
3. Sprinkle with garlic powder, onion powder, salt, and pepper.
4. Cover. Cook on Low 6 hours. After 6 hours, remove meat and trim fat. Shred meat and return to slow cooker, cooking until desired tenderness. Add more water if roast isn't covered with liquid when returning it to cooker.

## Dripped Beef

**Mitzi McGlynchey**
Downingtown, PA

*Makes 8 servings*

3-4-lb. chuck roast
1 tsp. salt
1 tsp. seasoned salt
1 tsp. white pepper
1 Tbsp. rosemary
1 Tbsp. dried oregano
1 Tbsp. garlic powder
1 cup water

1. Combine all ingredients in slow cooker.
2. Cover. Cook on Low 6-7 hours.
3. Shred meat using two forks. Strain liquid and return liquid and meat to slow cooker. Serve meat and au jus over mashed potatoes, noodles, or rice.

If you use ground herbs and spices, add them during the last hour of cooking.

**Darlene Raber**
Wellman, IA

**103**

# Deep Pit Beef

**Kristina Shull**
Timberville, VA

*Makes 6-8 servings*

1 tsp. garlic salt, *or* powder
1 tsp. celery salt
1 tsp. lemon pepper
1½ Tbsp. liquid smoke
2 Tbsp. Worcestershire
    sauce
3-4-lb. beef roast

1. Combine seasonings in small bowl. Spread over roast as a marinade. Cover tightly with foil. Refrigerate for at least 8 hours.
2. Place roast in slow cooker. Cover with marinade sauce.
3. Cover. Cook on Low 6-7 hours. Save juice for gravy and serve with roast.

**Note:**
This is also good served cold, along with picnic foods.

# Barbecued Roast Beef

**Kim Stoltzfus**
New Holland, PA

*Makes 10-12 servings*

4-lb. chuck roast
1 cup ketchup
1 cup barbecue sauce
2 cups chopped celery
2 cups water
1 cup chopped onions
4 Tbsp. vinegar
2 Tbsp. brown sugar
2 Tbsp. Worcestershire
    sauce
1 tsp. chili powder
1 tsp. garlic powder
1 tsp. salt

1. Combine all ingredients in large bowl. Spoon into 5-quart cooker, or 2 3½-quart cookers.
2. Cover. Cook on Low 6-8 hours, or High 3-4 hours.
3. Slice meat into thin slices and serve in barbecue sauce over mashed potatoes or rice.

# Italian Roast Beef

**Elsie Russett**
Fairbank, IA

*Makes 6-8 servings*

4-lb. beef rump roast
flour
1 onion
2 garlic cloves
1 large rib celery
2-oz. salt pork, *or* bacon
1 onion, sliced

1. Lightly flour roast.
2. In blender, grind onion, garlic, celery, and salt pork together. Rub ground mixture into roast.
3. Place sliced onion in slow cooker. Place roast on top of onion.
4. Cover. Cook on Low 8-10 hours.

# Diane's Gutbuster

**Joyce Cox**
Port Angeles, WA

*Makes 10-15 servings*

5-lb. chuck roast
1 large onion, sliced
2 tsp. salt
¾ tsp. pepper
28-oz. can stewed tomatoes
1 Tbsp. brown sugar
1 cup water
half a bottle barbecue sauce
1 Tbsp. Worcestershire sauce

1. Combine all ingredients except barbecue sauce and Worcestershire sauce in slow cooker.

2. Cover. Cook on Low 6-7 hours. Refrigerate for at least 8 hours.

3. Shred meat and place in slow cooker. Add barbecue sauce and Worcestershire sauce.

4. Cover. Cook on Low 4-5 hours.

5. Serve as main dish or in hamburger buns.

# Barbecue Brisket

### Patricia Howard
### Albuquerque, NM

*Makes 8-10 servings*

**4-5-lb. beef brisket**
**1/8 tsp. celery salt**
**1/4 tsp. garlic salt**
**1/4 tsp. onion salt**
**1/4 tsp. salt**
**1.5-oz. bottle liquid smoke**
**1 1/2 cups barbecue sauce**

1. Place brisket in slow cooker.

2. Sprinkle with celery salt, garlic salt, onion salt, and salt.

3. Pour liquid smoke over brisket. Cover. Refrigerate for 8 hours.

4. Cook on Low 8-10 hours, or until tender. During last hour pour barbecue sauce over brisket.

# Beef Ribs

### Maryann Westerberg
### Rosamond, CA

*Makes 8-10 servings*

**3-4-lb. boneless beef, *or* short ribs**
**1 1/2 cups barbecue sauce, divided**
**1/2 cup apricot, *or* pineapple, jam**
**1 Tbsp. soy sauce**

1. Place ribs in baking pan.

2. Combine 3/4 cup barbecue sauce, jam, and soy sauce. Pour over ribs. Bake at 450° for 30 minutes to brown.

3. Take out of oven. Layer beef and sauce used in oven in slow cooker.

4. Cover. Cook on Low 8 hours.

5. Mix remaining 3/4 cup barbecue sauce with sauce from slow cooker. Pour over ribs and serve.

# Reuben Sandwiches

### Maryann Markano
### Wilmington, DE

*Makes 3-4 servings*

**1-lb. can sauerkraut**
**1 lb. sliced corned beef brisket**
**1/4-lb. Swiss cheese, sliced**
**sliced rye bread**
**sandwich spread, *or* Thousand Island Dressing**

1. Drain sauerkraut in sieve, then on paper towels until very day. Place in bottom of slow cooker.

2. Arrange layer of corned beef slices over sauerkraut. Top with cheese slices.

3. Cover. Cook on Low 3-4 hours.

4. Toast bread. Spread generously with sandwich spread or dressing. Spoon ingredients from slow cooker onto toasted bread, maintaining layers of sauerkraut, meat, and cheese.

---

If I want to have a hot dish at noon time on Sunday, I bake a casserole on Saturday. Then on Sunday morning I put it into a slow cooker, turn it on High for 30 minutes, then on Low while I'm at church.

**Ruth Hershey**
Paradise, PA

# Smoky Brisket

**Angeline Lang**
Greeley, CO

*Makes 8-10 servings*

**2 medium onions, sliced**
**3-4-lb. beef brisket**
**1 Tbsp. smoke-flavored salt**
**1 tsp. celery seed**
**1 Tbsp. mustard seed**
**1/2 tsp. pepper**
**12-oz. bottle chili sauce**

1. Arrange onions in bottom of slow cooker.
2. Sprinkle both sides of meat with smoke-flavored salt.
3. Combine celery seed, mustard seed, pepper, and chili sauce. Pour over meat.
4. Cover. Cook on Low 10-12 hours.

# Easy Barbecued Venison

**Tracey B. Stenger**
Gretna, LA

*Makes 6 servings*

**2-3-lb. venison, *or* beef, roast, cubed**
**2 large onions, sliced in rings**
**1-2 18-oz. bottles barbecue sauce**

1. Put layer of meat and layer of onion rings in slow cooker. Drizzle generously with barbecue sauce. Repeat layers until meat and onion rings are all in place.
2. Cover. Cook on Low 8-10 hours.
3. Eat with au gratin potatoes and a vegetable, or slice thin and pile into steak rolls, drizzled with juice.

## Note:

To be sure venison cooks tender, marinate overnight in 1 cup vinegar and 2 Tbsp. dried rosemary. In the morning, discard marinade, cut venison into cubes, and proceed with recipe.

# Sour Beef

**Rosanne Hankins**
Stevensville, MD

*Makes 6-8 servings*

**3-4-lb. pot roast**
**1/3 cup cider vinegar**
**1 large onion, sliced**
**3 bay leaves**
**1/2 tsp. salt**
**1/4 tsp. ground cloves**
**1/4 tsp. garlic powder**

1. Place roast in slow cooker. Add remaining ingredients.
2. Cover. Cook on Low 8-10 hours.

# Old World Sauerbraten

**C.J. Slagle**
Roann, IN
**Angeline Lang**
Greeley, CO

*Makes 8 servings*

**3 1/2-4-lb. beef rump roast**
**1 cup water**
**1 cup vinegar**
**1 lemon, sliced but unpeeled**
**10 whole cloves**
**1 large onion, sliced**
**4 bay leaves**
**6 whole peppercorns**
**2 Tbsp. salt**
**2 Tbsp. sugar**
**12 gingersnaps, crumbled**

1. Place meat in deep ceramic or glass bowl.
2. Combine water, vinegar, lemon, cloves, onion, bay leaves, peppercorns, salt, and sugar. Pour over meat. Cover and refrigerate 24-36 hours. Turn meat several times during marinating.
3. Place beef in slow cooker. Pour 1 cup marinade over meat.
4. Cover. Cook on Low 6-8 hours. Remove meat.
5. Strain meat juices and return to pot. Turn to High. Stir in gingersnaps. Cover and cook on High 10-14 minutes. Slice meat. Pour finished sauce over meat.

# Meatloaf Dinner

**Esther Lehman**
Croghan, NY

*Makes 4 servings*

6 potatoes, cubed
4 carrots, thinly sliced
1/4 tsp. salt
1 egg, slightly beaten
1 large shredded wheat
   biscuit, crushed
1/4 cup chili sauce
1/4 cup finely chopped
   onion
1/2 tsp. salt
1/4 tsp. dried marjoram
1/8 tsp. pepper
1 lb. ground beef

1. Place potatoes and carrots in slow cooker. Season with salt.
2. Combine egg, shredded wheat, chili sauce, onion, salt, marjoram, and pepper. Add ground beef. Mix well. Shape into loaf, slightly smaller in diameter than the cooker. Place on top of vegetables, not touching sides of cooker.
3. Cover. Cook on Low 9-10 hours.

**Variation:**
Substitute 1/2 cup bread crumbs or dry oatmeal for crushed shredded wheat biscuit.

# Easy, All-Day Meatloaf and Vegetables

**Ann Sunday McDowell**
Newtown, PA

*Makes 6 servings*

4 large, *or* 6 medium,
   potatoes, sliced
6 carrots, sliced
1/4 tsp. salt
1 1/2 lbs. ground beef
2 eggs, beaten
3/4 cup cracker crumbs
1/3 cup ketchup
1/3 cup finely chopped
   onions
3/4 tsp. salt
1/4 tsp. dried marjoram
1/4 tsp. black pepper

1. Place potatoes and carrots in slow cooker. Sprinkle with 1/4 tsp. salt.
2. Combine remaining ingredients. Mix well and shape into loaf. Place loaf on top of vegetables, making sure that it doesn't touch sides of slow cooker.
3. Cover. Cook on Low 8-10 hours.

# Ruth Ann's Meatloaf

**Ruth Ann Hoover**
New Holland, PA

*Makes 4 servings*

1 egg
1/4 cup milk
2 slices day-old bread,
   cubed
1/4 cup chopped onions
2 Tbsp. chopped green
   peppers
1 tsp. salt
1/4 tsp. pepper
1 1/2 lbs. ground beef
1/4 cup ketchup
8 small red potatoes
4-6 medium carrots, cut in
   1-inch chunks

1. Beat together eggs and milk.
2. Stir in bread cubes, onions, green peppers, salt, and pepper. Add beef and mix well.
3. Shape into loaf that is about an inch smaller in circumference than the inside of the slow cooker. Place loaf into slow cooker.
4. Spread top with ketchup.
5. Peel strip around the center of each potato. Place carrots and potatoes around Meatloaf.
6. Cover. Cook on High 1 hour. Reduce heat to Low. Cook 7-8 hours longer.

---

Don't peek. It takes 15-20 minutes for the cooker to regain lost steam and return to the right temperature.
**Janet V. Yocum**
Elizabethtown, PA

# Betty's Meatloaf

**Betty B. Dennison**
Grove City, PA

*Makes 4-6 servings*

2 lbs. ground beef
1/2 cup chopped green
  peppers
1/2 cup chopped onions
1/2 tsp. salt
1 cup cracker crumbs
1 egg
7/8-oz. envelope brown
  gravy mix
1 cup milk
4-6 small potatoes, cut up,
  optional

1. Combine all ingredients
except potatoes in large bowl.
Shape into loaf. Place in slow
cooker.
2. Place potatoes alongside
meatloaf.
3. Cover. Cook on Low 8-
10 hours, or High 4-5 hours.

# Tracey's Italian Meatloaf

**Tracey Yohn**
Harrisburg, PA

*Makes 8 servings*

2 lbs. ground beef
2 cups soft bread crumbs
1/2 cup spaghetti sauce
1 large egg
2 Tbsp. dried onion
1/4 tsp. pepper
1 1/4 tsp. salt
1 tsp. garlic salt
1/2 tsp. dried Italian herbs
1/4 tsp. garlic powder
2 Tbsp. spaghetti sauce

1. Fold a 30"-long piece of
foil in half lengthwise. Place in
bottom of slow cooker with
both ends hanging over the
edge of cooker. Grease foil.
2. Combine beef, bread
crumbs, 1/2 cup spaghetti
sauce, egg, onion, and seasonings. Shape into loaf. Place on
top of foil in slow cooker.
Spread 2 Tbsp. spaghetti
sauce over top.
3. Cover. Cook on High
2 1/2-3 hours, or Low 5-6
hours.

# Mary Ann's Italian Meatloaf

**Mary Ann Wasick**
West Allis, WI

*Makes 8-10 servings*

2 lbs. ground beef
2 eggs, beaten
2/3 cup quick-cooking oats
1 envelope dry onion soup
  mix
1/2 cup pasta sauce (your
  favorite)
1 tsp. garlic powder
onion slices

1. Combine ground beef,
eggs, oats, soup mix, pasta
sauce, and garlic powder.
Shape into a loaf. Place in
slow cooker. Garnish top of
loaf with onion slices.
2. Cover. Cook on Low 8
hours.
3. Serve with pasta and
more of the sauce that you
mixed into the meatloaf.

To remove meatloaf or other meats from your cooker,
make foil handles to lift the food out. Use double strips of
heavy foil to make 3 strips, each about 20" x 3". Crisscross
them in the bottom of the pot and bring them up the sides in
a spoke design before putting in the food.
**John D. Allen**
Rye, CO
**Esther Lehman**
Croghan, NY

## Meatloaf Sensation

**Andrea O'Neil**
Fairfield, CT

*Makes 8 servings*

2½ lbs. ground beef
half of an 8-oz. jar salsa
1 pkg. dry taco seasoning,
   divided
1 egg, slightly beaten
1 cup bread crumbs
12-oz. pkg. shredded
   Mexican-mix cheese
2 tsp. salt
½ tsp. pepper

1. Combine all ingredients,
except half of taco seasoning.
Mix well. Shape into loaf and
place in slow cooker. Sprinkle
with remaining taco seasoning.
2. Cover. Cook on Low 8-
10 hours.

## Barbecue Hamburger Steaks

**Jeanette Oberholtzer**
Manheim, PA

*Makes 4 servings*

1 lb. ground beef
1 tsp. salt
1 tsp. pepper
½ cup milk
1 cup soft bread crumbs
2 Tbsp. brown sugar
2 Tbsp. vinegar
3 Tbsp. Worcestershire
   sauce
1 cup ketchup

1. Combine beef, salt, pepper, milk, and bread crumbs.
Mix well. Form into patties.
Brown in saucepan and drain.
2. Combine brown sugar,
vinegar, Worcestershire sauce,
and ketchup in slow cooker.
Add ground beef patties,
pushing them down into the
sauce, so that each one is
well covered.
3. Cover. Cook on Low 4-6
hours.

## Nutritious Meatloaf

**Elsie Russett**
Fairbank, IA

*Makes 6 servings*

1 lb. ground beef
2 cups finely shredded
   cabbage
1 medium green pepper,
   diced
1 Tbsp. dried onion flakes
½ tsp. caraway seeds
1 tsp. salt

1. Combine all ingredients.
Shape into loaf and place on
rack in slow cooker.
2. Cover. Cook on High 3-4
hours.

# Poor Man's Steak

**Elsie Schlabach**
Millersburg, OH

*Makes 8-10 servings*

1 1/2 lbs. ground beef
1 cup milk
1/4 tsp. pepper
1 tsp. salt
1 small onion, finely
  chopped
1 cup cracker crumbs
1 tsp. brown sugar
10 3/4-oz. can cream of
  mushroom soup
1 soup can water

1. Mix together all ingredients except soup and water. Shape into narrow loaf. Refrigerate for at least 8 hours.
2. Slice and fry until brown in skillet.
3. Mix soup and water together until smooth. Spread diluted soup on each piece. Place slices into cooker. Pour any remaining soup over slices in cooker.
4. Cover. Cook on Low 2-3 hours.

# Beef Stroganoff

**Julette Leaman**
Harrisonburg, VA

*Makes 6 servings*

2 lbs. ground beef
2 medium onions, chopped
2 garlic cloves, minced
6 1/2-oz. can mushrooms
1 1/2 cups sour cream
4 Tbsp. flour
2 1/2 tsp. salt
1/4 tsp. pepper
1 cup bouillon
3 Tbsp. tomato paste

1. In skillet, brown beef, onions, garlic, and mushrooms until meat and onions are brown. Drain. Pour into slow cooker.
2. Combine sour cream and flour. Add to mixture in slow cooker. Stir in remaining ingredients.
3. Cover. Cook on Low 6-8 hours.
4. Serve over hot buttered noodles.

# Chili and Cheese on Rice

**Dale and Shari Mast**
Harrisonburg, VA

*Makes 6 servings*

1 lb. ground beef
1 onion, diced
1 tsp. dried basil
1 tsp. dried oregano
16-oz. can light red kidney
  beans
15 1/2-oz. can chili beans
1 pint stewed tomatoes,
  drained
cooked rice
grated cheddar cheese

1. Brown ground beef and onion in skillet. Season with basil and oregano.
2. Combine all ingredients except rice and cheese in slow cooker.
3. Cover. Cook on Low 4 hours.
4. Serve over cooked rice. Top with cheese.

---

Roasting bags work well in the slow cooker. Simply fill with meat and vegetables and cook as directed in slow cooker recipes. Follow manufacturer's directions for filling and sealing bags.

**Charlotte Shaffer**
East Earl, PA

## Loretta's Spanish Rice

**Loretta Krahn**
Mt. Lake, MN

---

*Makes 8 servings*

2 lbs. ground beef,
  browned
2 medium onions, chopped
2 green peppers, chopped
28-oz. can tomatoes
8-oz. can tomato sauce
1½ cups water
2½ tsp. chili powder
2 tsp. salt
2 tsp. Worcestershire sauce
1½ cups rice, uncooked

1. Combine all ingredients
in slow cooker.
2. Cover. Cook on Low 8-
10 hours, or High 6 hours.

## Evie's Spanish Rice

**Evie Hershey**
Atglen, PA

---

*Makes 10-12 servings*

2 lbs. lean ground beef
2 onions, chopped
2 green peppers, chopped
1 qt. canned tomatoes
8-oz. can tomato sauce
1 cup water
2½ tsp. chili powder
2 tsp. salt

2 tsp. Worcestershire sauce
1 cup converted rice,
  uncooked

1. Brown beef in skillet.
Drain.
2. Combine all ingredients
in slow cooker. Stir.
3. Cover. Cook on Low 7-9
hours.

## A Hearty Western Casserole

**Karen Ashworth**
Duenweg, MO

---

*Makes 5 servings*

1 lb. ground beef, browned
16-oz. can whole corn,
  drained
16-oz. can red kidney
  beans, drained
10¾-oz. can condensed
  tomato soup
1 cup (4 oz.) Colby cheese
¼ cup milk
1 tsp. minced dry onion
  flakes
½ tsp. chili powder

1. Combine beef, corn,
beans, soup, cheese, milk,
onion, and chili powder in
slow cooker.
2. Cover. Cook on Low
1 hour.

**Variation:**
1 pkg. (of 10) refrigerator
  biscuits
2 Tbsp. margarine
¼ cup yellow cornmeal

Dip biscuits in margarine
and then in cornmeal. Bake
20 minutes or until brown.
Top beef mixture with biscuits before serving.

## Green Chili Stew

**Jeanne Allen**
Rye, CO

---

*Makes 6-8 servings*

3 Tbsp. oil
2 garlic cloves, minced
1 large onion, diced
1 lb. ground sirloin
½ lb. ground pork
3 cups chicken broth
2 cups water
2 4-oz. cans diced green
  chilies
4 large potatoes, diced
10-oz. pkg. frozen corn
1 tsp. black pepper
1 tsp. crushed dried
  oregano
½ tsp. ground cumin
1 tsp. salt

1. Brown onion, garlic, sirloin, and pork in oil in skillet.
Cook until meat is no longer
pink.
2. Combine all ingredients
in slow cooker.
3. Cover. Cook on Low 4-6
hours, or until potatoes are
soft.

**Note:**
Excellent served with
warm tortillas or corn bread.

# Cowboy Casserole

Lori Berezovsky
Salina, KS

*Makes 4-6 servings*

1 onion, chopped
1½ lbs. ground beef,
    browned and drained
6 medium potatoes, sliced
1 clove garlic, minced
16-oz. can kidney beans
15-oz. can diced tomatoes
    mixed with 2 Tbsp.
    flour, *or* 10¾-oz. can
    tomato soup
1 tsp. salt
¼ tsp. pepper

1. Layer onions, ground
beef, potatoes, garlic, and
beans in slow cooker.
2. Spread tomatoes or soup
over all. Sprinkle with salt
and pepper.
3. Cover. Cook on Low 5-6
hours, or until potatoes are
tender.

# 10-Layer Slow-Cooker Dish

Norma Saltzman
Shickley, NE

*Makes 6-8 servings*

6 medium potatoes, thinly
    sliced
1 medium onion, thinly
    sliced
salt to taste
pepper to taste
15-oz. can corn
15-oz. can peas
¼ cup water
1½ lbs. ground beef,
    browned
10¾-oz. can cream of
    mushroom soup

1. Layer 1: ¼ of potatoes,
½ of onion, salt, and pepper
2. Layer 2: ½ can of corn
3. Layer 3: ¼ of potatoes
4. Layer 4: ½ can of peas
5. Layer 5: ¼ of potatoes,
½ of onion, salt, and pepper
6. Layer 6: remaining corn
7. Layer 7: remaining potatoes
8. Layer 8: remaining peas
and water
9. Layer 9: ground beef
10. Layer 10: soup
11. Cover. Cook on High 4
hours.

# Hamburger Potatoes

Juanita Marner
Shipshewana, IN

*Makes 3-4 servings*

3 medium potatoes, sliced
3 carrots, sliced
1 small onion, sliced
2 Tbsp. dry rice
1 tsp. salt
½ tsp. pepper
1 lb. ground beef, browned
    and drained
1½-2 cups tomato juice, as
    needed to keep dish
    from getting too dry

1. Combine all ingredients
in slow cooker.
2. Cover. Cook on Low 6-8
hours.

When cooking meats and vegetables together, especially
when cooking on Low, place the vegetables on the bottom
where they will be kept moist.

**Roseann Wilson**
Albuquerque, NM

# Shipwreck

**Betty Lahman**
Elkton, VA

*Makes 8 servings*

1 lb. ground beef, browned
4-5 potatoes, cut in French-
    fry-like strips
1-2 onions, chopped
16-oz. can light red kidney
    beans, drained
1/4-lb. Velveeta cheese,
    cubed
10 3/4-oz. can tomato soup
1 1/2 tsp. salt
1/4 tsp. pepper
butter

1. Layer in slow cooker in
this order: ground beef, potatoes, onions, kidney beans,
and cheese. Pour soup over
top. Season with salt and pepper. Dot with butter.
2. Cover. Cook on Low 6-8
hours.

**Note:**
This is particularly good
served with Parmesan cheese
sprinkled on top at the table.

# Beef and Lentils

**Esther Porter**
Minneapolis, MN

*Makes 12 servings*

1 medium onion
3 whole cloves
5 cups water
1 lb. lentils
1 tsp. salt
1 bay leaf
1 lb. (or less) ground beef,
    browned and drained
1/2 cup ketchup
1/4 cup molasses
2 Tbsp. brown sugar
1 tsp. dry mustard
1/4 tsp. Worcestershire
    sauce
1 onion, finely chopped

1. Stick cloves into whole
onion. Set aside.
2. In large saucepan, combine water, lentils, salt, bay
leaf, and whole onion with
cloves. Simmer 30 minutes.
3. Meanwhile, combine all
remaining ingredients in slow
cooker. Stir in simmered
ingredients from saucepan.
Add additional water if mixture seems dry.
4. Cover. Cook on Low 6-8
hours (check to see if lentils
are tender).

**Note:**
Freezes well.

**Variation:**
Top with sour cream
and/or salsa when serving.

# Judy's
# Hamburger Stew

**Judy Koczo**
Plano, IL

*Makes 6-8 servings*

3 large potatoes, sliced
3 carrots, sliced
1 lb. frozen peas
1 onion, diced
2 ribs celery, sliced thin
salt to taste
pepper to taste
1 1/2 lbs. ground beef,
    browned and drained
10 3/4-oz. can tomato soup
1 soup can water

1. Put vegetables in slow
cooker in layers as listed.
Season each layer with salt
and pepper.
2. Layer beef on top of celery. Mix together soup and
water. Pour over ground beef.
3. Cover. Cook on Low 6-8
hours, or High 2-4 hours, stirring occasionally.

**Variation:**
Substitute 28-oz. can
whole or diced tomatoes in
place of tomato soup and
water.

**Ann Bender**
Fort Defiance, VA

# Taters n' Beef

**Maryland Massey**
Millington, MD

---

*Makes 6-8 servings*

2 lbs. ground beef,
  browned
1 tsp. salt
1/2 tsp. pepper
1/4 cup chopped onions
1 cup canned tomato soup
6 potatoes, sliced
1 cup milk

1. Combined beef, salt, pepper, onions, and soup.
2. Place a layer of potatoes in bottom of slow cooker. Cover with a portion of the meat mixture. Repeat layers until ingredients are used.
3. Cover. Cook on Low 4-6 hours. Add milk and cook on High 15-20 minutes.

**Variations:**
1. Use home-canned spaghetti sauce instead of tomato soup.
2. Add a layer of chopped raw cabbage after each layer of sliced potatoes to add to the flavor, texture, and nutritional value of the meal.

# Jeanne's Hamburger Stew

**Jeanne Heyerly**
Chenoa, IL

---

*Makes 8 servings*

2 lbs. ground beef
1 medium onion, chopped
1 garlic clove, minced
2 cups tomato juice
2-3 carrots, sliced
2-3 ribs celery, sliced
half a green pepper,
  chopped
2 cups green beans
2 medium potatoes, cubed
2 cups water
1 Tbsp. Worcestershire
  sauce
1/4 tsp. dried oregano
1/4 tsp. dried basil
1/4 tsp. dried thyme
dash of hot pepper sauce
2 Tbsp. dry onion soup
  mix, *or* 1 beef bouillon
  cube
1 tsp. salt
1/4 tsp. pepper

1. Brown meat and onion in saucepan. Drain. Stir in garlic and tomato juice. Heat to boiling.
2. Combine all ingredients in slow cooker.
3. Cover. Cook on Low 8-10 hours.

**Variation:**
Use 1 cup barley in place of potatoes.

# Supper-in-a-Dish

**Martha Hershey**
Ronks, PA

---

*Makes 8 servings*

1 lb. ground beef, browned
  and drained
1 1/2 cups sliced raw
  potatoes
1 cup sliced carrots
1 cup peas
1/2 cup chopped onions
1/2 cup chopped celery
1/4 cup chopped green
  peppers
1 tsp. salt
1/4 tsp. pepper
10 3/4 -oz. can cream of
  chicken, *or* mushroom,
  soup
1/4 cup milk
2/3 cup grated sharp cheese

1. Layer ground beef, potatoes, carrots, peas, onions, celery, green peppers, salt, and pepper in slow cooker.
2. Combine soup and milk. Pour over layered ingredients. Sprinkle with cheese.
3. Cover. Cook on High 4 hours.

# Working-Woman Favorite

**Martha Ann Auker**
Landisburg, PA

*Makes 6-8 servings*

2 lbs. ground beef,
  browned and drained
4 ribs celery, chopped
1 small green pepper,
  chopped
1 onion, chopped
2 tsp. sugar
1/2 tsp. salt
dash of pepper
10 3/4-oz. can cream of
  mushroom soup

1. Combine all ingredients in slow cooker.
2. Cover. Cook on Low 8-10 hours.
3. Serve over warm biscuits.

**Note:**

Sprinkle individual servings with shredded cheddar cheese.

# Ground Beef Casserole

**Lois J. Cassidy**
Willow Street, PA

*Makes 6-8 servings*

1 1/2 lbs. ground beef
6-8 potatoes, sliced
1 medium onion, sliced
14 1/2-oz. can cut green
  beans with juice
1/2 tsp. salt
dash of pepper
10 3/4-oz. can cream of
  mushroom soup

1. Crumble uncooked ground beef in bottom of slow cooker. Add potatoes, onion, salt, and pepper. Pour beans over all. Spread can of mushroom soup over beans.
2. Cover. Cook on Low 6-8 hours.

**Variation:**

Brown the beef before putting in the slow cooker. Mix half a soup can of water with the mushroom soup before placing over beans.

# Chinese Hamburger

**Esther J. Yoder**
Hartville, OH

*Makes 8 servings*

1 lb. ground beef, browned
  and drained
1 onion, diced
2 ribs celery, diced
10 3/4-oz. can chicken
  noodle soup
10 3/4-oz. can cream of
  mushroom soup
12-oz. can Chinese
  vegetables
salt to taste, about 1/4-1/2
  tsp.
pepper to taste, about 1/4
  tsp.
1 green pepper, diced
1 tsp. soy sauce

1. Combine all ingredients in slow cooker.
2. Cover. Cook on High 3-4 hours.
3. Serve over rice.

You may want to revise herb amounts when using a slow cooker. Whole herbs and spices increase their flavoring power, while ground spices tend to lose some flavor. It's a good idea to season to taste before serving.
**Irma H. Schoen**
Windsor, CT

## Tater Tot Casserole

**Shirley Hinh**
Wayland, IA

*Makes 6-8 servings*

32-oz. bag frozen tater tots
1 lb. ground beef, browned
1/2 tsp. salt
1/4 tsp. pepper
2 14 1/2-oz. cans green
 beans, drained
10 3/4-oz. can cream of
 mushroom soup
1 Tbsp. dried onions
1/4 cup milk

1. Line slow cooker with frozen tater tots.
2. Combine remaining ingredients. Pour over potatoes.
3. Cover. Cook on High 3 hours.

**Note:**
 Sprinkle individual servings with your choice of grated cheese.

## Bean Tator Tot Casserole

**Marjora Miller**
Archbold, OH

*Makes 6 servings*

1 lb. ground beef
1/2 tsp. salt
1/4 tsp. pepper
1 onion, chopped
1-lb. bag frozen string
 beans
10 3/4-oz. can cream of
 mushroom soup
1 cup shredded cheese
21-oz. bag. frozen tator tots

1. Crumble raw ground beef in bottom of slow cooker. Sprinkle with salt and pepper.
2. Layer remaining ingredients on beef in order listed.
3. Cover. Cook on High 1 hour. Reduce heat to Low and cook 3 hours.

**Variation:**
 In order to reduce the calorie content of this dish, use raw shredded potatoes instead of tater tots.

## Meal-in-One-Casserole

**Elizabeth Yoder**
Millersburg, OH
**Marcella Stalter**
Flanagan, IL

*Makes 4-6 servings*

1 lb. ground beef
1 medium onion, chopped
1 medium green pepper,
 chopped
15 1/4-oz. can whole kernel
 corn, drained
4-oz. can mushrooms,
 drained
1 tsp. salt
1/4 tsp. pepper
11-oz. jar salsa
5 cups uncooked medium
 egg noodles
28-oz. can diced tomatoes,
 undrained
1 cup shredded cheddar
 cheese

1. Cook beef and onion in saucepan over medium heat until meat is no longer pink. Drain. Transfer to slow cooker.
2. Top with green pepper, corn, and mushrooms. Sprinkle with salt and pepper. Pour salsa over mushrooms. Cover and cook on Low 3 hours.
3. Cook noodles according to package in separate pan. Drain and add to slow cooker after mixture in cooker has cooked for 3 hours. Top with tomatoes. Sprinkle with cheese.

4. Cover. Cook on Low 1 more hour.

**Variation:**

Add uncooked noodles after salsa. Pour tomatoes and 1 cup water over all. Sprinkle with cheese. Cover and cook on Low 4 hours, or until noodles are tender.

Nadine Martinitz
Salina, KS

# Noodle Hamburger Dish

Esther J. Yoder
Hartville, OH

*Makes 10 servings*

1½ lbs. ground beef, browned and drained
1 green pepper, diced
1 qt. whole tomatoes
10¾-oz. can cream of mushroom soup
1 large onion, diced
1½ Tbsp. Worcestershire sauce
8-oz. pkg. noodles, uncooked
1 tsp. salt
¼ tsp. pepper
1 cup shredded cheese

1. Combine all ingredients except cheese in slow cooker.
2. Cover. Cook on High 3-4 hours.
3. Sprinkle with cheese before serving.

# Yum-e-setti

Elsie Schlabach
Millersburg, OH

*Makes 6-8 servings*

1½ lbs. ground beef, browned and drained
10¾-oz. can tomato soup
8-oz. pkg. wide noodles, cooked
10¾-oz. can cream of chicken soup
1 cup chopped celery, cooked tender
2 tsp. salt
1 lb. frozen mixed vegetables
½ lb. Velveeta cheese, cubed

1. Combine ground beef and tomato soup.
2. Combine chicken soup, noodles, and celery.
3. Layer beef mixture, chicken mixture, and vegetables. Sprinkle with salt. Lay cheese over top.
4. Cover. Cook on Low 2-3 hours.

**Variation:**

For more "bite," use shredded cheddar cheese instead of cubed Velveeta.

# Shell Casserole

Jean Butzer
Batavia, NY

*Makes 4-5 servings*

1 lb. ground beef
1 small onion, chopped
¾ tsp. salt
¼ tsp. garlic powder
1 tsp. Worcestershire sauce
¼ cup flour
1¼ cups hot water
2 tsp. beef bouillon granules
2 Tbsp. red wine
6 oz. medium-sized shell pasta, uncooked
4-oz. can sliced mushrooms, drained
1 cup sour cream

1. Brown ground beef and onion in saucepan. Drain. Place in slow cooker.
2. Stir in salt, garlic powder, Worcestershire sauce, and flour.
3. Add water, bouillon, and wine. Mix well.
4. Cover. Cook on Low 2-3 hours.
5. Cook pasta in separate pan according to package directions. Stir cooked pasta, mushrooms, and sour cream into slow cooker. Cover. Cook on High 10-15 minutes.

# Family Favorite Casserole

**Lizzie Weaver**
Ephrata, PA

*Makes 6-8 servings*

1 1/2 lbs. ground beef
1 onion, chopped
1 1/2 cups diced potatoes
1 1/2 cups sliced carrots
1 1/2 cups peas
1 1/2 cups macaroni, cooked
10 3/4-oz. can cream of
  celery soup
1/2 lb. cheddar cheese,
  grated
2 cups milk
1 1/2 tsp. salt

1. Fry beef and onion in saucepan until brown. Drain.
2. Cook vegetables just until soft.
3. Combine all ingredients in slow cooker.
4. Cover. Cook on High 2 hours, or Low 4-5 hours.

**Variation:**
Skip pre-cooking the vegetables; add them raw to the slow cooker. Increase cooking time to 4 hours on High, or 8-10 hours on Low. Add the cooked macaroni and the milk during the last 15 minutes if cooking on High, or during the last 30 minutes if cooking on Low.

# Tastes-Like-Turkey

**Lizzie Weaver**
Ephrata, PA

*Makes 6 servings*

2 lbs. hamburger, browned
1 tsp. salt
1/2 tsp. pepper
2 10 3/4-oz. cans cream of
  chicken soup
10 3/4-oz. can cream of
  celery soup
4 scant cups milk
1 large pkg. bread stuffing,
  *or* large loaf of bread,
  torn in pieces

1. Combine all ingredients in large buttered slow cooker.
2. Cover. Cook on High 3 hours, or Low 6-8 hours.

# Meatball Stew

**Nanci Keatley**, Salem, OR
**Ada Miller**, Sugarcreek, OH

*Makes 8 servings*

2 lbs. ground beef
1/2 tsp. salt
1/2 tsp. pepper
6 medium potatoes, cubed
1 large onion, sliced
6 medium carrots, sliced
1 cup ketchup
1 cup water
1 1/2 tsp. balsamic vinegar
1 tsp. dried basil
1 tsp. dried oregano
1/2 tsp. salt
1/2 tsp. pepper

1. Combine beef, 1/2 tsp. salt, and 1/2 tsp. pepper. Mix well. Shape into 1-inch balls. Brown meatballs in saucepan over medium heat. Drain.
2. Place potatoes, onion, and carrots in slow cooker. Top with meatballs.
3. Combine ketchup, water, vinegar, basil, oregano, 1/2 tsp. salt, and 1/2 tsp. pepper. Pour over meatballs.
4. Cover. Cook on High 4-5 hours, or until vegetables are tender.

Here's a real time-saver from our house: Brown large quantities (10 lbs.) of ground beef, seasoned with onion, basil, and oregano to taste. Drain and cool. Freeze in pint freezer containers. The meat is readily available with no prep time or cleanup need when preparing a slow cooker recipe or casserole that calls for browned ground beef.
**Dale and Shari Mast**
Harrisonburg, VA

# Sweet and Sour Meatballs

**Barbara Katrine Rose**
Woodbridge, VA

*Makes 4-6 servings*

4 tsp. Worcestershire sauce
2 tsp. vinegar
1 tsp. dried Italian
  seasoning
1/4 tsp. garlic powder
1/4 tsp. cinnamon
1/4 tsp. pepper
2 4-oz. cans sliced
  mushrooms, undrained
2 cups sliced carrots
3 cups tomato juice
4 tsp. instant minced
  onion
4 Tbsp. minced green
  peppers
1 recipe Meatballs (see
  next recipe)

1. Combine all ingredients
in slow cooker.
2. Cover. Cook on High 3-4
hours.
3. Serve over rice.

# Meatballs

*Makes 24 small meatballs*

1 lb. ground beef
1 cup drained,
  unsweetened crushed
  pineapple
2 slices crumbled whole
  wheat bread
2 tsp. instant minced
  onion
2 tsp. Worcestershire sauce
1/4 tsp. garlic powder
1/4 tsp. dry mustard
1/4 tsp. pepper

1. Combine all ingredients.
Shape into meatballs, using 1
heaping tablespoon mixture
for each. Place on rack in
baking pan.
2. Bake at 350° for 30 minutes, or until done.

# BBQ Meatballs

**Kathryn Yoder**
Minot, ND

*Makes 12-15 main-dish servings,
or 20-25 appetizer servings*

**Meatballs:**
3 lbs. ground beef
5-oz. can evaporated milk
1 cup dry oatmeal (rolled
  *or* instant)
1 cup cracker crumbs
2 eggs

1/2 cup chopped onions
1/2 tsp. garlic powder
2 tsp. salt
1/2 tsp. pepper
2 tsp. chili powder

**Sauce:**
2 cups ketchup
1 cup brown sugar
1 1/2 tsp. liquid smoke
1/2 tsp. garlic powder
1/4 cup chopped onions

1. Combine all meatball
ingredients. Shape into wal-
nut-sized balls. Place on
waxed paper-lined cookie
sheets. Freeze. When fully
frozen, place in plastic bag
and store in freezer until
needed.
2. When ready to use,
place frozen meatballs in
slow cooker. Cover. Cook on
High as you mix up sauce.
3. Pour combined sauce
ingredients over meatballs.
Stir.
4. Cover. Continue cooking
on High 1 hour. Stir. Turn to
Low and cook 6-9 hours.

**Variation:**
Instead of using barbecue
sauce, cook meatballs with
spaghetti sauce or cream of
mushroom soup.

# Mary Ellen's Barbecued Meatballs

**Mary Ellen Wilcox**
Scatia, NY

*Makes about 60 small meatballs*

**Meatballs:**
¾-lb. ground beef
¾ cup bread crumbs
1½ Tbsp. minced onion
½ tsp. horseradish
3 drops Tabasco sauce
2 eggs, beaten
¾ tsp. salt
½ tsp. pepper
butter

**Sauce:**
¾ cup ketchup
½ cup water
¼ cup cider vinegar
2 Tbsp. brown sugar
1 Tbsp. minced onion
2 tsp. horseradish
1 tsp. salt
1 tsp. dry mustard
3 drops Tabasco
dash pepper

1. Combine all meatball ingredients except butter. Shape into ¾-inch balls. Brown in butter in skillet. Place in slow cooker.
2. Combine all sauce ingredients. Pour over meatballs.
3. Cover. Cook on Low 5 hours.

# Cocktail Meatballs

**Irene Klaeger**
Inverness, FL

*Makes 6 main-dish servings, or 12 appetizer servings*

2 lbs. ground beef
⅓ cup ketchup
3 tsp. dry bread crumbs
1 egg, beaten
2 tsp. onion flakes
¾ tsp. garlic salt
½ tsp. pepper
1 cup ketchup
1 cup packed brown sugar
6-oz. can tomato paste
¼ cup soy sauce
¼ cup cider vinegar
1-1½ tsp. hot pepper
   sauce

1. Combine ground beef, ⅓ cup ketchup, bread crumbs, egg, onion flakes, garlic salt, and pepper. Mix well. Shape into 1-inch meatballs. Place on jelly roll pan. Bake at 350° for 18 minutes, or until brown. Place in slow cooker.
2. Combine 1 cup ketchup, brown sugar, tomato paste, soy sauce, vinegar, and hot pepper sauce. Pour over meatballs.
3. Cover. Cook on Low 4 hours.

# Sweet and Sour Meatballs

**Elaine Unruh**
Minneapolis, MN

*Makes 6-8 main-dish servings, or 20-30 appetizer servings*

**Meatballs:**
2 lbs. ground beef
1¼ cups bread crumbs
1½ tsp. salt
1 tsp. pepper
2-3 Tbsp. Worcestershire
   sauce
1 egg
½ tsp. garlic salt
¼ cup finely chopped
   onions

**Sauce:**
1 can pineapple chunks,
   juice reserved
3 Tbsp. cornstarch
¼ cup cold water
1-1¼ cups ketchup
¼ cup Worcestershire
   sauce
¼ tsp. salt
¼ tsp. pepper
¼ tsp. garlic salt
½ cup chopped green
   peppers

1. Combine all meatball ingredients. Shape into 60-80 meatballs. Brown in skillet, rolling so all sides are browned. Place meatballs in slow cooker.
2. Pour juice from pineapples into skillet. Stir into drippings.
3. Combine cornstarch and cold water. Add to skillet and

stir until thickened.

4. Stir in ketchup and Worcestershire sauce. Season with salt, pepper, and garlic salt. Add green peppers and pineapples. Pour over meatballs.

5. Cover. Cook on Low 6 hours.

## Festive Cocktail Meatballs

**Sharon Timpe**
Mequon, WI

*Makes about 4 dozen meatballs*

**Sauce:**
2 cups ketchup
1 cup brown sugar
2 Tbsp. Worcestershire sauce

**Meatballs:**
2 lbs. ground beef
1 envelope dry onion soup mix
1/2 cup milk

1. Mix together ketchup, brown sugar, and Worcestershire sauce in slow cooker. Turn on High while mixing up meatballs.

2. Combine ground beef, soup mix, and milk. Mix well. Shape into 1-inch balls. Bake at 325° for 20 minutes. Drain. Add to slow cooker.

3. Cover. Cook on Low 2-2½ hours, stirring gently, twice throughout the cooking time.

## Barbecued Meatballs

**Esther Becker**
Gordonville, Pa
**Ruth Shank**, Gridley, IL

*Makes 30 small meatballs*

1½ cups chili sauce
1 cup grape, *or* apple, jelly
3 tsp. brown spicy mustard
1 lb. ground beef
1 egg
3 Tbsp. dry bread crumbs
1/2 tsp. salt

1. Combine chili sauce, jelly, and mustard in slow cooker. Mix well.

2. Cover. Cook on High while preparing meatballs.

3. Mix together remaining ingredients. Shape into 30 balls. Place in baking pan and bake at 400° for 15-20 minutes. Drain well. Spoon into slow cooker. Stir gently to coat well.

4. Cover. Cook on Low 6-10 hours.

**Variations:**
1. To increase flavor, add 1/4 tsp. pepper, 1/4 tsp. Italian spice, and a dash of garlic powder to the meatball mixture.

**Sandra Thom**
Jenks, OK

2. Use Italian or seasoned bread crumbs in meatball mixture. Add 1 tsp. Worcestershire sauce and 1½ Tbsp.

fresh parsley to meatball mixture.

**Barbara Sparks**
Glen Burnie, MD

3. Make meatballs larger and serve with rice or noodles.

## Great Meatballs

**Judy Denney**
Lawrenceville, GA

*Makes 12-16 main dish-size servings,* or *24 appetizer-size servings*

4 lbs. ground beef
2 eggs
4 slices fresh bread, torn into bread crumbs
1½ tsp. salt
1/2 tsp. pepper
1 cup tomato juice
2 10-oz. jars chili sauce
2 cans whole cranberry sauce

1. Mix together beef, eggs, bread crumbs, seasonings, and tomato juice. Form into small meatballs. Place in slow cooker.

2. Pour chili sauce and cranberry sauce on top of meatballs. Stir lightly.

3. Cover. Cook on High 2 hours. Reduce heat to Low and cook 3 more hours.

# Nancy's Meatballs
**Betty Richards**
Rapid City, SD

*Makes 8 main-dish servings*

3-4-lb. bag prepared
  meatballs (or make your
  own, using recipe for
  meatballs with BBQ
  Meatballs, page 119)
3 10¾-oz. cans cream of
  mushroom, *or* cream of
  celery, soup
4-oz. can button mushrooms
16-oz. jar Cheese Whiz
1 medium onion, diced

1. Combine all ingredients
in slow cooker.
2. Cover. Cook on Low 6-8
hours.
3. Use as an appetizer, or
as a main dish served over
noodles or rice.

# Party Meatballs
**Marie Miller**
Scotia, NY

*Makes 8-10 main-dish servings*

16-oz. jar salsa
16-oz. can jellied cranberry
  sauce
2 lbs. frozen meatballs (see
  recipe for making BBQ
  Meatballs on page 119)

1. Melt cranberry sauce in
saucepan. Stir in salsa and
meatballs. Bring to boil. Stir.
Pour into slow cooker.
2. Cover. Cook on Low 2-4
hours.

# Swedish Cabbage Rolls
**Jean Butzer**, Batavia, NY
**Pam Hochstedler**, Kalona, IA

*Makes 6 servings*

12 large cabbage leaves
1 egg, beaten
¼ cup milk
¼ cup finely chopped onions
1 tsp. salt
¼ tsp. pepper
1 lb. ground beef, browned
  and drained
1 cup cooked rice
8-oz. can tomato sauce
1 Tbsp. brown sugar
1 Tbsp. lemon juice
1 tsp. Worcestershire sauce

1. Immerse cabbage leaves
in boiling water for about 3
minutes or until limp. Drain.
2. Combine egg, milk,
onions, salt, pepper, beef, and
rice. Place about ¼ cup meat
mixture in center of each leaf.
Fold in sides and roll ends over
meat. Place in slow cooker.
3. Combine tomato sauce,
brown sugar, lemon juice,
and Worcestershire sauce.
Pour over cabbage rolls.
4. Cover. Cook on Low 7-9
hours.

# Cabbage Dinner
**Kathi Rogge**
Alexandria, IN

*Makes 6-8 servings*

medium head of cabbage
6-8 medium-sized potatoes
2 lbs. smoked sausage, *or*
  turkey sausage
salt to taste
1 qt. water

1. Cut cabbage into 1-2
inch-wide wedges. Place in
slow cooker.
2. Wash and quarter pota-
toes. Do not peel. Add to cabbage in slow cooker.
3. Cut sausage into bite-
sized pieces. Add to slow
cooker. Add salt and mix
well.
4. Pour water into slow
cooker.
5. Cover. Cook on High
2 hours, and then on Low 6-8
hours, or until vegetables are
tender.

# Stuffed Cabbage
**Barbara Nolan**
Pleasant Valley, NY

*Makes 6 servings*

4 cups water
12 large cabbage leaves
1 lb. ground beef, lamb, *or* turkey
1/2 cup cooked rice
1/2 tsp. salt
1/8 tsp. pepper
1/4 tsp. dried thyme
1/4 tsp. nutmeg
1/4 tsp. cinnamon
6-oz. can tomato paste
3/4 cup water

1. Boil 4 cups water in deep kettle. Remove kettle from heat. Soak cabbage leaves in hot water 5 minutes, or just until softened. Remove. Drain. Cool.
2. Combine ground beef, rice, salt, pepper, thyme, nutmeg, and cinnamon. Place 2 Tbsp. of mixture on each leaf. Roll up firmly. Stack stuffed leaves in slow cooker.
3. Combine tomato paste and 3/4 cup water until smooth. Pour over cabbage rolls.
4. Cover. Cook on Low 6-8 hours.

# Stuffed Green Peppers
**Lois Stoltzfus**
Honey Brook, PA

*Makes 6 servings*

6 large green peppers
1 lb. ground beef, browned
2 Tbsp. minced onion
1 tsp. salt
1/8 tsp. garlic powder
2 cups cooked rice
15-oz. can tomato sauce
3/4 cup shredded mozzarella cheese

1. Cut peppers in half and remove seeds.
2. Combine all ingredients except peppers and cheese.
3. Stuff peppers with ground beef mixture. Place in slow cooker.
4. Cover. Cook on Low 6-8 hours, or High 3-4 hours. Sprinkle with cheese during last 30 minutes.

# Stuffed Bell Peppers
**Mary Puterbaugh**
Elwood, IN

*Makes 8 servings*

8 large bell peppers
2 lbs. ground beef, lightly browned
1 large onion, chopped
1 cup cooked rice
2 eggs, beaten
1/2 cup milk
1/2 cup ketchup
dash hot pepper sauce
2 tsp. salt
1/2 tsp. pepper

1. Combine all ingredients except peppers. Gently pack mixture into peppers which have been capped and seeded. Place in greased slow cooker.
2. Cover. Cook on Low 9-11 hours, or High 5-6 hours.

I often start the slow cooker on High until I'm ready for work, then switch it to Low as I go out the door. It may only be 45 minutes to 1 hour on High, but I feel it starts the cooking process faster, thus preserving flavor.
**Evie Hershey**
Atglen, PA

# Stuffed Peppers

**Eleanor J. Ferreira**
N. Chelmsford, MA

*Makes 6-8 servings*

6-8 green peppers
1-2 lbs. ground beef
1 onion, chopped
1/4 tsp. salt
1/4 tsp. pepper
1 egg
1 slice white bread
28-oz. can whole, *or*
stewed, tomatoes

1. Cut peppers in half and remove seeds.
2. Combine ground beef, onion, salt, pepper, and egg. Tear bread into small pieces. Add to ground beef mixture. Stuff into peppers.
3. Form remaining meat into oblong shape. Place meatloaf and peppers into slow cooker. Pour in tomatoes.
4. Cover. Cook on Low 6-12 hours, or High 4-5 hours.

# Helen's Lasagna

**Helen King,** Fairbank, IA
**Clarice Williams,**
Fairbank, IA
**Nancy Zimmerman**
Loysville, PA

*Makes 6-8 servings*

1 lb. ground beef
1 medium onion, chopped
2 cloves garlic, minced
29-oz. can tomato sauce
1 cup water
6-oz. can tomato paste
1 tsp. salt
1 tsp. dried oregano
8-oz. pkg. lasagna noodles,
uncooked
4 cups (16 oz.) shredded
mozzarella cheese
1 1/2 cups (12 oz.) small-
curd cottage cheese
1/2 cup grated Parmesan
cheese

1. Cook beef, onion, and garlic together in saucepan until browned. Drain.
2. Stir in tomato sauce, water, tomato paste, salt, and oregano. Mix well.
3. Spread one-fourth of meat sauce in ungreased slow cooker. Arrange one third of noodles over sauce.
4. Combine the cheeses. Spoon one-third of mixture over noodles. Repeat layers twice. Top with remaining meat sauce.
5. Cover. Cook on Low 4-5 hours.

**Variation:**
For a fuller flavor, use 24-oz. can tomato sauce instead of 6-oz. can tomato paste and water. Add 1/2 tsp. garlic powder, 1 tsp. dried basil, and 1/4 tsp. pepper.
**Dolores S. Kratz**
Souderton, PA

# Spicy Lasagna

**Kathy Hertzler,** Lancaster, PA
**L. Jean Moore,** Pendleton, IN
**Mary Ellen Musser**
Reinholds, PA

*Makes 6 servings*

10-oz. pkg. lasagna
noodles, broken into
bite-sized pieces, cooked
1 lb. ground beef, browned
1/2 lb. Italian sausage,
sliced and browned
1 onion, chopped
1 clove garlic, minced
12 oz. mozzarella cheese,
shredded
12 oz. cottage, *or* ricotta,
cheese
16-oz. can tomato sauce
1 tsp. dried basil
1/2 tsp. dried oregano
1 1/2 Tbsp. dried parsley
flakes
1/2 tsp. pepper
1 1/2 tsp. salt

1. Combine all ingredients in greased slow cooker.
2. Cover. Cook on Low 7-9 hours, or High 3-5 hours.

**Variation:**
Replace mix of ground beef and sausage with 1½ lbs. ground beef.

# Violette's Lasagna

Violette Harris Denney
Carrollton, GA

*Makes 8 servings*

8 lasagna noodles, uncooked
1 lb. ground beef
1 tsp. Italian seasoning
28-oz. jar spaghetti sauce
⅓ cup water
4-oz. can sliced mushrooms
15 oz. ricotta cheese
2 cups shredded mozzarella cheese

1. Break noodles. Place half in bottom of greased slow cooker.
2. Brown ground beef in saucepan. Drain. Stir in Italian seasoning. Spread half over noodles in slow cooker.
3. Layer half of sauce and water, half of mushrooms, half of ricotta cheese, and half of mozzarella cheese over beef. Repeat layers.
4. Cover. Cook on Low 5 hours.

# Rigatoni

Susan Alexander
Baltimore, MD

*Makes 10 servings*

28-oz. jar spaghetti sauce
12 oz. rigatoni, cooked
1-1½ lbs. ground beef, browned
3 cups shredded mozzarella cheese
½ lb. pepperoni slices
sliced mushrooms, optional
sliced onions, optional

1. In 4-quart slow cooker, layer half of each ingredient in order listed. Repeat.
2. Cover. Cook on Low 4-5 hours.

**Variation:**
Use 1 lb. ground beef and 1 lb. sausage.

# Beef Enchiladas

Jane Talso
Albuquerque, NM

*Makes 12-16 servings*

4-lb. boneless chuck roast
2 Tbsp. oil
4 cups sliced onions
2 tsp. salt
2 tsp. black pepper
2 tsp. cumin seeds
2 4½-oz. cans peeled, diced green chilies
14½-oz. can peeled, diced tomatoes
8 large tortillas (10-12 inch size)
1 lb. cheddar cheese, shredded
4 cups green, *or* red, enchilada sauce

1. Brown roast on all sides in oil in saucepan. Place roast in slow cooker.
2. Add remaining ingredients except tortillas, cheese, and sauce.
3. Cover. Cook on High 4-5 hours.
4. Shred meat with fork and return to slow cooker.
5. Warm tortillas in oven. Heat enchilada sauce. Fill each tortilla with ¾ cup beef mixture and ½ cup cheese. Roll up and serve with sauce.

**Variation:**
Use 2 lbs. ground beef instead of chuck roast. Brown without oil in saucepan, along with chopped onions.

# Slow Cooker Enchiladas

**Lori Berezovsky**, Salina, KS
**Tracy Clark**,
Mt. Crawford, VA
**Mary E. Herr and Michelle Reineck**, Three Rivers, MI
**Marcia S. Myer**, Manheim, PA
**Renee Shirk**, Mt. Joy, PA
**Janice Showalter**, Flint, MI

*Makes 4 servings*

1 lb. ground beef
1 cup chopped onions
1/2 cup chopped green peppers
16-oz. can red kidney beans, rinsed and drained
15-oz. can black beans, rinsed and drained
10-oz. can diced tomatoes with green chilies, undrained
1/3 cup water
1 1/2 tsp. chili powder
1/2 tsp. ground cumin
1/2 tsp. salt
1/4 tsp. pepper
1 cup (4 ozs.) shredded sharp cheddar cheese
1 cup (4 ozs.) shredded Monterey Jack, *or* pepper Monterey Jack, cheese
6 flour tortillas (6-7 inches in diameter)

1. Cook beef, onions, and green peppers in skillet until beef is browned and vegetables are tender. Drain.
2. Add next 8 ingredients and bring to boil. Reduce heat. Cover and simmer 10 minutes.
3. Combine cheeses.
4. In slow cooker, layer about 3/4 cup beef mixture, one tortilla, and about 1/3 cup cheese. Repeat layers.
5. Cover. Cook on Low 5-7 hours or until heated through.
6. To serve, reach to bottom with each spoonful to get all the layers, or carefully invert onto large platter and cut into wedges. Serve with sour cream and/or guacamole.

# Shredded Beef for Tacos

**Dawn Day**
Westminster, CA

*Makes 6-8 servings*

2-3-lb. round roast, cut into large chunks
1 large onion, chopped
3 Tbsp. oil
2 serrano chilies, chopped
3 garlic cloves, minced
1 tsp. salt
1 cup water

1. Brown meat and onion in oil. Transfer to slow cooker.
2. Add chilies, garlic, salt, and water.
3. Cover. Cook on High 6-8 hours.
4. Pull meat apart with two forks until shredded.
5. Serve with fresh tortillas, lettuce, tomatoes, cheese, and guacamole.

# Southwestern Flair

**Phyllis Attig**
Reynolds, IL

*Makes 8-12 servings*

3-4-lb. chuck roast, *or* flank steak
1 envelope dry taco seasoning
1 cup chopped onions
1 Tbsp. white vinegar
1 1/4 cup green chilies
flour tortillas
grated cheese
refried beans
shredded lettuce
chopped tomatoes
salsa
sour cream
guacamole

1. Combine meat, taco seasoning, onions, vinegar, and chilies in slow cooker.
2. Cover. Cook on Low 9 hours.
3. Shred meat with fork.
4. Serve with tortillas and your choice of the remaining ingredients.

# Tostadas

Elizabeth L. Richards
Rapid City, SD

*Makes 6-10 servings*

1 lb. ground beef, browned
2 cans refried beans
1 envelope dry taco
    seasoning mix
8-oz. can tomato sauce
1/2 cup water
10 tostada shells
1 1/2 cups shredded lettuce
2 tomatoes, diced
1/2 lb. shredded cheddar
    cheese
1 can sliced black olives
1 pint sour cream
guacamole
salsa

   1. Combine ground beef, refried beans, taco seasoning mix, tomato sauce, and water in slow cooker.
   2. Cover. Cook on Low 6 hours.
   3. Crisp tostada shells.
   4. Spread hot mixture on tostada shells. Top with remaining ingredients.

# Pecos River Red Frito Pie

Donna Barnitz
Jerks, OK

*Makes 6 servings*

1 large onion, chopped
    coarsely
3 lbs. coarsely ground
    hamburger
2 garlic cloves, minced
3 Tbsp. ground hot red
    chili peppers
2 Tbsp. ground mild red
    chili peppers
1 1/2 cups water
corn chips
shredded Monterey Jack
    cheese
shredded cheddar cheese

   1. Combine onion, hamburger, garlic, chilies, and water in slow cooker.
   2. Cover. Cook on Low 8-10 hours. Drain.
   3. Serve over corn chips. Top with mixture of Monterey Jack and cheddar cheeses.

# Nachos

Arlene Miller
Hutchinson, KS

*Makes 8 servings*

1 lb. ground beef
1/4 cup diced onions
1/4 cup diced green peppers
1 pint taco sauce
1 can refried beans
10 3/4-oz. can cream of
    mushroom soup
1 envelope dry taco
    seasoning
salt to taste
2 cups Velveeta, *or*
    cheddar, cheese
tortilla chips
lettuce
chopped tomatoes
sour cream

   1. Brown ground beef, onions, and green peppers in saucepan. Drain.
   2. Combine all ingredients except tortilla chips, lettuce, tomatoes, and sour cream in slow cooker.
   3. Cover. Cook on High 1 hour, stirring occasionally until cheese is fully melted.
   4. Pour into serving bowl and serve immediately with chips, lettuce, tomatoes, and sour cream, or turn to Low to keep warm and serve from cooker.

---

   If a recipe calls for cooked noodles, macaroni, etc., cook them before adding to the cooker. Don't overcook; instead, cook just till slightly tender.
   If cooked rice is called for, stir in raw rice with the other ingredients. Add 1 cup extra liquid per cup of raw rice. Use long grain converted rice for best results in all-day cooking.
**Mrs. Don Martins**
Fairbank, IA

# Mexican Corn Bread

Jeanne Heyerly
Chenoa, IL

*Makes 6 servings*

16-oz. can cream-style corn
1 cup cornmeal
1/2 tsp. baking soda
1 tsp. salt
1/4 cup oil
1 cup milk
2 eggs, beaten
1/2 cup taco sauce
2 cups shredded cheddar
   cheese
1 medium onion, chopped
1 garlic clove, minced
4-oz. can diced green
   chilies
1 lb. ground beef, lightly
   cooked and drained

1. Combine corn, corn-
meal, baking soda, salt, oil,
milk, eggs, and taco sauce.
Pour half of mixture into slow
cooker.
2. Layer cheese, onion,
garlic, green chilies, and
ground beef on top of cornmeal mixture. Cover with
remaining cornmeal mixture.
3. Cover. Cook on High
1 hour and on Low 31/2-4
hours, or only on Low 6
hours.

# Tamale Pie

Jeannine Janzen
Elbing, KS

*Makes 8 servings*

3/4 cup cornmeal
1 1/2 cups milk
1 egg, beaten
1 lb. ground beef, browned
   and drained
1 envelope dry chili
   seasoning mix
16-oz. can diced tomatoes
16-oz. can corn, drained
1 cup grated cheddar
   cheese

1. Combine cornmeal,
milk, and egg.
2. Stir in meat, chili seasoning mix, tomatoes, and
corn until well blended. Pour
into slow cooker.
3. Cover. Cook on High 1
hour, then on Low 3 hours.
4. Sprinkle with cheese.
Cook another 5 minutes until
cheese is melted.

# Piquant French Dip

Marcella Stalter
Flanagan, IL

*Makes 8 servings*

3-lb. chuck roast
2 cups water
1/2 cup soy sauce
1 tsp. dried rosemary
1 tsp. dried thyme
1 tsp. garlic powder
1 bay leaf
3-4 whole peppercorns
8 French rolls

1. Place roast in slow
cooker. Add water, soy sauce,
and seasonings.
2. Cover. Cook on High 5-6
hours, or until beef is tender.
3. Remove beef from
broth. Shred with fork. Keep
warm.
4. Strain broth. Skim fat.
Pour broth into small cups for
dipping. Serve beef on rolls.

**Note:**
If you have leftover broth,
freeze it to use later for gravy
or as a soup base.

# Carol's Italian Beef

### Carol Findling
### Princeton, IL

*Makes 6-8 servings*

3-4-lb. lean rump roast
2 tsp. salt, divided
4 garlic cloves
2 tsp. Romano, *or*
   Parmesan, cheese,
   divided
12-oz. can beef broth
1 tsp. dried oregano

1. Place roast in slow cooker. Cut 4 slits in top of roast. Fill each slit with ½ tsp. salt, 1 garlic clove, and ½ tsp. cheese.

2. Pour broth over meat. Sprinkle with oregano.

3. Cover. Cook on Low 10-12 hours, or High 4-6 hours.

4. Remove meat and slice or shred. Serve on buns with meat juices on the side.

# Lauren's Italian Beef

### Lauren Eberhard
### Seneca, IL

*Makes 16 servings*

4-5-lb. boneless roast,
   cubed
1 medium onion, chopped
1-2 garlic cloves, minced
2-3 pkgs. dry Good Seasons
   Italian dressing mix
½ cup water
16 steak rolls
mozzarella cheese,
   shredded

1. Combine first five ingredients in slow cooker.

2. Cover. Cook on Low 10 hours. Stir occasionally.

3. Slice meat into thin slices. Pile on rolls, top with cheese, and serve immediately.

# Tangy Barbecue Sandwiches

### Lavina Hochstedler
### Grand Blanc, MI
### Lois M. Martin, Lititz, PA

*Makes 14-18 sandwiches*

3 cups chopped celery
1 cup chopped onions
1 cup ketchup
1 cup barbecue sauce
1 cup water
2 Tbsp. vinegar
2 Tbsp. Worcestershire
   sauce
2 Tbsp. brown sugar
1 tsp. chili powder
1 tsp. salt
½ tsp. pepper
½ tsp. garlic powder
3-4-lb. boneless chuck
   roast
14-18 hamburger buns

1. Combine all ingredients except roast and buns in slow cooker. When well mixed, add roast.

2. Cover. Cook on High 6-7 hours.

3. Remove roast. Cool and shred meat. Return to sauce. Heat well.

4. Serve on buns.

---

Always defrost meat or poultry before putting it into the slow cooker, or cook recipes containing frozen meats an additional 4-6 hours on Low, or 2 hours on High.
**Rachel Kauffman**
Alto, MI

# Mile-High Shredded Beef Sandwiches

Miriam Christophel
Battle Creek, MI
**Mary Seielstad**, Sparks, NV

*Makes 8 servings*

3-lb. chuck roast, *or* round
   steak
2 Tbsp. oil
1 cup chopped onions
1/2 cup sliced celery
2 cups beef broth, *or*
   bouillon
1 garlic clove
1 tsp. salt
3/4 cup ketchup
4 Tbsp. brown sugar
2 Tbsp. vinegar
1 tsp. dry mustard
1/2 tsp. chili powder
3 drops Tabasco sauce
1 bay leaf
1/4 tsp. paprika
1/4 tsp. garlic powder
1 tsp. Worcestershire sauce

1. In skillet brown both
sides of meat in oil. Add
onions and celery and saute
briefly. Transfer to slow
cooker. Add broth or bouillon.

2. Cover. Cook on Low 6-8
hours, or until tender.
Remove meat from cooker
and cool. Shred beef.

3. Remove vegetables from
cooler and drain, reserving
1 1/2 cups broth. Combine vegetables and meat.

4. Return shredded meat
and vegetables to cooker. Add

broth and remaining ingredients and combine well.

5. Cover. Cook on High 1
hour. Remove bay leaf.

6. Pile into 8 sandwich
rolls and serve.

# Slow-Cooker Beef Sandwiches

Elaine Unruh
Minneapolis, MN
**Winifred Ewy**, Newton, KS

*Makes 6-8 servings*

2-3-lb. chuck roast, cubed
1 pkg. dry onion soup mix
12-oz. can cola

1. Place meat in slow
cooker.

2. Sprinkle soup mix over
meat. Pour cola over all.

3. Cover. Cook on Low 8-
10 hours.

4. Serve as roast or shred
the beef, mix with sauce, and
serve on buns.

**Variation:**

Layer 4 medium potatoes,
sliced, and 4 carrots, sliced,
in bottom of pot. Place meat
and rest of ingredients on
top, and follow recipe for
cooking.

# Barbecue Beef

Elizabeth Yoder
Millersburg, OH

*Makes 12 servings*

3-lb. boneless chuck roast
1 cup barbecue sauce
1/2 cup apricot preserves
1/3 cup chopped green
   peppers
1 small onion, chopped
1 Tbsp. Dijon mustard
2 tsp. brown sugar
12 sandwich rolls

1. Cut roast into quarters.
Place in greased slow cooker.

2. Combine barbecue
sauce, preserves, green peppers, onion, mustard, and
brown sugar. Pour over roast.

3. Cover. Cook on Low 6-8
hours. Remove roast and slice
thinly. Return to slow cooker.
Stir gently.

4. Cover. Cook 20-30 min-
utes.

5. Serve beef and sauce on
rolls.

Fill the cooker no more than 2/3 full and no less than half-
full.

**Rachel Kauffman**
Alto, MI

# Barbecue Beef Sandwiches

**Eleanor Larson**
Glen Lyon, PA

*Makes 18-20 sandwiches*

3 1/2-4-lb. beef round steak, cubed
1 cup finely chopped onions
1/2 cup firmly packed brown sugar
1 Tbsp. chili powder
1/2 cup ketchup
1/3 cup cider vinegar
12-oz. can beer
6-oz. can tomato paste
buns

1. Combine all ingredients except buns in slow cooker.
2. Cover. Cook on Low 10-12 hours.
3. Remove beef from sauce with slotted spoon. Place in large bowl. Shred with 2 forks.
4. Add 2 cups sauce from slow cooker to shredded beef. Mix well.
5. Pile into buns and serve immediately.
6. Reserve any remaining sauce for serving over pasta, rice, or potatoes.

# Hearty Italian Sandwiches

**Rhonda Lee Schmidt**
Scranton, PA
**Robin Schrock**
Millersburg, OH

*Makes 8 servings*

1 1/2 lbs. ground beef
1 1/2 lbs. bulk Italian sausage
2 large onions, chopped
2 large green peppers, chopped
2 large sweet red peppers, chopped
1 tsp. salt
1 tsp. pepper
shredded Monterey Jack cheese
8 sandwich rolls

1. In skillet brown beef and sausage. Drain.
2. Place one-third onions and peppers in slow cooker. Top with half of meat mixture. Repeat layers. Sprinkle with salt and pepper.
3. Cover. Cook on Low 6 hours, or until vegetables are tender.
4. With a slotted spoon, serve about 1 cup mixture on each roll. Top with cheese.

**Note:**
For some extra flavor, add a spoonful of salsa to each roll before topping with cheese.

# Barbecued Spoonburgers

**Mrs. Paul Gray**
Beatrice, NE

*Makes 8-10 servings*

2 Tbsp. oil
1 1/2 lbs. ground beef
1/2 cup chopped onions
1/2 cup diced celery
half a green pepper, chopped
1 Tbsp. Worcestershire sauce
1/2 cup ketchup
1 garlic clove, minced
1 tsp. salt
3/4 cup water
1/8 tsp. pepper
1/2 tsp. paprika
6-oz. can tomato paste
2 Tbsp. vinegar
2 tsp. brown sugar
1 tsp. dry mustard

1. Brown beef in oil in saucepan. Drain.
2. Combine all ingredients in slow cooker.
3. Cover. Cook on Low 6-8 hours, or High 3-4 hours.
4. Serve on buns or over mashed potatoes, pasta, or rice.

## Jean & Tammy's Sloppy Joes

**Jean Shaner**, York, PA
**Tammy Smoker**
Cochranville, PA

*Makes 12 servings*

3 lbs. ground beef,
   browned and drained
1 onion, finely chopped
1 green pepper, chopped
2 8-oz. cans tomato sauce
3/4 cup ketchup
1 Tbsp. Worcestershire
   sauce
1 tsp. chili powder
1/4 tsp. pepper
1/4 tsp. garlic powder
sandwich rolls

1. Combine all ingredients
except rolls in slow cooker.
2. Cover. Cook on Low 8-
10 hours, or High 3-4 hours.
3. Serve in sandwich rolls.

## Penny's Sloppy Joes

**Penny Blosser**
Beavercreek, OH

*Makes 6 servings*

1 lb. ground beef, browned
   and drained
10 3/4-oz. can cream of
   mushroom soup
1/4 cup ketchup
1 small onion, diced

1. Combine all ingredients
in slow cooker.
2. Cover. Cook on Low 1-2
hours.
3. Serve on rolls or over
baked potatoes.

## Nan's Sloppy Joes

**Nan Decker**
Albuquerque, NM

*Makes 4-6 servings*

1 lb. ground beef
1 onion, chopped
3/4 cup ketchup
2 Tbsp. chili sauce
1 Tbsp. Worcestershire
   sauce
1 Tbsp. prepared mustard
1 Tbsp. vinegar
1 Tbsp. sugar
whole wheat buns

1. Brown beef and onion
in saucepan. Drain.

2. Combine all ingredients
in slow cooker.
3. Cover. Cook on Low 4-5
hours.
4. Serve on buns.

## Corned Beef

**Margaret Jarrett**
Anderson, IN

*Makes 6-7 servings*

2-3-lb. cut of marinated
   corned beef
2-3 garlic cloves, minced
10-12 peppercorns

1. Place meat in bottom of
cooker. Top with garlic and
peppercorns. Cover with
water.
2. Cover. Cook on High 4-5
hours, or until tender.
3. Cool meat, slice thin,
and use to make Reuben
sandwiches along with sliced
Swiss cheese, sauerkraut, and
Thousand Island dressing on
toasted pumpernickel bread.

# Corned Beef and Cabbage

**Rhoda Burgoon**
Collingswood, NJ
**Jo Ellen Moore**, Pendleton, IN

*Makes 6-8 servings*

3 carrots, cut in 3" pieces
3-4-lb. corned beef brisket
2-3 medium onions,
    quartered
3/4-1 1/4 cups water
half a small head of
    cabbage, cut in wedges

1. Layer all ingredients except cabbage in slow cooker.

2. Cover. Cook on Low 8-10 hours, or High 5-6 hours.

3. Add cabbage wedges to liquid, pushing down to moisten. Turn to High and cook an additional 2-3 hours.

**Note:**
To cook more cabbage than slow cooker will hold, cook separately in skillet. Remove 1 cup broth from slow cooker during last hour of cooking. Pour over cabbage wedges in skillet. Cover and cook slowly for 20-30 minutes.

**Variations:**
1. Add 4 medium potatoes, halved, with the onions.

2. Top individual servings with mixture of sour cream and horseradish.
**Kathi Rogge**
Alexandria, IN

# Eleanor's Corned Beef and Cabbage

**Eleanor J. Ferreira**
N. Chelmsford, MA

*Makes 6 servings*

2 medium onions, sliced
2 1/2-3-lb. corned beef
    brisket
1 cup apple juice
1/4 cup brown sugar,
    packed
2 tsp. finely shredded
    orange peel
6 whole cloves
2 tsp. prepared mustard
6 cabbage wedges

1. Place onions in slow cooker. Place beef on top of onions.

2. Combine apple juice, brown sugar, orange peel, cloves, and mustard. Pour over meat.

3. Place cabbage on top.

4. Cover. Cook on Low 10-12 hours, or High 5-6 hours.

# Cranberry Pork Roast

**Barbara Aston**
Ashdown, AR

*Makes 6-8 servings*

3-4-lb. pork roast
salt to taste
pepper to taste
1 cup ground, *or* finely
    chopped, cranberries
1/4 cup honey
1 tsp. grated orange peel
1/8 tsp. ground cloves
1/8 tsp. ground nutmeg

1. Sprinkle roast with salt and pepper. Place in slow cooker.

2. Combine remaining ingredients. Pour over roast.

3. Cover. Cook on Low 8-10 hours.

Use your slow cooker to cook a hen, turkey, or roast beef for use in salads or casseroles. The meat can even be frozen when you put it in the slow cooker. Set the cooker on Low, and let the meat cook all night while you sleep.
**Julia B. Boyd**
Memphis, TN

# Cranberry Pork Roast

**Phyllis Attig**, Reynolds, IL
**Mrs. J.E. Barthold**
Bethlehem, PA
**Kelly Bailey**
Mechanicsburg, PA
**Joyce Kaut**, Rochester, NY

*Makes 4-6 servings*

2½-3-lb. boneless rolled
  pork loin roast
16-oz. can jellied cranberry
  sauce
½ cup sugar
½ cup cranberry juice
1 tsp. dry mustard
¼ tsp. ground cloves
2 Tbsp. cornstarch
2 Tbsp. cold water
1 tsp. salt

1. Place roast in slow cooker.
2. Combine cranberry sauce, sugar, cranberry juice, mustard, and cloves. Pour over roast.
3. Cover. Cook on Low 6-8 hours, or until meat is tender.
4. Remove roast and keep warm.
5. Skim fat from juices. Measure 2 cups, adding water if necessary. Pour into saucepan. Bring to boil over medium heat. Combine the cornstarch and cold water to make a paste. Stir into gravy. Cook and stir until thickened. Season with salt.
6. Serve with sliced pork.

# Savory Pork Roast

**Betty A. Holt**
St. Charles, MO

*Makes 8-10 servings*

4-5-lb. pork loin roast
large onion, sliced
1 bay leaf
2 Tbsp. soy sauce
1 Tbsp. garlic powder

1. Place roast and onion in slow cooker. Add bay leaf, soy sauce, and garlic powder.
2. Cover. Cook on High 1 hour and then on Low 6 hours.
3. Slice and serve.

# Teriyaki Pork Roast

**Janice Yoskovich**
Carmichaels, PA

*Makes 8 servings*

¾ cup unsweetened apple
  juice
2 Tbsp. sugar
2 Tbsp. soy sauce
1 Tbsp. vinegar
1 tsp. ground ginger
¼ tsp. garlic powder
⅛ tsp. pepper
3-lb. boneless pork loin
  roast, halved
2½ Tbsp. cornstarch
3 Tbsp. cold water

1. Combine apple juice, sugar, soy sauce, vinegar, ginger, garlic powder, and pepper in greased slow cooker.
2. Add roast. Turn to coat.
3. Cover. Cook on Low 7-8 hours. Remove roast and keep warm.
4. In saucepan, combine cornstarch and cold water until smooth. Stir in juices from roast. Bring to boil. Cook and stir for 2 minutes, or until thickened. Serve with roast.

---

Since I work full-time, I often put my dinner into the slow cooker to cook until I get home. My three teenagers and umpire/referee husband can all get a hot nutritious meal no matter what time they get home.

**Rhonda Burgoon**
Collingswood, NJ

# Pork Roast with Potatoes and Onions

Trudy Kutter
Corfu, NY

*Makes 6-8 servings*

2½-3-lb. boneless pork
  loin roast
1 large garlic clove, slivered
5-6 potatoes, cubed
1 large onion, sliced
¾ cup broth, tomato juice,
  *or* water
1½ Tbsp. soy sauce
1 Tbsp. cornstarch
1 Tbsp. cold water

1. Make slits in roast and insert slivers of garlic. Put under broiler to brown.
2. Put potatoes in slow cooker. Add half of onions. Place roast on onions and potatoes. Cover with remaining onions.
3. Combine broth and soy sauce. Pour over roast.
4. Cover. Cook on Low 8 hours. Remove roast and vegetables from liquid.
5. Combine cornstarch and water. Add to liquid in slow cooker. Turn to High until thickened. Serve over sliced meat and vegetables.

**Variation:**
Use sweet potatoes instead of white potatoes.

# Chalupa

Jeannine Janzen
Elbing, KS

*Makes 12-16 servings*

3-lb. pork roast
1 lb. dry pinto beans
2 garlic cloves, minced
1 Tbsp. ground cumin
1 Tbsp. dried oregano
2 Tbsp. chili powder
1 Tbsp. salt
4-oz. can chopped green
  chilies
water

1. Cover beans with water and soak overnight in slow cooker.
2. In the morning, remove beans (reserve soaking water), and put roast in bottom of cooker. Add remaining ingredients (including the beans and their soaking water) and more water if needed to cover all the ingredients.
3. Cook on High 1 hour, and then on Low 6 hours. Remove meat and shred with two forks. Return meat to slow cooker.
4. Cook on High 1 more hour.
5. Serve over a bed of lettuce. Top with grated cheese and chopped onions and tomatoes.

# Tangy Pork Chops

Tracy Clark, Mt. Crawford, VA
**Lois M. Martin**, Lititz, PA
Becky Oswald, Broadway, PA

*Makes 4 servings*

4 ½-inch thick pork chops
½ tsp. salt
⅛ tsp. pepper
2 medium onions, chopped
2 celery ribs, chopped
1 large green pepper, sliced
14½-oz. can stewed
  tomatoes
½ cup ketchup
2 Tbsp. cider vinegar
2 Tbsp. brown sugar
2 Tbsp. Worcestershire sauce
1 Tbsp. lemon juice
1 beef bouillon cube
2 Tbsp. cornstarch
2 Tbsp. water

1. Place chops in slow cooker. Sprinkle with salt and pepper.
2. Add onions, celery, pepper, and tomatoes.
3. Combine ketchup, vinegar, brown sugar, Worcestershire sauce, lemon juice, and bouillon. Pour over vegetables.
4. Cover. Cook on Low 5-6 hours.
5. Combine cornstarch and water until smooth. Stir into slow cooker.
6. Cover. Cook on High 30 minutes, or until thickened.
7. Serve over rice.

**Variation:**
Use chunks of beef or chicken legs and thighs instead of pork.

## Spicy Pork Chops

**Mary Puskar**
Forest Hill, MD

*Makes 5 servings*

5-6 center-cut loin pork
  chops
3 Tbsp. oil
1 onion, sliced
1 green pepper, cut in
  strips
8-oz. can tomato sauce
3-4 Tbsp. brown sugar
1 Tbsp. vinegar
1½ tsp. salt
1-2 tsp. Worcestershire
  sauce

1. Brown chops in oil in skillet. Transfer to slow cooker.
2. Add remaining ingredients to cooker.
3. Cover. Cook on Low 6-8 hours.
4. Serve over rice.

## Saucy Pork Chops

**Bonita Ensenberger**
Albuquerque, NM

*Makes 4 servings*

4 pork chops
salt to taste
pepper to taste
1 tsp. garlic powder
1 Tbsp. oil
2-2½ cups ketchup
½ cup brown sugar
1 Tbsp. hickory-flavored
  liquid smoke
1 cup onions, chopped

1. Season chops with salt, pepper, and garlic powder. Brown on both sides in oil in skillet. Drain.
2. Combine ketchup, brown sugar, and liquid smoke in bowl.
3. Place onions in slow cooker. Dip browned pork chops in sauce mixture and place on onions. Pour remaining sauce over chops.
4. Cover. Cook on Low 7-9 hours, or High 4-5 hours.
5. Makes a great meal served with cole slaw and oven-roasted, cut-up root vegetables.

## Barbecue Pork Chops

**Annabelle Unternahrer**
Shipshewana, IN
**Evelyn L. Ward**
Greeley, CO

*Makes 8 servings*

8 pork chops
1 cup (or more) barbecue,
  *or* sweet-sour, sauce

1. Brush each pork chop generously with sauce, then place in slow cooker.
2. Cover. Cook on Low 7-8 hours.

Trim as much visible fat from meat as possible before placing it in the slow cooker in order to avoid greasy gravy.
**Carolyn Baer**
Conrath, WI

# Pork Chops in Bean Sauce

**Shirley Sears**
Tiskilwa, IL

*Makes 6 servings*

6 pork chops
1/3 cup chopped onions
1/2 tsp. salt
1/3 tsp. garlic salt
1/8 tsp. pepper
28-oz. can vegetarian, *or* baked, beans
1/4 tsp. hot pepper sauce
13 1/2-oz. can crushed pineapple, undrained
1/3 cup chili sauce

1. Brown pork chops in skillet five minutes per side. Place in slow cooker.
2. Saute onion in skillet in meat juices. Spread over pork chops.
3. Sprinkle with salt, garlic salt, and pepper.
4. Combine beans and hot sauce. Pour over chops.
5. Combine pineapple and chili sauce. Spread evenly over beans.
6. Cover. Cook on Low 7-8 hours.

# Chops and Beans

**Mary L. Casey**
Scranton, PA

*Makes 4-6 servings*

2 1-lb. cans pork and beans
1/2 cup ketchup
2 slices bacon, browned and crumbled
1/2 cup chopped onions, sauteed
1 Tbsp. Worcestershire sauce
1/4 cup firmly packed brown sugar
4-6 pork chops
2 tsp. prepared mustard
1 Tbsp. brown sugar
1/4 cup ketchup
one lemon

1. Combine beans, 1/2 cup ketchup, bacon, onions, Worcestershire sauce, and 1/4 cup brown sugar in slow cooker.
2. Brown chops in skillet. In separate bowl, mix together 2 tsp. mustard, 1 Tbsp. brown sugar, and 1/4 cup ketchup. Brush each chop with sauce, then carefully stack into cooker, placing a slice of lemon on each chop. Submerge in bean/bacon mixture.
3. Cover. Cook on Low 4-6 hours.

# Italian Chops

**Jan Moore**
Wellsville, KS

*Makes 2-4 servings*

16-oz. bottle Italian salad dressing (use less if cooking only 2 chops)
2-4 pork chops

1. Place pork chops in slow cooker. Pour salad dressing over chops.
2. Cover. Cook on High 6-8 hours.

**Variation:**
Add cubed potatoes and thinly sliced carrots and onions to meat before pouring dressing over top.

# Cooker Chops

**Lucille Metzler**
Wellsboro, PA

*Makes 4 servings*

4 pork chops
10¾-oz. can cream of
  mushroom soup
¼ cup ketchup
2 tsp. Worcestershire sauce

1. Put chops in slow cooker.
2. Combine remaining ingredients. Pour over chops.
3. Cover. Cook on High 3-4 hours, or Low 8-10 hours.

**Variation:**
Add one sliced onion to mixture.

**Maryland Massey**
Mellington, MD

# Easy Sweet and Sour Pork Chops

**Jeanne Hertzog**
Bethlehem, PA

*Makes 6 servings*

16-oz. bag frozen Oriental
  vegetables
6 pork chops
12-oz. bottle sweet and
  sour sauce
½ cup water
1 cup frozen pea pods

1. Place partially thawed Oriental vegetables in slow cooker. Arrange chops on top.
2. Combine sauce and water. Pour over chops
3. Cover. Cook on Low 7-8 hours.
4. Turn to High and add pea pods.
5. Cover. Cook on High 5 minutes.

# Chicken-Fried Pork Chops

**Martha Ann Auker**
Landisburg, PA

*Makes 6 servings*

½ cup flour
¾ tsp. salt
1½ tsp. dry mustard
¾ tsp. garlic powder
6 pork chops
2 Tbsp. oil
10¾-oz. can cream of
  chicken soup
1 soup can water

1. Combine flour, salt, dry mustard, and garlic powder. Dredge pork chops in flour mixture. Brown in oil in skillet. Place in slow cooker.
2. Combine soup and water. Pour over meat.
3. Cover. Cook on High 6-8 hours.

# Golden Glow Pork Chops

**Pam Hochstedler**
Kalona, IA

*Makes 5-6 servings*

5-6 pork chops
salt to taste
pepper to taste
29-oz. can cling peach
  halves, drained (reserve
  juice)
¼ cup brown sugar
½ tsp. ground cinnamon
¼ tsp. ground cloves
8-oz. can tomato sauce
¼ cup vinegar

1. Lightly brown pork chops on both sides in saucepan. Drain. Arrange in slow cooker. Sprinkle with salt and pepper.
2. Place drained peach halves on top of pork chops.
3. Combine brown sugar, cinnamon, cloves, tomato sauce, ¼ cup peach syrup, and vinegar. Pour over peaches and pork chops.
4. Cover. Cook on Low 3-4 hours.

# Perfect Pork Chops

**Brenda Pope**
Dundee, OH

*Makes 2 servings*

2 small onions
2 ¾-inch thick, boneless,
  center loin pork chops,
  frozen
fresh ground pepper to
  taste
1 chicken bouillon cube
¼ cup hot water
2 Tbsp. prepared mustard
  with white wine
fresh parsley sprigs, *or*
  lemon slices, optional

1. Cut off ends of onions
and peel. Cut onions in half
crosswise to make 4 thick
"wheels." Place in bottom of
slow cooker.
2. Sear both sides of frozen
chops in heavy skillet. Place
in cooker on top of onions.
Sprinkle with pepper.
3. Dissolve bouillon cube
in hot water. Stir in mustard.
Pour into slow cooker.
4. Cover. Cook on High 3-4
hours.
5. Serve topped with fresh
parsley sprigs or lemon slices,
if desired.

# Pork Chops and Gravy

**Sharon Wantland**
Menomonee Falls, WI

*Makes 8 servings*

8 pork chops
salt to taste
pepper to taste
2 Tbsp. oil
2 10¾-oz. cans cream of
  mushroom soup
1 large onion, sliced
12-oz. can evaporated milk

1. Season pork chops with
salt and pepper. Brown in oil.
Drain. Transfer to slow
cooker.
2. In separate bowl, whisk
together mushroom soup,
onion, and evaporated milk
until smooth. Pour over
chops.
3. Cook on High 3-4 hours,
or Low 6-8 hours.

**Variations:**

To increase flavor, stir ½-1
cup sour cream, or ¼ cup
sherry, into mixture during
last 30 minutes of cooking
time.

# Pork Chops and Mushrooms

**Michele Ruvola**
Selden, NY

*Makes 4 servings*

4 boneless pork chops,
  ½-inch thick
2 medium onions, sliced
4-oz. can sliced
  mushrooms, drained
1 envelope dry onion soup
  mix
¼ cup water
10¾-oz. can golden cream
  of mushroom soup

1. Place pork chops in
greased slow cooker. Top with
onions and mushrooms.
2. Combine soup mix,
water, and mushroom soup.
Pour over mushrooms.
3. Cover. Cook on Low 6-8
hours.

Lightly grease your slow cooker before adding casserole
ingredients.

**Sara Wilson**
Blainstown, MO

**139**

# Pork Chops with Mushroom Sauce

**Jennifer J. Gehman**
Harrisburg, PA

*Makes 4-6 servings*

4-6 boneless thin or thick
  pork chops
10³/4-oz. can cream of
  mushroom soup
³/4 cup white wine
4-oz. can sliced
  mushrooms
2 Tbsp. quick cooking
  tapioca
2 tsp. Worcestershire sauce
1 tsp. beef bouillon
  granules, *or* 1 beef
  bouillon cube
¹/4 tsp. minced garlic
³/4 tsp. dried thyme,
  optional

1. Place pork chops in
slow cooker.
2. Combine remaining
ingredients and pour over
pork chops.
3. Cook on Low 8-10
hours, or on High 4¹/2-5
hours.
4. Serve over rice.

# Pork Chops and Gravy

**Barbara J. Fabel**
Wausau, WI

*Makes 3-4 servings*

3 large onions, quartered
  *or* sliced
3 ribs of celery, chunked *or*
  sliced
3-4 pork chops
10³/4-oz. can cream of
  mushroom, *or* cream of
  celery, soup

1. Place onions and celery
in slow cooker. Wash pork
chops and place on top of
onions and celery. Pour soup
over all.
2. Cover. Cook on High 1
hour. Reduce heat to Low
and cook 3-4 hours, or until
chops are tender.

# Pork Chop Surprise

**Jan Moore**
Wellsville, KS

*Makes 4 servings*

4 pork chops
6 potatoes, sliced
10³/4-oz. can cream of
  mushroom soup
water

1. Brown pork chops on
both sides in skillet. Transfer
to slow cooker.
2. Add potatoes. Pour soup
over top. Add enough water
to cover all ingredients.
3. Cover. Cook on High 6-8
hours.

**Variation:**
Combine 1 envelope dry
onion soup mix with mush-
room soup before pouring
over chops and potatoes.
  **Trudy Kutter**
  Corfu, NY

# Pork Chop Casserole

**Doris Bachman**
Putnam, IL

*Makes 4-6 servings*

4-6 pork chops
3 cups water
1 cup rice, uncooked
10³/4-oz. can cream of
  mushroom soup
1 tsp. salt
1 tsp. dried parsley
¹/4 tsp. pepper

1. Saute pork chops in skillet until brown. Transfer to
slow cooker.
2. Mix remaining ingredi-
ents and pour over chops in
cooker.
3. Cover. Cook on Low 6-8
hours, or High 3-4 hours.

# Jean's Pork Chops

**Jean Weller**
State College, PA

*Makes 6 servings*

½ cup flour
1 Tbsp. salt
1½ tsp. dry mustard
½ tsp. garlic powder
6-8 1-inch thick pork
    chops
2 Tbsp. oil
15½-oz. can chicken and
    rice soup

1. Combine flour, salt, dry mustard, and garlic powder. Dredge pork chops in flour mixture. Brown in oil in skillet. Transfer to slow cooker. Add soup.
2. Cover. Cook on Low 6-8 hours, or on High 3½ hours.

**Variation:**
For increased flavor, step up the dry mustard to 1 Tbsp. and add 1 tsp. pepper.
**Mary Puskar**
Forest Hill, MD

# Tender Pork Chops

**Dawn M. Propst**
Levittown, PA
**Kim McEuen**
Lincoln University, PA

*Makes 6 servings*

6 pork chops
½ cup flour
1 tsp. salt
½ tsp. garlic powder
1½ tsp dry mustard
2 Tbsp. oil
15-oz. can chicken gumbo
    soup

1. Coat chops with a combination of flour, salt, garlic powder, and mustard. Brown chops in skillet. Place in slow cooker. Drain drippings from skillet.
2. Add soup to skillet. Stir to loosen brown bits from pan. Pour over pork chops.
3. Cover. Cook on Low 6-8 hours.

# Pork and Cabbage Dinner

**Mrs. Paul Gray**
Beatrice, NE

*Makes 8 servings*

2 lbs. pork steaks, *or*
    chops, *or* shoulder
¾ cup chopped onions
¼ cup chopped fresh
    parsley, *or* 2 Tbsp. dried
    parsley
4 cups shredded cabbage
1 tsp. salt
⅛ tsp. pepper
½ tsp. caraway seeds
⅛ tsp. allspice
½ cup beef broth
2 cooking apples, cored
    and sliced ¼-inch thick

1. Place pork in slow cooker. Layer onions, parsley, and cabbage over pork.
2. Combine salt, pepper, caraway seeds, and allspice. Sprinkle over cabbage. Pour broth over cabbage.
3. Cover. Cook on Low 5-6 hours.
4. Add apple slices 30 minutes before serving.

Put your cooker meal together the night before you want to cook it. The following morning put the mixture in the slow cooker, cover, and cook.
**Sara Wilson**
Blairstown, MO

141

# Ham and Cabbage Supper

**Louise Stackhouse**
Benten, PA

*Makes 4 servings*

1 medium-size cabbage
   head, cut into quarters
4-lb. smoked picnic ham
1/4 cup water

1. Place cabbage quarters
in bottom of slow cooker.
Place ham on top. Pour in
water.
   2. Cover. Cook on Low 8-
10 hours.

**Variation:**
   To cabbage quarters, add
2 sliced carrots, 1 sliced
onion, 2 potatoes cut into
cubes, and 2 bay leaves for
additional flavor and nutri-
tion.

# Ham and Scalloped Potatoes

**Penny Blosser**
Beavercreek, OH
**Jo Haberkamp**, Fairbank, IA
**Ruth Hofstetter**
Versailles, Missouri
**Rachel Kauffman**, Alto, MI
**Mary E. Martin**, Goshen, IN
**Brenda Pope**, Dundee, OH
**Joyce Slaymaker**
Strasburg, PA

*Makes 6-8 servings*

6-8 slices ham
8-10 medium potatoes,
   thinly sliced
2 onions, thinly sliced
salt to taste
pepper to taste
1 cup grated cheddar, *or*
   American, cheese
10 3/4-oz. can cream of
   celery, *or* mushroom,
   soup
paprika

1. Put half of ham, pota-
toes, and onions in slow
cooker. Sprinkle with salt, pepper, and cheese. Repeat layers.
   2. Spoon soup over top.
Sprinkle with paprika.
   3. Cover. Cook on Low 8-
10 hours, or High 4 hours.

**Variation:**
   If you like a lot of creamy
sauce with your ham and
potatoes, stir 3/4 soup can of
milk into the soup before
pouring it over the layers.
   **Alma Z. Weaver**
Ephrata, PA

# Miriam's Scalloped Potatoes with Ham

**Miriam Christophel**
Battle Creek, MI

*Makes 6 servings*

6 cups raw potatoes, cut
   into small cubes
1 medium onion, minced
1 tsp. salt
1/2 lb. cooked ham, cubed
4 Tbsp. butter
4 Tbsp. flour
1 tsp. salt
2 cups milk
1 1/2 cups shredded cheddar
   cheese

1. Layer potatoes, onion,
1 tsp. salt, and ham into slow
cooker.
   2. Melt butter in saucepan.
Stir in flour and 1 tsp. salt.
Cook until bubbly. Gradually
add milk. Cook until smooth
and thickened. Add cheese
and stir until melted. Pour
over potato-ham mixture, stirring lightly.
   3. Cover. Cook on Low 6-7
hours, or High 3-4 hours.

# Michelle's Scalloped Potatoes and Ham

**Michelle Strite**
Harrisonburg, VA

*Makes 6-8 servings*

6 cups cooked, shredded
  potatoes
4 cups diced ham
dash pepper, if desired
10¾-oz. can cream of
  mushroom soup
10¾-oz. can cream of
  celery soup
1 cup milk

1. Combine all ingredients
in slow cooker.
2. Cover. Cook on Low 3-4
hours.

# Potatoes and Ham

**Janice Martins**
Fairbank, IA

*Makes 8 serving*

5 potatoes, sliced
½ lb. ham, diced
¼-lb. Velveeta cheese,
  cubed
half a small onion, diced
10¾-oz. can cream of
  chicken soup

1. Layer potatoes, ham,
cheese, and onion in slow
cooker. Top with soup.
2. Cover. Cook on Low 6
hours.

# Barbara's Scalloped Potatoes with Ham

**Barbara Katrine Rose**
Woodbridge, VA

*Makes 10-12 servings*

4-lb. potatoes, sliced
1½ lbs. cooked ham, cut
  into ¼-inch strips
3 Tbsp. minced dried
  onions
1 cup water
2 11-oz. cans condensed
  cheddar cheese soup

1. Layer potatoes, ham,
and onions in very large slow
cooker.
2. Combine soup and
water. Pour over layers in pot.
3. Cover. Cook on Low 6-8
hours.

# Country Scalloped Potatoes and Ham

**Deb Unternahrer**
Wayland, IA

*Makes 10 servings*

8 potatoes, thinly sliced
1 onion, chopped
1 lb. fully-cooked ham,
  cubed
1-oz. pkg. dry country-style
  gravy mix
10¾-oz. can cream of
  mushroom soup
2 cups water
2 cups shredded cheddar
  cheese

1. Combine potatoes,
onion, and ham in lightly
greased slow cooker.
2. Combine gravy mix,
mushroom soup, and water.
Whisk until combined. Pour
over potaotes.
3. Cover. Cook on Low 7-9
hours, or High 3-4 hours.
4. Top with cheese during
last 30 minutes of cooking.

**Variation:**
  Put half the potatoes,
onion, and ham in cooker.
Top with half the grated
cheese. Repeat layers. Spoon
undiluted soup over top.
Cover and cook on Low 7-9
hours, or High 3-4 hours.
Sprinkle individual servings
with paprika.
  **Doris Bachman**
  Putnam, IL

## Au Gratin Potatoes and Ham

**Donna Lantgen**
Rapid City, SD

*Makes 6-8 servings*

10 potatoes, thinly sliced
1 onion, chopped
2 Tbsp. flour
1/4 tsp. pepper, optional
1/2 lb. Velveeta cheese,
   cubed
1/2 cup milk
1/2-1 cup fully cooked ham,
   *or* sliced hot dogs

1. Combine all ingredients
in slow cooker.
2. Cover. Cook on Low 7-8
hours.

## Ham and Potatoes

**Ruth Shank**
Gridley, IL

*Makes 6-8 servings*

6-8 medium red, *or* russet,
   potatoes, cut into
   chunks
2-3-lb. boneless ham
1/2 cup brown sugar
1 tsp. dry mustard

1. Prick potato pieces with
fork. Place in slow cooker.
2. Place ham on top of
potatoes. Crumble brown
sugar over ham. Sprinkle
with dry mustard.
3. Cover. Cook on Low 10
or more hours, until potatoes
are tender.
4. Pour juices over ham
and potatoes to serve.

## Ham 'n Cola

**Carol Peachey**
Lancaster, PA

*Makes 8-10 servings*

1/2 cup brown sugar
1 tsp. dry mustard
1 tsp. prepared horseradish
1/4 cup cola-flavored soda
3-4-lb. precooked ham

1. Combine brown sugar,
mustard, and horseradish.
Moisten with just enough

cola to make a smooth paste.
Reserve remaining cola.
2. Rub entire ham with
mixture. Place ham in slow
cooker and add remaining
cola.
3. Cover. Cook on Low 6-
10 hours, or High 2-3 hours.

## Ham in Cider

**Dorothy M. Van Deest**
Memphis, TN

*Makes 6-8 servings*

3-lb. ham (or larger;
   whatever fits your slow
   cooker)
4 cups sweet cider, *or*
   apple juice
1 cup brown sugar
2 tsp. dry mustard
1 tsp. ground cloves
2 cups white seedless
   raisins

1. Place ham and cider in
slow cooker.
2. Cover. Cook on Low 8-
10 hours.
3. Remove ham from cider
and place in baking pan.
4. Make a paste of sugar,
mustard, cloves, and a little
hot cider. Brush over ham.
Pour a cup of juice from slow
cooker into baking pan. Stir
in raisins.
5. Bake at 375° for 30 minutes, until the paste has
turned into a glaze.

# Sweet-Sour Pork

**Mary W. Stauffer**
Ephrata, PA

*Makes 4-6 servings*

2 lbs. pork shoulder, cut in
  strips
1 green pepper, cut in
  strips
half a medium onion,
  thinly sliced
3/4 cup shredded carrots
2 Tbsp. coarsely chopped
  sweet pickles
1/4 cup brown sugar,
  packed
2 Tbsp. cornstarch
1/4 cup water
1 cup pineapple syrup
  (reserved from
  pineapple chunks)
1/4 cup cider vinegar
1 Tbsp. soy sauce
2 cups pineapple chunks

1. Place pork strips in slow
cooker.
2. Add green pepper,
onion, carrots, and pickles.
3. In bowl, mix together
brown sugar and cornstarch.
Add water, pineapple syrup,
vinegar, and soy sauce. Stir
until smooth.
4. Pour over ingredients in
slow cooker.
5. Cover. Cook on Low 5-7
hours. One hour before serving, add pineapple chunks.
Stir.
6. Serve over buttered noodles with an additional dash
of vinegar or garlic to taste.

# Barbecued Spareribs

**Mrs. Paul Gray**
Beatrice, NE

*Makes 4 servings*

4-lb. country-style
  spareribs, cut into
  serving-size pieces
10 3/4-oz. can tomato soup
1/2 cup cider vinegar
1/2 cup brown sugar
1 Tbsp. soy sauce
1 tsp. celery seed
1 tsp. salt
1 tsp. chili powder
dash cayenne pepper

1. Place ribs in slow
cooker.
2. Combine remaining
ingredients and pour over
ribs.
3. Cover. Cook on Low 6-8
hours.
4. Skim fat from juices
before serving.

# Tender and Tangy Ribs

**Betty Moore**, Plano, IL
**Renee Shirk**, Mount Joy, PA

*Makes 2-3 servings*

3/4-1 cup vinegar
1/2 cup ketchup
2 Tbsp. sugar
2 Tbsp. Worcestershire
  sauce
1 garlic clove, minced
1 tsp. dry mustard
1 tsp. paprika
1/2 tsp. salt
1/8 tsp. pepper
2 lbs. pork spareribs
1 Tbsp. oil

1. Combine all ingredients
except spareribs and oil in
slow cooker.
2. Brown ribs in oil in skillet. Transfer to slow cooker.
3. Cover. Cook on Low 4-6
hours.

"High" on most slow cookers is approximately 300°F.
"Low" is approximately 200°F.
**Annabelle Unternahrer**
Shipshewana, IN

# Michele's Barbecued Ribs

**Michele Ruvola**
Selden, NY

*Makes 8 servings*

3 lbs. pork loin back ribs,
  cut into serving-size
  pieces
2 Tbsp. instant minced
  onion
1 tsp. crushed red pepper
1/2 tsp. ground cinnamon
1/2 tsp. garlic powder
1 medium onion, sliced
1/2 cup water
1 1/2 cups barbecue sauce

1. Combine onion, red
pepper, cinnamon, and garlic
powder. Rub mixture into
ribs. Layer ribs and onion in
slow cooker. Pour water
around ribs.
2. Cover. Cook on Low 8-9
hours.
3. Remove ribs from slow
cooker. Drain and discard liquid. Pour barbecue sauce in
bowl and dip ribs in sauce.
Return ribs to slow cooker.
Pour remaining sauce over
ribs.
4. Cover. Cook on Low 1
hour.

# Sharon's Barbecued Ribs

**Sharon Easter**
Yuba City, CA

*Makes 4-6 servings*

3-4-lb. boneless pork ribs,
  cut into serving-size
  pieces
1 cup barbecue sauce
1 cup Catalina salad
  dressing

1. Place ribs in slow
cooker.
2. Combine barbecue
sauce and salad dressing.
Pour over ribs.
3. Cover. Cook on Low 8
hours.

**Variation:**
Add 1 garlic clove sliced
thin to top of sauce before
cooking.

# Awfully Easy Barbecued Ribs

**Sara Harter Fredette,**
Williamsburg, MA
**Colleen Konetzni,**
Rio Rancho, NM
**Mary Mitchell,**
Battle Creek, MI
**Audrey Romonosky**
Austin, TX
**Iva Schmidt,** Fergus Falls, MN
**Susan Tjon**
Austin, TX

*Makes 4-6 servings*

3-4-lb. baby back, *or*
  country-style, spareribs
1/2 tsp. salt, optional
1/2 tsp. pepper, optional
2 onions, sliced
16-24-oz. bottle barbecue
  sauce (depending upon
  how saucy you like your
  chops)

1. Brown ribs under
broiler. Slice into serving-size
pieces, season, and place in
slow cooker.
2. Add onions and barbe-
cue sauce.
3. Cover. Cook on Low 6
hours. These are good served
with baked beans and corn
on the cob.

**Variation:**
Instead of broiling the ribs,
place them in slow cooker
with other ingredients and
cook on High 1 hour. Turn to
Low and cook 8 more hours.

# Barbecued Pork Ribs

**Julia B. Boyd**
Memphis, TN

*Makes 4 servings*

3 lbs. spareribs, cut into
　serving-size pieces
water
1/4 tsp. salt
1/4 tsp. pepper
1 large onion, diced
1 garlic clove, minced
2 cups barbecue sauce

1. Place ribs in slow
cooker. Cover with water.
2. Cover. Cook on Low 3-4
hours. Drain water, reserving
it to make Dumplings (see
below), if desired.
3. Add remaining ingredi-
ents to slow cooker.
4. Cover. Cook on Low 3-5
hours.

**Dumplings:**
2 Tbsp. butter, *or*
　margarine
1/2 cup boiling broth (from
　parboiling spareribs,
　above)
flour
remaining broth
salt to taste
pepper to taste

1. Pour 1/2 cup broth over
butter to melt. Add flour to
make dough. Roll out on
floured board until pastry-
thin.
2. Pour remaining reserved
broth into soup pot and add

salt and pepper to taste. Bring
to boil.
3. Slice dough into 1 1/2"
strips and drop into boiling
broth in soup pot. Cover, but
watch carefully that the broth
does not boil over. The
dumplings will rise to the
surface and be done within 5-
10 minutes. Serve with barbe-
cued ribs.

# Just Peachy Ribs

**Amymarlene Jensen**
Fountain, CO

*Makes 4-6 servings*

4-lb. boneless pork
　spareribs
1/2 cup brown sugar
1/4 cup ketchup
1/4 cup white vinegar
1 garlic clove, minced
1 tsp. salt
1 tsp. pepper
2 Tbsp. soy sauce
15-oz. can spiced cling
　peaches, cubed, with
　juice

1. Cut ribs in serving-size
pieces and brown in broiler
or in saucepan in oil. Drain.
Place in slow cooker.
2. Combine remaining
ingredients. Pour over ribs.
3. Cover. Cook on Low 8-
10 hours.

# Sesame Pork Ribs

**Joette Droz**
Kalona, IA

*Makes 6 servings*

1 medium onion, sliced
3/4 cup packed brown
　sugar
1/4 cup soy sauce
1/2 cup ketchup
1/4 cup honey
2 Tbsp. cider, *or* white
　vinegar
3 garlic cloves, minced
1 tsp. ground ginger
1/4-1/2 tsp. crushed red
　pepper flakes
5 lbs. country-style pork
　ribs
2 Tbsp. sesame seeds,
　toasted
2 Tbsp. chopped green
　onions

1. Place onions in bottom
of slow cooker.
2. Combine brown sugar,
soy sauce, ketchup, honey,
vinegar, garlic, ginger, and
red pepper flakes in large
bowl. Add ribs and turn to
coat. Place on top of onions
in slow cooker. Pour sauce
over meat.
3. Cover. Cook on Low 5-6
hours.
4. Place ribs on serving
platter. Sprinkle with sesame
seeds and green onions. Serve
sauce on the side.

# Barbecued Pork

**Grace Ketcham**, Marietta, GA
**Mary Seielstad**, Sparks, NV

*Makes 6 servings*

3 lbs. pork, cubed
2 cups chopped onions
3 green peppers, chopped
1/2 cup brown sugar
1/4 cup vinegar
6-oz. can tomato paste
1 1/2 Tbsp. chili powder
1 tsp. dry mustard
2 tsp. Worcestershire sauce
2 tsp. salt

1. Combine all ingredients in slow cooker.
2. Cover. Cook on High 8 hours.
3. Shred meat with fork. Mix into sauce and heat through.
4. Serve on hamburger buns with grated cheese and cole slaw on top.

**Variation:**

Substitute cubed chuck roast or stewing beef for the pork, or use half beef, half pork.

# Barbecued Pork in the Slow Cooker

**Dawn Day**
Westminster, CA

*Makes 6-8 servings*

2-3-lb. boneless pork roast, cubed
2 onions, chopped
12-oz. bottle barbecue sauce
1/4 cup honey
sandwich rolls

1. Place meat in slow cooker. Add onions, barbecue sauce, and honey.
2. Cover. Cook on Low 6-8 hours.
3. Use 2 forks to shred meat.
4. Serve on rolls with sauce.

# Pork Barbecue

**Mary Sommerfeld**
Lancaster, PA

*Makes 8-12 sandwiches*

2 onions, sliced
4-5-lb. pork roast, *or* fresh picnic ham
5-6 whole cloves
2 cups water

Sauce:
1 large onion, chopped
16-oz. bottle barbecue sauce

1. Put half of sliced onions in bottom of slow cooker. Add meat, cloves, and water. Cover with remaining sliced onions.
2. Cover. Cook on Low 8-12 hours.
3. Remove bone from meat. Cut up meat. Drain liquid.
4. Return meat to slow cooker. Add chopped onion and barbecue sauce.
5. Cover. Cook on High 1-3 hours, or Low 4-8 hours, stirring two or three times.
6. Serve on buns.

**Note:**
This freezes well.

---

A word of caution—it is a common mistake to add too much liquid.

**Mrs. J.E. Barthold**
Bethlehem, PA

# Shredded Pork

**Sharon Easter**
Yuba City, CA

*Makes 4-6 servings*

**2-3-lb. pork butt roast,** *or*
**boneless country-style
spareribs**
**1/2-1 cup water**
**1 pkg. dry taco seasoning
mix**

1. Place meat in slow cooker. Add water and seasoning mix.
2. Cover. Cook on Low 24 hours. Shred meat with two forks.
3. Use in tacos or in rolls, or use the sauce as gravy and serve over rice.

# Melt-in-Your-Mouth Sausages

**Ruth Ann Gingrich,**
New Holland, PA
**Ruth Hershey,** Paradise, PA
**Carol Sherwood,** Batavia, NY
**Nancy Zimmerman**
Loysville, PA

*Makes 6-8 servings*

**2 lbs. sweet Italian
sausage, cut into 5-inch
lengths**
**48-oz. jar spaghetti sauce**
**6-oz. can tomato paste**
**1 large green pepper,
thinly sliced**
**1 large onion, thinly sliced**
**1 Tbsp. grated Parmesan
cheese**
**1 tsp. dried parsley,** *or*
**1 Tbsp. chopped fresh
parsley**
**1 cup water**

1. Place sausage in skillet. Cover with water. Simmer 10 minutes. Drain.
2. Combine remaining ingredients in slow cooker. Add sausage.
3. Cover. Cook on Low 6 hours.
4. Serve in buns, or cut sausage into bite-sized pieces and serve over cooked spaghetti. Sprinkle with more Parmesan cheese.

# Sauerkraut & Trail Bologna

**Carol Sommers**
Millersburg, OH

*Makes 10 servings*

**32-oz. bag sauerkraut,
rinsed**
**1/4-1/2 cup brown sugar**
**1 ring Trail Bologna**

1. Combine sauerkraut and brown sugar in slow cooker.
2. Remove casing from bologna and cut into 1/4-inch slices. Add to sauerkraut. Stir.
3. Cover. Cook on Low 6-8 hours.

**Note:**
If you don't have access to Holmes County, Ohio's specialty Trail Bologna, use 1 large ring bologna.

## Kraut and Sausage

Kathi Rogge
Alexandria, IN

*Makes 4 servings*

2 16-oz. cans sauerkraut,
  drained and rinsed
2 Tbsp. dark brown sugar
1 large onion, chopped
2 strips bacon, diced
1 lb. fully-cooked sausage,
  sliced

1. Combine sauerkraut and brown sugar. Place in slow cooker. Add layers of onion, bacon, and sausage. Add enough water to cover half of sausage.
2. Cover. Cook on Low 5-6 hours, or on High 3 hours.

## Sauerkraut and Kielbasa

Mary Ellen Wilcox
Scotia, NY

*Makes 4-6 servings*

64-oz. can sauerkraut
1 medium onion, chopped
1 large bay leaf
1 lb. kielbasa, cut into
  serving-sized pieces

1. Combine all ingredients in slow cooker. Add enough water to cover all ingredients.

2. Cover. Cook on High 30 minutes, and then on Low 6 hours. Remove bay leaf before serving.

## Polish Kraut 'n Apples

Lori Berezovsky, Salina, KS
Marie Morucci,
Glen Lyon, PA

*Makes 4 servings*

1 lb. fresh, *or* canned,
  sauerkraut
1 lb. lean smoked Polish
  sausage
3 tart cooking apples,
  thinly sliced
1/2 cup packed brown
  sugar
3/4 tsp. salt
1/8 tsp. pepper
1/2 tsp. caraway seeds,
  optional
3/4 cup apple juice, *or* cider

1. Rinse sauerkraut and squeeze dry. Place half in slow cooker.
2. Cut sausage into 2-inch lengths and add to cooker.
3. Continue to layer remaining ingredients in slow cooker in order given. Top with remaining sauerkraut. Do not stir.
4. Cover. Cook on High 3-3 1/2 hours, or Low 6-7 hours. Stir before serving.

## Old World Sauerkraut Supper

Josie Bollman, Maumee, OH
Joyce Bowman, Lady Lake, FL
Vera Schmucker, Goshen, IN

*Makes 8 servings*

3 strips bacon, cut into
  small pieces
2 Tbsp. flour
2 15-oz. cans sauerkraut
2 small potatoes, cubed
2 small apples, cubed
3 Tbsp. brown sugar
1 1/2 tsp. caraway seeds
3 lbs. Polish sausage, cut
  into 3-inch pieces
1/2 cup water

1. Fry bacon until crisp. Drain, reserving drippings.
2. Add flour to bacon drippings. Blend well. Stir in sauerkraut and bacon. Transfer to slow cooker.
3. Add remaining ingredients.
4. Cover. Cook on Low 6-8 hours, or High 3-4 hours.

# Polish Sausage Stew

**Jeanne Heyerly,** Chenoa, IL
**Joyce Kaut,** Rochester, NY
**Joyce B. Suiter,**
Garysburg, NC

*Makes 6-8 servings*

10³/4-oz. can cream of
celery soup
1/3 cup packed brown
sugar
27-oz. can sauerkraut,
drained
1¹/2 lbs. Polish sausage, cut
into 2-inch pieces and
browned
4 medium potatoes, cubed
1 cup chopped onions
1 cup (4 oz.) shredded
Monterey Jack cheese

1. Combine soup, sugar,
and sauerkraut. Stir in
sausage, potatoes, and onions.
2. Cover. Cook on Low 8
hours, or on High 4 hours.
3. Stir in cheese and serve.

# Sausage Sauerkraut Supper

**Ruth Ann Hoover,**
New Holland, PA
**Robin Schrock,**
Millersburg, OH

*Makes 10-12 servings*

4 cups cubed carrots
4 cups cubed red potatoes
2 14-oz. cans sauerkraut,
rinsed and drained
2¹/2 lbs. fresh Polish
sausage, cut into 3-inch
pieces
1 medium onion, thinly
sliced
3 garlic cloves, minced
1¹/2 cups dry white wine,
*or* chicken broth
1/2 tsp. pepper
1 tsp. caraway seeds

1. Layer carrots, potatoes,
and sauerkraut in slow
cooker.
2. Brown sausage in skil-
let. Transfer to slow cooker.
Reserve 1 Tbsp. drippings in
skillet.
3. Saute onion and garlic
in drippings until tender. Stir
in wine. Bring to boil. Stir to
loosen brown bits. Stir in pepper and caraway seeds. Pour
over sausage.
4. Cover. Cook on Low 8-9
hours.

# Kielbasa and Cabbage

**Barbara McGinnis**
Jupiter, FL

*Makes 6 servings*

1¹/2 lb.-head green cabbage,
shredded
2 medium onions, chopped
3 medium red potatoes,
peeled and cubed
1 red bell pepper, chopped
2 garlic cloves, minced
2/3 cup dry white wine
1¹/2 lbs. Polish kielbasa,
cut into 3-inch long
links
28-oz. can cut-up tomatoes
with juice
1 Tbsp. Dijon mustard
3/4 tsp. caraway seeds
1/2 tsp. pepper
3/4 tsp. salt

1. Combine all ingredients
in slow cooker.
2. Cover. Cook on Low 7-8
hours, or until cabbage is tender.

# Aunt Lavina's Sauerkraut

**Pat Unternahrer**
Wayland, IA

*Makes 8-12 servings*

2-3 lbs. smoked sausage, cut into 1-inch pieces
2 Tbsp. water, *or* oil
2 bell peppers, chopped
2 onions, sliced
1/2 lb. fresh mushrooms, sliced
1 qt. sauerkraut, drained
2 14 1/2-oz. cans diced tomatoes with green peppers
1 tsp. salt
1/2 tsp. pepper
2 Tbsp. brown sugar

1. Place sausage in slow cooker. Heat on Low while you prepare other ingredients.
2. Saute peppers, onions, and mushrooms in small amount of water or oil in saucepan.
3. Combine all ingredients in slow cooker.
4. Cover. Cook on Low 5-6 hours, or High 3-4 hours.
5. Serve with mashed potatoes.

# Pork and Kraut

**Joyce B. Suiter**
Garysburg, NC

*Makes 6 servings*

4-lb. pork loin
29-oz. can sauerkraut
1/4 cup water
1 onion, sliced
1 large white potato, sliced
10 3/4-oz. can cheddar cheese soup
1 Tbsp. caraway seeds
1 large Granny Smith apple, peeled and sliced
salt to taste
pepper to taste

1. Brown roast on all sides in skillet. Place in slow cooker.
2. Rinse sauerkraut and drain well. Combine sauerkraut, water, onion, potato, soup, caraway seeds, and apple. Pour over roast.
3. Cover. Cook on Low 10 hours.
4. Season with salt and pepper before serving.

**Note:**
Apple and potato disappear into the cheese soup as they cook, making a good sauce.

# Pork Roast with Sauerkraut

**Gail Bush**
Landenberg, PA

*Makes 8 servings*

2 3-lb. pork shoulder roasts
1 large can sweet Bavarian sauerkraut with caraway seeds
1/4 cup brown sugar
1 envelope dry onion soup mix
1/2 cup water

1. Place roasts in slow cooker.
2. Rinse and drain sauerkraut. Combine sauerkraut, brown sugar, and onion soup mix. Layer over roasts. Pour water over all.
3. Cover. Cook on Low 7 hours.

**Note:**
If you can't find Bavarian sauerkraut with caraway seeds, substitute with a 27-oz. can regular sauerkraut and 1/2 tsp. caraway seeds.

---

Browning the meat, onions, and vegetables before putting them in the cooker improves their flavor, but this extra step can be skipped in most recipes. The flavor will still be good.
**Dorothy M. Van Deest**
Memphis, TN

# Pork and Sauerkraut

**Carole Whaling**
New Tripoli, PA

*Makes 6 servings*

4 large potatoes, cubed
32-oz. bag sauerkraut, drained
1 large onion, chopped
1 large tart apple, chopped
2 Tbsp. packed brown sugar
1 tsp. caraway seeds
1 tsp. minced garlic
1/2 tsp. pepper
2 1/2-lb. boneless pork loin roast

1. Put potatoes in slow cooker.
2. Combine remaining ingredients, except pork, in slow cooker. Place half of the sauerkraut mixture on top of the potatoes. Add roast. Top with remaining sauerkraut mixture.
3. Cover. Cook on High 3-4 hours.

# Country Ribs and Sauerkraut

**Andrea O'Neil**
Fairfield, CT

*Makes 4-6 servings*

2 27-oz. cans sauerkraut, drained and rinsed
2-3 lbs. country-style pork ribs, cut into serving-size pieces
6 slices bacon, browned
3-4 Tbsp. caraway seeds
2 cups water

1. Place alternating layers of sauerkraut and ribs in slow cooker, starting and ending with sauerkraut.
2. Crumble bacon and mix gently into top layer of sauerkraut. Sprinkle with caraway seeds. Pour water over all.
3. Cover. Cook on Low 7-8 hours.

# Sauerkraut and Ribs

**Margaret H. Moffitt**
Bartlett, TN

*Makes 6 servings*

27-oz. can sauerkraut with juice
1 small onion, chopped
2 lbs. pork, *or* beef, ribs, cut into serving-size pieces
1 tsp. salt
1/4 tsp. pepper
half a sauerkraut can of water

1. Pour sauerkraut and juice into slow cooker. Add onion.
2. Season ribs with salt and pepper. Place on top of kraut. Add water.
3. Cover. Cook on High until mixture boils. Reduce heat to Low and cook 4 hours.
4. Serve with mashed potatoes.

# Pork Spareribs with Sauerkraut

Char Hagner
Montague, MI

*Makes 4-6 servings*

2 small cooking apples, sliced in rings
1 1/2-2 lbs. spareribs, cut into serving-size pieces and browned
1 qt. sauerkraut
1/2 cup apple cider, *or* juice
1/2 tsp. caraway seeds, optional

1. Layer apples, ribs, and sauerkraut into slow cooker. Pour on juice. Sprinkle with caraway seeds.
2. Cover. Cook on Low 8 hours, or High 4 hours.

# Pork Rib and Kraut Dinner

Betty A. Holt
St. Charles, MO

*Makes 6-8 servings*

3-4 lbs. country-style ribs
4 Tbsp. brown rice
1 Tbsp. caraway seeds
28-oz. can sauerkraut, rinsed
12-oz. can V-8 juice

1. Place ingredients in slow cooker in order listed.
2. Cover. Cook on Low 6-8 hours, or High 3-4 hours.

**Variation:**
To take the edge off the sour flavor of sauerkraut, stir in 3 Tbsp. mild molasses or honey before cooking.

# Ham Hock and Sauerkraut

Bernice M. Gnidovec
Streator, IL

*Makes 2 servings*

2 small ham hocks, *or* pork chops
14-oz. can sauerkraut, rinsed
1 large potato, cubed
1 Tbsp. butter
half a small onion, diced
1 Tbsp. flour
2 Tbsp. cold water

1. Place ham hocks or chops in slow cooker. Top with sauerkraut. Add enough water to cover meat and sauerkraut.
2. Cover. Cook on High 4 hours, or Low 6-8 hours.
3. Saute onions in butter in saucepan until transparent. Stir in flour and brown. Add 2 Tbsp. cold water, stirring until thickened. Pour over ingredients in slow cooker. Cover and cook on High 5-10 minutes.

In recipes calling for rice, don't use minute or quick-cooking rice.

**Mary Puskar**
Forest Hill, MD

# Simply Pork and Sauerkraut

Gladys Longacre
Susquehanna, PA

*Makes 2-4 servings*

2-4 pork chops
14-oz. can sauerkraut, *or* more if you like sauerkraut

1. Place pork chops in slow cooker. Cover with sauerkraut.
2. Cover. Cook on Low 7-8 hours.

**Variations:**
1. Brown pork chops before placing in slow cooker.
2. Substitute spareribs for pork chops.

# Chops and Kraut

Willard E. Roth
Elkhart, IN

*Makes 6 servings*

1-lb. bag fresh sauerkraut
2 large Vidalia onions, sliced
6 pork chops

1. Make 3 layers in well-greased cooker: kraut, onions, and chops.
2. Cover. Cook on Low 6 hours.
3. Serve with mashed potatoes and applesauce or cranberry sauce.

# Sauerkraut and Pork

Ethel Mumaw
Berlin, OH

*Makes 6-8 servings*

2 lbs. pork cutlets
2 14-oz. cans sauerkraut
2 apples, chopped
2 Tbsp. brown sugar

1. Cut pork into serving-size pieces. Brown under broiler or in 2 Tbsp. oil in skillet. Place in slow cooker.
2. Add remaining ingredients.
3. Cover. Cook on Low 7-8 hours.

# Smothered Lentils

Tracey B. Stenger
Gretna, LA

*Makes 6 servings*

2 cups dry lentils, rinsed and sorted
1 medium onion, chopped
1/2 cup chopped celery
2 garlic cloves, minced
1 cup ham, cooked and chopped
1/2 cup chopped carrots
1 cup diced tomatoes
1 tsp. dried marjoram
1 tsp. ground coriander
salt to taste
pepper to taste
3 cups water

1. Combine all ingredients in slow cooker.
2. Cover. Cook on Low 8 hours. (Check lentils after 5 hours of cooking. If they've absorbed all the water, stir in 1 more cup water.)

# Green Beans and Sausage

**Alma Weaver**
Ephrata, PA

*Makes 4-6 servings*

1 qt. green beans, cut into
   2-inch pieces
1 carrot, chopped
1 small green pepper,
   chopped
8-oz. can tomato sauce
1/4 tsp. dried thyme
1/2 tsp. salt
1 lb. bulk pork sausage, *or*
   link sausage cut into 1-
   inch pieces

1. Combine all ingredients
except sausage in slow
cooker.
2. Cover. Cook on High 3-4
hours. Add sausage and cook
another 2 hours on Low.

# Sausage Supreme

**Jan Moore**
Wellsville, KS

*Makes 4 servings*

1 lb. fresh sausage, cut into
   1-inch pieces and
   browned
2 10³/₄-oz. cans cream of
   mushroom soup
1 onion, chopped
4 potatoes, cubed

1. Combine all ingredients
in slow cooker.
2. Cover. Cook on Low 8
hours. If mixture becomes too
dry, stir in half a soup can or
more of water.

**Variation:**
   Substitute 1 can cheese
soup for 1 can cream of
mushroom soup.

# Sausage and Apples

**Evelyn L. Ward**
Greeley, CO

*Makes 4 servings*

20-oz. can apple pie filling
1/4 cup water
ground nutmeg
10-oz. pkg. fully cooked
   and browned sausage
   patties

1. Spoon pie filling into
slow cooker. Stir in water.
Sprinkle with nutmeg. Top
with sausage.
2. Cover. Cook on Low 4-6
hours.

# Kielbasa and Cheese Casserole

**Dolores S. Kratz**
Souderton, PA

*Makes 4-5 servings*

3 cups uncooked noodles
oil
2 beef bouillon cubes
1 cup boiling water
1/4 cup flour
2 Tbsp. butter, melted
4 oz. cheese, shredded
1 lb. kielbasa, sliced
1 small onion, chopped
2 ribs celery, diced
2 carrots, grated
2-oz. jar pimentos

1. Cook noodles until
barely tender. Drain. Toss
with small amount of oil.
2. Dissolve bouillon in
boiling water.
3. Combine all ingredients
in slow cooker.
4. Cover. Cook on Low 8
hours.

**Variation:**
   Instead of noodles, use
gnocchi.

# Supreme Sausage Dish

**Shirley Thieszen**
Lakin, KS

*Makes 6 servings*

1 lb. smoky wieners, cut in 1-inch pieces
2 cups cooked macaroni
1 cup frozen peas, *or* corn
½ cup chopped onions
1 tsp. dry parsley
1 small jar chopped pimentos (about 3 Tbsp.)
¾ cup shredded American, *or* Velveeta, cheese
3 Tbsp. flour
¾ tsp. salt
¼ tsp. pepper
1 cup milk
1 cup water
½ Tbsp. vinegar

1. Combine wieners, macaroni, peas, onions, parsley, and pimentos in greased slow cooker.
2. In saucepan, combine cheese, flour, salt, pepper, milk, water, and vinegar. Cook until smooth and thickened. Pour into slow cooker. Mix well.
3. Cover. Cook on High 1 hour, and then on Low 3-4 hours.

**Variation:**
Use smoked sausage instead of smoky wieners.

# Barbecued Sausage Pieces

**Elizabeth Yutzy**
Wauseon, OH

*Makes 4-5 main-dish servings, or 8-10 snack-sized servings*

1 lb. smoked sausage
1 cup hickory-flavored barbecue sauce
¼ cup honey
2 Tbsp. brown sugar

1. Cut sausage in ½-inch pieces. Brown in skillet. Place in slow cooker.
2. Combine remaining ingredients. Pour over sausage.
3. Cover. Cook on Low 2 hours.
4. Serve over rice or noodles as a main dish or with toothpicks as a party snack.

# Perfection Hot Dogs

**Audrey L. Kneer**
Williamsfield, IL

*Makes 12 servings*

12 hot dogs, bratwurst, *or* Polish sausage links

1. Place hot dogs or sausages in slow cooker.
2. Cover. Cook on High 1-2 hours.

# Beer Brats

**Mary Ann Wasick**
West Allis, WI

*Makes 6 servings*

6 fresh bratwurst
2 garlic cloves, minced
2 Tbsp. olive oil
12-oz. can beer

1. Brown sausages and garlic in olive oil in skillet. Pierce sausage casings and cook 5 more minutes. Transfer to slow cooker.
2. Pour beer into cooker to cover sausages.
3. Cover. Cook on Low 6-7 hours.

## Spiced Hot Dogs

Tracey Yohn
Harrisburg, PA

*Makes 3-4 servings*

1 lb. hot dogs, cut in pieces
2 Tbsp. brown sugar
3 Tbsp. vinegar
1/2 cup ketchup
2 tsp. prepared mustard
1/2 cup water
1/2 cup chopped onions

1. Place hot dogs in slow cooker.
2. Combine all ingredients except hot dogs in saucepan. Simmer. Pour over hot dogs.
3. Cover. Cook on Low 2 hours.

## Barbecued Hot Dogs

Jeanette Oberholtzer
Manheim, PA

*Makes 8 servings*

1 cup apricot preserves
4 oz. tomato sauce
1/3 cup vinegar
2 Tbsp. soy sauce
2 Tbsp. honey
1 Tbsp. oil
1 tsp. salt
1/4 tsp. ground ginger
2 lbs. hot dogs, cut into
    1-inch pieces

1. Combine all ingredients except hot dogs in slow cooker.
2. Cover. Cook on High 30 minutes. Add hot dog pieces. Cook on Low 4 hours.
3. Serve over rice as a main dish, or as an appetizer.

## Bits and Bites

Betty Richards
Rapid City, SD

*Makes 12 servings*

12-oz. can beer
1 cup ketchup
1 cup light brown sugar
1/2-1 cup barbecue sauce
1 lb. all-beef hot dogs,
    sliced 1 1/2-inches thick
2 lbs. cocktail sausages

1. Combine beer, ketchup, brown sugar, and barbecue sauce. Pour into slow cooker.
2. Add hot dogs and sausages. Mix well.
3. Cover. Cook on Low 3-4 hours.

## Barbecued Mini-Franks

Zona Mae Bontrager
Kokomo, IN

*Makes 8-10 full-sized servings, or
16-20 appetizer-sized servings*

1 cup finely chopped
    onions
1 cup ketchup
1/3 cup Worcestershire
    sauce
1/4 cup sugar
1/4 cup vinegar
4 tsp. prepared mustard
1 tsp. pepper
4-lbs. miniature hot dogs

1. Combine all ingredients except hot dogs in slow cooker.
2. Cover. Heat on High 1 1/2 hours, or until hot. Add hot dogs.
3. Reduce heat to Low and simmer 4 hours.

**Variations:**
1. Add 1 Tbsp. finely chopped green pepper and 2 garlic cloves, pressed.
2. Use miniature smoked sausages instead of mini-hot dogs.

# Spicy Franks
**Char Hagner**
Montague, MI

*Makes 4-6 full-sized servings, or 32 appetizer-sized servings*

2 1-lb. pkgs. cocktail
   wieners
1 cup chili sauce
1 cup bottled barbecue
   sauce
8-oz. can jellied cranberry
   sauce

1. Place wieners in slow cooker.
2. In separate bowl, combine chili sauce, barbecue sauce, and cranberry sauce. Pour over wieners.
3. Cover. Cook on Low 3-4 hours, or High 1½-2 hours.

# Little Smokies
**Sharon Kauffman**
Harrisonburg, VA

*Makes 6-8 full-sized servings, or 12-15 appetizer-sized servings*

2 pkgs. Li'l Smokies
1 bottle chili sauce
1 small jar grape jelly

1. Combine all ingredients in slow cooker.
2. Cover. Cook on Low 1-2 hours, or until heated through.

# Sweet and Sour Vienna Sausages
**Judy Denney**
Lawrenceville, GA

*Makes 10 full-sized servings, or 20 appetizer-sized servings*

8 cans Vienna sausages,
   drained
2 cups grape jelly
2 cups ketchup

1. Put sausages in slow cooker.
2. Combine jelly and ketchup. Pour over sausages. Stir lightly. (Add more jelly and ketchup if sausages are not covered.)
3. Cover. Cook on High 1 hour, then turn to Low for 5 hours.

**Variations:**
   Instead of Vienna sausages, use smoky links. Add 1 can pineapple chunks and juice to jelly and ketchup.

# Barbecued Ham Sandwiches
**Jane Steiner**
Orrville, OH

*Makes 4-6 full-sized servings*

1 lb. turkey ham chipped,
   *or* chipped honey-glazed
   ham
1 small onion, finely diced
½ cup ketchup
1 Tbsp. vinegar
3 Tbsp. brown sugar
buns

1. Place half of meat in greased slow cooker.
2. Combine other ingredients. Pour half of mixture over meat. Repeat layers.
3. Cover. Cook on Low 5 hours.
4. Fill buns and serve.

---

A slow cooker set on Low does not burn food and will not spoil a meal if cooked beyond the designated time.
**Eleanor J. Ferreira**
North Chelmsford, MA

# Ham Barbecue

**Janet V. Yocum**
Elizabethtown, PA

*Makes 6-8 servings*

1 lb. boiled ham, cut into
 cubes
1 cup cola-flavored soda
1 cup ketchup

1. Place ham in slow
cooker. Pour cola and ketchup
over ham.
2. Cover. Cook on Low 8
hours.
3. Serve in hamburger
rolls.

# Spaghetti Sauce

**Doris Perkins**
Mashpee, MA

*Makes 18-24 servings*

1/4-lb. bacon, diced
1 1/4-lb. ground beef
1/2 lb. ground pork
1 cup chopped onions
1/2 cup chopped green
 peppers
3 garlic cloves, minced
2 2-lb., 3-oz. cans Italian
 tomaoes
2 6-oz. cans tomao paste
1 cup dry red wine, *or*
 water
2 1/2 tsp. dried oregano
2 1/2 tsp. dried basil
1 bay leaf, crumbled
3/4 cup water
1/4 cup chopped fresh
 parsley
1 tsp. dried thyme
1 Tbsp. salt
1/4 tsp. pepper
1/4 cup dry red wine, *or*
 water

1. Brown bacon in skillet
until crisp. Remove. Add
ground beef and pork.
Crumble and cook until
brown. Stir in onions, green
peppers, and garlic. Cook 10
minutes.
2. Pour tomatoes into slow
cooker and crush with back
of spoon.
3. Add all other ingredi-
ents, except 1/4 cup wine, in
slow cooker.
4. Cover. Bring to boil on
High. Reduce heat to Low for
3-4 hours.

5. During last 30 minutes,
stir in 1/4 cup red wine *or*
water.

# Italian
# Spaghetti Sauce

**Michele Ruvola**
Selden, NY

*Makes 8-10 servings*

2 lbs. sausage, *or* ground
 beef
3 medium onions, chopped
 (about 2 1/4 cups)
2 cups sliced mushrooms
6 garlic cloves, minced
2 14 1/2-oz. cans diced
 tomatoes, undrained
29-oz. can tomato sauce
12-oz. can tomato paste
2 Tbsp. dried basil
1 Tbsp. dried oregano
1 Tbsp. sugar
1 tsp. salt
1/2 tsp. crushed red pepper
 flakes

1. Cook sausage, onions,
mushrooms, and garlic in
skillet over medium heat for
10 minutes. Drain. Transfer
to slow cooker
2. Stir in remaining ingredients.
3. Cover. Cook on Low 8-9
hours.

**Note:**
This is also a good sauce to
use in lasagna.

# Chunky Spaghetti Sauce

**Patti Boston**
Newark, OH

*Makes 6 cups*

1 lb. ground beef, browned and drained
1/2 lb. bulk sausage, browned and drained
14 1/2-oz. can Italian tomatoes with basil
15-oz. can Italian tomato sauce
1 medium onion, chopped
1 green pepper, chopped
8-oz. can sliced mushrooms
1/2 cup dry red wine
2 tsp. sugar
1 tsp. minced garlic

1. Combine all ingredients in slow cooker.
2. Cover. Cook on High 3 1/2-4 hours, or Low 7-8 hours.

**Variations:**
1. For added texture and zest, add 3 fresh, medium-sized tomatoes, chopped, and 4 large fresh basil leaves, torn. Stir in 1 tsp. salt and 1/2 tsp. pepper.
2. To any leftover sauce, add chickpeas or kidney beans and serve chili!

# Sausage-Beef Spaghetti Sauce

**Jeannine Janzen**
Elbing, KS

*Makes 16-20 servings*

1 lb. ground beef
1 lb. Italian sausage, sliced
2 28-oz. cans crushed tomatoes
3/4 can (28-oz. tomato can) water
2 tsp. garlic powder
1 tsp. pepper
2 Tbsp. or more parsley
2 Tbsp. dried oregano
2 12-oz. cans tomato paste
2 12-oz. cans tomato puree

1. Brown ground beef and sausage in skillet. Drain. Transfer to large slow cooker.
2. Add crushed tomatoes, water, garlic powder, pepper, parsley, and oregano.
3. Cover. Cook on High 30 minutes. Add tomato paste and tomato puree. Cook on Low 6 hours.

**Note:**
Leftovers freeze well.

# Italian Sausage Spaghetti

**Eleanor Larson**
Glen Lyon, PA

*Makes 12 servings*

6 Italian turkey sausage links (1 1/2 lbs.), cut into 1 1/2-inch pieces
1 cup diced onions
3 Tbsp. sugar
1 tsp. dried oregano
1/2 tsp. salt
2 garlic cloves, minced
28-oz. can crushed tomatoes, undrained
15-oz. can tomato sauce
12-oz. can tomato paste
1 1/2 lbs. dry spaghetti

1. Combine all ingredients except spaghetti in slow cooker.
2. Cover. Cook on Low 8-10 hours.
3. Cook spaghetti in large soup pot. Drain and top with sauce.

Cooked pasta and rice should be added during the last 1-1 1/2 hours of cooking time to prevent them from disintegrating.
**John D. Allen**
Rye, CO

# Easy-Does-It Spaghetti

**Rachel Kauffman**, Alto, MI
**Lois Stoltzfus**, Honey Brook, PA
**Deb Unternahrer**, Wayland, IA

*Makes 8 servings*

2 lbs. ground chuck, browned and drained
1 cup chopped onions
2 cloves garlic, minced
2 15-oz. cans tomato sauce
2-3 tsp. Italian seasoning
1½ tsp. salt
¼ tsp. pepper
2 4-oz. cans sliced mushrooms, drained
6 cups tomato juice
16-oz. dry spaghetti, broken into 4-5-inch pieces
grated Parmesan cheese

1. Combine all ingredients except spaghetti and cheese in 4-quart (or larger) slow cooker.
2. Cover. Cook on Low 6-8 hours, or High 3-5 hours. Turn to High during last 30 minutes and stir in dry spaghetti. (If spaghetti is not fully cooked, continue cooking another 10 minutes, checking to make sure it is not becoming over-cooked.)
3. Sprinkle individual servings with Parmesan cheese.

**Variation:**
Add 1 tsp. dry mustard and ½ tsp. allspice in Step 1.
**Kathy Hertzler**
Lancaster, PA

# Mom's Spaghetti and Meatballs

**Mary C. Casey**
Scranton, PA

*Makes 8-10 servings*

Sauce:
2 Tbsp. oil
¼-½ cup chopped onions
3 garlic cloves, minced
29-oz. can tomato puree
29-oz. can water
12-oz. can tomato paste
12-oz. can water
1 tsp. salt
1 Tbsp. sugar
2 tsp. dried oregano
¼ tsp. Italian seasoning
½ tsp. dried basil
⅛ tsp. pepper
¼ cup diced green peppers

Meatballs:
1 lb. ground beef
1 egg
2 Tbsp. water
¾ cup Italian bread crumbs
⅛ tsp. black pepper
½ tsp. salt
2 Tbsp. oil

1. Saute onions and garlic in oil in saucepan.
2. Combine all sauce ingredients in slow cooker.
3. Cover. Cook on Low.
4. Mix together all meatball ingredients except oil. Form into small meatballs, then brown on all sides in oil in saucepan. Drain on paper towels. Add to sauce.
5. Cover. Cook on Low 4-5 hours.

# Spaghetti with Meat Sauce

**Esther Lehman**
Croghan, NY

*Makes 8-10 servings*

1 lb. ground beef, browned
2 28-oz. cans tomatoes
2 medium onions, quartered
2 medium carrots, cut into chunks
2 garlic cloves, minced
6-oz. can tomato paste
2 Tbsp. chopped fresh parsley
1 bay leaf
1 Tbsp. sugar
1 tsp. dried basil
¾ tsp. salt
½ tsp. dried oregano
dash pepper
2 Tbsp. cold water
2 Tbsp. cornstarch
hot cooked spaghetti
grated Parmesan cheese

1. Place meat in slow cooker.
2. In blender, combine 1 can tomatoes, onions, carrots, and garlic. Cover and blend until finely chopped. Stir into meat.
3. Cut up the remaining can of tomatoes. Stir into meat mixture. Add tomato paste, parsley, bay leaf, sugar, basil, salt, oregano, and pepper. Mix well.
4. Cover. Cook on Low 8-10 hours.
5. To serve, turn to High. Remove bay leaf. Cover and heat until bubbly, about 10 minutes.

6. Combine water and corn-starch. Stir into tomato mixture. Cook 10 minutes longer.

7. Serve with spaghetti and cheese.

# Slow Cooker Spaghetti Sauce

**Lucille Amos**, Greensboro, NC
**Julia Lapp**, New Holland, PA

*Makes 6-8 servings*

1 lb. ground beef
1 medium onion, chopped
2 14-oz. cans diced
   tomatoes, with juice
6-oz. can tomato paste
8-oz. can tomato sauce
1 bay leaf
4 garlic cloves, minced
2 tsp. dried oregano
1 tsp. salt
2 tsp. dried basil
1 Tbsp. brown sugar
1/2-1 tsp. dried thyme

1. Brown meat and onion in saucepan. Drain well. Transfer to slow cooker.
2. Add remaining ingredients.
3. Cover. Cook on Low 7 hours. If the sauce seems too runny, remove lid during last hour of cooking.

# Nancy's Spaghetti Sauce

**Nancy Graves**
Manhattan, KS

*Makes 4-6 servings*

1/4 cup minced onion
garlic powder to taste
3 cups chopped fresh
   tomatoes, *or* 1-lb., 12-oz.
   can diced tomatoes with
   juice
6-oz. can tomato paste
3 1/2 tsp. salt
dash of pepper
1 basil leaf
1 chopped green pepper
1 lb. ground beef, browned
   and drained
4-oz. can sliced
   mushrooms

1. Combine all ingredients in slow cooker.
2. Cover. Cook on Low 3 hours.

# Pasta Sauce with Meat and Veggies

**Marla Folkerts**
Holland, OH

*Makes 6 servings*

1/2 lb. ground turkey
1/2 lb. ground beef
1 rib celery, chopped
2 medium carrots,
   chopped
1 garlic clove, minced
1 medium onion, chopped
28-oz. can diced tomatoes
   with juice
1/2 tsp. salt
1/4 tsp. dried thyme
6-oz. can tomato paste
1/8 tsp. pepper

1. Combine turkey, beef, celery, carrots, garlic, and onion in slow cooker.
2. Add remaining ingredients. Mix well.
3. Cover. Cook on Low 7-8 hours.
4. Serve over pasta or rice.

## Katelyn's Spaghetti Sauce
**Katelyn Bailey**
Mechanicsburg, PA

*Makes 10-12 servings*

1 lb. ground beef, browned
  and drained
3/4 cup chopped onions
1 garlic clove, minced
3 Tbsp. oil
2 6-oz. cans tomato paste
1 Tbsp. sugar
1 1/2 tsp. salt
1-1 1/2 tsp. dried oregano
1/2 tsp. pepper
1 bay leaf
2 qts. tomatoes, *or* tomato
  sauce

1. Combine all ingredients
in slow cooker.
2. Cover. Cook on Low 8-
10 hours. Remove bay leaf
before serving.

**Note:**
This sauce freezes well.

## Char's Spaghetti Sauce
**Char Hagner**
Montague, MI

*Makes 16-20 servings*

4 lbs. ground beef
2 large onions, chopped
1/4-lb. bacon, cut into small
  squares
5 garlic cloves, minced
1 Tbsp. salt
1/4 tsp. celery salt
4 10 3/4-oz. cans tomato
  soup
2 6-oz. cans tomato paste
8-oz. can mushrooms
3 green peppers, chopped

1. Brown ground beef,
onions, bacon, and garlic in
saucepan. Drain.
2. Combine all ingredients
in large slow cooker.
3. Cover. Cook on Low 6
hours.

## So-Easy Spaghetti
**Ruth Ann Swartzendruber**
Hydro, OK

*Makes 4-6 servings*

1 lb. ground beef
1/2 cup diced onions
1 pkg. dry spaghetti sauce
  mix
8-oz. can tomato sauce
3 cups tomato juice
4 oz. dry spaghetti, broken
  into 4-inch pieces

1. Brown meat and onions
in skillet. Drain. Transfer to
greased slow cooker.
2. Add remaining ingredi-
ents, except spaghetti.
3. Cover. Cook on Low 6-8
hours, or High 3 1/2 hours.
4. During last hour, turn to
High and add spaghetti. Stir
frequently to keep spaghetti
from clumping together.

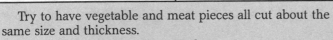
Try to have vegetable and meat pieces all cut about the
same size and thickness.
**Mary Puskar**
Forest Hill, MD

# Creamy Spaghetti

**Dale Peterson**
Rapid City, SD

*Makes 6 servings*

1 cup chopped onions
1 cup chopped green
  peppers
1 Tbsp. butter, *or*
  margarine
28-oz. can tomatoes with
  juice
4-oz. can mushrooms,
  chopped and drained
2¼-oz. can sliced ripe
  olives, drained
2 tsp. dried oregano
1 lb. ground beef, browned
  and drained
12 oz. spaghetti, cooked
  and drained
10¾-oz. can cream of
  mushroom soup
½ cup water
2 cups (8 oz.) shredded
  cheddar cheese
¼ cup grated Parmesan
  cheese

1. Saute onions and green
peppers in butter in skillet
until tender. Add tomatoes,
mushrooms, olives, oregano,
and beef. Simmer for 10 minutes. Transfer to slow cooker.
2. Add spaghetti. Mix well.
3. Combine soup and
water. Pour over casserole.
Sprinkle with cheeses.
4. Cover. Cook on Low 4-6
hours.

# Tomato Spaghetti Sauce

**Jean Butzer**
Batavia, NY

*Makes 6 servings*

1 cup finely chopped
  onions
2 garlic cloves, minced
2 lbs. fresh tomatoes,
  peeled and chopped, *or*
  28-oz. can tomatoes, cut
  up, with juice
6-oz. can tomato paste
1 Tbsp. sugar
2 tsp. instant beef bouillon
  granules
1 tsp. dried oregano
½ tsp. dried basil
1 large bay leaf
salt to taste
pepper to taste
4-oz. can sliced
  mushrooms
2 Tbsp. cornstarch
2 Tbsp. cold water

1. Combine all ingredients
except mushrooms, corn-
starch, and water in slow
cooker.
2. Cover. Cook on Low 10-
12 hours.
3. Remove bay leaf. Stir in
mushrooms.
4. Combine cornstarch and
water. Stir into sauce.
5. Cover. Cook on High
until thickened and bubbly,
about 25 minutes.

# Italian Vegetable Pasta Sauce

**Sherril Bieberly**
Salina, KS

*Makes 2½ quarts sauce*

3 Tbsp. olive oil
1 cup packed chopped
  fresh parsley
3 ribs celery, chopped
1 medium onion, chopped
2 garlic cloves, minced
2-inch sprig fresh
  rosemary, *or* ½ tsp.
  dried rosemary
2 small fresh sage leaves,
  *or* ½ tsp. dried sage
32-oz. can tomato sauce
32-oz. can chopped
  tomatoes
1 small dried hot chili
  pepper
¼ lb. fresh mushrooms,
  sliced, *or* 8-oz. can sliced
  mushrooms, drained
1½ tsp. salt

1. Heat oil in skillet. Add
parsley, celery, onion, garlic,
rosemary, and sage. Saute
until vegetables are tender.
Place in slow cooker.
2. Add tomatoes, chili pepper, mushrooms, and salt.
3. Cover. Cook on Low 12-
18 hours, or on High 5-6
hours.

**Variation:**
Add 2 lbs. browned
ground beef to olive oil and
sauted vegetables. Continue
with recipe.

# Louise's Vegetable Spaghetti Sauce

Louise Stackhouse
Benton, PA

*Makes 4-6 servings*

6-7 fresh tomatoes, peeled and crushed
1 medium onion, chopped
2 green peppers, chopped
2 cloves garlic, minced
1/2 tsp. dried basil
1/2 tsp. dried oregano
1/4 tsp. salt
1/4 cup sugar
6-oz. can tomato paste, optional

1. Combine all ingredients in slow cooker.
2. Cover. Cook on Low 8-10 hours. If the sauce is too watery for your liking, stir in a 6-oz. can of tomato paste during the last hour of cooking.
3. Serve over cooked spaghetti or other pasta.

# Pizza in a Pot

Marianne J. Troyer
Millersburg, OH

*Makes 6-8 servings*

1 lb. bulk Italian sausage, browned and drained
28-oz. can crushed tomatoes
15 1/2-oz. can chili beans
2 1/4-oz. can sliced black olives, drained
1 medium onion, chopped
1 small green pepper, chopped
2 garlic cloves, minced
1/4 cup grated Parmesan cheese
1 Tbsp. quick-cooking tapioca
1 Tbsp. dried basil
1 bay leaf
1 tsp. salt
hot cooked pasta
shredded mozzarella cheese

1. Combine all ingredients in slow cooker except pasta and mozzarella cheese.
2. Cover. Cook on Low 8-9 hours.
3. Discard bay leaf. Stir well.
4. Serve over pasta. Top with mozzarella cheese.

# Slow-Cooker Pizza

**Marla Folkerts**, Holland, OH
**Ruth Ann Swartzendruber**
Hydro, OK
**Arlene Wiens**, Newton, KS

*Makes 6-8 servings*

1 1/2 lbs. ground beef, *or* bulk Italian sausage
1 medium onion, chopped
1 green pepper, chopped
half a box rigatoni, cooked
7-oz. jar sliced mushrooms, drained
3 oz. sliced pepperoni
16-oz. jar pizza sauce
10 oz. mozzarella cheese, shredded
10 oz. cheddar cheese, shredded

1. Brown ground beef and onions in saucepan. Drain.
2. Layer half of each of the following, in the order given, in slow cooker: ground beef and onions, green pepper, noodles, mushrooms, pepperoni, pizza sauce, cheddar cheese, and mozzarella cheese. Repeat layers.
3. Cover. Cook on Low 3-4 hours.

**Note:**
Keep rigatoni covered with sauce so they don't become dry and crunchy.

**Variation:**
Add a 10 3/4-oz. can cream of mushroom soup to the mix, putting half of it in as a layer after the first time the noodles appear, and the other

half after the second layer of noodles.

**Dorothy Horst**
Tiskilwa, IL

# Pizza Rice

**Sue Hamilton**
Minooka, IL

*Makes 6 servings*

2 cups rice, uncooked
3 cups chunky pizza sauce
2½ cups water
7-oz. can mushrooms, undrained
4 oz. pepperoni, sliced
1 cup grated cheese

1. Combine rice, sauce, water, mushrooms, and pepperoni. Stir.
2. Cover. Cook on Low 10 hours, or on High 6 hours. Sprinkle with cheese before serving.

# Wild Rice Hot Dish

**Barbara Tenney**
Delta, PA

*Makes 8-10 servings*

2 cups wild rice, uncooked
½ cup slivered almonds
½ cup chopped onions
½ cup chopped celery
8-12-oz. can mushrooms, drained
2 cups cut-up chicken
6 cups chicken broth
¼-½ tsp. salt
¼ tsp. pepper
¼ tsp. garlic powder
1 Tbsp. parsley

1. Wash and drain rice.
2. Combine all ingredients in slow cooker. Mix well.
3. Cover. Cook on Low 4-6 hours, or until rice is finished. Do not remove lid before rice has cooked 4 hours.

# Frances' Roast Chicken

**Frances Schrag**
Newton, KS

*Makes 6 servings*

3-4-lb. whole frying chicken
half an onion, chopped
1 rib celery, chopped
salt to taste
pepper to taste
½ tsp. poultry seasoning
¼ tsp. dried basil

1. Sprinkle chicken cavity with salt, pepper, and poultry seasoning. Put onion and celery inside cavity. Put chicken in slow cooker. Sprinkle with basil.
2. Cover. Cook on Low 8-10 hours, or High 4-6 hours.

> When adapting range-top recipes to slow cooking, reduce the amount of onion you normally use because the onion flavor gets stronger during slow cooking.
> **Beatrice Orgish**
> Richardson, TX

# Donna's Cooked Chicken

**Donna Treloar**
Gaston, IN

*Makes 1 chicken*

chicken (boneless, skinless
  breasts are the easiest,
  but any chicken pieces
  will do)
1 onion, sliced
seasoned salt
pepper
minced garlic, *or* garlic
  powder

1. Layer onion in bottom
of slow cooker. Add chicken
and sprinke with seasoned
salt, pepper, minced garlic, or
garlic powder.
2. Cook on Low 4 hours or
until done but not dry. (Time
will vary according to
amount of chicken and size of
pieces.)
3. Use in stir-frys, chicken
salads, or casseroles, slice for
sandwiches, shred for enchi-
ladas, or cut up and freeze for
later use.

**Variation:**
  Splash chicken with
2 Tbsp. soy sauce before
cooking.

# Valerie's & Stacy's Roast Chicken

**Valerie Hertzler**
Weyers Cave, VA
**Stacy Petersheim**
Mechanicsburg, PA

*Makes 4-6 servings*

3-4-lb. chicken
salt to taste
pepper to taste
butter
basil to taste

1. Wash chicken thor-
oughly. Pat dry. Sprinkle cavity
with salt and pepper. Place in
slow cooker. Dot with butter.
Sprinkle with basil.
2. Cover. Cook on High
1 hour, and then on Low 8-10
hours.

# Chicken-at-the-Ready

**Mary Mitchell**
Battle Creek, MI

*Makes 2-3 pints cooked chicken*

1 large whole chicken,
  skinned
1 cup water

1. Place chicken in greased
slow cooker. Add water.
2. Cover. Cook on Low 6-8
hours.

3. Remove meat from
bones, pack cooked meat into
plastic boxes, and store in
freezer to use in recipes that
call for cooked chicken.

**Note:**
  I frequently put this on
late at night so that it is done
when I wake up in the morning.

# Chicken in a Pot

**Carolyn Baer**, Conrath, WI
**Evie Hershey**, Atglen, PA
**Judy Koczo**, Plano, IL
**Mary Puskar**, Forest Hill, MD
**Mary Wheatley**, Mashpee, MA

*Makes 6 servings*

2 carrots, sliced
2 onions, sliced
2 celery ribs, cut in 1-inch
  pieces
3 lb. chicken, whole *or*
  cut up
2 tsp. salt
1/2 tsp. dried coarse black
  pepper
1 tsp. dried basil
1/2 cup water, chicken
  broth, *or* white cooking
  wine

1. Place vegetables in bottom of slow cooker. Place
chicken on top of vegetables.
Add seasonings and water.
2. Cover. Cook on Low 8-
10 hours, or High 3 1/2-5 hours
(use 1 cup liquid if cooking
on High).
3. This is a great founda-

tion for soups—chicken vegetable, chicken noodle . . .

**Note:**
To make this a full meal, add 2 medium-sized potatoes, quartered, to vegetables before cooking.

# Another Chicken in a Pot

Jennifer J. Gehman
Harrisburg, PA

*Makes 4-6 servings*

1-lb. bag baby carrots
1 small onion, diced
14½-oz. can green beans
3-lb. whole chicken, cut into serving-size pieces
2 tsp. salt
½ tsp. black pepper
½ cup chicken broth
¼ cup white wine
½-1 tsp. dried basil

1. Put carrots, onion, and beans on bottom of slow cooker. Add chicken. Top with salt, pepper, broth, and wine. Sprinkle with basil.
2. Cover. Cook on Low 8-10 hours, or High 3½-5 hours.

# Savory Slow-Cooker Chicken

Sara Harter Fredette
Williamsburg, MA

*Makes 4 servings*

2½ lbs. chicken pieces, skinned
1 lb. fresh tomatoes, chopped, *or* 15-oz. can stewed tomatoes
2 Tbsp. white wine
1 bay leaf
¼ tsp. pepper
2 garlic cloves, minced
1 onion, chopped
½ cup chicken broth
1 tsp. dried thyme
1½ tsp. salt
2 cups broccoli, cut into bite-sized pieces

1. Combine all ingredients except broccoli in slow cooker.
2. Cover. Cook on Low 8-10 hours.
3. Add broccoli 30 minutes before serving.

# Chicken and Vegetables

Rosanne Hankins
Stevensville, MD

*Makes 6 servings*

1 chicken, cut up
salt to taste
pepper to taste
1 bay leaf
2 tsp. lemon juice
¼ cup diced onions
¼ cup diced celery
1 lb. frozen mixed vegetables

1. Sprinkle salt and pepper over chicken and place chicken in slow cooker. Add bay leaf and lemon juice.
2. Cover. Cook on Low 6-8 hours, or High 3-5 hours. Remove chicken from bones. Reserve liquid, skimming fat if desired.
3. Cook ½ cup liquid, celery and onions in microwave on High for 2 minutes. Add frozen vegetables and microwave until cooked through.
4. Return all ingredients to slow cooker and cook on High 30 minutes.
5. Serve over cooked rice.

# Baked Chicken Breasts

**Janice Crist,** Quinter, KS
**Tracy Supcoe,** Barclay, MD

*Makes 4-6 servings*

2-3 whole chicken breasts, halved
2 Tbsp. butter, *or* margarine
10¾-oz. can cream of chicken soup
½ cup dry sherry
1 tsp. dried tarragon, *or* rosemary, *or* both
1 tsp. Worcestershire sauce
¼ tsp. garlic powder
4-oz. can sliced mushrooms, drained

1. Place chicken breasts in slow cooker.
2. In saucepan, combine remaining ingredients. Heat until smooth and hot. Pour over chicken.
3. Cover. Cook on Low 8-10 hours.

# Chicken Delicious

**Janice Crist**
Quinter, KS

*Makes 8-12 servings*

4-6 whole skinless chicken breasts, boned and halved
lemon juice
salt to taste
pepper to taste
celery salt to taste
paprika to taste
10¾-oz. can cream of mushroom soup
10¾-oz. can cream of celery soup
⅓ cup dry sherry, *or* white wine
grated Parmesan cheese

1. Season chicken with lemon juice, salt, pepper, celery salt, and paprika. Place in slow cooker.
2. Combine soups with sherry. Pour over chicken. Sprinkle with cheese.
3. Cover. Cook on Low 8-10 hours.
4. Serve with rice.

# Chicken in Wine

**Mary Seielstad**
Sparks, NV

*Makes 4-6 servings*

2-3 lbs. chicken breasts, *or* pieces
10¾-oz. can cream of mushroom soup
10¾-oz. can French onion soup
1 cup dry white wine, *or* chicken broth

1. Put chicken in slow cooker.
2. Combine soups and wine. Pour over chicken.
3. Cover. Cook on Low 6-8 hours.
4. Serve over rice, pasta, or potatoes.

In place of ground meat in a recipe, use vegetarian burgers. Cut them up, and you won't need to brown the meat.
**Sue Hamilton**
Minooka, IL

# Chicken in Mushroom Gravy

Rosemarie Fitzgerald
Gibsonia, PA
**Audrey L. Kneer**
Williamsfield, IL

*Makes 6 servings*

6 boneless, skinless
  chicken-breast halves
salt to taste
pepper to taste
1/4 cup dry white wine, *or*
  chicken broth
10³/4-oz. can cream of
  mushroom soup
4-oz. can sliced
  mushrooms, drained

1. Place chicken in slow cooker. Season with salt and pepper.
2. Combine wine and soup. Pour over chicken. Top with mushrooms.
3. Cover. Cook on Low 7-9 hours.

# Ruth's Slow-Cooker Chicken

**Sara Harter Fredette**
Williamsburg, MA

*Makes 6 servings*

6 boneless chicken-breast
  halves
10³/4-oz. can cream of
  mushroom soup
1 pkg. dry mushroom soup
  mix
1/4-1/2 cup sour cream
4-oz. can mushrooms,
  drained

1. Combine chicken and soups in slow cooker.
2. Cover. Cook on Low 6-8 hours.
3. Just before serving, stir in sour cream and mushrooms. Reheat briefly.
4. Serve on noodles.

**Note:**
  Leftover sauce makes a flavorful topping for grilled hamburgers.

# Creamy Cooker Chicken

**Violette Harris Denney**
Carrollton, GA

*Makes 6 servings*

1 envelope dry onion soup
  mix
2 cups sour cream
10³/4-oz. can cream of
  mushroom soup
6 boneless, skinless
  chicken-breast halves

1. Combine soup mix, sour cream, and cream of mushroom soup in slow cooker. Add chicken, pushing it down so it is submerged in the sauce.
2. Cover. Cook on Low 8 hours.
3. Serve over rice or noodles.

# Mushroom Chicken

**Brenda Pope**
Dundee, OH

*Makes 4 servings*

1 lb. boneless, skinless chicken breast
1 pkg. dry chicken gravy mix
10¾-oz. can cream of mushroom, *or* chicken, soup
1 cup white wine
8-oz. pkg. cream cheese, softened

1. Put chicken in slow cooker. Sprinkle gravy mix on top. In separate bowl, combine soup and wine and pour over gravy mix.
2. Cover. Cook on Low 8 hours.
3. During last 30 minutes of cooking time, stir in cream cheese. Before serving, remove chicken (keeping it warm) and whisk the sauce until smooth.
4. Serve chicken and sauce over noodles or rice.

# Creamy Mushroom Chicken

**Patricia Howard**
Albuquerque, NM

*Makes 4-5 servings*

2-3 lbs. chicken parts, skinned
4-oz. can mushrooms
2 10¾-oz. cans cream of chicken soup
1 envelope dry onion soup mix
½-1 cup chicken broth

1. Place chicken in slow cooker.
2. Combine remaining ingredients and pour over chicken.
3. Cover. Cook on Low 5-6 hours.

# So You Forgot to Defrost!

**Mary Seielstad**
Sparks, NV

*Makes 6 servings*

6 boneless, skinless frozen chicken-breast halves
2 10¾-oz. cans cream of chicken soup
4-oz. can sliced mushrooms, *or* ½ cup sliced fresh mushrooms
¾ tsp. salt
¼ tsp. pepper

1. Place frozen chicken in slow cooker.
2. Mix together soup, mushrooms, salt, and pepper and pour over chicken.
3. Cover. Cook on Low 10-12 hours.
4. Serve over rice.

# Continental Chicken

**Jennifer J. Gehman,**
Harrisburg, PA
**Gladys M. High,** Ephrata, PA
**L. Jean Moore,** Pendleton, IN

*Makes 4-6 servings*

2¼-oz. pkg. dried beef
3-4 whole chicken breasts, halved, skinned, and boned
6-8 slices bacon
10¾-oz. can cream of mushroom soup, undiluted
¼ cup sour cream
¼ cup flour

1. Arrange dried beef in bottom of slow cooker.
2. Wrap each piece of chicken with a strip of bacon. Place on top of dried beef.
3. Combine soup, sour cream, and flour. Pour over chicken.
4. Cover. Cook on Low 7-9 hours, or High 3-4 hours.
5. Serve over hot buttered noodles.

# Wanda's Chicken and Rice Casserole

Wanda Roth
Napoleon, OH

*Makes 6-8 servings*

1 cup long-grain rice, uncooked
3 cups water
2 tsp. chicken bouillon granules
10³/4-oz can cream of chicken soup
16-oz. bag frozen broccoli
2 cups chopped, cooked chicken
1/4 tsp. garlic powder
1 tsp. onion salt
1 cup grated cheddar cheese

1. Combine all ingredients in slow cooker.
2. Cook on High 3-4 hours.

**Note:**

If casserole is too runny, remove lid from slow cooker for 15 minutes while continuing to cook on High.

# Chicken Rice Dish

Esther Porter
Minneapolis, MN

*Makes 4 servings*

1 cup cooked rice
10³/4-oz. can cream of chicken soup
1 cup chicken broth
4 chicken thighs, partially cooked
10-oz. pkg. broccoli, frozen

1. Combine rice, soup, chicken broth, and chicken thighs. Place mixture in slow cooker.
2. Cover. Cook on Low 4 hours.
3. During last hour of cooking time, stir in broccoli.

# Sharon's Chicken and Rice Casserole

Sharon Anders
Alburtis, PA

*Makes 2 servings*

10³/4-oz. can cream of celery soup
2-oz. can sliced mushrooms, undrained
1/2 cup raw long grain rice
2 chicken-breast halves, skinned and boned
1 Tbsp. dry onion soup mix

1. Combine soup, mushrooms, and rice in greased slow cooker. Mix well.
2. Layer chicken breasts on top of mixture. Sprinkle with onion soup mix.
3. Cover. Cook on Low 4-6 hours.

# Barbara's Chicken Rice Casserole

Barbara A. Yoder
Goshen, IN

*Makes 6-8 servings*

2 chicken bouillon cubes
2 cups hot water
1/2 cup margarine, melted
6-oz. box Uncle Ben's Long Grain and Wild Rice (Original Recipe), uncooked
4¹/2-oz. jar sliced mushrooms
10-oz. can cooked chicken

1. Dissolve bouillon in hot water.
2. Combine all ingredients, including rice seasoning packet, in slow cooker.
3. Cover. Cook on High 2 hours, or until rice is tender.

**Note:**

To reduce salt in recipe, use 2 cups low- or no-sodium chicken broth instead of 2 chicken bouillon cubes and water.

# Scalloped Potatoes and Chicken

**Carol Sommers**
Millersburg, OH

*Makes 6-8 servings*

1/4 cup chopped green
peppers
1/2 cup chopped onions
1 1/2 cups diced Velveeta
cheese
7-8 medium potatoes,
sliced
salt to taste
10 3/4-oz. can cream of
celery soup
1 soup can milk
3-4 whole boneless,
skinless chicken breasts
salt to taste

1. Place layers of green peppers, onions, cheese, and potatoes and a sprinkling of salt in slow cooker.
2. Sprinkle salt over chicken breasts and lay on top of potatoes.
3. Combine soup and milk and pour into slow cooker, pushing meat down into liquid.
4. Cover. Cook on High 1 1/2 hours. Reduce temperature to Low and cook 3-4 hours. Test that potatoes are soft. If not, continue cooking on Low another hour and test again, continuing to cook until potatoes are finished.

# Scalloped Chicken

**Carolyn W. Carmichael**
Berkeley Heights, NJ

*Makes 4 servings*

5-oz. pkg. scalloped
potatoes
scalloped potatoes dry
seasoning pack
4 chicken-breast halves, *or*
8 legs
10-oz. pkg. frozen peas
2 cups water

1. Put potatoes, seasoning pack, chicken, and peas in slow cooker. Pour water over all.
2. Cover. Cook on Low 8-10 hours, or High 4 hours.

# Chicken-Vegetable Dish

**Cheri Jantzen**
Houston, TX

*Makes 4 servings*

4 skinless chicken-breast
halves, with bone in
15-oz. can crushed
tomatoes
10-oz. pkg. frozen green
beans
2 cups water, *or* chicken
broth
1 cup brown rice,
uncooked
1 cup sliced mushrooms

2 carrots, chopped
1 onion, chopped
1/2 tsp. minced garlic
1/2 tsp. herb-blend
seasoning
1/4 tsp. dried tarragon

1. Combine all ingredients in slow cooker.
2. Cover. Cook on High 2 hours, and then on Low 3-5 hours.

# Chicken and Vegetables

**Jeanne Heyerly**
Chenoa, IL

*Makes 2 servings*

2 medium potatoes,
quartered
2-3 carrots, sliced
2 frozen chicken breasts, *or*
2 frozen drumstick/thigh
pieces
salt to taste
pepper to taste
1 medium onion, chopped
2 garlic cloves, minced
1-2 cups shredded cabbage
16-oz. can chicken broth

1. Place potatoes and carrots in slow cooker. Layer chicken on top. Sprinkle with salt, pepper, onion, and garlic. Top with cabbage. Carefully pour chicken broth around edges.
2. Cover. Cook on Low 8-9 hours.

# California Chicken

**Shirley Sears**
Tiskilwa, IL

*Makes 4-6 servings*

3-lb. chicken, quartered
1 cup orange juice
1/3 cup chili sauce
2 Tbsp. soy sauce
1 Tbsp. molasses
1 tsp. dry mustard
1 tsp. garlic salt
2 Tbsp. chopped green
  peppers
3 medium oranges, peeled
  and separated into
  slices, *or* 13½-oz. can
  mandarin oranges

1. Arrange chicken in slow cooker.
2. In separate bowl, combine juice, chili sauce, soy sauce, molasses, dry mustard, and garlic salt. Pour over chicken.
3. Cover. Cook on Low 8-9 hours.
4. Stir in green peppers and oranges. Heat 30 minutes longer.

**Variation:**
Stir 1 tsp. curry powder in with sauces and seasonings. Stir 1 small can pineapple chunks and juice in with green peppers and oranges.

# Orange Chicken Leg Quarters

**Kimberly Jensen**
Bailey, CO

*Makes 4-5 servings*

4 chicken drumsticks
4 chicken thighs
1 cup strips of green and
  red bell peppers
1/2 cup canned chicken
  broth
1/2 cup prepared orange
  juice
1/2 cup ketchup
2 Tbsp. soy sauce
1 Tbsp. light molasses
1 Tbsp. prepared mustard
1/2 tsp. garlic salt
11-oz. can mandarin
  oranges
2 tsp. cornstarch
1 cup frozen peas
2 green onions, sliced

1. Place chicken in slow cooker. Top with pepper strips.
2. Combine broth, juice, ketchup, soy sauce, molasses, mustard, and garlic salt. Pour over chicken.
3. Cover. Cook on Low 6-7 hours.
4. Remove chicken and vegetables from slow cooker. Keep warm.
5. Measure out 1 cup of cooking sauce. Put in saucepan and bring to boil.
6. Drain oranges, reserving 1 Tbsp. juice. Stir cornstarch into reserved juice. Add to boiling sauce in pan.

7. Add peas to sauce and cook, stirring for 2-3 minutes until sauce thickens and peas are warm. Stir in oranges.
8. Arrange chicken pieces on platter of cooked white rice, fried cellophane noodles, or lo mein noodles. Pour orange sauce over chicken and rice or noodles. Top with sliced green onions.

# Cranberry Chicken

**Teena Wagner**
Waterloo, ON

*Makes 6-8 servings*

3-4-lb. chicken pieces
1/2 tsp. salt
1/4 tsp. pepper
1/2 cup diced celery
1/2 cup diced onions
16-oz. can whole berry
  cranberry sauce
1 cup barbecue sauce

1. Combine all ingredients in slow cooker.
2. Cover. Bake on High for 4 hours, or on Low 6-8 hours.

## Chicken Sweet and Sour

**Willard E. Roth**
Elkhart, IN

*Makes 8 servings*

4 medium potatoes, sliced
8 boneless, skinless
 chicken-breast halves
2 Tbsp. cider vinegar
1/4 tsp. ground nutmeg
1 tsp. dry basil, *or* 1 Tbsp.
 chopped fresh basil
2 Tbsp. brown sugar
1 cup orange juice
dried parsley flakes
17-oz. can waterpack
 sliced peaches, drained
fresh parsley
fresh orange slices

1. Place potatoes in greased slow cooker. Arrange chicken on top.
2. In separate bowl, combine vinegar, nutmeg, basil, brown sugar, and orange juice. Pour over chicken. Sprinkle with parsley.
3. Cover. Cook on Low 6 hours.
4. Remove chicken and potatoes from sauce and arrange on warm platter.
5. Turn cooker to High. Add peaches. When warm, spoon peaches and sauce over chicken and potatoes. Garnish with fresh parsley and orange slices.

## Chicken with Tropical Barbecue Sauce

**Lois Stoltzfus**
Honey Brook, PA

*Makes 6 servings*

1/4 cup molasses
2 Tbsp. cider vinegar
2 Tbsp. Worcestershire
 sauce
2 tsp. prepared mustard
1/8-1/4 tsp. hot pepper sauce
2 Tbsp. orange juice
3 whole chicken breasts,
 halved

1. Combine molasses, vinegar, Worcestershire sauce, mustard, hot pepper sauce, and orange juice. Brush over chicken.
2. Place chicken in slow cooker.
3. Cover. Cook on Low 7-9 hours, or High 3-4 hours.

## Fruited Barbecue Chicken

**Barbara Katrine Rose**
Woodbridge, VA

*Makes 4-6 servings*

29-oz. can tomato sauce
20-oz. can unsweetened
 crushed pineapple,
 undrained
2 Tbsp. brown sugar
3 Tbsp. vinegar
1 Tbsp. instant minced
 onion
1 tsp. paprika
2 tsp. Worcestershire sauce
1/4 tsp. garlic powder
1/8 tsp. pepper
3 lbs. chicken, skinned and
 cubed
11-oz. can mandarin
 oranges, drained

1. Combine all ingredients except chicken and oranges. Add chicken pieces.
2. Cover. Cook on High 4 hours.
3. Just before serving, stir in oranges. Serve over hot rice.

When I use mushrooms or green peppers in the slow cooker, I usually stir them in during the last hour so they don't get too mushy.

**Trudy Kutter**
Corfu, NY

# Orange Chicken and Sweet Potatoes

**Kimberlee Greenawalt**
Harrisonburg, VA

*Makes 6 servings*

2-3 sweet potatoes, peeled and sliced
3 whole chicken breasts, halved
2/3 cup flour
1 tsp. salt
1 tsp. nutmeg
1/2 tsp. cinnamon
dash pepper
dash garlic powder
10¾-oz. can cream of celery, *or* cream of chicken, soup
4-oz. can sliced mushrooms, drained
1/2 cup orange juice
1/2 tsp. grated orange rind
2 tsp. brown sugar
3 Tbsp. flour

1. Place sweet potatoes in bottom of slow cooker.
2. Rinse chicken breasts and pat dry. Combine flour, salt, nutmeg, cinnamon, pepper, and garlic powder. Thoroughly coat chicken in flour mixture. Place on top of sweet potatoes.
3. Combine soup with remaining ingredients. Stir well. Pour over chicken breasts.
4. Cover. Cook on Low 8-10 hours, or High 3-4 hours.
5. Serve over rice.

# Orange-Glazed Chicken Breasts

**Leona Miller**
Millersburg, OH

*Makes 6 servings*

6-oz. can frozen orange juice concentrate, thawed
1/2 tsp. dried marjoram
6 boneless, skinless chicken-breast halves
1/4 cup cold water
2 Tbsp. cornstarch

1. Combine orange juice and marjoram in shallow dish. Dip each breast in orange-juice mixture and place in slow cooker. Pour remaining sauce over breasts.
2. Cover. Cook on Low 7-9 hours, or High 3½-4 hours.
3. Remove chicken from slow cooker. Turn cooker to High and cover.
4. Combine water and cornstarch. Stir into liquid in slow cooker. Place cover slightly ajar on slow cooker. Cook until sauce is thick and bubbly, about 15-20 minutes. Serve over chicken.

**Variation:**
To increase "spice" in dish, add 1/2-1 tsp. Worcestershire sauce to orange juice-marjoram glaze.

# Sweet and Sour Chicken

**Bernice A. Esau**
North Newton, KS

*Makes 6 servings*

1½ cups sliced carrots
1 large green pepper, chopped
1 medium onion, chopped
2 Tbsp. quick-cooking tapioca
2½-3 lb. chicken, cut into serving-size pieces
8-oz. can pineapple chunks in juice
1/3 cup brown sugar
1/3 cup vinegar
1 Tbsp. soy sauce
1/2 tsp. instant chicken bouillon
1/4 tsp. garlic powder
1/4 tsp. ground ginger, *or* 1/2 tsp. freshly grated ginger
1 tsp. salt

1. Place vegetables in bottom of slow cooker. Sprinkle with tapioca. Add chicken.
2. In separate bowl, combine pineapple, brown sugar, vinegar, soy sauce, bouillon, garlic powder, ginger, and salt. Pour over chicken.
3. Cover. Cook on Low 8-10 hours.
4. Serve over cooked rice.

## Easy Teriyaki Chicken

**Barbara Shie**
Colorado Springs, CO

*Makes 5-6 servings*

2-3 lbs. skinless chicken pieces
20-oz. can pineapple chunks
dash of ground ginger
1 cup teriyaki sauce

1. Place chicken in slow cooker. Pour remaining ingredients over chicken.
2. Cover. Cook on Low 6-8 hours, or High 4-6 hours.

## Creamy Chicken Italiano

**Sharon Easter,** Yuba City, CA
**Rebecca Meyerkorth,** Wamego, KS
**Bonnie Milller,** Cochranville, PA

*Makes 4 servings*

4 boneless, skinless chicken-breast halves
1 envelope dry Italian salad dressing mix
1/4 cup water
8-oz. pkg. cream cheese, softened
10 3/4-oz. can cream of chicken soup
4-oz. can mushroom stems and pieces, drained

1. Place chicken in slow cooker.
2. Combine salad dressing mix and water. Pour over chicken.
3. Cover. Cook on Low 3 hours.
4. Combine cheese and soup until blended. Stir in mushrooms. Pour over chicken.
5. Cover. Cook on Low 1 hour, or until chicken juices run clear.
6. Serve over noodles or rice.

## Creamy Mushroom Chicken

**Barbara Shie**
Colorado Springs, CO

*Makes 4-6 servings*

4-6 boneless, skinless chicken-breast halves
12-oz. jar mushroom gravy
1 cup milk
8-oz. pkg. cream cheese, cubed
4 1/2-oz. can chopped green chilies
1 pkg. dry Italian salad dressing

1. Combine all ingredients in slow cooker.
2. Cover. Cook on Low 6 hours.
3. Serve over noodles or rice.

## Super Easy Chicken

**Mary Seielstad**
Sparks, NV

*Makes 4 servings*

4 frozen chicken-breast halves
1 pkg. dry Italian dressing mix
1 cup warm water, *or* chicken stock

1. Place chicken in slow cooker. Sprinkle with dressing mix. Pour water over chicken.
2. Cover. Cook on Low 8-10 hours.

## Ann's Chicken Cacciatore

**Ann Driscoll**
Albuquerque, NM

*Makes 6-8 servings*

1 large onion, thinly sliced
2 1/2-3 lb. chicken, cut up
2 6-oz. cans tomato paste
4-oz. can sliced mushrooms, drained
1 tsp. salt
1/4 cup dry white wine
1/4 tsp. pepper
1-2 garlic cloves, minced
1-2 tsp. dried oregano
1/2 tsp. dried basil

½ tsp. celery seed,
   optional
1 bay leaf

1. Place onion in slow cooker. Add chicken.
2. Combine remaining ingredients. Pour over chicken.
3. Cover. Cook on Low 7-9 hours, or High 3-4 hours.
4. Serve over spaghetti.

# Darla's Chicken Cacciatore

**Darla Sathre**
Baxter, MN

*Makes 6 servings*

2 onions, thinly sliced
4 boneless chicken breasts, cubed
3 garlic cloves, minced
¼ tsp. pepper
2 tsp. dried oregano
1 tsp. dried basil
1 bay leaf
2 15-oz. cans diced tomatoes
8-oz. can tomato sauce
4-oz. can sliced mushrooms

1. Place onions in bottom of slow cooker. Add remaining ingredients.
2. Cover. Cook on Low 8 hours.
3. Serve over hot spaghetti.

# Dorothea's Chicken Cacciatore

**Dorothea K. Ladd**
Ballston Lake, NY

*Makes 4-6 servings*

1 frying chicken, cut into serving-size pieces
¼ cup flour
2 Tbsp. oil
1 garlic clove, minced
46-oz. can tomato juice, *or* V-8 juice
12-oz. can tomato paste
2 Tbsp. dried parsley
2 Tbsp. sugar
2 tsp. salt
1 Tbsp. dried oregano
½ tsp. dried thyme
1 bay leaf

1. Put flour and chicken pieces in bag and shake to coat. Brown chicken and garlic in oil in skillet. Transfer chicken pieces and garlic to slow cooker.
2. Mix together tomato juice, tomato paste, parsley, sugar, salt, oregano, thyme, and bay leaf. Pour over chicken and garlic.
3. Cover. Cook on Low 8-10 hours.
4. Serve over spaghetti or rice.

# Dale & Shari's Chicken Cacciatore

**Dale and Shari Mast**
Harrisonburg, VA

*Makes 4 servings*

4 chicken quarters, *or* 4 boneless, skinless chicken-breast halves
15-oz. can tomato, *or* spaghetti, sauce
4-oz. can sliced mushrooms, drained
½ cup water
1 tsp. dry chicken broth granules
½ tsp. Italian seasoning

1. Place chicken in slow cooker. Pour on sauce, mushrooms, and water. Sprinkle with granules and seasoning.
2. Cover. Cook on High 3-4 hours, or Low 6-8 hours.
3. Serve over rice.

# Chicken Parmigiana

**Brenda Pope**
Dundee, OH

*Makes 6 servings*

1 egg
1 tsp. salt
1/4 tsp. pepper
6 boneless, skinless
    chicken-breast halves
1 cup Italian bread crumbs
2-4 Tbsp. butter
14-oz. jar pizza sauce
6 slices mozzarella cheese
grated Parmesan cheese

1. Beat egg, salt, and pepper together. Dip chicken into egg and coat with bread crumbs. Saute chicken in butter in skillet. Arrange chicken in slow cooker.
2. Pour pizza sauce over chicken.
3. Cover. Cook on Low 6-8 hours.
4. Layer mozzarella cheese over top and sprinkle with Parmesan cheese. Cook an additional 15 minutes.

# Easy Chicken A la King

**Jenny R. Unternahrer**
Wayland, IA

*Makes 4 servings*

1 1/2 lbs. boneless, skinless
    chicken breasts
10 3/4-oz. can cream of
    chicken soup
3 Tbsp. flour
1/4 tsp. pepper
9-oz. pkg. frozen peas and
    onions, thawed and
    drained
2 Tbsp. chopped pimentos
1/2 tsp. paprika

1. Cut chicken into bite-sized pieces and place in slow cooker.
2. Combine soup, flour, and pepper. Pour over chicken. Do not stir.
3. Cover. Cook on High 2 1/2 hours, or Low 5-5 1/2 hours.
4. Stir in peas and onions, pimentos, and paprika.
5. Cover. Cook on High 20-30 minutes.

**Variation:**
    Add 1/4-1/2 cup chopped green peppers to Step 2.
        **Sharon Brubaker**
        Myerstown, PA

# Coq au Vin

**Kimberlee Greenawalt**
Harrisonburg, VA

*Makes 6 servings*

2 cups frozen pearl onions,
    thawed
4 thick slices bacon, fried
    and crumbled
1 cup sliced button
    mushrooms
1 garlic clove, minced
1 tsp. dried thyme leaves
1/8 tsp. black pepper
6 boneless, skinless
    chicken-breast halves
1/2 cup dry red wine
3/4 cup chicken broth
1/4 cup tomato paste
3 Tbsp. flour

1. Layer ingredients in slow cooker in the following order: onions, bacon, mushrooms, garlic, thyme, pepper, chicken, wine, broth.
2. Cover. Cook on Low 6-8 hours.
3. Remove chicken and vegetables. Cover and keep warm.
4. Ladle 1/2 cup cooking liquid into small bowl. Cool slightly. Turn slow cooker to High. Cover. Mix reserved liquid, tomato paste, and flour until smooth. Return mixture to slow cooker, cover, and cook 15 minutes, or until thickened.
5. Serve chicken, vegetables, and sauce over noodles.

---

When using raw meat, begin by cooking it for 1-2 hours on High to avoid cooking it too slowly.
**Joy Sutter**
Iowa City, IA

# Lemon Garlic Chicken

**Cindy Krestynick**
Glen Lyon, PA

*Makes 4 servings*

1 tsp. dried oregano
1/2 tsp. seasoned salt
1/4 tsp. pepper
2 lbs. chicken-breast halves, skinned and rinsed
2 Tbsp. butter, *or* margarine
1/4 cup water
3 Tbsp. lemon juice
2 garlic cloves, minced
1 tsp. chicken bouillon granules
1 tsp. minced fresh parsley

1. Combine oregano, salt, and pepper. Rub all of mixture into chicken. Brown chicken in butter or margarine in skillet. Transfer to slow cooker.
2. Place water, lemon juice, garlic, and bouillon cubes in skillet. Bring to boil, loosening browned bits from skillet. Pour over chicken.
3. Cover. Cook on High 2-2 1/2 hours, or Low 4-5 hours.
4. Add parsley and baste chicken. Cover. Cook on High 15-30 minutes, until chicken is tender.

# Lemon Honey Chicken

**Carolyn W. Carmichael**
Berkeley Heights, NJ

*Makes 4-6 servings*

1 lemon
1 whole roasting chicken, rinsed
1/2 cup orange juice
1/2 cup honey

1. Pierce lemon with fork. Place in chicken cavity. Place chicken in slow cooker.
2. Combine orange juice and honey. Pour over chicken.
3. Cover. Cook on Low 8 hours. Remove lemon and squeeze over chicken.
4. Carve chicken and serve.

# Melanie's Chicken Cordon Bleu

**Melanie Thrower**
McPherson, KS

*Makes 6 servings*

3 whole chicken breasts, split and deboned
6 pieces thinly sliced ham
6 slices Swiss cheese
salt to taste
pepper to taste
6 slices bacon
1/4 cup water
1 tsp. chicken bouillon granules
1/2 cup white cooking wine
1 tsp. cornstarch
1/4 cup cold water

1. Flatten chicken to 1/8-1/4-inch thickness. Place a slice of ham and a slice of cheese on top of each flattened breast. Sprinkle with salt and pepper. Roll up and wrap with strip of bacon. Secure with toothpick. Place in slow cooker.
2. Combine 1/4 cup water, granules, and wine. Pour into slow cooker.
3. Cover. Cook on High 4 hours.
4. Combine cornstarch and 1/4 cup cold water. Add to slow cooker. Cook until sauce thickens.

# Chicken Cordon Bleu

**Barbara Nolan**
Pleasant Valley, NY
**Jenny R. Unternahrer,**
Wayland, IA

*Makes 6 servings*

3 whole boneless, skinless chicken breasts
3 large Swiss cheese slices, halved
3 large, thin ham slices, halved
2 Tbsp. margarine
10³⁄4-oz. can cream of mushroom soup, *or* cream of chicken soup
3 Tbsp. milk
3 Tbsp. sherry, optional
1/4 tsp. pepper

1. Cut whole breasts in half. Flatten each half with wooden mallet. Cover each half breast with half slice of cheese and ham. Roll up and secure with toothpicks. Brown each chicken roll in margarine in skillet. Transfer to slow cooker.
2. Combine remaining ingredients. Pour over chicken, making sure chicken pieces are fully covered.
3. Cover. Cook on Low 4-5 hours.

# Stuffed Chicken Rolls

**Lois M. Martin**, Lititz, PA
**Renee Shirk**, Mount Joy, PA

*Makes 6 servings*

6 large boneless, skinless chicken-breast halves
6 slices fully cooked ham
6 slices Swiss cheese
1/4 cup flour
1/4 cup grated Parmesan cheese
1/2 tsp. rubbed sage
1/4 tsp. paprika
1/4 tsp. pepper
1/4 cup oil
10³⁄4-oz. can cream of chicken soup
1/2 cup chicken broth
chopped fresh parsley, optional

1. Flatten chicken to 1/8-inch thickness. Place ham and cheese slices on each breast. Roll up and tuck in ends. Secure with toothpick.
2. Combine flour, Parmesan cheese, sage, paprika, and pepper. Coat chicken on all sides. Cover and refrigerate for 1 hour.
3. Brown chicken in oil in skillet. Transfer to slow cooker.
4. Combine soup and broth. Pour over chicken.
5. Cover. Cook on Low 4-5 hours.
6. Remove toothpicks. Garnish with parsley.

# Ham and Swiss Chicken

**Nanci Keatley**, Salem, OR
**Janice Yoskovich**
Carmichaels, PA

*Makes 6 servings*

2 eggs, beaten
1 1/2 cups milk
2 Tbsp. butter, melted
1/2 cup chopped celery
1/4 cup diced onion
10 slices bread, cubed
12 thin slices deli ham, rolled up
2 cups grated Swiss cheese
2 1/2 cups cubed cooked chicken
10³⁄4-oz. can cream of chicken soup
1/2 cup milk

1. Combine eggs and milk. Add butter, celery, and onion. Stir in bread cubes. Place half of mixture in greased slow cooker. Top with half the ham, cheese, and chicken.
2. Combine soup and milk. Pour half over chicken. Repeat layers.
3. Cover. Cook on Low 4-5 hours.

# Dawn's Barbecued Chicken

**Dawn M. Propst**
Levittown, PA

*Makes 6 servings*

3 whole boneless, skinless chicken breasts, cut in half
1/4 cup flour
1/4 cup oil
1 medium onion, sliced
1 green, *or* yellow, pepper, sliced
1/2 cup chopped celery
2 Tbsp. Worcestershire sauce
1 cup ketchup
2 cups water
1/4 tsp. salt
1/4 tsp. paprika

1. Roll chicken breasts in flour. Brown in oil in skillet. Transfer chicken to slow cooker.

2. Saute onion, peppers, and celery in skillet, also, cooking until tender. Add remaining ingredients and bring to boil. Pour over chicken.

3. Cover. Cook on Low 8 hours.

4. Serve over noodles or rice.

# Marcy's Barbecued Chicken

**Marcy Engle**
Harrisonburg, VA

*Makes 6 servings*

2 lbs. chicken pieces
1/4 cup flour
1 cup ketchup
2 cups water
1/3 cup Worcestershire sauce
1 tsp. chili powder
1/2 tsp. salt
1/2 tsp. pepper
2 drops Tabasco sauce
1/4 tsp. garlic salt
1/4 tsp. onion salt

1. Dust chicken with flour. Transfer to slow cooker.

2. Combine remaining ingredients. Pour over chicken.

3. Cover. Cook on Low 5 hours.

# Oriental Chicken

**Marcia S. Myer**
Manheim, PA

*Makes 6 servings*

2 2 1/2-3 lb. broiler/fryer chickens, cut up
1/4 cup flour
1 1/2 tsp. salt
2 Tbsp. oil
6-oz. can lemonade concentrate, thawed
2 Tbsp. brown sugar
3 Tbsp. ketchup
1 Tbsp. vinegar
2 Tbsp. cold water
2 Tbsp. cornstarch

1. Combine flour with salt. Coat chicken. Brown chicken in oil in skillet. Transfer to slow cooker.

2. Combine lemonade concentrate, brown sugar, ketchup, and vinegar. Pour over chicken.

3. Cover. Cook on High 3-4 hours.

4. Remove chicken. Pour liquid into saucepan. Return chicken to cooker and cover to keep warm. Skim fat from liquid.

5. Combine water and cornstarch. Stir into hot liquid. Cook and stir until thick and bubbly.

6. Serve chicken and sauce over rice.

# Awfully Easy Chicken

**Martha Hershey**
Ronks, PA

*Makes 8 servings*

½ cup water
4-lb. chicken legs and
  thighs
14-oz. bottle barbecue
  sauce

1. Place water in bottom of slow cooker. Add chicken. Pour barbecue sauce over top.
2. Cover. Cook on Low 8 hours.

**Note:**
Serve any additional sauce over mashed potatoes.
  **Judy Denney**
  Lawrenceville, GA

**Variation:**
Place 3 large onions, quartered or sliced, in bottom of slow cooker. Then add chicken and sauce.
  **Barbara J. Fabel**
  Wausau, WI

# Tracy's Barbecued Chicken Wings

**Tracy Supcoe**
Barclay, MD

*Makes 8 full-sized servings*

4-lb. chicken wings
2 large onions, chopped
2 6-oz. cans tomato paste
2 large garlic cloves,
  minced
¼ cup Worcestershire
  sauce
¼ cup cider vinegar
½ cup brown sugar
½ cup sweet pickle relish
½ cup red, *or* white, wine
2 tsp. salt
2 tsp. dry mustard

1. Cut off wing tips. Cut wings at joint. Place in slow cooker.
2. Combine remaining ingredients. Add to slow cooker. Stir.
3. Cover. Cook on Low 5-6 hours.

# Mary's Chicken Wings

**Mary Casey**
Scranton, PA

*Makes 8-12 full-sized servings*

3-6 lbs. chicken wings
1-3 Tbsp. oil
¾-1 cup vinegar
½ cup ketchup
2 Tbsp. sugar
2 Tbsp. Worcestershire
  sauce
3 garlic cloves, minced
1 Tbsp. dry mustard
1 tsp. paprika
½-1 tsp. salt
⅛ tsp. pepper

1. Brown wings in oil in skillet, or brush wings with oil and broil, watching carefully so they do not burn.
2. Combine remaining ingredients in 5-6½-quart slow cooker. Add wings. Stir gently so that they are all well covered with sauce.
3. Cover. Cook on Low 4-6 hours, or until tender.

---

Don't have enough time? A lot of dishes can be made in less time by increasing the temperature to High and cooking the dish for about half the time as is necessary on Low.
**Jenny R. Unternahrer**
Wayland, IA

# Rosemarie's Barbecued Chicken Wings

**Rosemarie Fitzgerald**
Gibsonia, PA

*Makes 10 full-sized servings*

5 lbs. chicken wings, tips
 cut off
12-oz. bottle chili sauce
1/3 cup lemon juice
1 Tbsp. Worcestershire
 sauce
2 Tbsp. molasses
1 tsp. salt
2 tsp. chili powder
1/4 tsp. hot pepper sauce
dash garlic powder

1. Place wings in cooker.
2. Combine remaining ingredients and pour over chicken.
3. Cover. Cook on Low 6-8 hours, or High 2-3 hours.

**Note:**
 These wings are also a great appetizer, yielding about 15 appetizer-size servings.
 Take any leftover chicken off the bone and combine with leftover sauce. Serve over cooked pasta for a second meal.

# Donna's Chicken Wings

**Donna Conto**
Saylorsburg, PA

*Makes 10 full-sized servings*

5 lbs. chicken wings
28-oz. jar spaghetti sauce
1 Tbsp. Worcestershire
 sauce
1 Tbsp. molasses
1 Tbsp. prepared mustard
1 tsp. salt
1/2 tsp. pepper

1. Place wings in slow cooker.
2. Combine remaining ingredients. Pour over wings and stir them gently, making sure all are covered with sauce.
3. Cover. Cook on High 3-4 hours.

# Sweet Aromatic Chicken

**Anne Townsend**
Albuquerque, NM

*Makes 4 servings*

1/2 cup coconut milk
1/2 cup water
8 chicken thighs, skinned
1/2 cup brown sugar
2 Tbsp. soy sauce
1/8 tsp. ground cloves
2 garlic cloves, minced

1. Combine coconut milk and water. Pour into greased slow cooker.
2. Add remaining ingredients in order listed.
3. Cover. Cook on Low 5-6 hours.

**Note:**
 What to do with leftover coconut milk?
 1. Two or three spoonfuls over vanilla ice cream, topped with a cherry, makes a flavorful, quick dessert.
 2. Family Pina Coladas are good. Pour the coconut milk into a pitcher and add one large can pineapple juice, along with some ice cubes. Decorate with pineapple chunks and cherries.

# Chicken Casablanca

**Joyce Kaut**
Rochester, NY

*Makes 6-8 servings*

2 Tbsp. oil
2 large onions, sliced
1 tsp. ground ginger
3 garlic cloves, minced
3 large carrots, diced
2 large potatoes, diced
3 lbs. skinless chicken
 pieces
1/2 tsp. ground cumin
1/2 tsp. salt
1/2 tsp. pepper
1/4 tsp. cinnamon
2 Tbsp. raisins
14 1/2-oz. can chopped
 tomatoes
3 small zucchini, sliced
15-oz. can garbanzo beans,
 drained
2 Tbsp. chopped parsley

1. Saute onions, ginger, and garlic in oil in skillet. (Reserve oil.) Transfer to slow cooker. Add carrots and potatoes.

2. Brown chicken over medium heat in reserved oil. Transfer to slow cooker. Mix gently with vegetables.

3. Combine seasonings in separate bowl. Sprinkle over chicken and vegetables. Add raisins and tomatoes.

4. Cover. Cook on High 4-6 hours.

5. Add sliced zucchini, beans, and parsley 30 minutes before serving.

6. Serve over cooked rice or couscous.

**Variation:**

Add 1/2 tsp. turmeric and 1/4 tsp. cayenne pepper to Step 3.

**Michelle Mann**
Mt. Joy, PA

# Chicken Kapaman

**Judy Govotsus**
Monrovia, MD

*Makes 4-6 servings*

4-6 potatoes, quartered
4-6 carrots, sliced
2-3-lbs. chicken pieces
2 onions, chopped
1 whole garlic bulb,
 minced
2 Tbsp. tomato paste
1 1/2 cups water
1 cinnamon stick
1/2 tsp. salt
1/4 tsp. pepper

1. Layer potatoes and carrots in slow cooker. Add chicken.

2. In separate bowl, mix remaining ingredients together and pour over vegetables and chicken in cooker.

3. Cover. Cook on High 4 hours. Remove lid and cook on Low an additional 1-1 1/2 hours.

# Greek Chicken

**Judy Govotsus**
Monrovia, MD

*Makes 4-6 servings*

4-6 potatoes, quartered
2-3 lbs. chicken pieces
2 large onions, quartered
1 whole bulb garlic,
 minced
3 tsp. dried oregano
1 tsp. salt
1/2 tsp. pepper
1 Tbsp. olive oil

1. Place potatoes in bottom of slow cooker. Add chicken, onions, and garlic. Sprinkle with seasonings. Top with oil.

2. Cover. Cook on High 5-6 hours, or on Low 9-10 hours.

# Cathy's Chicken Creole

**Cathy Boshart**

Lebanon, PA

*Makes 6 servings*

2 Tbsp. butter
half a medium green
  pepper, chopped
2 medium onions, chopped
1/2 cup chopped celery
1 lb. 4 oz.-can tomatoes
1/2 tsp. pepper, *or* your
  choice of dried herbs
1 1/2 tsp. salt, *or* your
  choice of dried herbs
1/8 tsp. red pepper
1 cup water
2 Tbsp. cornstarch
1 tsp. sugar
1 1/2 Tbsp. cold water
2 cups cooked and cubed
  chicken
6 green, *or* black, olives,
  sliced
1/2 cup sliced mushrooms

1. Melt butter in slow
cooker. Add green pepper,
onions, and celery. Heat.
2. Add tomatoes, pepper,
salt and 1 cup water.
3. Cover. Cook on High
while preparing remaining
ingredients.
4. Combine cornstarch and
sugar. Add 1 1/2 Tbsp. cold
water and make a smooth
paste. Stir into mixture in
slow cooker. Add chicken,
olives, and mushrooms.
5. Cover. Cook on Low 2-3
hours.

# Barbara's Creole Chicken

**Barbara McGinnis**

Jupiter, FL

*Makes 4 servings*

2 (.9-oz.) pkgs. dry
  bearnaise sauce mix
1/2 cup dry white wine
1 lb. boneless, skinless
  chicken breasts, cut into
  bite-sized cubes
9-oz. pkg. frozen mixed
  vegetables
1 lb. cooked ham, cubed
1 lb. red potatoes, cubed
1 red bell pepper, chopped
1 green bell pepper,
  chopped
3 shallots, minced
1/2 tsp. garlic powder
1/2 tsp. turmeric powder
1/2 tsp. dried tarragon

1. Combine all ingredients
in slow cooker.
2. Cover. Cook on Low 6
hours.

# Chicken Curry

**Maricarol Magill**

Freehold, NJ

*Makes 4 servings*

4 boneless, skinless
  chicken-breast halves
1 small onion, chopped
2 sweet potatoes (about
  1 1/2 lbs.), cubed
2/3 cup orange juice
1 garlic clove, minced
1 tsp. chicken bouillon
  granules
1 tsp. salt
1/4 tsp. pepper
4 tsp. curry powder
2 Tbsp. cornstarch
2 Tbsp. cold water
rice

Toppings:
sliced green onions
shredded coconut
peanuts
raisins

1. Place chicken in slow
cooker. Cover with onions
and sweet potatoes.
2. Combine orange juice,
garlic, chicken bouillon granules, salt, pepper, and curry
powder. Pour over vegetables.
3. Cover. Cook on Low 5-6
hours.
4. Remove chicken and
vegetables and keep warm.
5. Turn slow cooker to
High. Dissolve cornstarch in
cold water. Stir into sauce in
slow cooker. Cover. Cook on
High 15-20 minutes.
6. Serve chicken and sauce
over rice. Sprinkle with your
choice of toppings.

## Groundnut Stew

Cathy Boshart
Lebanon, PA

*Makes 8 servings*

2 green peppers, cut into
  rings
1 medium onion, cut into
  rings
2 Tbsp. shortening
6-oz. can tomato paste
3/4 cup peanut butter
3 cups chicken broth
1 1/2 tsp. salt
1 tsp. chili powder
1 tsp. sugar
1/2 tsp. ground nutmeg
4 cups cubed, cooked
  chicken
6 cups hot cooked rice

Toppings:
coconut
peanuts
raisins
hard-boiled eggs, chopped
bananas, chopped
oranges, cut up
eggplant, chopped
apples, chopped
tomatoes, chopped
carrots, shredded
green pepper, chopped
onion, chopped
pineapple, crushed

1. Cook and stir green pepper and onion rings in shortening in hot slow cooker.
2. Combine tomato paste and peanut butter. Stir into slow cooker.
3. Add broth and seasonings. Stir in chicken.
4. Cover. Cook on Low 3 hours.

5. Serve over hot rice with your choice of toppings.

## Mulligan Stew

Carol Ambrose
Ripon, CA

*Makes 8-10 servings*

3-lb. stewing hen, cut up,
  *or* 4 lbs. chicken legs
  and thighs
1 1/2 tsp. salt
1/4-lb. salt pork, *or* bacon,
  cut in 1-inch squares
4 cups tomatoes, peeled
  and sliced
2 cups fresh corn, *or* 1-lb.
  pkg. frozen corn
1 cup coarsely chopped
  potatoes
10-oz. pkg. lima beans,
  frozen
1/2 cup chopped onions
1 tsp. salt
1/4 tsp. pepper
dash of cayenne pepper

1. Place chicken in very large slow cooker. Add water to cover. Add 1 1/2 tsp. salt.
2. Cover. Cook on Low 2 hours. Add more water if needed.
3. Add remaining ingredients. (If you don't have a large cooker, divide the stew between 2 average-sized ones.) Simmer on Low 5 hours longer.

**Notes:**
1. Flavor improves if stew is refrigerated and reheated

the next day. May also be made in advance and frozen.
2. You can debone the chicken after the first cooking for 2 hours. Stir chicken pieces back into cooker with other ingredients and continue with directions above.

## African Chicken Treat

Anne Townsend
Albuquerque, NM

*Makes 4 servings*

1 1/2 cups water
2 tsp. chicken bouillon
  granules
2 ribs celery, thinly sliced
2 onions, thinly sliced
1 red bell pepper, sliced
1 green bell pepper, sliced
8 chicken thighs, skinned
1/2 cup extra crunchy
  peanut butter
crushed chili pepper of
  your choice

1. Combine water, chicken bouillon granules, celery, onions, and peppers in slow cooker.
2. Spread peanut butter over both sides of chicken pieces. Sprinkle with chili pepper. Place on top of ingredients in slow cooker.
3. Cover. Cook on Low 5-6 hours.

# Gran's Big Potluck
Carol Ambrose
Ripon, CA

*Makes 10-15 servings*

2½-3 lb. stewing hen, cut into pieces
½ lb. stewing beef, cubed
½-lb. veal shoulder, *or* roast, cubed
1½ qts. water
½ lb. small red potatoes, cubed
½ lb. small onions, cut in half
1 cup sliced carrots
1 cup chopped celery
1 green pepper, chopped
1-lb. pkg. frozen lima beans
1 cup okra, whole *or* diced, fresh *or* frozen
1 cup whole kernel corn
8-oz. can whole tomatoes with juice
15-oz. can tomato puree
1 tsp. salt
¼-½ tsp. pepper
1 tsp. dry mustard
½ tsp. chili powder
¼ cup chopped fresh parsley

1. Combine all ingredients except last 5 seasonings in one very large slow cooker, or divide between two medium-sized ones.
2. Cover. Cook on Low 10-12 hours. Add seasonings during last hour of cooking.

**Note:**
You may want to debone the chicken and mix it back into the cooker before serving the meal.

# Marsha's Chicken Enchilada Casserole
Marsha Sabus
Fallbrook, CA

*Makes 4-6 servings*

1 onion, chopped
1 garlic clove, minced
1 Tbsp. oil
10-oz. can enchilada sauce
8-oz. can tomato sauce
salt to taste
pepper to taste
8 corn tortillas
3 boneless chicken-breast halves, cooked and cubed
15-oz. can ranch-style beans, drained
11-oz. can Mexicorn, drained
¾-lb. cheddar cheese, grated
2¼-oz. can sliced black olives, drained

1. Saute onion and garlic in oil in saucepan. Stir in enchilada sauce and tomato sauce. Season with salt and pepper.
2. Place two tortillas in bottom of slow cooker. Layer one-third chicken on top. Top with one-third sauce mixture, one-third beans, one-third corn, one-third cheese, and one-third black olives. Repeat layers 2 more times. Top with 2 tortillas.
3. Cover. Cook on Low 6-8 hours.

**Variation:**
Substitute 1 lb. cooked and drained hamburger for the chicken.

# Chicken Olé
Barb Yoder
Angola, IN

*Makes 8 servings*

10¾-oz. can cream of mushroom soup
10¾-oz. can cream of chicken soup
1 cup sour cream
2 Tbsp. grated onion
1½ cups grated cheddar cheese
12 flour tortillas, each torn into 6-8 pieces
3-4 cups cubed, cooked chicken
7-oz. jar salsa
½ cup grated cheddar cheese

1. In separate bowl, combine soups, sour cream, onion, and 1½ cups cheese.
2. Place one-third of each of the following in layers in slow cooker: torn tortillas, soup mixture, chicken, and salsa. Repeat layers 2 more times.
3. Cover. Cook on Low 4-5 hours. (This recipe does not respond well to cooking on High.)
4. Gently stir. Sprinkle with remaining ½ cup cheese. Cover. Cook on Low another 15-30 minutes.
5. Serve with tortilla chips and lettuce.

# Chicken Enchilada Casserole

### Jane Talso
Albuquerque, NM

*Makes 6-8 servings*

3-4-lb. chicken
1 medium onion, finely
   chopped
1 Tbsp. oil
10¾-oz. can cream of
   mushroom soup
10¾-oz. can cream of
   chicken soup
1 cup sour cream
10-oz. can green enchilada
   sauce
4.5-oz. can peeled, diced
   green chilies
20 corn tortillas
3 cups shredded cheddar
   cheese

1. Boil chicken. Shred meat and discard bones and skin.
2. Saute onion in oil in saucepan until translucent. Stir in soups, sour cream, green enchilada sauce, and chilies. Heat until warm.
3. Tear tortillas into bite-sized pieces.
4. Layer half of sauce, chicken, tortillas, and cheese in slow cooker, alternating layers. Repeat, ending with cheese and sauce.
5. Cover. Cook on Low 5-6 hours, or High 2-3 hours.

# Chicken Tortillas

### Julette Leaman
Harrisonburg, VA

*Makes 4 servings*

1 fryer chicken, cooked
   and cubed
10¾-oz. can cream of
   chicken soup
½ cup (can) tomatoes with
   chilies
2 Tbsp. quick-cooking
   tapioca
6-8 tortillas, torn into
   pieces
1 medium onion, chopped
2 cups grated cheddar
   cheese

1. Combine chicken, soup, tomatoes with chilies, and tapioca.
2. Line bottom of slow cooker with one-third tortilla pieces. Add one-third chicken mixture. Sprinkle with one-third onion and cheese. Repeat layers.
3. Cover. Cook on Low 6-8 hours. (This recipe does not respond well to being cooked on High.)

**Note:**
   Serve, if you wish, with shredded lettuce, chopped fresh tomatoes, diced raw onions, sour cream, and salsa.

# Chicken at a Whim

### Colleen Heatwole
Burton, MI

*Makes 6-8 servings*

6 medium-sized, boneless,
   skinless chicken-breast
   halves
1 small onion, sliced
1 cup dry white wine,
   chicken broth, *or* water
15-oz. can chicken broth
2 cups water
6-oz. can sliced black
   olives, with juice
1 small can artichoke
   hearts, with juice
5 garlic cloves, minced
1 cup dry elbow macaroni,
   *or* small shells
1 envelope dry savory
   garlic soup

1. Place chicken in slow cooker. Spread onion over chicken.
2. Combine remaining ingredients, except dry soup mix, and pour over chicken. Sprinkle with dry soup.
3. Cover. Cook on Low 4½ hours.

---

Browning meat in another pan means an extra step, but it adds a lot to a recipe's appearance and flavor.
**Mary Puskar**
Forest Hill, MD

# Joyce's Chicken Tetrazzini

**Joyce Slaymaker**
Strasburg, PA

*Makes 4 servings*

2-3 cups diced cooked chicken
2 cups chicken broth
1 small onion, chopped
1/4 cup sauterne, white wine, *or* milk
1/2 cup slivered almonds
2 4-oz. cans sliced mushrooms, drained
103/4-oz. can cream of mushroom soup
1 lb. cooked spaghetti
grated Parmesan cheese

1. Combine all ingredients except spaghetti and cheese in slow cooker.
2. Cover. Cook on Low 6-8 hours.
3. Serve over buttered spaghetti. Sprinkle with Parmesan cheese.

**Variations:**
1. Place spaghetti in large baking dish. Pour sauce in center. Sprinkle with Parmesan cheese. Broil until lightly browned.
2. Add 10-oz. pkg. frozen peas to Step 1.
**Darlene Raber**
Wellman, IA

# Dorothy's Chicken Tetrazzini

**Dorothy Shank**
Sterling, IL

*Makes 6 servings*

3-4 cups diced, cooked chicken
2 cups chicken broth
103/4-oz. can cream of mushroom soup
1/2 lb. fresh mushrooms, sliced
1 cup half-and-half
1 lb. cooked spaghetti

1. Combine chicken, broth, and soup in slow cooker.
2. Cover. Cook on Low 4-6 hours.
3. During last hour of cooking, stir in half-and-half.
4. Serve chicken and sauce over cooked spaghetti.

# Chickenetti

**Miriam Nolt**, New Holland, PA
**Ruth Hershey**, Paradise, PA

*Makes 10 servings*

1 cup chicken broth
16-oz. pkg. spaghetti, cooked
4-6 cups cubed and cooked chicken, *or* turkey, breast
103/4-oz. can cream of mushroom soup, *or* cream of celery soup
1 cup water
1/4 cup green peppers, chopped
1/2 cup diced celery
1/2 tsp. pepper
1 medium onion, grated
1/2 lb. white, *or* yellow, American cheese, cubed

1. Put cup of chicken broth into very large slow cooker. Add spaghetti and meat.
2. In large bowl, combine soup and water until smooth. Stir in remaining ingredients, then pour into slow cooker.
3. Cover. Cook on Low 2-3 hours.

**Variations:**
1. For a creamier dish, add a 103/4-oz. can cream of chicken soup to Step 2.
**Arlene Miller**
Hutchinson, KS

2. Add 41/2-oz. can chopped green chilies to Step 2, for more zest.

# Golden Chicken and Noodles

Sue Pennington
Bridgewater, VA

*Makes 6 servings*

6 boneless, skinless
   chicken-breast halves
2 10¾-oz. cans broccoli
   cheese soup
2 cups milk
1 small onion, chopped
½-1 tsp. salt
½-1 tsp. dried basil
⅛ tsp. pepper

1. Place chicken pieces in slow cooker.
2. Combine remaining ingredients. Pour over chicken.
3. Cover. Cook on High 1 hour. Reduce heat to Low. Cook 5-6 hours.
4. Serve over noodles.

---

# Easy Casserole

Ruth Conrad Liechty
Goshen, IN

*Makes 6-8 servings*

2 10¾-oz. cans chicken
   gumbo soup
2 10¾-oz. cans cream of
   mushroom soup
1-2 cups cut up chicken, *or*
   turkey
1 cup milk
6-oz. can chow mein
   noodles
1 pint frozen green beans,
   *or* corn, cooked

1. Combine all ingredients in slow cooker.
2. Cover. Cook on Low 7-8 hours, or High 3-4 hours.

---

# Chicken and Stuffing

Janice Yoskovich
Carmichaels, PA
**Jo Ellen Moore**, Pendleton, IN

*Makes 14-16 servings*

2½ cups chicken broth
1 cup butter, *or* margarine,
   melted
½ cup chopped onions
½ cup chopped celery
4-oz. can mushrooms, stems
   and pieces, drained
¼ cup dried parsley flakes
1½ tsp. rubbed sage
1 tsp. poultry seasoning
1 tsp. salt
½ tsp. pepper
12 cups day-old bread
   cubes (½-inch pieces)
2 eggs
10¾-oz. can cream of
   chicken soup
5-6 cups cubed cooked
   chicken

1. Combine all ingredients except bread, eggs, soup, and chicken in saucepan. Simmer for 10 minutes.
2. Place bread cubes in large bowl.
3. Combine eggs and soup. Stir into broth mixture until smooth. Pour over bread and toss well.
4. Layer half of stuffing and then half of chicken into very large slow cooker (or two medium-sized cookers). Repeat layers.
5. Cover. Cook on Low 4½-5 hours.

---

When using fresh herbs you may want to experiment with the amounts to use, because the strength is enhanced in the slow cooker, rather than becoming weaker.
**Annabelle Unternahrer**
Shipshewana, IN

# Chicken Dressing
Mary V. Warye
West Liberty, OH

*Makes 25-30 servings*

12-13 cups bread cubes
1 tsp. poultry seasoning
1½ tsp. salt
1 tsp. dried thyme
½ tsp. pepper
½ tsp. dried marjoram
¾ cup margarine, *or*
   butter
2 cups chopped onions
2 cups chopped celery
¼ cup chopped fresh
   parsley
8-oz. can mushrooms,
   drained
3½-4½ cups chicken broth
4 cups diced, cooked
   chicken
2 eggs, beaten
1 tsp. baking powder

1. Put bread cubes in large bowl. Add all seasonings and mix well.
2. Melt margarine in skillet. Saute onions, celery, parsley, and mushrooms. Add to bread cubes.
3. Heat broth and pour into bread cubes, stirring until well moistened. Fold in chicken.
4. Add eggs. Toss well. Add baking powder. Toss well.
5. Pack lightly into very large slow cooker, or two medium-sized cookers.
6. Cover. Cook on Low 5-6 hours.

# One-Dish Chicken Supper
Louise Stackhouse
Benton, PA

*Makes 4 servings*

4 boneless, skinless
   chicken-breast halves
10¾-oz. can cream of
   chicken, *or* celery, *or*
   mushroom, soup
⅓ cup milk
1 pkg. Stove Top stuffing
   mix and seasoning
   packet
1⅔ cups water

1. Place chicken in slow cooker.
2. Combine soup and milk. Pour over chicken.
3. Combine stuffing mix, seasoning packet, and water. Spoon over chicken.
4. Cover. Cook on Low 6-8 hours.

# Chicken and Dumplings
Elva Ever
North English, IA

*Makes 8-10 servings*

4 whole chicken breasts, *or*
   1 small chicken
¾ cup sliced carrots
¼ cup chopped onions
¼ cup chopped celery
1½ cups peas
4-6 Tbsp. flour
1 cup water
salt to taste
pepper to taste
buttermilk baking mix
   dumplings
paprika to taste

1. Cook chicken in water in soup pot. Cool, skin, and debone chicken. Return broth to boiling in soup pot.
2. Cook vegetables in microwave on High for 5 minutes.
3. Meanwhile, combine flour and water until smooth. Add to boiling chicken broth. Add enough extra water to make 4 cups broth, making sure gravy is fairly thick. Season with salt and pepper.
4. Combine chicken, vegetables, and gravy in slow cooker.
5. Mix dumplings as directed on baking mix box. Place dumplings on top of chicken in slow cooker. Sprinkle with paprika.
6. Cover. Cook on High 3 hours.

# Sloppy Chicken

**Marjora Miller**
Archbold, OH

*Makes 4-6 servings*

28-oz. can boneless
  chicken
10³/4-oz. can cream of
  chicken soup
1 stack butter crackers,
  crushed
15-oz. can chicken broth
10³/4-oz. can cream of
  mushroom soup

1. Combine all ingredients
in slow cooker.
2. Cover. Cook on Low 5-6
hours, stirring occasionally.

# Elizabeth's
# Hot Chicken
# Sandwiches

**Elizabeth Yutzy**
Wauseon, OH

*Makes 8 servings*

3 cups cubed cooked
  chicken
2 cups chicken broth
1 cup crushed soda
  crackers
¹/4-¹/2 tsp. salt
dash pepper
8 sandwich buns

1. Combine chicken,
broth, crackers, and seasoning in slow cooker.
2. Cover. Cook on Low 2-3
hours, until mixture thickens
and can be spread.
3. Fill sandwich buns and
serve while warm.

# Loretta's
# Hot Chicken
# Sandwiches

**Loretta Krahn**
Mt. Lake, MN

*Makes 12 servings*

8 cups cubed cooked
  chicken, *or* turkey
1 medium onion, chopped
1 cup chopped celery
2 cups mayonnaise
1 cup cubed American
  cheese
buns

1. Combine all ingredients
except buns in slow cooker.
2. Cover. Cook on High 2
hours.
3. Serve on buns.

# Barbecue Chicken
# for Buns

**Linda Sluiter**
Schererville, IN

*Makes 16-20 servings*

6 cups diced cooked
  chicken
2 cups chopped celery
1 cup chopped onions
1 cup chopped green
  peppers
4 Tbsp. butter
2 cups ketchup
2 cups water
2 Tbsp. brown sugar
4 Tbsp. vinegar
2 tsp. dry mustard
1 tsp. pepper
1 tsp. salt

1. Combine all ingredients
in slow cooker.
2. Cover. Cook on Low 8
hours.
3. Stir chicken until it
shreds.
4. Pile into steak rolls and
serve.

# Chicken Reuben Bake

**Gail Bush**
Landenberg, PA

*Makes 4 servings*

4 boneless, skinless
chicken-breast halves
2-lb. bag sauerkraut,
drained and rinsed
4-5 slices Swiss cheese
1¼ cups Thousand Island
salad dressing
2 Tbsp. chopped fresh
parsley

1. Place chicken in slow
cooker. Layer sauerkraut over
chicken. Add cheese. Top
with salad dressing. Sprinkle
with parsley.
2. Cover. Cook on Low 6-8
hours.

# No-Fuss Turkey Breast

**Dorothy Miller**
Gulfport, MI

*Makes 3-4 pints cooked meat*

1 turkey breast
olive oil
1-2 Tbsp. water

1. Rub turkey breast with
oil. Place in slow cooker. Add
water.

2. Cover. Cook on High 1
hour, or Low 4-5 hours.
3. Cool. Debone and cut
into bite-sized pieces and
store in pint-size plastic boxes
in freezer. Use when cooked
turkey or chicken is called
for.

# Turkey in a Pot

**Dorothy M. Pittman**
Pickens, SC

*Makes 10-12 servings*

4-5 lb. turkey breast (if
frozen, it doesn't have to
be thawed)
1 medium onion, chopped
1 rib celery, chopped
¼ cup melted margarine
salt to taste
lemon-pepper seasoning to
taste
1½ cups chicken broth

1. Wash turkey breast. Pat
dry. Place in greased slow
cooker. Put onion and celery
in cavity.
2. Pour margarine over
turkey. Sprinkle with seasonings. Pour broth around
turkey.
3. Cover. Cook on High 6
hours. Let stand 10 minutes
before carving.

# Turkey Breast

**Barbara Katrine Rose**
Woodbridge, VA

*Makes 6-8 servings*

1 large boneless turkey
breast
¼ cup apple cider, *or* juice
1 tsp. salt
¼ tsp. pepper

1. Put turkey breast in
slow cooker. Drizzle apple
cider over turkey. Sprinkle on
both sides with salt and pepper.
2. Cover. Cook on High 3-4
hours.
3. Remove turkey breast.
Let stand for 15 minutes
before slicing.

# Onion Turkey Breast

**Mary Ann Wasick**
West Allis, WI

*Makes 6-8 servings*

4-6-lb. boneless, skinless
   turkey breast
1 tsp. garlic powder
1 envelope dry onion soup
   mix

1. Place turkey in slow
cooker. Sprinkle garlic powder and onion soup mix over
breast.
2. Cover. Cook on Low 8-
10 hours.

**Note:**
   Use au jus over rice or
pasta.

# Easy and Delicious Turkey Breast

**Gail Bush**
Landenberg, PA

*Makes 4-6 servings*

1 turkey breast
15-oz. can whole berry
   cranberry sauce
1 envelope dry onion soup
   mix
1/2 cup orange juice
1/2 tsp. salt
1/4 tsp. pepper

1. Place turkey in slow
cooker.
2. Combine remaining
ingredients. Pour over turkey.
3. Cover. Cook on Low 6-8
hours.

# Turkey Stew

**Ruth S. Weaver**
Reinholds, PA

*Makes 8 servings*

2 lbs. skinless turkey
   thighs
1 lb., *or* 5 large, carrots,
   sliced
2 medium onions, chopped
8 medium potatoes, cubed
4 ribs celery, chopped
3 garlic cloves, minced
1 tsp. salt
1/4 tsp. pepper
2 Tbsp. Worcestershire
   sauce
15-oz. can tomato sauce
2 bay leaves

1. Place turkey in large
slow cooker.
2. In separate bowl, mix
together carrots, onions, potatoes, celery, garlic, salt, pepper, Worcestershire sauce,
tomato sauce, and bay.
3. Pour over turkey. Cover.
Cook on Low 8-12 hours, or
High 6-8 hours. Remove bay
leaves before serving.

# Pheasant a la Elizabeth

**Elizabeth L. Richards**
Rapid City, SD

*Makes 4 servings*

6 pheasant breasts,
   deboned and cubed
3/4 cup teriyaki sauce
1/3-1/2 cup flour
1 1/2 tsp. garlic salt
pepper to taste
1/3 cup olive oil
1 large onion, sliced
12-oz. can beer
3/4 cup fresh mushrooms,
   sliced

1. Marinate pheasant in
teriyaki sauce for 2-4 hours.
2. Combine flour, garlic
salt, and pepper. Dredge
pheasant in flour. Brown in
olive oil in skillet. Add onion
and saute for 3 minutes, stirring frequently. Transfer to
slow cooker.
3. Add beer and mush-
rooms.
4. Cover. Cook on Low 6-8
hours.

**Variation:**
   Instead of pheasant, use
chicken.

# Pot-Roasted Rabbit

**Donna Treloar**
Gaston, IN

*Makes 4 servings*

2 onions, sliced
4-5-lb. roasting rabbit
salt to taste
pepper to taste
1 garlic clove, sliced
2 bay leaves
1 whole clove
1 cup hot water
2 Tbsp. soy sauce
2 Tbsp. flour
1/2 cup cold water

1. Place onion in bottom of slow cooker.
2. Rub rabbit with salt and pepper. Insert garlic in cavity. Place rabbit in slow cooker.
3. Add bay leaves, clove, hot water, and soy sauce.
4. Cover. Cook on Low 10-12 hours.
5. Remove rabbit and thicken gravy by stirring 2 Tbsp. flour blended into 1/2 cup water into simmering juices in cooker. Continue stirring until gravy thickens. Cut rabbit into serving-size pieces and serve with gravy.

# Baked Lamb Shanks

**Irma H. Schoen**
Windsor, CT

*Makes 4-6 servings*

1 medium onion, thinly sliced
2 small carrots, cut in thin strips
1 rib celery, chopped
3 lamb shanks, cracked
1-2 cloves garlic, split
1 1/2 tsp. salt
1/4 tsp. pepper
1 tsp. dried oregano
1 tsp. dried thyme
2 bay leaves, crumbled
1/2 cup dry white wine
8-oz. can tomato sauce

1. Place onions, carrots, and celery in slow cooker.
2. Rub lamb with garlic and season with salt and pepper. Add to slow cooker.
3. Mix remaining ingredients together in separate bowl and add to meat and vegetables.
4. Cover. Cook on Low 8-10 hours, or High 4-6 hours.

# Herb Potato-Fish Bake

**Barbara Sparks**
Glen Burnie, MD

*Makes 4 servings*

10 3/4-oz. can cream of celery soup
1/2 cup water
1-lb. perch fillet, fresh *or* thawed
2 cups cooked, diced potatoes, drained
1/4 cup grated Parmesan cheese
1 Tbsp. chopped parsley
1/2 tsp. salt
1/2 tsp. dried basil
1/4 tsp. dried oregano

1. Combine soup and water. Pour half in slow cooker. Spread fillet on top. Place potatoes on fillet. Pour remaining soup mix over top.
2. Combine cheese and herbs. Sprinkle over ingredients in slow cooker.
3. Cover. Cook on High 1-2 hours, being careful not to overcook fish.

If you have them available, use whole or leaf herbs and spices rather than crushed or ground ones.
**Barbara Sparks**
Glen Burnie, MD

# Shrimp Jambalaya

Karen Ashworth
Duenweg, MO

*Makes 6-8 servings*

2 Tbsp. margarine
2 medium onions, chopped
2 green bell peppers,
  chopped
3 ribs celery, chopped
1 cup chopped cooked
  ham
2 garlic cloves, chopped
1½ cups minute rice
1½ cups beef broth
28-oz. can chopped
  tomatoes
2 Tbsp. chopped parsley
1 tsp. dried basil
½ tsp. dried thyme
¼ tsp. pepper
⅛ tsp. cayenne pepper
1 lb. shelled, deveined,
  medium-size shrimp
1 Tbsp. chopped parsley
  for garnish

1. Melt margarine in slow cooker set on High. Add onions, peppers, celery, ham, and garlic. Cook 30 minutes.

2. Add rice. Cover and cook 15 minutes.

3. Add broth, tomatoes, 2 Tbsp. parsley, and remaining seasonings. Cover and cook on High 1 hour.

4. Add shrimp. Cook on High 30 minutes, or until liquid is absorbed.

5. Garnish with 1 Tbsp. parsley.

# Jambalaya

Doris M. Coyle-Zipp
South Ozone Park, NY

*Makes 5-6 servings*

3½-4-lb. roasting chicken,
  cut up
3 onions, diced
1 carrot, sliced
3-4 garlic cloves, minced
1 tsp. dried oregano
1 tsp. dried basil
1 tsp. salt
⅛ tsp. white pepper
14-oz. can crushed
  tomatoes
1 lb. shelled raw shrimp
2 cups cooked rice

1. Combine all ingredients except shrimp and rice in slow cooker.

2. Cover. Cook on Low 2-3½ hours, or until chicken is tender.

3. Add shrimp and rice.

4. Cover. Cook on High 15-20 minutes, or until shrimp are done.

# Shrimp Creole

Carol Findling
Princeton, IL

*Makes 8-10 servings*

½ cup butter
⅓ cup flour
1¾ cups sliced onions
1 cup diced green peppers
1 cup diced celery
1½ large carrots, shredded
2¾-lb. can tomatoes
¾ cup water
½ tsp. dried thyme
1 garlic clove, minced
pinch of rosemary
1 Tbsp. sugar
3 bay leaves
1 Tbsp. Worcestershire
  sauce
1 Tbsp. salt
⅛ tsp. dried oregano
2 lbs. shelled shrimp,
  deveined

1. Melt butter in skillet. Add flour and brown, stirring constantly. Add onions, green peppers, celery, and carrots. Cook 5-10 minutes. Transfer to slow cooker.

2. Add remaining ingredients, except shrimp, and stir well.

3. Cover. Cook on Low 6-8 hours.

4. Add shrimp during last hour.

5. Serve over rice.

# Seafood Gumbo

**Barbara Katrine Rose**
Woodbridge, VA

*Makes 10 servings*

1 lb. okra, sliced
2 Tbsp. butter, melted
¼ cup butter, melted
¼ cup flour
1 bunch green onions, sliced
½ cup chopped celery
2 garlic cloves, minced
16-oz. can tomatoes and juice
1 bay leaf
1 Tbsp. chopped fresh parsley
1 fresh thyme sprig
1½ tsp. salt
½-1 tsp. red pepper
3-5 cups water, depending upon the consistency you like
1 lb. peeled and deveined fresh shrimp
½ lb. fresh crabmeat

1. Saute okra in 2 Tbsp. butter until okra is lightly browned. Transfer to slow cooker.
2. Combine remaining butter and flour in skillet. Cook over medium heat, stirring constantly until roux is the color of chocolate, 20-25 minutes. Stir in green onions, celery, and garlic. Cook until vegetables are tender. Add to slow cooker. Gently stir in remaining ingredients.
3. Cover. Cook on High 3-4 hours.
4. Serve over rice.

# Seafood Medley

**Susan Alexander**
Baltimore, MD

*Makes 10-12 servings*

1 lb. shrimp, peeled and deveined
1 lb. crabmeat
1 lb. bay scallops
2 10¾-oz. cans cream of celery soup
2 soup cans milk
2 Tbsp. butter, melted
1 tsp. Old Bay seasoning
¼-½ tsp. salt
¼ tsp. pepper

1. Layer shrimp, crab, and scallops in slow cooker.
2. Combine soup and milk. Pour over seafood.
3. Mix together butter and spices and pour over top.
4. Cover. Cook on Low 3-4 hours.
5. Serve over rice or noodles.

# Salmon Cheese Casserole

**Wanda S. Curtin**
Bradenton, FL

*Makes 6 servings*

14¾-oz. can salmon with liquid
4-oz. can mushrooms, drained
1½ cups bread crumbs
2 eggs, beaten
1 cup grated cheese
1 Tbsp. lemon juice
1 Tbsp. minced onion

1. Flake fish in bowl, removing bones. Stir in remaining ingredients. Pour into lightly greased slow cooker.
2. Cover. Cook on Low 3-4 hours.

# Tuna Barbecue

**Esther Martin**
Ephrata, PA

*Makes 4 servings*

12-oz. can tuna, drained
2 cups tomato juice
1 medium green pepper,
  finely chopped
2 Tbsp. onion flakes
2 Tbsp. Worcestershire
  sauce
3 Tbsp. vinegar
2 Tbsp. sugar
1 Tbsp. prepared mustard
1 rib celery, chopped
dash chili powder
1/2 tsp. cinnamon
dash of hot sauce, optional

1. Combine all ingredients
in slow cooker.
2. Cover. Cook on Low 8-
10 hours, or High 4-5 hours.
If mixture becomes too dry
while cooking, add 1/2 cup
tomato juice.
3. Serve on buns.

# Tuna Salad Casserole

**Charlotte Fry**, St. Charles, MO
**Esther Becker,** Gordonville, PA

*Makes 4 servings*

2 7-oz. cans tuna
10 3/4-oz. can cream of
  celery soup
3 hard-boiled eggs,
  chopped
1/2 to 1 1/2 cups diced celery
1/2 cup diced onions
1/2 cup mayonnaise
1/4 tsp. ground pepper
1 1/2 cups crushed potato
  chips

1. Combine all ingredients
except 1/4 cup potato chips in
slow cooker. Top with
remaining chips.
2. Cover. Cook on Low 5-8
hours.

# Tuna Noodle Casserole

**Leona Miller**
Millersburg, OH

*Makes 6 servings*

2 6 1/2-oz. cans water-
  packed tuna, drained
2 10 1/2-oz. cans cream of
  mushroom soup
1 cup milk
2 Tbsp. dried parsley
10-oz. pkg. frozen mixed
  vegetables, thawed
10-oz. pkg. noodles, cooked
  and drained
1/2 cup toasted sliced
  almonds

1. Combine tuna, soup,
milk, parsley, and vegetables.
Fold in noodles. Pour into
greased slow cooker. Top with
almonds.
2. Cover. Cook on Low 7-9
hours, or High 3-4 hours.

If your recipe turns out to have too much liquid, remove
the cover and use the High setting for about 45 minutes.
**Esther Porter**
Minneapolis, MN

# Tempeh-Stuffed Peppers

**Sara Harter Fredette**
Williamsburg, MA

*Makes 4 servings*

4 oz. tempeh, cubed
1 garlic clove, minced
28-oz. can crushed
   tomatoes
2 tsp. soy sauce
1/4 cup chopped onions
1 1/2 cups cooked rice
1 1/2 cups shredded cheese
Tabasco sauce, optional
4 green, red, *or* yellow, bell
   peppers, tops removed
   and seeded
1/4 cup shredded cheese

1. Steam tempeh 10 minutes in saucepan. Mash in bowl with the garlic, half the tomatoes, and soy sauce.
2. Stir in onions, rice, 1 1/2 cups cheese, and Tabasco sauce. Stuff into peppers.
3. Place peppers in slow cooker, 3 on the bottom and one on top. Pour remaining half of tomatoes over peppers.
4. Cover. Cook on Low 6-8 hours, or High 3-4 hours. Top with remaining cheese in last 30 minutes.

# Tastes-Like-Chili-Rellenos

**Roseann Wilson**
Albuquerque, NM

*Makes 6 servings*

2 tsp. butter
2 4-oz. cans whole green
   chilies
1/2 lb. grated cheddar
   cheese
1/2 lb. grated Monterey Jack
   cheese
14 1/2-oz. can stewed
   tomatoes
4 eggs
2 Tbsp. flour
3/4 cup evaporated milk

1. Grease sides and bottom of slow cooker with butter.
2. Cut chilies into strips. Layer chilies and cheeses in slow cooker. Pour in stewed tomatoes.
3. Combine eggs, flour, and milk. Pour into slow cooker.
4. Cover. Cook on High 2-3 hours.

# Barbecued Lentils

**Sue Hamilton**
Minooka, IL

*Makes 8 servings*

2 cups barbecue sauce
3 1/2 cups water
1 lb. dry lentils
1 pkg. vegetarian hot dogs,
   sliced

1. Combine all ingredients in slow cooker.
2. Cover. Cook on Low 6-8 hours.

# Cheryl's Macaroni and Cheese

**Cheryl Bartel**
Hillsboro, KS

*Makes 6 servings*

8 oz. dry elbow macaroni, cooked
3-4 cups (about 3/4-lb.) shredded sharp cheddar cheese, divided
13-oz. can evaporated milk
1 1/2 cups milk
2 eggs
1 tsp. salt
1/4 tsp. black pepper
chopped onion to taste

1. Combine all ingredients, except 1 cup cheese, in greased slow cooker. Sprinkle reserved cup of cheese over top.
2. Cover. Cook on Low 3-4 hours. Do not remove the lid or stir until the mixture has finished cooking.

**Variation:**

For some extra zest, add 1/2 tsp. dry mustard when combining all ingredients. Add thin slices of cheese to top of cooker mixture.
**Dorothy M. Pittman**
Pickens, SC

# Macaroni and Cheese

**Martha Hershey**, Ronks, PA
**Marcia S. Myer**, Manheim, PA
**LeAnne Nolt**, Leola, PA
**Ellen Ranck**, Gap, PA
**Mary Sommerfeld**, Lancaster, PA
**Kathryn Yoder**, Minot, ND

*Makes 6 servings*

8-oz. pkg. dry macaroni, cooked
2 Tbsp. oil
13-oz. can evaporated milk (fat-free will work)
1 1/2 cups milk
1 tsp. salt
3 cups (about 1/2 lb.) shredded cheese: cheddar, American, Velveeta, *or* a combination
2-4 Tbsp. melted butter
2 Tbsp. onion, chopped fine
4 hot dogs, sliced, optional

1. In slow cooker, toss macaroni in oil. Stir in remaining ingredients except hot dogs.
2. Cover. Cook on Low 2-3 hours. Add hot dogs, if desired, and cook 1 hour longer.

**Variations:**

1. Use 3 cups evaporated milk, instead of 13-oz. evaporated milk and 1 1/2 cups milk.
2. Add more onion, up to 1/4 cup total.
3. Add 1/2 tsp. pepper
**Stacy Petersheim**
Mechanicsburg, PA
**Sara Wilson**, Blairstown, MO

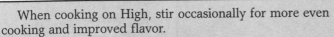

When cooking on High, stir occasionally for more even cooking and improved flavor.
**Roseann Wilson**
Albuquerque, NM

# Bean Main Dishes

## From-Scratch Baked Beans

**Wanda Roth**
Napoleon, OH

*Makes 6 servings*

2½ cups Great Northern dried beans
4 cups water
1½ cups tomato sauce
½ cup brown sugar
2 tsp. salt
1 small onion, chopped
½ tsp. chili powder

1. Wash and drain dry beans. Combine beans and water in slow cooker. Cook on Low 8 hours, or overnight.
2. Stir in remaining ingredients. Cook on Low 6 hours.

## New England Baked Beans

**Mary Wheatley**
Mashpee, MA
**Jean Butzer**
Batavia, NY

*Makes 8 servings*

1 lb. dried beans—Great Northern, pea beans, *or* navy beans
¼ lb. salt pork, sliced *or* diced
1 qt. water
1 tsp. salt
1-4 Tbsp. brown sugar, according to your preference
½ cup molasses
½-1 tsp. dry mustard, according to your preference
½ tsp. baking soda
1 onion, coarsely chopped
5 cups water

1. Wash beans and remove any stones or shriveled beans.
2. Meanwhile, simmer salt pork in 1 quart water in saucepan for 10 minutes. Drain. Do not reserve liquid.
3. Combine all ingredients in slow cooker.
4. Cook on High until contents come to boil. Turn to Low. Cook 14-16 hours, or until beans are tender.

**Variations:**
1. Add ½ tsp. pepper to Step 3.

**Rachel Kauffman**
Alton, MI

2. Add ¼ cup ketchup to Step 3.

**Cheri Jantzen**
Houston, TX

# Mom's New England Baked Beans

**Debbie Zeida**
Mashpee, MA

*Makes 6-8 servings*

3 cups dried navy beans
9 cups water
1 medium onion, chopped
1 cup ketchup
1 cup brown sugar
1 cup water
2 tsp. dry mustard
2 Tbsp. dark molasses
1 Tbsp. salt
1/4 lb. salt pork, ground *or* diced

1. Cook beans in water in soup pot until softened, or bring to boil, cover, and let stand for 1 1/2 hours. Drain. Pour beans into slow cooker.
2. Stir in remaining ingredients. Mix well.
3. Cover. Cook on Low 8 hours, or High 4 hours, stirring occasionally.

**Variation:**
Use 1 lb. dried Great Northern beans instead of 3 cups navy beans.
**Dorothy Miller**
Gulfport, MI

# Home-Baked Beans

**Carolyn Baer**
Conrath, WI

*Makes 15-25 servings*

2 lbs. (4 cups) dried navy, *or* pea, beans
1 lb. salt pork, *or* bacon, chopped
1 lb. (2 1/2 cups), *or less,* brown sugar
1-lb. 3-oz. can tomatoes
2 medium onions, chopped
2 Tbsp. prepared mustard
1/2 tsp. salt
1/2 tsp. pepper

1. Wash and pick over beans. Cover generously with water and soak overnight. Simmer in salted water until tender. Drain. Save liquid.
2. Place pork or bacon in bottom of slow cooker.
3. Mix together brown sugar, tomatoes, onions, mustard, salt, and pepper. Alternately layer sauce mixture and beans over pork.
4. Add enough reserved water to cover beans.
5. Cover. Cook on Low 8-10 hours, stirring occasionally.

**Note:**
These beans freeze well.

# Barbecued Lima Beans

**Hazel L. Propst**
Oxford, PA

*Makes 10 servings*

1 1/2 lbs. dried lima beans
6 cups water
2 1/4 cups chopped onions
1 1/4 cups brown sugar
1 1/2 cups ketchup
13 drops Tabasco sauce
1 cup dark corn syrup
1 Tbsp. salt
1/2 lb. bacon, diced

1. Soak washed beans in water overnight. Do not drain.
2. Add onion. Bring to boil. Simmer 30-60 minutes, or until beans are tender. Drain beans, reserving liquid.
3. Combine all ingredients except bean liquid in slow cooker. Mix well. Pour in enough liquid so that beans are barely covered.
4. Cover. Cook on Low 10 hours, or High 4-6 hours. Stir occasionally.

# Refried Beans with Bacon

**Arlene Wengerd**
Millersburg, OH

*Makes 8 servings*

2 cups dried red, *or* pinto, beans
6 cups water
2 garlic cloves, minced
1 large tomato, peeled, seeded, and chopped, *or* 1 pint tomato juice
1 tsp. salt
1/2 lb. bacon
shredded cheese

1. Combine beans, water, garlic, tomato, and salt in slow cooker.
2. Cover. Cook on High 5 hours, stirring occasionally. When the beans become soft, drain off some liquid.
3. While the beans cook, brown bacon in skillet. Drain, reserving drippings. Crumble bacon. Add half of bacon and 3 Tbsp. drippings to beans. Stir.
4. Mash or puree beans with a food processor. Fry the mashed bean mixture in the remaining bacon drippings. Add more salt to taste.
5. To serve, sprinkle the remaining bacon and shredded cheese on top of beans.

**Variations:**
1. Instead of draining off liquid, add 1/3 cup dry minute rice and continue cooking about 20 minutes. Add a dash of hot sauce and a dollop of sour cream to individual servings.
2. Instead of frying the mashed bean mixture, place several spoonfuls on flour tortillas, roll up, and serve.
**Susan McClure**
Dayton, VA

# Red Beans and Rice

**Margaret A. Moffitt**
Bartlett, TN

*Makes 8-10 servings*

1-lb. pkg. dried red beans
water
salt pork, ham hocks, *or* sausage, cut into small chunks
2 tsp. salt
1 tsp. pepper
3-4 cups water
6-oz. can tomato paste
8-oz. can tomato sauce
4 garlic cloves, minced

1. Soak beans for 8 hours. Drain. Discard soaking water.
2. Mix together all ingredients in slow cooker.
3. Cover. Cook on Low 10-12 hours, or until beans are soft. Serve over rice.

**Variation:**
Use canned red kidney beans. Cook 1 hour on High and then 3 hours on Low.

**Note:**
These beans freeze well.

# New Mexico Pinto Beans

**John D. Allen**
Rye, CO

*Makes 8-10 servings*

2 1/2 cups dried pinto beans
3 qts. water
1/2 cup ham, *or* salt pork, diced, *or* a small ham shank
2 garlic cloves, crushed
1 tsp. crushed red chili peppers, optional
salt to taste
pepper to taste

1. Sort beans. Discard pebbles, shriveled beans, and floaters. Wash beans under running water. Place in saucepan, cover with 3 quarts water, and soak overnight.
2. Drain beans and discard soaking water. Pour beans into slow cooker. Cover with fresh water.
3. Add meat, garlic, chili, salt, and pepper. Cook on Low 6-10 hours, or until beans are soft.

# Scandinavian Beans

**Virginia Bender**
Dover, DE

*Makes 8 servings*

1 lb. dried pinto beans
6 cups water
12 ozs. bacon, *or* 1 ham hock
1 onion, chopped
2-3 garlic cloves, minced
1/4 tsp. pepper
1 tsp. salt
1/4 cup molasses
1 cup ketchup
Tabasco to taste
1 tsp. Worcestershire sauce
3/4 cup brown sugar
1/2 cup cider vinegar
1/4 tsp. dry mustard

1. Soak beans in water in soup pot for 8 hours. Bring beans to boil and cook 1 1/2-2 hours, or until soft. Drain, reserving liquid.

2. Combine all ingredients in slow cooker, using just enough bean liquid to cover everything. Cook on Low 5-6 hours. If using ham hock, debone, cut ham into bite-sized pieces, and mix into beans.

# New Orleans Red Beans

**Cheri Jantzen**
Houston, TX

*Makes 6 servings*

2 cups dried kidney beans
5 cups water
2 Tbsp. bacon drippings
1/2 lb. hot sausage, cut in small pieces
2 onions, chopped
2 cloves garlic, minced
1 tsp. salt

1. Wash and sort beans. In saucepan, combine beans and water. Boil 2 minutes. Remove from heat. Soak 1 hour.

2. Heat bacon drippings in skillet. Add sausage and brown slowly. Add onions and garlic and saute until tender.

3. Combine all ingredients, including the bean water, in slow cooker.

4. Cover. Cook on Low 8-10 hours. During last 20 minutes of cooking, stir frequently and mash lightly with spoon.

5. Serve over hot cooked white rice.

# No Meat Baked Beans

**Esther Becker**
Gordonville, PA

*Makes 8-10 servings*

1 lb. dried navy beans
6 cups water
1 small onion, chopped
3/4 cup ketchup
3/4 cup brown sugar
3/4 cup water
1 tsp. dry mustard
2 Tbsp. dark molasses
1 tsp. salt

1. Soak beans in water overnight in large soup kettle. Cook beans in water until soft, about 1 1/2 hours. Drain, discarding bean water.

2. Mix together all ingredients in slow cooker. Mix well.

3. Cover. Cook on Low 10-12 hours.

## Hot Bean Dish Without Meat

**Jeannine Janzen**
Elbing, KS

*Makes 8-10 servings*

16-oz. can kidney beans,
  drained
15-oz. can lima beans,
  drained
1/4 cup vinegar
2 Tbsp. molasses
2 heaping Tbsp. brown
  sugar
2 Tbsp. minced onion
mustard to taste
Tabasco sauce to taste

1. Place beans in slow
cooker.
2. Combine remaining
ingredients. Pour over beans.
3. Cover. Cook on Low 3-4
hours.

**Variation:**
  Add 1 lb. browned ground
beef to make this a meaty
main dish.

## Barbecued Beans

**Jane Steiner**
Orrville, OH

*Makes 12-15 servings*

4 11-oz. cans pork and
  beans
3/4 cup brown sugar
1 tsp. dry mustard
1/2 cup ketchup
6 slices bacon, diced

1. Pour 2 cans pork and
beans into slow cooker.
2. Combine brown sugar
and mustard. Sprinkle half of
mixture over beans.
3. Cover with remaining
cans of pork and beans.
Sprinkle with rest of brown
sugar and mustard.
4. Layer bacon over top.
Spread ketchup over all.
5. Cut through bean mix-
ture a bit before heating.
6. Cover. Cook on Low 4
hours.

## Frances' Slow-Cooker Beans

**Frances B. Musser**
Newmanstown, PA

*Makes 6-8 servings*

1/2 cup ketchup
1 Tbsp. prepared mustard
1/2 cup brown sugar
1 small onion, chopped
1 tsp. salt
1/4 tsp. ground ginger
1/2 cup molasses
1 lb. turkey bacon,
  browned and crumbled
2-lb., 8-oz. can Great
  Northern beans, drained

1. Combine all ingredients
in slow cooker.
2. Cover. Cook on Low 4
hours.

If there is too much liquid in your cooker, stick a toothpick under the edge of the lid to tilt it slightly and to allow
the steam to escape.

**Carol Sherwood**
Batavia, NY

207

# Kelly's Baked Beans

**Kelly Bailey**
Mechanicsburg, PA

*Makes 6 servings*

40-oz. can Great Northern
  beans, juice reserved
15½-oz. can Great
  Northern beans, juice
  reserved
¾ cup brown sugar
¼ cup white corn syrup
½ cup ketchup
½ tsp. salt
half a medium-sized
  onion, chopped
8-9 slices bacon, browned
  and crumbled, optional

1. Drain beans overnight
in colander. Save ¼ cup liquid.
2. Mix together brown
sugar, corn syrup, and
ketchup. Mix well. Add salt
and onion.
3. Stir in beans and pour
into greased slow cooker. If
beans appear dry while cooking, add some of the ¼ cup
reserved bean juice.
4. Cover. Cook on Low 6-8
hours.

# Four Beans and Sausage

**Mary Seielstad**
Sparks, NV

*Makes 8 servings*

15-oz. can Great Northern
  beans, drained
15½-oz. can black beans,
  rinsed and drained
16-oz. can red kidney
  beans, drained
15-oz. can butter beans,
  drained
1½ cups ketchup
½ cup chopped onions
1 green pepper, chopped
1 lb. smoked sausage,
  cooked and cut into
  ½-inch slices
¼ cup brown sugar
2 garlic cloves, minced
1 tsp. Worcestershire sauce
½ tsp. dry mustard
½ tsp. Tabasco sauce

1. Combine all ingredients
in slow cooker.
2. Cover. Cook on Low 9-
10 hours, or High 4-5 hours.

# Mary Ellen's Three-Bean Dish

**Mary Ellen Musser**
Reinholds, PA

*Makes 10-20 servings*

10-oz. pkg. frozen lima
  beans, cooked
3 16-oz. cans baked beans
40-oz. can kidney beans,
  drained
1 lb. sausage links,
  browned and cut into
  pieces
½ lb. cooked ham, cubed
1 medium onion, chopped
8-oz. can tomato sauce
½ cup ketchup
¼ cup packed brown sugar
1 tsp. salt
½ tsp. pepper
½ tsp. prepared mustard

1. Combine lima beans,
baked beans, kidney beans,
sausage, and ham in 3½-4-
quart slow cooker.
2. In separate bowl, com-
bine onion, tomato sauce,
ketchup, brown sugar, salt,
pepper, and mustard and
pour into slow cooker. Mix
gently.
3. Cover. Cook on Low 4-6
hours.

# Sausage Bean Casserole

**Juanita Marner**
Shipshewana, IN

*Makes 8 servings*

1 lb. ground pork sausage
1/2 cup chopped onions
1/2 cup chopped green
  peppers
1 lb. cooked speckled
  butter beans
2 cups diced canned
  tomatoes
1/2 cup tomato sauce
1/4 tsp. salt
1/8 tsp. pepper

1. Brown sausage, onions, and green peppers in saucepan.
2. Combine all ingredients in slow cooker.
3. Cover. Cook on High 2 hours, or Low 4 hours.

# Cajun Sausage and Beans

**Melanie Thrower**
McPherson, KS

*Makes 4-6 servings*

1 lb. smoked sausage,
  sliced into 1/4-inch pieces
16-oz. can red beans
16-oz. can crushed
  tomatoes with green
  chilies
1 cup chopped celery
half an onion, chopped
2 Tbsp. Italian seasoning
Tabasco sauce to taste

1. Combine all ingredients in slow cooker.
2. Cover. Cook on Low 8 hours.
3. Serve over rice or as a thick zesty soup.

# Sausage Bean Quickie

**Ellen Ranck**
Gap, PA

*Makes 4 servings*

4-6 cooked brown 'n serve
  sausage links, cut into 1-
  inch pieces
2 tsp. cider vinegar
2 16-oz. cans red kidney *or*
  baked, beans, drained
7-oz. can pineapple
  chunks, undrained
2 tsp. brown sugar
3 Tbsp. flour

1. Combine sausage, vinegar, beans, and pineapple in slow cooker.
2. Combine brown sugar with flour. Add to slow cooker. Stir well.
3. Cover. Cook on Low 5-10 hours, or High 1-2 hours.

# Beans with Rice

**Miriam Christophel**
Battle Creek, MI

*Makes 8 servings*

3 cups dried small red
  beans
8 cups water
3 garlic cloves, minced
1 large onion, chopped
8 cups fresh water
1-2 ham hocks
1/2- 3/4 cup ketchup
2 tsp. salt
pinch of pepper
1 1/2-2 tsp. ground cumin
1 Tbsp. parsley
1-2 bay leaves

1. Soak beans overnight in
8 cups water. Drain. Place
soaked beans in slow cooker
with garlic, onion, 8 cups
fresh water, and ham hocks.
2. Cover. Cook on High 12-
14 hours.
3. Take ham hocks out of
cooker and allow to cool.
Remove meat from bones.
Cut up and return to slow
cooker. Add remaining ingredients.
4. Cover. Cook on High 2-3
hours.
5. Serve over rice with dollop of sour cream.

# Nan's Barbecued Beans

**Nan Decker**
Albuquerque, NM

*Makes 10-12 servings*

1 lb. ground beef
1 onion, chopped
5 cups canned baked
  beans
2 Tbsp. cider vinegar
1 Tbsp. Worcestershire
  sauce
2 Tbsp. brown sugar
1/2 cup ketchup

1. Brown ground beef and
onion in skillet. Drain.
2. Combine all ingredients
in slow cooker.
3. Cover. Cook on Low 4-6
hours.

# Betty's Calico Beans

**Betty Lahman**
Elkton, VA

*Makes 6-8 servings*

1 lb. ground beef, browned
  and drained
14 3/4-oz. can lima beans
15 1/2-oz. can pinto beans
15 1/4-oz. can corn
1/4 cup brown sugar
1 cup ketchup
1 Tbsp. vinegar
2 tsp. prepared mustard
1 medium onion, chopped

1. Combine all ingredients
in slow cooker.
2. Cover. Cook on High 3-4
hours.

# Three-Bean Barbecue

**Ruth Hofstetter**
Versailles, MO
**Kathryn Yoder**
Minot, ND

*Makes 6-8 servings*

1 1/2-2 lbs. ground beef
3/4 lb. bacon
1 cup chopped onions
2 31-oz. cans pork and
  beans
1-lb. can kidney beans,
  drained
1-lb. can lima beans,
  drained
1 cup ketchup
1/4 cup brown sugar
1 Tbsp. liquid smoke
3 Tbsp. white vinegar
1 tsp. salt
dash of pepper

1. Brown beef in
saucepan. Drain.
2. Fry bacon and onions in
saucepan. Drain.
3. Combine all ingredients
in slow cooker.
4. Cover. Cook on Low 4-6
hours.

**Note:**
  This is good served with
baked potatoes.

## Baked Beans in Slow Cooker

**Ruth Hershey**
Paradise, PA

*Makes 12 servings*

1½ lbs. ground beef
½-1 cup chopped onions,
  according to your
  preference
3 lbs. pork and beans
1-lb. can kidney beans,
  drained
1 cup ketchup
¼ cup brown sugar,
  packed
3 Tbsp. cider vinegar

1. Brown ground beef and onion in skillet. Drain.
2. Combine all ingredients in slow cooker. Mix well.
3. Cover. Cook on Low 4-6 hours. Stir occasionally.

## Roseann's Baked Beans

**Roseann Wilson**
Albuquerque, NM

*Makes 12 servings*

2 42-oz. cans baked beans,
  drained
l lb. ground beef, cooked
  and drained
½ cup barbecue sauce
¼ cup ketchup

1 Tbsp. prepared mustard
3 strips bacon, diced
¼ cup brown sugar
2 Tbsp. minced onion
3 strips bacon, cut in half

1. Combine all ingredients except half strips of bacon in slow cooker. Place 6 half-strips of bacon over top.
2. Cover. Cook on Low 3 hours.

## Carla's Baked Beans

**Carla Koslowsky**
Hillsboro, KS

*Makes 8-10 servings*

½ lb. ground beef
½ lb. bacon, chopped
1 medium onion, minced
1 tsp. salt
½ tsp. pepper
16-oz. can red kidney
  beans, drained
16-oz. can pork and beans,
  drained
15-oz. can butter, or green
  lima, beans
⅓ cup brown sugar
¼ cup sugar
¼ cup barbecue sauce
¼ cup ketchup
1 Tbsp. prepared mustard
2 Tbsp. molasses

1. Brown meats and onion in skillet. Drain.
2. Add salt, pepper, and beans. Stir in remaining ingredients. Mix well. Pour into slow cooker.

3. Cover. Cook on High 4-5 hours.

## Five-Bean Hot Dish

**Dede Peterson**
Rapid City, SD

*Makes 10 servings*

1 lb. ground beef
1 tsp. prepared mustard
2 tsp. vinegar
½ lb. bacon, finely diced
¾ cup brown sugar
15-oz. can lima beans,
  drained
1 tsp. salt
15-oz. can butter beans,
  drained
1 cup ketchup
16-oz. can kidney beans,
  drained
32-oz. can pork & beans,
  undrained
15-oz. can red beans,
  drained

1. Brown ground beef in deep saucepan. Drain.
2. Stir in mustard, vinegar, and bacon.
3. Add remaining ingredients. Mix well. Pour into large cooker.
4. Cover. Cook on Low 3-5 hours.

**Note:**
These beans freeze well.

# Char's Calico Beans
Char Hagner
Montague, MI

*Makes 10-12 servings*

¼ lb. bacon
1 onion, chopped
1 lb. ground beef
½ cup brown sugar
½ cup ketchup
1 Tbsp. prepared mustard
1 tsp. salt
2 15-oz. cans lima beans,
    drained
28-oz. can Boston baked
    beans
2 16-oz. cans kidney beans,
    drained

1. Cut bacon in pieces.
Brown in skillet and drain.
Brown onion with beef in
skillet. Drain.
2. Combine all ingredients
in slow cooker.
3. Cover. Cook on Low 6
hours.

# Casey's Beans
Cheryl Bartel
Hillsboro, KS

*Makes 10-12 servings*

½ lb. ground beef
10 slices bacon, diced
½ cup chopped onions
⅓ cup brown sugar
⅓ cup sugar, optional
¼ cup ketchup
¼ cup barbecue sauce
2 Tbsp. prepared mustard
2 Tbsp. molasses
½ tsp. salt
½ tsp. chili powder
½ tsp. pepper
1-lb. can kidney beans,
    drained
1-lb. can butter beans,
    drained
1-lb. can black beans,
    drained
1-lb. can pork and beans

1. Brown ground beef,
bacon, and onion in deep
saucepan. Drain.
2. Stir in remaining ingredients, except beans. Mix
well. Stir in beans. Pour into
slow cooker.
3. Cover. Cook on Low 5-6
hours.

# Hearty Slow-Cooker Beans
Kim McEuen
Lincoln University, PA

*Makes 10 servings*

1 lb. ground beef
½ lb. bacon, diced
1 onion, chopped
16-oz. can red kidney
    beans, drained
15-oz. can butter beans,
    drained
15-oz. can pork and beans
15-oz. can hot chili beans
½ cup brown sugar
½ cup sugar
1 Tbsp. prepared mustard
1 Tbsp. cider vinegar
½ cup ketchup

1. Brown beef, bacon, and
onion in skillet. Drain.
2. Combine all ingredients
in slow cooker. Mix well.
3. Cover. Cook on High 3
hours, or Low 5-6 hours.

# Allen's Beans

### John D. Allen
### Rye, CO

*Makes 10-12 servings*

1 large onion, chopped
1 lb. ground beef, browned
15-oz. can pork and beans
15-oz. can ranch-style
    beans, drained
16-oz. can kidney beans,
    drained
1 cup ketchup
1 tsp. salt
1 Tbsp. prepared mustard
2 Tbsp. brown sugar
2 Tbsp. hickory-flavored
    barbecue sauce
1/2-1 lb. small smoky link
    sausages, optional

1. Brown ground beef and onion in skillet. Drain. Transfer to slow cooker set on High.

2. Add remaining ingredients. Mix well.

3. Reduce heat to Low and cook 4-6 hours. Use a paper towel to absorb oil that's risen to the top before stirring and serving.

# Six-Bean Barbecued Beans

### Gladys Longacre
### Susquehanna, PA

*Makes 15-18 servings*

1-lb. can kidney beans,
    drained
1-lb. can pinto beans,
    drained
1-lb. can Great Northern
    beans, drained
1-lb. can butter beans,
    drained
1-lb. can navy beans,
    drained
1-lb. can pork and beans
1/4 cup barbecue sauce
1/4 cup prepared mustard
1/3 cup ketchup
1 small onion, chopped
1 small pepper, chopped
1/4 cup molasses, *or*
    sorghum molasses
1 cup brown sugar

1. Mix together all ingredients in slow cooker.

2. Cook on Low 4-6 hours.

# Four-Bean Medley

### Sharon Brubaker
### Myerstown, PA

*Makes 8 servings*

8 bacon slices, diced and
    browned until crisp
2 medium onions, chopped
3/4 cup brown sugar
1/2 cup vinegar
1 tsp. salt
1 tsp. dry mustard
1/2 tsp. garlic powder
16-oz. can baked beans,
    undrained
16-oz. can kidney beans,
    drained
15 1/2-oz. can butter beans,
    drained
14 1/2-oz. can green beans,
    drained
2 Tbsp. ketchup

1. Mix together all ingredients. Pour into slow cooker.

2. Cover. Cook on Low 6-8 hours.

**Variation:**

Make this a main dish by adding 1 lb. hamburger to the bacon, browning it along with the bacon and chopped onions in skillet, then adding that mixture to the rest of the ingredients before pouring into slow cooker.

---

I generally spray the inside of my slow cooker with non-stick cooking spray prior to putting my ingredients in. It helps with cleanup.

**Barb Yoder**
Angola, IN

## Lauren's Calico Beans

**Lauren Eberhard**
Seneca, IL

*Makes 12-16 servings*

8 slices bacon
1 cup chopped onions
1/2 cup brown sugar
1/2 cup ketchup
2 Tbsp. vinegar
1 tsp. dry mustard
14 1/2-oz. can green beans, drained
16-oz. can kidney beans, drained
15 1/2-oz. can butter beans, drained
15 1/2-oz. can pork and beans

1. Brown bacon in saucepan, reserving drippings. Crumble bacon. Cook onions in bacon drippings. Drain.
2. Combine all ingredients in slow cooker.
3. Cover. Cook on Low 6-8 hours.

## Sweet and Sour Beans

**Julette Leaman**
Harrisonburg, VA

*Makes 6-8 servings*

10 slices bacon
4 medium onions, cut in rings
1/2-1 cup brown sugar, according to your preference
1 tsp. dry mustard
1 tsp. salt
1/4 cup cider vinegar
1-lb. can green beans, drained
2 1-lb. cans butter beans, drained
1-lb., 11-oz. can pork and beans

1. Brown bacon in skillet and crumble. Drain all but 2 Tbsp. bacon drippings. Stir in onions, brown sugar, mustard, salt, and vinegar. Simmer 20 minutes.
2. Combine all ingredients in slow cooker.
3. Cover. Cook on Low 3 hours.

## Mixed Slow-Cooker Beans

**Carol Peachey**
Lancaster, PA

*Makes 6 servings*

16-oz. can kidney beans, drained
15 1/2-oz. can baked beans
1 pint home-frozen, *or* 1-lb. pkg. frozen, lima beans
1 pint home-frozen green beans, *or* 1-lb. pkg. frozen green beans
4 slices bacon, browned and crumbled
1/2 cup ketchup
1/2 cup sugar
1/2 cup brown sugar
2 Tbsp. vinegar
salt to taste

1. Combine beans and bacon in slow cooker.
2. Stir together remaining ingredients. Add to beans and mix well.
3. Cover. Cook on Low 8-10 hours.

# Lizzie's California Beans

**Lizzie Weaver**
Ephrata, PA

*Makes 12 servings*

2 medium onions, cut in rings
1 cup brown sugar
1 tsp. dry mustard
1 tsp. salt
1/4 cup vinegar
1/3 cup ketchup
1 lb. bacon, browned and crumbled
16-oz. can green beans, drained
40-oz. can butter beans, drained
2 16-oz. cans baked beans

1. In saucepan, mix together onions, brown sugar, dry mustard, salt, vinegar, and ketchup. Simmer in covered pan for 20 minutes. Add bacon and beans.
2. Pour into slow cooker. Cover. Cook on High 2 hours.

# Marcia's California Beans

**Marcia S. Myer**
Manheim, PA

*Makes 10-12 servings*

16-oz. can barbecue beans, *or* pork and beans
16-oz. can baked beans
16-oz. can kidney beans
14 1/2-oz. can green beans
15-oz. can lima beans
15 1/2-oz. can Great Northern beans
1 onion, chopped
1 tsp. prepared mustard
1 cup brown sugar
1 tsp. salt
1/4 cup vinegar
1/2 lb. bacon, browned until crisp and crumbled

1. Drain juice from beans. Combine beans in slow cooker.
2. In saucepan, combine onion, mustard, brown sugar, salt, vinegar, and bacon. Simmer for 10 minutes. Pour sauce over beans.
3. Cover. Cook on Low 3 hours.

# LeAnne's Calico Beans

**LeAnne Nolt**
Leola, PA

*Makes 10 servings*

1/4-1/2 lb. bacon
1 lb. ground beef
1 medium onion, chopped
2-lb. can pork and beans
1-lb. can Great Northern beans, drained
14 1/2-oz. can French-style green beans, drained
1/2 cup brown sugar
1/2 cup ketchup
1/2 tsp. salt
2 Tbsp. cider vinegar
1 Tbsp. prepared mustard

1. Brown bacon, ground beef, and onion in skillet until soft. Drain.
2. Combine all ingredients in slow cooker.
3. Cover. Cook on Low 5-6 hours, or on High 2-3 hours.

## Mixed Bean Casserole

**Margaret Rich**
North Newton, KS

*Makes 8 servings*

3 slices bacon, cut up
2 Tbsp. grated onion
31-oz. can pork and beans
    in tomato sauce
16-oz. can kidney beans,
    drained
15-oz. can lima beans, *or*
    butter beans, drained
3 Tbsp. brown sugar,
    packed
1/2 tsp. dry mustard
3 Tbsp. ketchup

1. Combine all ingredients in slow cooker.
2. Cover. Cook on Low 7-8 hours.

## LaVerne's Baked Beans

**LaVerne Olson**
Willow Street, PA

*Makes 16 servings*

1/2 lb. bacon
1 medium onion, chopped
1/2 cup molasses
1/2 cup brown sugar
1/2 tsp. dry mustard
40-oz. can butter beans,
    drained

2 16-oz. cans kidney beans,
    drained
40-oz. can Great Northern
    beans, drained

1. Brown bacon and onion in skillet until bacon is crisp and crumbly. Drain.
2. Combine all ingredients in slow cooker.
3. Cover. Cook on Low 1-3 hours.

## Joan's Calico Beans

**Joan Becker**
Dodge City, KS

*Makes 10-12 servings*

1/4-1/3 lb. bacon, diced
1/2 cup chopped onions
2 16-oz. cans pork and
    beans
15-oz. can butter beans,
    drained
16-oz. can kidney beans,
    drained
1/2 cup packed brown sugar
1/2 cup ketchup
1/2 tsp. salt
1 tsp. dry mustard

1. Brown bacon in skillet until crisp. Drain, reserving 2 Tbsp. drippings. Cook onion in drippings until tender. Add bacon and onion to slow cooker.
2. Stir in beans, brown sugar, ketchup, salt, and mustard. Mix well.
3. Cover. Cook on Low

41/2-51/2 hours, or on High 3-31/2 hours.

## Pat's Calico Baked Beans

**Pat Bishop**
Bedminster, PA

*Makes 10-12 servings*

2 cups green lima beans
2 cups limas, cooked
2 cups kidney beans
2 cups baked beans
6 slices bacon
11/2 cups onion, diced
3/4 cup brown sugar
2 tsp. salt
1 tsp. dry mustard
1 clove garlic, minced
1/2 cup vinegar
1/2 cup ketchup

1. Combine beans in slow cooker.
2. Brown bacon in skillet and crumble. Add to beans. Stir in onion.
3. Mix together brown sugar, salt, mustard, garlic, vinegar, and ketchup. Pour over beans. Mix well.
4. Cover. Cook on High 4 hours, or Low 6 hours.

**Variation:**
Add a chopped green pepper to the mixture in Step 2.
**Barbara Tenney**
Delta, PA

# Barbara's Calico Beans

**Barbara Kuhns**
Millersburg, OH

*Makes 12 servings*

1 lb. bacon, diced
1 onion, chopped
1/2 cup ketchup
1/3-1/2 cup brown sugar, according to taste
3 Tbsp. cider vinegar
28-oz. can pork and beans, drained
16-oz. can kidney beans, drained
16-oz. can butter beans, drained

1. Brown bacon in skillet. Drain, reserving 2 Tbsp. drippings. Saute onion in bacon drippings.
2. Mix together ketchup, sugar, and vinegar.
3. Combine all ingredients in slow cooker.
4. Cover Cook on Low 3-4 hours.

# Doris' Sweet-Sour Bean Trio

**Doris Bachman**
Putnam, IL

*Makes 6-8 large servings*

4 slices bacon
1 onion, chopped
1/4 cup brown sugar
1 tsp. crushed garlic
1 tsp. salt
3 Tbsp. cider vinegar
1 tsp. dry mustard
1-lb. can lima beans, drained
1-lb. can baked beans, drained
1-lb. can kidney beans, drained

1. Cook bacon in skillet. Reserve 2 Tbsp. bacon drippings. Crumble bacon.
2. In slow cooker, combine bacon, bacon drippings, onion, brown sugar, garlic, salt, and vinegar. Add beans. Mix well.
3. Cover. Cook on Low 6-8 hours.

# Carol's Calico Beans

**Carol Sommers**
Millersburg, OH

*Makes 10-12 servings*

1/2 lb. bacon, *or ground beef*
32-oz. can pork and beans
1-lb. can green limas, drained
16-oz. can kidney beans, drained
1-lb. can whole kernel corn, drained
1 tsp. prepared mustard
2 medium onions, chopped
3/4 cup brown sugar
1 cup ketchup

1. Brown bacon or ground beef in skillet. Drain and crumble.
2. Combine beans and meat in slow cooker.
3. Combine mustard, onions, brown sugar, and ketchup. Pour over beans. Mix well.
4. Cover. Cook on Low 4-6 hours.

# Ethel's Calico Beans

**Ethel Mumaw**
Berlin, OH

*Makes 6-8 servings*

1/2 lb. ground beef
1 onion, chopped
1/2 lb. bacon, diced
1/2 cup ketchup
2 Tbsp. cider vinegar
1/2 cup brown sugar,
    packed
16-oz. can red kidney
    beans, drained
14 1/2-oz. can pork and
    beans, undrained
15-oz. can butter beans,
    drained

1. Brown ground beef,
onion, and bacon in skillet.
Drain.
2. Combine all ingredients
in slow cooker.
3. Cover. Cook on Low 8
hours.

# Mary Ellen's and Nancy's Calico Beans

**Mary Ellen Wilcox**
Scotia, NY
**Nancy W. Huber**
Green Park, PA

*Makes 12-15 servings*

1/2 lb. bacon
1 lb. ground beef
2 15 1/2-oz. cans pork and
    beans
2 15 1/2-oz. cans butter
    beans, drained
2 16-oz. cans kidney beans,
    drained
1/2 cup sugar
1/2 cup brown sugar
1/4 cup ketchup
1 tsp. prepared mustard
1 tsp. garlic, finely
    chopped

1. Brown bacon in skillet
and then crumble. Drain
drippings. Add ground beef
and brown. Drain.
2. Combine all ingredients
in slow cooker.
3. Cover. Cook on Low 4-6
hours.

**Variation:**
Add 1 Tbsp. liquid smoke
in Step 2.
**Jan Pembleton**
Arlington, TX

# Sara's Bean Casserole

**Sara Harter Fredette**
Williamsburg, MA

*Makes 6 servings*

16-oz. can kidney beans,
    drained
2 1-lb. cans pork and
    beans
1 cup ketchup
1 Tbsp. Worcestershire
    sauce
1 tsp. salt
2 cups chopped onions
1 Tbsp. prepared mustard
1 tsp. cider vinegar

1. Combine all ingredients
in slow cooker.
2. Cover. Cook on High 2
hours, or Low 4 hours.

# Main Dish Baked Beans

**Sue Pennington**
Bridgewater, VA

*Makes 6-8 main-dish servings, or 12-16 side-dish servings*

1 lb. ground beef
28-oz. can baked beans
8-oz. can pineapple tidbits, drained
4½-oz. can sliced mushrooms, drained
1 large onion, chopped
1 large green pepper, chopped
½ cup barbecue sauce
2 Tbsp. soy sauce
1 clove garlic, minced
½ tsp. salt
¼ tsp. pepper

1. Brown ground beef in skillet. Drain. Place in slow cooker.
2. Stir in remaining ingredients. Mix well.
3. Cover. Cook on Low 4-8 hours, or until bubbly. Serve in soup bowls.

# Fruity Baked Bean Casserole

**Elaine Unruh**
Minneapolis, MN

*Makes 6-8 servings*

½ lb. bacon
3 medium onions, chopped
16-oz. can lima beans, drained
16-oz. can kidney beans, drained
2 16-oz. cans baked beans
15½-oz. can pineapple chunks
¼ cup brown sugar
¼ cup cider vinegar
¼ cup molasses
½ cup ketchup
2 Tbsp. prepared mustard
½ tsp. garlic salt
1 green pepper, chopped

1. Cook bacon in skillet. Crumble. Reserve 2 Tbsp. drippings in skillet. Place bacon in slow cooker.
2. Add onions to drippings and saute until soft. Drain. Add to bacon in slow cooker.
3. Add beans and pineapple to cooker. Mix well.
4. Combine brown sugar, vinegar, molasses, ketchup, mustard, garlic salt, and green pepper. Mix well. Stir into mixture in slow cooker.
5. Cover. Cook on High 2-3 hours.

# Apple Bean Bake

**Barbara A. Yoder**
Goshen, IN

*Makes 10-12 servings*

4 Tbsp. butter
2 large Granny Smith apples, cubed
½ cup brown sugar
¼ cup sugar
½ cup ketchup
1 tsp. cinnamon
1 Tbsp. molasses
1 tsp. salt
24-oz. can Great Northern beans, undrained
24-oz. can pinto beans, undrained
ham chunks, optional

1. Melt butter in skillet. Add apples and cook until tender.
2. Stir in brown sugar and sugar. Cook until they melt. Stir in ketchup, cinnamon, molasses, and salt.
3. Add beans and ham chunks. Mix well. Pour into slow cooker.
4. Cover. Cook on High 2-4 hours.

# Apple-Bean Pot

**Charlotte Bull**
Cassville, MO

*Makes 12 servings*

53-oz. can baked beans,
  well drained
1 large onion, chopped
3 tart apples, peeled and
  chopped
1/2 cup ketchup, *or*
  barbecue sauce
1/2 cup firmly packed
  brown sugar
1 pkg. smoky cocktail
  sausages, *or* chopped
  hot dogs, *or* chopped
  ham chunks, optional

1. Place beans in slow
cooker.
2. Add onions and apples.
Mix well.
3. Stir in ketchup or barbecue sauce, brown sugar, and
meat. Mix.
4. Cover. Heat on Low 3-4
hours, and then on High 30
minutes.

# Linda's Baked Beans

**Linda Sluiter**
Schererville, IN

*Makes 12 servings*

16-oz. can red kidney
  beans, drained
15 1/2-oz. can butter beans,
  drained
18-oz. jar B&M beans
1/4 lb. Velveeta cheese,
  cubed
1/2 lb. bacon, diced
1/2 cup brown sugar
1/3 cup sugar
2 dashes Worcestershire
  sauce

1. Combine all ingredients
in slow cooker.
2. Cover. Cook on Low 6
hours. Do not stir until nearly
finished cooking.

# Ann's Boston Baked Beans

**Ann Driscoll**
Albuquerque, MN

*Makes 20 servings*

1 cup raisins
2 small onions, diced
2 tart apples, diced
1 cup chili sauce
1 cup chopped ham, *or*
  crumbled bacon
2 1-lb., 15-oz. cans baked
  beans
3 tsp. dry mustard
1/2 cup sweet pickle relish

1. Mix together all ingredients.
2. Cover. Cook on Low 6-8
hours.

# Vegetables

## Very Special Spinach

Jeanette Oberholtzer
Manheim, PA

*Makes 8 servings*

3 10-oz. boxes frozen
  spinach, thawed and
  drained
2 cups cottage cheese
1½ cups grated cheddar
  cheese
3 eggs
¼ cup flour
1 tsp. salt
½ cup butter, *or*
  margarine, melted

1. Mix together all ingredients.
2. Pour into slow cooker.
3. Cook on High 1 hour.
Reduce heat to Low and cook
4 more hours.

## Spinach Casserole

Ann Bender
Ft. Defiance, VA

*Makes 6 servings*

2 10-oz. pkgs. frozen
  spinach, thawed and
  drained
2 cups white sauce, *or*
  cottage cheese
¼ cup butter, cubed
1¼ cups American cheese,
  cut into squares
2 eggs, beaten
¼ cup flour
1 tsp. salt
1 clove garlic, *or* ¼ tsp.
  garlic power

1. Combine all ingredients.
Mix well. Pour into greased
slow cooker.
2. Cover. Cook on High 1
hour. Reduce heat to Low
and cook 4-5 hours.

## Caramelized Onions

Mrs. J.E. Barthold
Bethlehem, PA

*Makes 6-8 servings*

6-8 large Vidalia *or* other
  sweet onions
4 Tbsp. butter, *or*
  margarine
10-oz. can chicken, *or*
  vegetable, broth

1. Peel onions. Remove
stems and root ends. Place in
slow cooker.
2. Pour butter and broth
over.
3. Cook on Low 12 hours.

**Note:**
Serve as a side dish, or use
onions and liquid to flavor
soups or stews, or as topping
for pizza.

# Barbecued Green Beans

**Arlene Wengerd**
Millersburg, OH

*Makes 4-6 servings*

1 lb. bacon
1/4 cup chopped onions
3/4 cup ketchup
1/2 cup brown sugar
3 tsp. Worcestershire sauce
3/4 tsp. salt
4 cups green beans

1. Brown bacon in skillet until crisp and then break into pieces. Reserve 2 Tbsp. bacon drippings.
2. Saute onions in bacon drippings.
3. Combine ketchup, brown sugar, Worcestershire sauce, and salt. Stir into bacon and onions.
4. Pour mixture over green beans and mix lightly.
5. Pour into slow cooker and cook on High 3-4 hours, or on Low 6-8 hours.

# Dutch Green Beans

**Edwina Stoltzfus**
Narvon, PA

*Makes 4-6 servings*

1/2 lb. bacon, *or* ham chunks
4 medium onions, sliced
2 qts. fresh, frozen, *or* canned, green beans
4 cups canned stewed tomatoes, *or* diced fresh tomatoes
1/2 -3/4 tsp. salt
1/4 tsp. pepper

1. Brown bacon until crisp in skillet. Drain, reserving 2 Tbsp. drippings. Crumble bacon into small pieces.
2. Saute onions in bacon drippings.
3. Combine all ingredients in slow cooker.
4. Cover. Cook on Low 4 1/2 hours.

# Orange Glazed Carrots

**Cyndie Marrara**
Port Matilda, PA

*Makes 6 servings*

32-oz. (2 lbs.) pkg. baby carrots
1/2 cup packed brown sugar
1/2 cup orange juice
3 Tbsp. butter, *or* margarine
3/4 tsp. cinnamon
1/4 tsp. nutmeg
2 Tbsp. cornstarch
1/4 cup water

1. Combine all ingredients except cornstarch and water in slow cooker.
2. Cover. Cook on Low 3-4 hours until carrots are tender crisp.
3. Put carrots in serving dish and keep warm, reserving cooking juices. Put reserved juices in small saucepan. Bring to boil.
4. Mix cornstarch and water in small bowl until blended. Add to juices. Boil one minute or until thickened, stirring constantly.
5. Pour over carrots and serve.

Vegetables do not overcook as they do when boiled on your range. Therefore, everything can go into the cooker at one time, with the exception of milk, sour cream, and cream, which should be added during the last hour.
**Darlene Raber**
Wellman, IA

# Glazed Root Vegetable Medley

**Teena Wagner**
Waterloo, ON

*Makes 6 servings*

**2 medium parsnips**
**4 medium carrots**
**1 turnip, about 4½ inches around**
**½ cup water**
**1 tsp. salt**
**½ cup sugar**
**3 Tbsp. butter**
**½ tsp. salt**

1. Clean and peel vegetables. Cut in 1-inch pieces.
2. Dissolve salt in water in saucepan. Add vegetables and boil for 10 minutes. Drain, reserving ½ cup liquid.
3. Place vegetables in slow cooker. Add liquid.
4. Stir in sugar, butter, and salt.
5. Cover. Cook on Low 3 hours.

# Acorn Squash

**Valerie Hertzler**
Weyers Cave, VA

*Makes 2 servings*

**1 acorn squash**
**salt**
**cinnamon**
**butter**

1. Place whole, rinsed squash in slow cooker.
2. Cover. Cook on Low 8-10 hours.
3. Split and remove seeds. Sprinkle each half with salt and cinnamon, dot with butter, and serve.

# Zucchini Special

**Louise Stackhouse**
Benten, PA

*Makes 4 servings*

**1 medium to large zucchini, peeled and sliced**
**1 medium onion, sliced**
**1 qt. stewed tomatoes with juice, *or* 2 14½-oz. cans stewed tomatoes with juice**
**¼ tsp. salt**
**1 tsp. dried basil**
**8 oz. mozzarella cheese, shredded**

1. Layer zucchini, onion, and tomatoes in slow cooker.
2. Sprinkle with salt, basil, and cheese.
3. Cover. Cook on Low 6-8 hours.

# Squash Casserole

**Sharon Anders**
Alburtis, PA

*Makes 4-6 servings*

**2 lbs. yellow summer squash, *or* zucchini, thinly sliced (about 6 cups)**
**half a medium onion, chopped**
**1 cup peeled, shredded carrot**
**10¾-oz. can condensed cream of chicken soup**
**1 cup sour cream**
**¼ cup flour**
**8-oz. pkg. seasoned stuffing crumbs**
**½ cup butter, *or* margarine, melted**

1. Combine squash, onion, carrots, and soup.
2. Mix together sour cream and flour. Stir into vegetables.
3. Toss stuffing mix with butter. Spread half in bottom of slow cooker. Add vegetable mixture. Top with remaining crumbs.
4. Cover. Cook on Low 7-9 hours.

## Doris' Broccoli and Cauliflower with Cheese

Doris G. Herr
Manheim, PA

*Makes 8 servings*

1 lb. frozen cauliflower
2 10-oz. pkgs. frozen
  broccoli
1/2 cup water
2 cups shredded cheddar
  cheese

1. Place cauliflower and broccoli in slow cooker.
2. Add water. Top with cheese.
3. Cook on Low 1 1/2-3 hours, depending upon how crunchy or soft you want the vegetables.

## Julia's Broccoli and Cauliflower with Cheese

Julia Lapp
New Holland, PA

*Makes 6 servings*

5 cups raw broccoli and
  cauliflower
1/4 cup water
2 Tbsp. butter, *or* margarine
2 Tbsp. flour
1/2 tsp. salt
1 cup milk

1 cup shredded cheddar
cheese

1. Cook broccoli and cauliflower in saucepan in water, until just crispy tender. Set aside.
2. Make white sauce by melting the butter in another pan over low heat. Blend in flour and salt. Add milk all at once. Cook quickly, stirring constantly until mixture thickens and bubbles. Add cheese. Stir until melted and smooth.
3. Combine vegetables and sauce in slow cooker. Mix well.
4. Cook on Low 1 1/2 hours.

**Variation:**
Substitute green beans and carrots or other vegetables for broccoli and cauliflower.

## Golden Cauliflower

Carol Peachey
Lancaster, PA

*Makes 4-6 servings*

2 10-oz. pkgs. frozen
  cauliflower, thawed
8-oz. jar cheese sauce
4 slices bacon, crisply
  browned and crumbled

1. Place cauliflower in slow cooker
2. Pour cheese over top. Top with bacon.
3. Cover. Cook on High 1 1/2 hours and then reduce to Low for an additional 2 hours. Or cook only on Low 4-5 hours.

## Broccoli Cheese Casserole

Janie Steele
Moore, OK

*Makes 8-10 servings*

10-oz. pkg. frozen chopped
  broccoli, thawed
1 cup cooked rice
1/4 cup chopped celery
10 3/4-oz. can cream of
  chicken soup
4-oz. jar cheese sauce
4-oz. can mushrooms,
  optional
1/8 tsp. garlic powder
1/8 tsp. pepper
1/4-1/2 tsp. salt

1. Mix together all ingredients in slow cooker.
2. Cook on Low 1 1/2 hours, or until heated through.

## Sweet-Sour Cabbage

Irma H. Schoen
Windsor, CT

*Makes 6 servings*

1 medium-sized head red,
  *or* green, cabbage,
  shredded
2 onions, chopped
4 tart apples, pared,
  quartered
1/2 cup raisins
1/4 cup lemon juice

¼ cup cider, *or* apple juice
3 Tbsp. honey
1 Tbsp. caraway seeds
⅛ tsp. allspice
½ tsp. salt

1. Combine all ingredients in slow cooker.
2. Cook on High 3-5 hours, depending upon how crunchy or soft you want the cabbage and onions.

# Bavarian Cabbage

Joyce Shackelford
Green Bay, WI

*Makes 4-8 servings, depending upon the size of the cabbage head*

1 small head red cabbage, sliced
1 medium onion, chopped
3 tart apples, cored and quartered
2 tsp. salt
1 cup hot water
2 Tbsp. sugar
⅓ cup vinegar
3 Tbsp. bacon drippings

1. Place all ingredients in slow cooker in order listed.
2. Cover. Cook on Low 8 hours, or High 3 hours. Stir well before serving.

**Variation:**
Add 6 slices bacon, browned until crisp and crumbled.

**Jean M. Butzer**
Batavia, NY

# Cabbage Casserole

Edwina Stoltzfus
Narvon, PA

*Makes 6 servings*

1 large head cabbage, chopped
2 cups water
1 Tbsp. salt
⅓ cup butter
¼ cup flour
½-1 tsp. salt
¼ tsp. pepper
1⅓ cups milk
1⅓ cups shredded cheddar cheese

1. Cook cabbage in saucepan in boiling water and salt for 5 minutes. Drain. Place in slow cooker.
2. In saucepan, melt butter. Stir in flour, salt, and pepper. Add milk, stirring constantly on low heat for 5 minutes. Remove from heat. Stir in cheese. Pour over cabbage.
3. Cover. Cook on Low 4-5 hours.

**Variation:**
Replace cabbage with cauliflower.

# Vegetable Curry

Sheryl Shenk
Harrisonburg, VA

*Makes 8-10 servings*

16-oz. pkg. baby carrots
3 medium potatoes, cubed
1 lb. fresh, *or* frozen, green beans, cut in 2-inch pieces
1 green pepper, chopped
1 onion, chopped
1-2 cloves garlic, minced
15-oz. can garbanzo beans, drained
28-oz. can crushed tomatoes
3 Tbsp. minute tapioca
3 tsp. curry powder
2 tsp. salt
1¾ cups boiling water
2 tsp. chicken bouillon granules, *or* 2 chicken bouillon cubes

1. Combine carrots, potatoes, green beans, pepper, onion, garlic, garbanzo beans, and crushed tomatoes in large bowl.
2. Stir in tapioca, curry powder, and salt.
3. Dissolve bouillon in boiling water. Pour over vegetables. Mix well. Spoon into large cooker, or two medium-sized ones.
4. Cover. Cook on Low 8-10 hours, or High 3-4 hours. Serve with cooked rice.

**Variation:**
Substitute canned green beans for fresh beans but add toward the end of the cooking time.

# Wild Mushrooms Italian

**Connie Johnson**
Loudon, NH

*Makes 4-5 servings*

2 large onions, chopped
3 large red bell peppers, chopped
3 large green bell peppers, chopped
2-3 Tbsp. oil
12-oz. pkg. oyster mushrooms, cleaned and chopped
4 garlic cloves, minced
3 fresh bay leaves
10 fresh basil leaves, chopped
1 Tbsp. salt
1½ tsp. pepper
28-oz. can Italian plum tomatoes, crushed *or* chopped

1. Saute onions and peppers in oil in skillet until soft. Stir in mushrooms and garlic. Saute just until mushrooms begin to turn brown. Pour into slow cooker.
2. Add remaining ingredients. Stir well.
3. Cover. Cook on Low 6-8 hours.

**Note:**
Good as an appetizer or on pita bread, or serve over rice or pasta for main dish.

# Corn Pudding

**Barbara A. Yoder**
Goshen, IN

*Makes 10 plus servings*

2 10-oz. cans whole kernel corn with juice
2 1-lb. cans creamed corn
2 boxes corn muffin mix
1 stick (¼ lb.) margarine
8-oz. box sour cream

1. Combine all ingredients in slow cooker.
2. Cover. Heat on Low 2-3 hours until thickened and set.

# Corn on the Cob

**Donna Conto**
Saylorsburg, PA

*Makes 3-4 servings*

6-8 ears of corn (in husk)
½ cup water

1. Remove silk from corn, as much as possible, but leave husks on.
2. Cut off ends of corn so ears can stand in the cooker.

3. Add water.
4. Cover. Cook on Low 2-3 hours.

# Cheesy Corn

**Tina Snyder**
Manheim, PA
**Jeannine Janzen**
Elbing, KS
**Nadine Martinitz**
Salina, KS

*Makes 10 servings*

3 16-oz. pkgs. frozen corn
8-oz. pkg. cream cheese, cubed
¼ cup butter, cubed
3 Tbsp. water
3 Tbsp. milk
2 Tbsp. sugar
6 slices American cheese, cut into squares

1. Combine all ingredients in slow cooker. Mix well.
2. Cover. Cook on Low 4 hours, or until heated through and the cheese is melted.

Be careful about adding liquids to food in a slow cooker. Foods have natural juices in them, and unlike oven cooking which is dry, food juices remain in the slow cooker as the food cooks.

**Ann Sunday McDowell**
Newtown, PA

# Slow-Cooker Rice

**Dorothy Horst**
Tiskilwa, IL

*Makes 10 servings*

1 Tbsp. butter
4 cups converted long
 grain rice, uncooked
10 cups water
4 tsp. salt

1. Pour rice, water, and salt into greased slow cooker.
2. Cover. Cook on High 2-3 hours, or until rice is tender, but not overcooked. Stir occasionally.

# Risi Bisi
# (Peas and Rice)

**Cyndie Marrara**
Port Matilda, PA

*Makes 6 servings*

1 1/2 cups converted long
 grain white rice,
 uncooked
3/4 cup chopped onions
2 garlic cloves, minced
2 14 1/2-oz. cans reduced-
 sodium chicken broth
1/3 cup water
3/4 tsp. Italian seasoning
1/2 tsp. dried basil leaves
1/2 cup frozen baby peas,
 thawed
1/4 cup grated Parmesan
 cheese

1. Combine rice, onions, and garlic in slow cooker.
2. In saucepan, mix together chicken broth and water. Bring to boil. Add Italian seasoning and basil leaves. Stir into rice mixture.
3. Cover. Cook on Low 2-3 hours, or until liquid is absorbed.
4. Stir in peas. Cover. Cook 30 minutes. Stir in cheese.

# Green Rice
# Casserole

**Ruth Hofstetter**
Versailles, Missouri

*Makes 6 servings*

1 1/3 cups evaporated milk
2 Tbsp. vegetable oil
3 eggs
one-fourth of a small
 onion, minced
half a small carrot,
 minced, optional
2 cups minced fresh
 parsley, *or* 10-oz. pkg.
 frozen chopped spinach,
 thawed and drained
2 tsp. salt
1/4 tsp. pepper
1 cup shredded sharp
 cheese
3 cups cooked long grain
 rice

1. Beat together milk, oil, and eggs until well combined.
2. Stir in remaining ingredients. Mix well. Pour into greased slow cooker.

3. Cover. Cook on High 1 hour. Stir. Reduce heat to Low and cook 4-6 hours.

# Wild Rice

**Ruth S. Weaver**
Reinholds, PA

*Makes 4-5 servings*

1 cup wild rice, *or* wild
 rice mixture, uncooked
1/2 cup sliced mushrooms
1/2 cup diced onions
1/2 cup diced green, *or* red,
 peppers
1 Tbsp. oil
1/2 tsp. salt
1/4 tsp. pepper
2 1/2 cups chicken broth

1. Layer rice and vegetables in slow cooker. Pour oil, salt, and pepper over vegetables. Stir.
2. Heat chicken broth. Pour over ingredients in slow cooker.
3. Cover. Cook on High 2 1/2-3 hours, or until rice is soft and liquid is absorbed.

# Baked Potatoes

**Lucille Metzler,** Wellsboro, PA
**Elizabeth Yutzy,** Wauseon, OH
**Glenda S. Weaver,** Manheim, PA
**Mary Jane Musser,** Manheim, PA
**Esther Becker,** Gordonville, PA

*Makes 6 servings*

6 medium baking potatoes
butter, *or* margarine

1. Prick potatoes with fork. Rub each with either butter or margarine. Place in slow cooker.
2. Cover. Cook on High 3-5 hours, or Low 6-10 hours.

# Baked Potatoes

**Valerie Hertzler**
Weyers Cave, VA
**Carol Peachey,** Lancaster, PA
**Janet L. Roggie,** Lowville, NY

Potatoes

1. Prick potatoes with fork and wrap in foil.
2. Cover. Do not add water. Cook on High 2½-4 hours, or Low 8-10 hours.

# Pizza Potatoes

**Margaret Wenger Johnson**
Keezletown, VA

*Makes 4-6 servings*

6 medium potatoes, sliced
1 large onion, thinly sliced
2 Tbsp. olive oil
2 cups grated mozzarella cheese
2 oz. sliced pepperoni
1 tsp. salt
8-oz. can pizza sauce

1. Saute potato and onion slices in oil in skillet until onions appear transparent. Drain well.
2. In slow cooker, combine potatoes, onions, cheese, pepperoni, and salt.
3. Pour pizza sauce over top.
4. Cover. Cook on Low 6-10 hours, or until potatoes are soft.

# Mustard Potatoes

**Frances B. Musser**
Newmanstown, PA
**Nancy Zimmerman**
Loysville, PA

*Makes 6 servings*

6 medium potatoes, peeled, cooked, cooled, and grated
½ cup chopped onions
¼ cup butter
1½ tsp. prepared mustard
1 tsp. salt
¼ tsp. pepper
½ cup milk
¼ lb. American, *or* cheddar, cheese

1. Put potatoes in greased slow cooker.
2. Saute onion in butter in skillet. Add mustard, salt, pepper, milk, and cheese. Pour over potatoes.
3. Cover. Cook on Low 3 hours. Stir or toss lightly when ready to serve.

Cut up vegetables for your slow-cooker dish the night before and place them in ziplock bags in the refrigerator. This cuts down on preparation time in the morning.
**Tracy Supcoe**
Barclay, MD

# Potatoes O'Brien

**Rebecca Meyerkorth**
Wamego, KS

*Makes 6 servings*

32-oz. pkg. shredded
  potatoes
1/4 cup chopped onions
1/4 cup chopped green
  peppers
2 Tbsp. chopped pimento,
  optional
1 cup chopped ham,
  optional
3/4 tsp. salt
1/4 tsp. pepper
3 Tbsp. butter
3 Tbsp. flour
1/2 cup milk
10 3/4-oz. can cream of
  mushroom soup
1 cup shredded cheddar
  cheese, divided

1. Place potatoes, onions, green peppers, pimento, and ham in slow cooker. Sprinkle with salt and pepper.
2. Melt butter in saucepan. Stir in flour; then add half of milk. Stir rapidly to remove all lumps. Stir in remaining milk. Stir in mushroom soup and 1/2 cup cheese. Pour over potatoes.
3. Cover. Cook on Low 4-5 hours. Sprinkle remaining cheese on top about 1/2 hour before serving.

# Potluck Potatoes

**Lovina Baer**
Conrath, WI

*Makes 6-8 servings*

4 cups potatoes, cooked,
  peeled, diced
10 3/4-oz. can cream of
  chicken soup
1 cup sour cream
1 cup shredded cheddar
  cheese
1/3 cup butter, *or*
  margarine, melted
1/4 cup chopped onions
1/2 tsp. garlic salt
1/2 tsp. salt
1/2 tsp. pepper

1. Combine all ingredients in slow cooker. Mix well.
2. Cover. Cook on Low 3-4 hours.

**Variations:**

1. If you prefer soft onions, saute in skillet in butter or margarine before combining with other ingredients.
    **Tracey Yohn**
    Harrisburg, PA

2. Add chopped ham or dried beef.

# German Potato Salad

**Lauren Eberhard**
Seneca, IL

*Makes 8 servings*

6 slices bacon
3/4 cup chopped onions
10 3/4-oz. can cream of
  chicken soup
1/4 cup water
2 Tbsp. cider vinegar
1/2 tsp. sugar
pepper to taste
4 cups parboiled, cubed
  potatoes
parsley

1. Brown bacon in skillet and then crumble. Reserve 2 Tbsp. bacon drippings. Saute onions in drippings.
2. Blend together soup, water, vinegar, sugar, and pepper. Add bacon and onions. Mix well.
3. Add potatoes and parsley. Mix well. Pour into slow cooker.
4. Cover. Cook on Low 4 hours.
5. Serve warm or at room temperature.

# Slow-Cooker Scalloped Potatoes

**Ruth S. Weaver**
Reinholds, PA

*Makes 10 servings*

1/2 tsp. cream of tartar
1 cup water
8-10 medium potatoes,
    thinly sliced
half an onion, chopped
salt to taste
pepper to taste
1 cup grated American, *or*
    cheddar, cheese
10¾-oz. can cream of
    celery, *or* mushroom, *or*
    chicken, soup
1 tsp. paprika

1. Dissolve cream of tartar
in water. Add potatoes and
toss together. Drain.
2. Place half of potatoes in
slow cooker. Sprinkle with
onions, salt, pepper, and half
of cheese.
3. Repeat with remaining
potatoes and cheese.
4. Spoon soup over the
top. Sprinkle with paprika.
5. Cover. Cook on Low 8-
10 hours, or High 4 hours.

**Variations:**
1. For thicker scalloped
potatoes, sprinkle each layer of
potatoes with 2 Tbsp. flour.
**Ruth Hershey**
Paradise, PA

2. Instead of sprinkling the
layers of potatoes with grated
cheese, place 1/4 lb. Velveeta,

or American cheese slices
over top during last 30 min-
utes of cooking.
**Pat Bishop**
Bedminster, PA
**Mary Ellen Musser**
Reinholds, PA
**Annabelle Unternahrer**
Shipshewana, IN

# Saucy Scalloped Potatoes

**Sue Pennington**
Bridgewater, VA

*Makes 4-6 servings*

4 cups peeled, thinly sliced
    potatoes
10¾-oz. can cream of
    celery, *or* mushroom,
    soup
12-oz. can evaporated milk
1 large onion, sliced
2 Tbsp. butter, *or*
    margarine
1/2 tsp. salt
1/4 tsp. pepper
1½ cups chopped, fully
    cooked ham

1. Combine potatoes, soup,
evaporated milk, onion, butter, salt, and pepper in slow
cooker. Mix well.
2. Cover. Cook on High 1
hour. Stir in ham. Reduce to

Low. Cook 6-8 hours, or until
potatoes are tender.

# Creamy Red Potatoes

**Mrs. J.E. Barthold**
Bethlehem, PA

*Makes 4-6 servings*

2 lbs. small red potatoes,
    quartered
8-oz. pkg. cream cheese,
    softened
10¾-oz. can cream of
    potato soup
1 envelope dry Ranch
    salad dressing mix

1. Place potatoes in slow
cooker.
2. Beat together cream
cheese, soup, and salad dressing mix. Stir into potatoes.
3. Cover. Cook on Low 8
hours, or until potatoes are
tender.

---

Be sure vegetables are thinly sliced or chopped because
they cook slowly in a slow cooker.
**Marilyn Yoder**
Archbold, OH

## Extra Good Mashed Potatoes

**Zona Mae Bontrager**
Kokomo, IN
**Mary Jane Musser**, Manheim, PA
**Elsie Schlabach**, Millersburg, OH
**Carol Sommers**, Millersburg, OH
**Edwina Stoltzfus**, Narvon, PA

*Makes 12 servings*

5 lbs. potatoes, peeled,
cooked, and mashed
8-oz. pkg. cream cheese,
softened
1½ cups sour cream
3 tsp. onion, *or* garlic, salt
1½ tsp. salt
¼-½ tsp. pepper
2 Tbsp. butter, melted

1. Combine all ingredients.
Pour into slow cooker.
2. Cover. Cook on Low 5-6
hours.

**Note:**

These potatoes may be
prepared 3-4 days in advance
of serving and kept in the
refrigerator until ready to
use.

**Variations:**

1. Add 1½ cups shredded
cheddar cheese to Step 1.
**Maricarol Magill**
Freehold, NJ

2. Sprinkle with paprika
before cooking.
**Pat Unternahrer**
Wayland, IA

## Potato Cheese Puff

**Mary Sommerfeld**
Lancaster, PA

*Makes 10 servings*

12 medium potatoes,
boiled and mashed
1 cup milk
6 Tbsp. butter
¾ tsp. salt
2¼ cups Velveeta cheese,
cubed
2 eggs, beaten

1. Combine all ingredients.
Pour into slow cooker.
2. Cover. Cook on High
2½ hours, or Low 3-4 hours.

## Creamy Hash Browns

**Judy Buller**, Bluffton, OH
**Elaine Patton**
West Middletown, PA
**Melissa Raber**, Millersburg, OH

*Makes 14 servings*

2-lb. pkg. frozen, cubed
hash brown potatoes
2 cups cubed *or* shredded
American cheese
1 pint (2 cups) sour cream
10¾-oz. can cream of
celery soup
10¾-oz. can cream of
chicken soup
½ lb. sliced bacon, cooked
and crumbled

1 medium onion, chopped
¼ cup margarine, melted
¼ tsp. pepper

1. Place potatoes in slow
cooker. Combine remaining
ingredients and pour over
potatoes. Mix well.
2. Cover. Cook on Low 4-5
hours, or until potatoes are
tender.

## Cheese and Potato Bake

**Ann Gouinlock**
Alexander, NY

*Makes 8 servings*

2-lb. bag frozen hash
browns
10¾-oz. can cheddar
cheese soup
10¾-oz. can cream of
chicken soup
1 cup milk
2.8-oz. can French-fried
onion rings
½ cup grated cheddar
cheese

1. Combine hash browns,
soups, and milk in slow
cooker. Mix well.
2. Top with half can of
onion rings.
3. Cover. Cook on Low 6-8
hours. Sprinkle with cheddar
cheese and remaining onion
rings about 1 hour before
serving.

## Cheesy Hash Brown Potatoes

**Clarice Williams**
Fairbank, IA

*Makes 6-8 servings*

2 10¾-oz. cans cheddar cheese soup
1⅓ cups buttermilk
2 Tbsp. butter, *or* margarine, melted
½ tsp. seasoned salt
¼ tsp. garlic powder
¼ tsp. pepper
2-lb. pkg. frozen, cubed hash brown potatoes
¼ cup grated Parmesan cheese
1 tsp. paprika

1. Combine soup, buttermilk, butter, seasoned salt, garlic powder, and pepper in slow cooker. Mix well.
2. Stir in hash browns. Sprinkle with Parmesan cheese and paprika.
3. Cover. Cook on Low 4-4½ hours, or until potatoes are tender.

## Slow-Cooker Cheese Potatoes

**Bernice M. Wagner**
Dodge City, KS
**Marilyn Yoder**
Archbold, OH

*Makes 6 servings*

2-lb. pkg. frozen hash browns
10¾-oz. can cream of potato soup
10¾-oz. can cream of mushroom soup
8 oz. (2 cups) shredded cheddar cheese
1 cup grated Parmesan cheese
1 pint sour cream

1. Mix together all ingredients in slow cooker.
2. Cover. Cook on Low 7 hours.

## Scalloped Taters

Sara Wilson
Blairstown, MD

*Makes 6-8 servings*

½ cup melted margarine
¼ cup dried onions
16-oz. pkg. frozen hash brown potatoes
10¾-oz. can cream of chicken soup
1½ cups milk
1 cup shredded cheddar cheese
⅛ tsp. black pepper
1 cup crushed cornflakes, divided

1. Stir together margarine, onions, potatoes, soup, milk, cheese, pepper, and ½ cup cornflakes. Pour into greased slow cooker. Top with remaining cornflakes.
2. Cover. Cook on High 3-4 hours.

To prevent potatoes from darkening, slice them, then stir a mixture of 1 cup water and ½ tsp. cream of tartar into them. Drain, then place potatoes in cooker and proceed with the recipe.

**Dale Peterson**
Rapid City, SD

## Slow-Cooker Cottage Potatoes

**Marjora Miller**
Archbold, OH

*Makes 10-12 servings*

2 lbs. frozen hash brown
potatoes
1 pint sour cream
10¾-oz. can cream of
chicken soup
dash of pepper
2 cups Velveeta cheese,
cubed
½ cup chopped onions
¾ tsp. salt
¼ tsp. pepper

1. Combine all ingredients
except potatoes in large bowl.
Then fold in potatoes. Spoon
into slow cooker.
2. Cover. Cook on High
1½ hours, and then on Low
2½ hours.

## Cheesy Potatoes

**Darla Sathre**
Baxter, MN

*Makes 6 servings*

2-lb. pkg. frozen hash
browns, partly thawed
2 10¾-oz.cans cheddar
cheese soup
12-oz. can evaporated milk
2.8-oz. can French-fried
onion rings
salt to taste
pepper to taste

1. Combine all ingredients.
Pour into greased slow
cooker.
2. Cover. Cook on Low 6-8
hours, or on High 3-4 hours.

## Slow-Cooker Potatoes

**Arlene Wiens**
Newton, KS

*Makes 8 servings*

32-oz. pkg. frozen hash
brown potatoes
2 10¾-oz. cans cheddar
cheese soup
2.8-oz. can French-fried
onion rings

1. Combine all ingredients
in greased slow cooker.
2. Cover. Cook on Low 7-8
hours.

## Au Gratin Hash Brown Potatoes

**Penny Blosser**
Beavercreek, OH

*Makes 12 servings*

2 lb.-pkg. frozen hash
brown potatoes, thawed
1 small onion, diced
1 stick butter, melted
16-oz. container French
onion dip
16-oz. jar Cheez Whiz,
heated

1. Place hash browns in
slow cooker.
2. Combine onion, butter,
dip, and Cheez Whiz. Pour
over hash browns. Mix well.
3. Cover. Cook on Low 4-6
hours, or High 2-3 hours.
(Use the greater number of
hours if potatoes are frozen.)

# Candied Sweet Potatoes
**Julie Weaver**
Reinholds, PA

*Makes 8 servings*

6-8 medium sweet potatoes
1/2 tsp. salt
1/4 cup butter, *or*
   margarine, melted
20-oz. can crushed
   pineapples, undrained
1/4 cup brown sugar
1 tsp. nutmeg
1 tsp. cinnamon

1. Cook sweet potatoes until soft. Peel. Slice and place in slow cooker.
2. Combine remaining ingredients. Pour over sweet potatoes.
3. Cover. Cook on High 4 hours.

# Potato Filling
**Miriam Nolt**
New Holland, PA

*Makes 16-20 servings*

1 cup celery, chopped fine
1 medium onion, minced
1 cup butter
2 15-oz. pkgs. bread cubes
6 eggs, beaten
1 qt. milk
1 qt. mashed potatoes
3 tsp. salt
2 pinches saffron
1 cup boiling water
1 tsp. pepper

1. Saute celery and onion in butter in skillet for about 15 minutes.
2. Combine sauted mixture with bread cubes. Stir in remaining ingredients. Add more milk if mixture isn't very moist.
3. Pour into large, or several medium-sized, slow cookers. Cook on High 3 hours, stirring up from bottom every hour or so to make sure the filling isn't sticking.

# Mild Dressing
**Jane Steiner**
Orrville, OH

*Makes 6 servings*

16-oz. loaf homemade
   white bread
2 eggs, beaten
1/2 cup celery
1/4 cup diced onions
3/4 tsp. salt
1/2 tsp. pepper
giblets, cooked and cut up
   fine
milk

1. Set bread slices out to dry the day before using. Cut into small cubes.
2. Combine all ingredients except milk.
3. Moisten mixture with enough milk to make bread cubes soft but not soggy.
4. Pour into greased slow cooker. Cook on Low 3 1/2 hours, stirring every hour. When stirring, add a small amount of milk to sides of cooker—if needed—to keep dressing moist and to prevent sticking.

---

It's quite convenient to use a slow cooker to cook potatoes for salads or for fried potatoes or as baked potatoes. Just fill the slow cooker with cleaned potatoes and cook all day until done.

**Darla Sathre**
Baxter, MN

# Slow Cooker Stuffing with Poultry

**Pat Unternahrer**
Wayland, IA

*Makes 18 servings*

1 large loaf dried bread, cubed
1½-2 cups chopped cooked turkey, *or* chicken, meat & giblets
1 large onion, chopped
3 ribs celery with leaves, chopped
½ cup butter, melted
4 cups chicken broth
1 Tbsp. poultry seasoning
1 tsp. salt
4 eggs, beaten
½ tsp. pepper

1. Mix together all ingredients. Pour into slow cooker.
2. Cover and cook on High 1 hour, then reduce to Low 6-8 hours.

# Moist Poultry Dressing

**Virginia Bender**, Dover, DE
**Josie Bollman**, Maumee, OH
**Sharon Brubaker**, Myerstown, PA
**Joette Droz**, Kalona, IA
**Jacqueline Stefl**, E. Bethany, NY

*Makes 14 servings*

2 4½-oz. cans sliced mushrooms, drained
4 celery ribs, chopped (about 2 cups)
2 medium onions, chopped
¼ cup minced fresh parsley
¼-¾ cup margarine (enough to flavor bread)
13 cups cubed day-old bread
1½ tsp. salt
1½ tsp. sage
1 tsp. poultry seasoning
1 tsp. dried thyme
½ tsp. pepper
2 eggs
1 *or* 2 14½-oz. cans chicken broth (enough to moisten bread)

1. In large skillet, saute mushrooms, celery, onions, and parsley in margarine until vegetables are tender.
2. Toss together bread cubes, salt, sage, poultry seasoning, thyme, and pepper. Add mushroom mixture.
3. Combine eggs and broth and add to bread mixture. Mix well.

4. Pour into greased slow cooker. Cook on Low 5 hours, or until meat thermometer reaches 160°.

**Note:**
This is a good way to free up the oven when you're making a turkey.

**Variations:**
1. Use 2 bags bread cubes for stuffing. Make one mixed bread (white and wheat) and the other corn bread cubes.
2. Add ½ tsp. dried marjoram to Step 2.
**Arlene Miller**
Hutchinson, KS

# Fresh Herb Stuffing

Barbara J. Fabel
Wausau, WI

*Makes 6-8 servings*

1/2 cup butter
2 onions, chopped
3 celery ribs, chopped
1/2 cup chopped fresh
   parsley
1 Tbsp. chopped fresh
   rosemary
1 Tbsp. chopped fresh
   thyme
1 Tbsp. chopped fresh
   marjoram
1 Tbsp. chopped fresh sage
1 tsp. salt
1/2 tsp. freshly ground
   pepper
1 loaf stale sourdough
   bread, cut in 1-inch
   cubes
1 1/2-2 cups chicken broth

1. Saute onions and celery
in butter in skillet for 10 minutes. Remove from heat and
stir in fresh herbs and seasonings.

2. Place bread cubes in
large bowl. Add onion/herb
mixture. Add enough broth to
moisten. Mix well. Turn into
greased slow cooker.

3. Cover. Cook on High 1
hour. Reduce heat to Low
and continue cooking 3-4
hours.

# Slow-Cooker Dressing

Helen King
Fairbank, IA

*Makes 10-12 servings*

14-15 cups bread cubes
3 cups chopped celery
1 1/2 cups chopped onions
1 1/2 tsp. sage
1 tsp. salt
1/2 tsp. pepper
1 1/2 cups *or more* chicken
   broth (enough to
   moisten the bread)
1/4-1 cup melted butter, *or*
   margarine (enough to
   flavor the bread)

1. Combine all ingredients
but butter. Mix well. Toss
with butter.

2. Spoon into slow cooker.
Cook on Low 4-5 hours.

# Slow Cooker Stuffing

Dede Peterson
Rapid City, SD

*Makes 10 servings*

12 cups toasted bread
   crumbs, *or* dressing mix
1 lb. bulk sausage,
   browned and drained
1/4-1 cup butter, *or*
   margarine (enough to
   flavor bread)

1 cup *or more* finely
   chopped onions
1 cup *or more* finely
   chopped celery
8-oz. can sliced
   mushrooms, with liquid
1/4 cup chopped fresh
   parsley
2 tsp. poultry seasoning
   (omit if using dressing
   mix)
dash of pepper
1/2 tsp. salt
2 eggs, beaten
4 cups chicken stock

1. Combine bread crumbs
and sausage.

2. Melt butter in skillet.
Add onions and celery and
saute until tender. Stir in
mushrooms and parsley. Add
seasonings. Pour over bread
crumbs and mix well.

3. Stir in eggs and chicken
stock.

4. Pour into slow cooker
and bake on High 1 hour, and
on Low an additional 3 hours.

**Variations:**

1. For a drier stuffing,
reduce the chicken stock to
1 1/2 cups (or 14 1/2-oz. can
chicken broth) and eliminate
the sausage.

2. For a less spicy stuffing,
reduce the poultry seasoning
to 1/2 tsp.

**Dolores Metzler**
Mechanicsburg, PA

3. Substitute 3 1/2-4 1/2 cups
cooked and diced giblets in
place of sausage. Add another
can mushrooms and 2 tsp.
sage in Step 2.

**Mrs. Don Martins**
Fairbank, IA

# Desserts

## Bread Pudding

**Winifred Ewy**, Newton, KS
**Helen King**, Fairbank, IA
**Elaine Patton**
West Middletown, PA

*Makes 6 servings*

8 slices bread (raisin bread
  is especially good),
  cubed
4 eggs
2 cups milk
¼ cup sugar
¼ cup melted butter, *or*
  margarine
½ cup raisins (use only
  ¼ cup if using raisin
  bread)
½ tsp. cinnamon

Sauce:
2 Tbsp. butter, *or*
  margarine
2 Tbsp. flour
1 cup water
¾ cup sugar
1 tsp. vanilla

1. Place bread cubes in greased slow cooker.
2. Beat together eggs and milk. Stir in sugar, butter, raisins, and cinnamon. Pour over bread and stir.
3. Cover and cook on High 1 hour. Reduce heat to Low and cook 3-4 hours, or until thermometer reaches 160°.
4. Make sauce just before pudding is done baking. Begin by melting butter in saucepan. Stir in flour until smooth. Gradually add water, sugar, and vanilla. Bring to boil. Cook, stirring constantly for 2 minutes, or until thickened.
5. Serve sauce over warm bread pudding.

**Variations:**
1. Use dried cherries instead of raisins. Use cherry flavoring in sauce instead of vanilla.
    **Char Hagnes**
    Montague, MI

2. Use ¼ tsp. ground cinnamon and ¼ tsp. ground nutmeg, instead of ½ tsp. ground cinnamon in pudding.
3. Use 8 cups day-old unfrosted cinnamon rolls instead of the bread.
    **Beatrice Orgist**
    Richardson, TX

4. Use ½ tsp. vanilla and ¼ tsp. ground nutmeg instead of ½ tsp. cinnamon.
    **Nanci Keatley**
    Salem, OR

To achieve the best volume in baked goods, always use large fresh eggs.
    **Sara Wilson**
    Blairstown, MO

# Old-Fashioned Rice Pudding

**Ann Bender**, Fort Defiance, VA
**Gladys M. High**, Ephrata, PA
**Mrs. Don Martins**, Fairbank, IA

*Makes 6 servings*

2 1/2 cups cooked rice
1 1/2 cups evaporated milk
   (or scalded milk)
2/3 cup brown, *or* white,
   sugar
3 Tbsp. soft butter
2 tsp. vanilla
1/2-1 tsp. nutmeg
3 eggs, beaten
1/2-1 cup raisins

1. Mix together all ingredients. Pour into lightly greased slow cooker.
2. Cover and cook on High 2 hours, or on Low 4-6 hours. Stir after first hour.
3. Serve warm or cold.

# Mama's Rice Pudding

**Donna Barnitz**, Jenks, OK
**Shari Jensen**, Fountain, CO

*Makes 4-6 servings*

1/2 cup white rice,
   uncooked
1/2 cup sugar
1 tsp. vanilla
1 tsp. lemon extract
1 cup plus 2 Tbsp. milk
1 tsp. butter
2 eggs, beaten
1 tsp. cinnamon
1/2 cup raisins
1 cup whipping cream,
   whipped
nutmeg

1. Combine all ingredients except whipped cream and nutmeg in slow cooker. Stir well.
2. Cover pot. Cook on Low 6-7 hours, until rice is tender and milk absorbed. Be sure to stir once every 2 hours during cooking.
3. Pour into bowl. Cover with plastic wrap and chill.
4. Before serving, fold in whipped cream and sprinkle with nutmeg.

# Ann's Rice Pudding

Ann Sunday McDowell
Newtown, PA

*Makes 6-8 servings*

1 cup uncooked, long grain
   white rice
3 cups milk
3 Tbsp. butter
1/2 tsp. salt
3/4 cup sugar
3 eggs, beaten
1/2 tsp. freshly ground
   nutmeg
1 tsp. vanilla

1. Cook rice according to package directions.
2. Mix together all ingredients in greased 1 1/2-qt. casserole dish. Cover with greased foil and set inside slow cooker. Add 1 cup water to slow cooker (around the outside of the casserole).
3. Cover and cook on High 2 hours.

Chopping dried fruit can be difficult. Make it easier by spraying your kitchen scissors with nonstick cooking spray before chopping. Fruits won't stick to the blade.
**Cyndie Marrara**
Port Matilda, PA

# Dolores' Rice Pudding

**Dolores Metzler**
Mechanicsburg, PA

*Makes 8-10 servings*

1 cup white uncooked rice
1 cup sugar
8 cups milk
3 eggs
1 1/2 cups milk
2 tsp. vanilla
1/4 tsp. salt
nutmeg, *or* cinnamon

1. In slow cooker, mix together rice, sugar, and 8 cups milk.
2. Cook on High 3 hours.
3. Beat together, eggs, 1 1/2 cups milk, vanilla, and salt. Add to slow cooker. Stir.
4. Cook on High 25-30 minutes.
5. Sprinkle with nutmeg *or* cinnamon. Serve warm.

# Custard Rice Pudding

**Iva Schmidt**
Fergus Falls, MN

*Makes 4-6 servings*

1/4 cup rice, uncooked
2 eggs
1/3 cup sugar
1/4 tsp. salt

1/2 tsp. vanilla
1 1/2 cups milk
1/3 cup raisins
nutmeg, *or* cinnamon
2 cups water

1. Cook rice according to package directions.
2. Beat together eggs, sugar, salt, vanilla, and milk. Stir in rice and raisins.
3. Put in 1-quart baking dish that will fit into your slow cooker. Sprinkle with nutmeg or cinnamon.
4. Cover with foil and set on metal trivet or a canning jar ring in bottom of slow cooker. Pour water around casserole.
5. Cover cooker. Cook on High 2-2 1/2 hours, or until set.
6. Serve warm or cold.

# Slow-Cooker Tapioca

**Nancy W. Huber**
Green Park, PA

*Makes 10-12 servings*

2 quarts milk
1 cup small pearl tapioca
1 to 1 1/2 cups sugar
4 eggs, beaten
1 tsp. vanilla
whipped cream, *or* fruit of choice, optional

1. Combine milk, tapioca, and sugar in slow cooker. Cook on High 3 hours.
2. Mix together eggs,

vanilla, and a little hot milk from slow cooker. Add to slow cooker. Cook on High 20 more minutes. Chill.
3. Serve with whipped cream or fruit.

# Tapioca Salad

**Karen Ashworth**
Duenweg, MO

*Makes 10-12 servings*

10 Tbsp. large pearl tapioca
1/2 cup sugar to taste
dash salt
4 cups water
1 cup grapes, cut in half
1 cup crushed pineapple
1 cup whipped cream

1. Mix together tapioca, sugar, salt, and water in slow cooker.
2. Cook on High 3 hours, or until tapioca pearls are almost translucent.
3. Cool thoroughly in refrigerator.
4. Stir in remaining ingredients. Serve cold.

**Variation:**
Add 1 small can mandarin oranges, drained, when adding rest of fruit.

# Blushing Apple Tapioca

**Julie Weaver**
Reinholds, PA

*Makes 8-10 servings*

8-10 tart apples
1/2 cup sugar
4 Tbsp. minute tapioca
4 Tbsp. red cinnamon
    candy
1/2 cup water
whipped topping, optional

1. Pare and core apples. Cut into eighths lengthwise and place in slow cooker.
2. Mix together sugar, tapioca, candy, and water. Pour over apples.
3. Cook on High 3- 4 hours.
4. Serve hot or cold. Top with whipped cream.

# Baked Apples with Raisins

**Vera Schmucker**
Goshen, IN
**Connie B. Weaver**
Bethlehem, PA

*Makes 6-8 servings*

6-8 medium-sized baking
    apples, cored
2 Tbsp. raisins
1/4 cup sugar
1 tsp. cinnamon
1 Tbsp. butter
1/2 cup water

1. Remove top inch of peel from each apple.
2. Mix together raisins and sugar. Spoon into center of apples.
3. Sprinkle with additional sugar and dot with butter.
4. Place apples in slow cooker. Add water. Cover and cook on Low 7-9 hours, or on High 2 1/2-3 1/2 hours.

# Raisin Nut-Stuffed Apples

**Margaret Rich**
North Newton, KS

*Makes 6 servings*

6 baking apples, cored
2 Tbsp. butter, *or*
    margarine, melted
1/4 cup packed brown sugar
3/4 cup raisins
3 Tbsp. chopped walnuts
1/2 cup water

1. Peel a strip around apple about one-third of the way below the stem end to prevent splitting.
2. Mix together butter and brown sugar. Stir in raisins and walnuts. Stuff into apple cavities.
3. Place apples in slow cooker. Add water.
4. Cover and cook on Low 6-8 hours.

"Bake" cakes in a cake pan set directly on the bottom of your slow cooker. Cover the top with 4-5 layers of paper towels to help absorb the moisture from the top of the cake. Leave the cooker lid open slightly to let extra moisture escape.

**Eleanor J. Ferreira**
North Chelmsford, MA

# Fruit/Nut Baked Apples

**Cyndie Marrara**
Port Matilda, PA

*Makes 4 servings*

4 large firm baking apples
1 Tbsp. lemon juice
1/3 cup chopped dried apricots
1/3 cup chopped walnuts, *or* pecans
3 Tbsp. packed brown sugar
1/2 tsp. cinnamon
2 Tbsp. melted butter
1/2 cup water, *or* apple juice
4 pecan halves, optional

1. Scoop out center of apples creating a cavity 1½ inches wide and stopping ½ inch from the bottom of each. Peel top of each apple down about 1 inch. Brush edges with lemon juice.
2. Mix together apricots, nuts, brown sugar, and cinnamon. Stir in butter. Spoon mixture evenly into apples.
3. Put ½ cup water or juice in bottom of slow cooker. Put 2 apples in bottom, and 2 apples above, but not squarely on top of other apples. Cover and cook on Low 1½-3 hours, or until tender.
4. Serve warm or at room temperature. Top each apple with a pecan half, if desired.

# Nut-Filled Baked Apples

**Joyce Cox**
Port Angeles, WA

*Makes 8 servings*

1 cup nuts of your choice, ground
1/4 cup (packed) brown sugar
1/2 tsp. cinnamon
1 egg, beaten
8 medium baking apples, kept whole, but cored
1 cup sugar
1/3 cup water
2 Tbsp. butter
1/2 cup water

1. Mix together nuts, brown sugar, cinnamon, and egg. Place apples on rack in large, rectangular slow cooker. Spoon nut-sugar mixture into apples until they are two-thirds full.
2. In saucepan, combine sugar, 1/3 cup water, and butter. Stir over medium heat until sugar dissolves. Pour syrup over the filling in the apples until their cavities are filled.
3. Add ½ cup water to slow cooker around apples.
4. Cover and cook on Low 8-10 hours, or on High 3-4 hours. Serve warm. Top with whipped cream, whipped topping, ice cream, or frozen yogurt, if you wish.

# Caramel Apples

**Elaine Patton**
West Middletown, PA
**Rhonda Lee Schmidt**
Scranton, PA
**Renee Shirk**
Mount Joy, PA

*Makes 4 servings*

4 very large tart apples, cored
1/2 cup apple juice
8 Tbsp. brown sugar
12 hot cinnamon candies
4 Tbsp. butter, *or* margarine
8 caramel candies
1/4 tsp. ground cinnamon
whipped cream

1. Remove ½-inch-wide strip of peel off the top of each apple and place apples in slow cooker.
2. Pour apple juice over apples.
3. Fill the center of each apple with 2 Tbsp. brown sugar, 3 hot cinnamon candies, 1 Tbsp. butter, or margarine, and 2 caramel candies. Sprinkle with cinnamon.
4. Cover and cook on Low 4-6 hours, or until tender.
5. Serve hot with whipped cream.

# Golden Fruit Compote

Cindy Krestynick
Glen Lyon, PA
**Judi Manos**
West Islip, NY

*Makes 6-8 servings*

1-lb. 13-oz. can peach, *or*
 pear, slices, undrained
1/2 cup dried apricots
1/4 cup golden raisins
1/8 tsp. cinnamon
1/8 tsp. nutmeg
3/4 cup orange juice

1. Combine undrained peach or pear slices, apricots, raisins, cinnamon, and nutmeg in slow cooker. Stir in orange juice. Completely immerse fruit in liquid.
2. Cover and cook on Low 6-8 hours.
3. Serve cold with angel food or pound cake, or ice cream. Serve warm as a side dish in the main meal.

**Variation:**

If you prefer a thicker compote, mix together 2 Tbsp. cornstarch and 1/4 cup cold water until smooth. Stir into hot fruit 15 minutes before end of cooking time. Stir until absorbed in juice.

# Fruit Compote Dessert

**Beatrice Orgish**
Richardson, TX

*Makes 8 servings*

2 medium tart apples,
 peeled
2 medium fresh peaches,
 peeled and cubed
2 cups unsweetened
 pineapple chunks
1 1/4 cups unsweetened
 pineapple juice
1/4 cup honey
2 1/4-inch thick lemon
 slices
3 1/2-inch cinnamon stick
1 medium firm banana,
 thinly sliced
whipped cream, optional
sliced almonds, optional
maraschino cherries,
 optional

1. Cut apples into 1/4-inch slices and then in half horizontally. Place in slow cooker.
2. Add peaches, pineapple, pineapple juice, honey, lemon, and cinnamon. Cover and cook on Low 3-4 hours.
3. Stir in banana slices just before serving. Garnish with whipped cream, sliced almonds, and cherries, if you wish.

# Hot Curried Fruit Compote

**Cathy Boshart**
Lebanon, PA

*Makes 12 servings*

1-lb. can peach halves
1-lb. can pear halves
1-lb. can apricot halves
1-lb. can pineapple chunks
4 medium bananas, sliced
15 maraschino cherries
1/3 cup walnut halves
1/3 cup margarine
2/3 cup brown sugar
1/2 tsp. curry powder (or to
 taste)

1. Drain fruit. Pour canned fruit into slow cooker. Add bananas.
2. Scatter cherries and walnuts on top.
3. In skillet, melt margarine. Mix in sugar and curry powder. Pour over fruit.
4. Cook on Low 2 hours.
5. Serve hot as a side dish to beef, pork, or poultry; serve warm as a dessert; or serve cold as a topping for ice cream.

# Scandinavian Fruit Soup

**Willard E. Roth**
Elkhart, IN

*Makes 12 servings*

1 cup dried apricots
1 cup dried sliced apples
1 cup dried pitted prunes
1 cup canned pitted red cherries
1/2 cup quick-cooking tapioca
1 cup grape juice, *or* red wine
3 cups water, *or* more
1/2 cup orange juice
1/4 cup lemon juice
1 Tbsp. grated orange peel
1/2 cup brown sugar

1. Combine apricots, apples, prunes, cherries, tapioca, and grape juice in slow cooker. Cover with water.
2. Cook on Low for at least 8 hours.
3. Before serving, stir in remaining ingredients.
4. Serve warm or cold, as a soup or dessert. Delicious served chilled over vanilla ice cream or frozen yogurt.

# Hot Fruit Compote

**Sue Williams**
Gulfport, MS

*Makes 4-6 servings*

1 lb. dried prunes
1 1/3 cups dried apricots
13 1/2-oz. can pineapple chunks, undrained
1-lb. can pitted dark sweet cherries, undrained
1/4 cup dry white wine
2 cups water
1 cup sugar

1. Mix together all ingredients in slow cooker.
2. Cover and cook on Low 7-8 hours, or High 3-4 hours.
3. Serve warm.

# Fruit Medley

**Angeline Lang**
Greeley, CO

*Makes 6-8 servings*

1 1/2 lbs. mixed dried fruit
2 1/2 cups water
1 cup sugar
1 Tbsp. honey
peel of half a lemon, cut into thin strips
1/8 tsp. nutmeg
1 cinnamon stick
3 Tbsp. cornstarch
1/4 cup cold water
1/4 cup Cointreau

1. Place dried fruit in slow cooker. Pour in water.
2. Stir in sugar, honey, lemon peel, nutmeg, and cinnamon.
3. Cover and cook on Low 2-3 hours. Turn cooker to High.
4. Mix cornstarch into water until smooth. Stir into fruit mixture. Cook on High 10 minutes, or until thickened.
5. Stir in Cointreau.
6. Serve warm or chilled. Serve as a side dish with the main course, as a dessert on its own, or as a topping for ice cream.

# Rhubarb Sauce

**Esther Porter**
Minneapolis, MN

*Makes 4-6 servings*

1 1/2 lbs. rhubarb
1/8 tsp. salt
1/2 cup water
1/2-2/3 cup sugar

1. Cut rhubarb into 1/2-inch slices.
2. Combine all ingredients in slow cooker. Cook on Low 4-5 hours.
3. Serve chilled.

**Variation:**
Add 1 pint sliced strawberries about 30 minutes before removing from heat.

## Strawberry Rhubarb Sauce

**Tina Snyder**
Manheim, PA

*Makes 6-8 servings*

6 cups chopped rhubarb
1 cup sugar
1 cinnamon stick
1/2 cup white grape juice
2 cups sliced strawberries

1. Place rhubarb in slow cooker. Pour sugar over rhubarb. Add cinnamon stick and grape juice. Stir well.
2. Cover and cook on Low 5-6 hours, or until rhubarb is tender.
3. Stir in strawberries. Cook 1 hour longer.
4. Remove cinnamon stick. Chill.
5. Serve over cake or ice cream.

## Old-Fashioned Rice Pudding

**Ann Bender**
Fort Defiance, VA

*Makes 6 servings*

2 1/2 cups cooked rice
1 1/2 cups whole milk
2/3 cup brown sugar
3 eggs, beaten
3 Tbsp. butter, melted
2 tsp. vanilla
1/2 tsp. ground nutmeg
1/2 tsp. ground cinnamon
1/2 cup raisins

1. Mix together all ingredients. Pour into a lightly greased slow cooker.
2. Cover and cook on High 1-2 hours, or on Low 4-6 hours. Stir once during last 30 minutes.
3. Serve warm or cold.

## Spiced Applesauce

**Judi Manos**
West Islip, NY

*Makes 6 cups*

12 cups pared, cored, thinly sliced, cooking apples
1/2 cup sugar
1/2 tsp. cinnamon
1 cup water
1 Tbsp. lemon juice
freshly grated nutmeg, optional

1. Place apples in slow cooker.
2. Combine sugar and cinnamon. Mix with apples. Stir in water and lemon juice, and nutmeg, if desired.
3. Cover. Cook on Low 5-7 hours, or High 2 1/2-3 1/2 hours.
4. Stir for a chunky sauce. Serve hot or cold.

---

Cook your favorite "Plum Pudding" recipe in a can set inside a slow cooker on a metal rack or trivet. Pour about 2 cups warm water around it. The water helps steam the pudding. Cover the can tightly with foil to keep the cake dry. Cover the cooker with its lid. Cook on High.

**Eleanor J. Ferreira**
North Chelmsford, MA

# Chunky Applesauce

**Joan Becker**
Dodge City, KS
**Rosanne Hankins**
Stevensville, MD

*Makes 8-10 servings*

**8 apples, peeled, cored,
and cut into chunks *or*
slices (6 cups)**
**1 tsp. cinnamon**
**1/2 cup water**
**1/2-1 cup sugar, *or*
cinnamon red hot
candies**

1. Combine all ingredients in slow cooker.
2. Cook on Low 8-10 hours, or High 3-4 hours.

# Applesauce

**Charmaine Caesar**
Lancaster, PA

*Makes 4 cups*

**10 medium Winesap, *or*
Golden Delicious,
cooking apples**
**1/2 cup water**
**3/4 cup sugar**
**cinnamon, optional**

1. Core, peel, and thinly slice apples.
2. Combine all ingredients in slow cooker.

3. Cover. Cook on Low 5 hours.
4. Stir until well blended. If you want a smooth sauce, put through blender or mix with a hand mixer. Cool and serve.

# Quick Yummy Peaches

**Willard E. Roth**
Elkhart, IN

*Makes 6 servings*

**1/3 cup buttermilk baking
mix**
**2/3 cup dry quick oats**
**1/2 cup brown sugar**
**1 tsp. cinnamon**
**4 cups sliced peaches
(canned *or* fresh)**
**1/2 cup peach juice, *or*
water**

1. Mix together baking mix, oats, brown sugar, and cinnamon in greased slow cooker.
2. Stir in peaches and peach juice.
3. Cook on Low for at least 5 hours. (If you like a drier cobbler, remove lid for last 15-30 minutes of cooking.)
4. Serve with frozen yogurt or ice cream.

# Scalloped Pineapples

**Shirley Hinh**
Wayland, IA

*Makes 8 servings*

**2 cups sugar**
**3 eggs**
**3/4 cup butter, melted**
**3/4 cup milk**
**1 large can crushed
pineapple, drained**
**8 slices bread (crusts
removed), cubed**

1. Mix together all ingredients in slow cooker.
2. Cook on High 2 hours. Reduce heat to Low and cook 1 more hour.
3. Delicious served as a side dish to ham or poultry, or as a dessert served warm or cold. Eat hot or chilled with vanilla ice cream or frozen yogurt.

# Black and Blue Cobbler

**Renee Shirk**
Mount Joy, PA

*Makes 6 servings*

1 cup flour
3/4 cup sugar
1 tsp. baking powder
1/4 tsp. salt
1/4 tsp. ground cinnamon
1/4 tsp. ground nutmeg
2 eggs, beaten
2 Tbsp. milk
2 Tbsp. vegetable oil
2 cups fresh, *or* frozen, blueberries
2 cups fresh, *or* frozen, blackberries
3/4 cup water
1 tsp. grated orange peel
3/4 cup sugar
whipped topping, *or* ice cream, optional

1. Combine flour, 3/4 cup sugar, baking powder, salt, cinnamon, and nutmeg.
2. Combine eggs, milk, and oil. Stir into dry ingredients until moistened.
3. Spread the batter evenly over bottom of greased 5-quart slow cooker.
4. In saucepan, combine berries, water, orange peel, and 3/4 cup sugar. Bring to boil. Remove from heat and pour over batter. Cover.
5. Cook on High 2-2 1/2 hours, or until toothpick inserted into batter comes out clean. Turn off cooker.
6. Uncover and let stand 30 minutes before serving. Spoon from cooker and serve with whipped topping or ice cream, if desired.

# Cranberry Pudding

**Margaret Wheeler**
North Bend, OR

*Makes 8-10 servings*

**Pudding:**
1 1/3 cups flour
1/2 tsp. salt
2 tsp. baking soda
1/3 cup boiling water
1/2 cup dark molasses
2 cups whole cranberries
1/2 cup chopped nuts

1/2 cup water

**Butter Sauce:**
1 cup confectioners sugar
1/2 cup heavy cream, *or* evaporated milk
1/2 cup butter
1 tsp. vanilla

1. Mix together flour and salt.
2. Dissolve soda in boiling water. Add to flour and salt.
3. Stir in molasses. Blend well.
4. Fold in cranberries and nuts.
5. Pour into well greased and floured bread or cake pan that will sit in your cooker. Cover with greased tin foil.
6. Pour 1/2 cup water into cooker. Place foil-covered pan in cooker. Cover with cooker lid and steam on High 3 to 4 hours, or until pudding tests done with a wooden pick.
7. Remove pan and uncover. Let stand 5 minutes, then unmold.
8. To make butter sauce, mix together all ingredients in saucepan. Cook, stirring over medium heat until sugar dissolves.
9. Serve warm butter sauce over warm cranberry pudding.

# Slow Cooker Pumpkin Pie Pudding

**Joette Droz**
Kalona, IA

*Makes 4-6 servings*

15-oz. can solid pack pumpkin
12-oz. can evaporated milk
3/4 cup sugar
1/2 cup buttermilk baking mix
2 eggs, beaten
2 Tbsp. melted butter, *or* margarine
1 Tbsp. pumpkin pie spice
2 tsp. vanilla
whipped cream

1. Mix together all ingredients except whipped cream. Pour into greased slow cooker.
2. Cover and cook on Low 6-7 hours, or until thermometer reads 160°.
3. Serve in bowls topped with whipped cream.

# Lemon Pudding Cake

**Jean Butzer**
Batavia, NY

---

*Makes 5-6 servings*

3 eggs, separated
1 tsp. grated lemon peel
¼ cup lemon juice
3 Tbsp. melted butter
1½ cups milk
¾ cup sugar
¼ cup flour
⅛ tsp. salt

1. Beat eggs whites until stiff peaks form. Set aside.
2. Beat eggs yolks. Blend in lemon peel, lemon juice, butter, and milk.
3. In separate bowl, combine sugar, flour, and salt. Add to egg-lemon mixture, beating until smooth.
4. Fold into beaten egg whites.
5. Spoon into slow cooker.
6. Cover and cook on High 2-3 hours.
7. Serve with spoon from cooker.

# Apple Cake

**Esther Becker**
Gordonville, PA
**Wanda S. Curtin**
Bradenton, FL

---

*Makes 8-10 servings*

2 cups sugar
1 cup oil
2 eggs
1 tsp. vanilla
2 cups chopped apples
2 cups flour
1 tsp. salt
1 tsp. baking soda
1 tsp. nutmeg
1 cup chopped walnuts, *or* pecans

1. Beat together sugar, oil, and eggs. Add vanilla.
2. Add apples. Mix well.
3. Sift together flour, salt, baking soda, and nutmeg. Add dry ingredients and nuts to apple mixture. Stir well.
4. Pour batter into greased and floured bread or cake pan that fits into your slow cooker. Cover with pan's lid, or greased tin foil. Place pan in slow cooker. Cover cooker.
5. Bake on High 3½-4 hours. Let cake stand in pan for 5 minutes after removing from slow cooker.
6. Remove cake from pan, slice, and serve.

**Variation:**
Instead of a bread or cake pan, pour batter into greased and floured 2-lb. coffee can. Cover top of can with 6 to 8 paper towels. Place can in

slow cooker. Cover cooker, tilting lid slightly to allow release of extra moisture. Continue with Step 5 above.

# Apple Peanut Crumble

**Phyllis Attig**, Reynolds, IL
**Joan Becker**, Dodge City, KS
**Pam Hochstedler**, Kalona, IA

---

*Makes 4-5 servings*

4-5 cooking apples, peeled and sliced
⅔ cup packed brown sugar
½ cup flour
½ cup quick-cooking dry oats
½ tsp. cinnamon
¼-½ tsp. nutmeg
⅓ cup butter, softened
2 Tbsp. peanut butter
ice cream, *or* whipped cream

1. Place apple slices in slow cooker.
2. Combine brown sugar, flour, oats, cinnamon, and nutmeg.
3. Cut in butter and peanut butter. Sprinkle over apples.
4. Cover cooker and cook on Low 5-6 hours.
5. Serve warm or cold, plain or with ice cream or whipped cream.

# Harvey Wallbanger Cake

**Roseann Wilson**
Albuquerque, NM

*Makes 8 servings*

Cake:
16-oz. pkg. pound cake mix
1/3 cup vanilla instant pudding (reserve rest of pudding from 3-oz. pkg. for glaze)
1/4 cup salad oil
3 eggs
2 Tbsp. Galliano liqueur
2/3 cup orange juice

Glaze:
remaining pudding mix
2/3 cup orange juice
1 Tbsp. Galliano liqueur

1. Mix together all ingredients for cake. Beat for 3 minutes. Pour batter into greased and floured bread or cake pan that will fit into your slow cooker. Cover pan.
2. Bake in covered slow cooker on High 2½-3½ hours.
3. Invert cake onto serving platter.
4. Mix together glaze ingredients. Spoon over cake.

# Cherry Delight

**Anna Musser**
Manheim, PA
**Marianne J. Troyer**
Millersburg, OH

*Makes 10-12 servings*

21-oz. can cherry pie filling
1 pkg. yellow cake mix
1/2 cup butter, melted
1/3 cup walnuts, optional

1. Place pie filling in greased slow cooker.
2. Combine dry cake mix and butter (mixture will be crumbly). Sprinkle over filling. Sprinkle with walnuts.
3. Cover and cook on Low 4 hours, or on High 2 hours.
4. Allow to cool, then serve in bowls with dips of ice cream.

**Note:**
For a less rich, less sweet dessert, use only half the cake mix and only 1/4 cup butter, melted.

# Chocolate Fondue

**Eleanor J. Ferriera**
North Chelmsford, MA

*Makes 6 servings*

1 pkg. (8 squares) semisweet chocolate
4-oz. pkg. sweet cooking chocolate
3/4 cup sweetened condensed milk
1/4 cup sugar
2 Tbsp. kirsch
fresh cherries with stems
squares of sponge cake

1. Break both chocolates into pieces and place in cooker. Set cooker to High and stir chocolate constantly until it melts.
2. Turn cooker to Low and stir in milk and sugar. Stir until thoroughly blended.
3. Stir in kirsch. Cover and cook on Low until fondue comes to a very gentle simmer.
4. Bring fondue to table, along with cherries and sponge cake squares to dip into it.

> You can use a 2-lb. coffee can, 2 1-lb. coffee cans, 3 16-oz. vegetable cans, a 6-7 cup mold, or a 1½-2-quart baking dish for "baking" cakes in a slow cooker. Leave the cooker lid slightly open to let extra moisture escape.
> **Eleanor J. Ferreira**
> North Chelmsford, MA

# Hot Fudge Cake

**Maricarol Magill**
Freehold, NJ

*Makes 6-8 servings*

1 cup packed brown sugar
1 cup flour
3 Tbsp. unsweetened cocoa
   powder
2 tsp. baking powder
1/2 tsp. salt
1/2 cup milk
2 Tbsp. melted butter
1/2 tsp. vanilla
3/4 cup packed brown sugar
1/4 cup unsweetened cocoa
   powder
13/4 cups boiling water
vanilla ice cream

1. Mix together 1 cup brown sugar, flour, 3 Tbsp. cocoa, baking powder, and salt.
2. Stir in milk, butter, and vanilla. Spread over the bottom of slow cooker.
3. Mix together 3/4 cup brown sugar and 1/4 cup cocoa. Sprinkle over mixture in slow cooker.
4. Pour in boiling water. Do not stir.
5. Cover and cook on High 2-3 hours, or until a toothpick inserted comes out clean.
6. Serve warm with vanilla ice cream.

# Self-Frosting Fudge Cake

**Mary Puterbaugh**
Elwood, IN

*Makes 8-10 servings*

2 1/2 cups of 18 1/2-oz. pkg.
   chocolate fudge pudding
   cake mix
2 eggs
3/4 cup water
3 Tbsp. oil
1/3 cup pecan halves
1/4 cup chocolate syrup
1/4 cup warm water
3 Tbsp. sugar

1. Combine cake mix, eggs, 3/4 cup water, and oil in electric mixer bowl. Beat 2 minutes.
2. Pour into greased and floured bread or cake pan that will fit into your slow cooker.
3. Sprinkle nuts over mixture.
4. Blend together chocolate syrup, 1/4 cup water, and sugar. Spoon over batter.
5. Cover. Bake on High 2-3 hours.
6. Serve warm from slow cooker.

# Chocolate Pudding Cake

**Lee Ann Hazlett**
Freeport, IL
**Della Yoder**
Kalona, IA

*Makes 10-12 servings*

18 1/2-oz. pkg. chocolate
   cake mix
3.9-oz. pkg. instant
   chocolate pudding mix
2 cups (16 oz.) sour cream
4 eggs
1 cup water
3/4 cup oil
1 cup (6 oz.) semisweet
   chocolate chips
whipped cream, *or* ice
   cream, optional

1. Combine cake mix, pudding mix, sour cream, eggs, water, and oil in electric mixer bowl. Beat on medium speed for 2 minutes. Stir in chocolate chips.
2. Pour into greased slow cooker. Cover and cook on Low 6-7 hours, or on High 3-4 hours, or until toothpick inserted near center comes out with moist crumbs.
3. Serve with whipped cream or ice cream.

# Peanut Butter and Hot Fudge Pudding Cake

**Sara Wilson**
Blairstown, MO

*Makes 6 servings*

½ cup flour
¼ cup sugar
¾ tsp. baking powder
⅓ cup milk
1 Tbsp. oil
½ tsp. vanilla
¼ cup peanut butter
½ cup sugar
3 Tbsp. unsweetened cocoa
   powder
1 cup boiling water
vanilla ice cream

1. Combine flour, ¼ cup sugar, and baking powder. Add milk, oil, and vanilla. Mix until smooth. Stir in peanut butter. Pour into slow cooker.
2. Mix together ½ cup sugar and cocoa powder. Gradually stir in boiling water. Pour mixture over batter in slow cooker. Do not stir.
3. Cover and cook on High 2-3 hours, or until toothpick inserted comes out clean.
4. Serve warm with ice cream.

# Seven Layer Bars

**Mary W. Stauffer**
Ephrata, PA

*Makes 6-8 servings*

¼ cup melted butter
½ cup graham cracker
   crumbs
½ cup chocolate chips
½ cup butterscotch chips
½ cup flaked coconut
½ cup chopped nuts
½ cup sweetened
   condensed milk

1. Layer ingredients in a bread or cake pan that fits in your slow cooker, in the order listed. Do not stir.
2. Cover and bake on High 2-3 hours, or until firm. Remove pan and uncover. Let stand 5 minutes.
3. Unmold carefully on plate and cool.

# Easy Chocolate Clusters

**Marcella Stalter**
Flanagan, IL

*Makes 3½ dozen clusters*

2 lbs. white coating
   chocolate, broken into
   small pieces
2 cups (12 oz.) semisweet
   chocolate chips
4-oz. pkg. sweet German
   chocolate
24-oz. jar roasted peanuts

1. Combine coating chocolate, chocolate chips, and German chocolate. Cover and cook on High 1 hour. Reduce heat to Low and cook 1 hour longer, or until chocolate is melted, stirring every 15 minutes.
2. Stir in peanuts. Mix well.
3. Drop by teaspoonfuls onto waxed paper. Let stand until set. Store at room temperature.

# Beverages

## Apple-Honey Tea

**Jeanne Allen**
Rye, CO

*Makes 6 1-cup servings*

12-oz. can frozen apple
   juice/cider concentrate
2 Tbsp. instant tea powder
1 Tbsp. honey
1/2 tsp. ground cinnamon

1. Reconstitute the apple
juice/cider concentrate
according to package directions. Pour into slow cooker.

2. Add tea powder, honey,
and cinnamon. Stir to blend.

3. Heat on Low 1-2 hours.
Stir well before serving since
cinnamon tends to settle on
bottom.

## Hot Mulled Cider

**Phyllis Attig**, Reynolds, IL
**Jean Butzer**, Batavia, NY
**Doris G. Herr**, Manheim, PA
**Mary E. Martin**, Goshen, IN
**Leona Miller**, Millersburg, OH
**Marjora Miller**, Archbold, OH
**Janet L. Roggie**, Lowville, NY
**Shirley Sears**, Tiskilwa, IL
**Charlotte Shaffer**, East Earl, PA
**Berenice M. Wagner**
Dodge City, KS
**Connie B. Weaver**
Bethlehem, PA
**Maryann Westerberg**
Rosamond, CA
**Carole Whaling**, New Tripoli, PA

*Makes 8 1-cup servings*

1/4-1/2 cup brown sugar
2 quarts apple cider
1 tsp. whole allspice
1 1/2 tsp. whole cloves
2 cinnamon sticks
2 oranges sliced, with peels
   on

1. Combine brown sugar
and cider in slow cooker.

2. Put spices in tea strainer
or tie in cheesecloth. Add to
slow cooker. Stir in orange
slices.

3. Cover and simmer on
Low 2-8 hours.

**Variation:**

Add a dash of ground nut-
meg and salt.

**Marsha Sabus**
Fallbrook, CA

251

# Autumn Sipper
### -- Shari Jensen
Fountain, CO

*Makes 8 1-cup servings*

1 Tbsp. whole allspice
3 3-inch cinnamon sticks
2 whole cloves
1 piece each lemon and
  orange peel, each about
  the size of a half dollar
1 piece crystallized ginger,
  about the size of a
  quarter
3 cups apricot nectar
5 cups apple juice
cinnamon sticks and
  orange slices, optional

1. Place spices, citrus
peels, and ginger in a cheesecloth or coffee filter. Tie
securely. Place in bottom of
slow cooker.
2. Pour in apple juice and
nectar. Cover.
3. Cook on High 1 hour,
then on Low 3 hours.
4. Garnish filled glasses
with cinnamon sticks and
orange slices.

# Hot Mulled Apple Tea
### Barbara Tenney
Delta, PA

*Makes 16 1-cup servings*

½ gallon apple cider
½ gallon strong tea
1 sliced lemon
1 sliced orange
3 3-inch cinnamon sticks
1 Tbsp. whole cloves
1 Tbsp. allspice
brown sugar to taste

1. Combine all in slow
cooker.
2. Heat on Low 2 hours.

# Spiced Apple Cider
### Janice Muller
Derwood, MD

*Makes 18-20 servings*

2 sticks cinnamon
1 cup orange juice
1 tsp. cinnamon
1 tsp. ground cloves
¼ cup lemon juice
2 tsp. whole cloves
1 gallon apple cider
2 tsp. ground nutmeg
½ cup pineapple juice
1 tsp. ginger
1 tsp. lemon peel
1 cup sugar

1. Mix all ingredients in 6-
quart slow cooker.
2. Simmer on Low 4-6
hours.

# Yummy Hot Cider
### Char Hagner
Montague, MI

*Makes 10-11 1-cup servings*

3 3-inch sticks cinnamon
2 tsp. whole cloves
1 tsp. whole nutmeg, *or*
  ½ tsp. ground nutmeg
½ gallon apple cider
1 cup sugar
2 cups orange juice
½ cup lemon juice

1. Tie spices in cheesecloth
or tea strainer and place in
slow cooker.
2. Add apple cider and
sugar, stirring well.
3. Cover. Simmer on Low
1 hour. Remove spices and
stir in orange juice and lemon
juice. Continue heating 1
more hour. Serve cider from
cooker, set on Low.

# Great Mulled Cider

**Charlotte Shaffer**
East Earl, PA
**Barbara Sparks**
Glen Burnie, MD

*Makes 8-10 1-cup servings*

**2 qts. apple cider**
**½ cup frozen orange juice concentrate**
**½ cup brown sugar**
**½ tsp. ground allspice, *or* 1 tsp. whole allspice**
**1½ tsp. whole cloves**
**2 cinnamon sticks**
**orange slices**

1. Tie all whole spices in cheesecloth bag, then combine all ingredients in slow cooker.
2. Cover and simmer on Low 3 hours.

# Hot Spiced Cider

**Elva Evers**
North English, IA

*Makes 6 1-cup servings*

**12-oz. can frozen apple juice**
**3 3-inch cinnamon sticks**
**6 whole cloves**

1. Combine all ingredients in slow cooker.
2. Cover and simmer on Low 4 hours.
3. Remove cinnamon and cloves before serving.

**Variation:**
Omit the cinnamon and cloves. Use ¼ cup fresh or dried mint tea leaves instead.

# Spiced Cider

**Mary Puterbaugh**
Elwood, IN

*Makes 12 1-cup servings*

**12 whole cloves**
**½ gallon apple cider**
**⅔ cup red hot candies**
**¼ cup dry orange drink mix**
**1 qt. water**

1. Place cloves in cheesecloth bag or tea ball.
2. Combine all ingredients in slow cooker.

3. Cover. Cook on Low 3-4 hours.
4. Serve hot from cooker during fall, or on Halloween.

# Hot Wassail Drink

**Dale Peterson**
Rapid City, SC

*Makes 24-27 1-cup servings*

**12-oz. can frozen orange juice**
**12-oz. can frozen lemonade**
**2 qts. apple juice**
**2 cups sugar, *or* less**
**3 Tbsp. whole cloves**
**2 tbsp. ground ginger**
**4 tsp. ground cinnamon**
**10 cups hot water**
**6 cups strong tea**

1. Mix juices, sugar, and spices in slow cooker.
2. Add hot water and tea.
3. Heat on High until Hot (1-2 hours), then on Low while serving.

# Holiday Wassail

**Dolores S. Kratz**
Souderton, PA

*Makes 8 1-cup servings*

16-oz. can apricot halves,
  undrained
4 cups unsweetened
  pineapple juice
2 cups apple cider
1 cup orange juice
18 whole cloves
6 3½-inch cinnamon
  sticks, broken

1. In blender or food
processor, blend apricots and
liquid until smooth.

2. Place cloves and cinnamon sticks in cheesecloth
bag.

3. Put all ingredients in
slow cooker. Cook on Low 3-
4 hours. Serve hot.

# Hot Cider

**Ilene Bontrager**
Arlington, KS

*Makes 18-20 1-cup servings*

1 gallon cider
1 qt. cranberry juice
5-6 cinnamon sticks
2 tsp. whole cloves
½ tsp. ginger
1 whole orange, sliced

1. Combine cider and
cranberry juice in slow
cooker.

2. Place cinnamon sticks
and cloves in cheesecloth bag
and add to slow cooker. Stir
in ginger.

3. Heat on High 5-6 hours.

4. Float orange slices on
top before serving.

# Wassail

**John D. Allen**, Rye, CO
**Susan Yoder Graber**
Eureka, IL
**Jan Pembleton**, Arlington, TX

*Makes 12 1-cup servings*

2 qts. cider
1 pint cranberry juice
⅓-⅔ cup sugar
1 tsp. aromatic bitters
2 sticks cinnamon
1 tsp. whole allspice
1 small orange, studded
  with whole coves
1 cup rum, optional

1. Put all ingredients into
cooker. Cover and cook on
High 1 hour, then on Low 4-8
hours.

2. Serve warm from
cooker.

**Note:**

If the wassail turns out to
be too sweet for you, add
more cranberry juice until
you find the flavor balance to
be more pleasing.

# Holiday Spice
Punch

**Maryland Massey**
Millington, MD

*Makes 10 1-cup servings*

2 qts. apple cider
2 cups cranberry juice
2 Tbsp. mixed whole
  spices — allspice, cloves,
  coriander, and ginger
2 3-inch cinnamon sticks,
  broken
lemon, *or* orange, slices
studded with whole
cloves

1. Pour cider and juice into
slow cooker. Place mixed
spices in muslin bag or tea
ball. Add to juice.

2. Cover and simmer on
Low 2 hours.

3. Float cinnamon sticks
and fruit slices in individual
mugs as you serve.

# Hot Cranberry-Apple Punch

**Barbara Sparks**
Glen Burnie, MD
**Shirley Thieszen**
Larkin, KS

*Makes 10-11 1-cup servings*

4½ cups cranberry juice
6 cups apple juice
¼ cup + 1 Tbsp. brown
  sugar
¼ tsp. salt
3 cinnamon sticks
1 tsp. whole cloves

1. Pour juices into slow cooker. Mix in brown sugar and salt. Stir until sugar is dissolved.
2. Tie cinnamon sticks and cloves in cheesecloth and drop into liquid.
3. Cover. Simmer on High 2 hours. Remove spice bag. Keep warm on Low.

# Hot Cranberry Tea

**Sherrill Bieberly**
Salina, KS

*Makes 14 1-cup servings*

1 cup sugar
2 qts. water
3 cinnamon sticks
1 qt. cranberry juice
6-oz. can frozen orange
  juice

1¼ cups water
3 Tbsp. lemon juice
fresh lemon and/or orange
  slices

1. In saucepan, mix together sugar, 2 quarts water, and cinnamon sticks. Bring to boil.
2. Pour into slow cooker along with remaining ingredients. Cover and cook on High 1 hour. Turn to Low. Serve warm.

# Josie's
# Hot Cranberry
# Punch

**Josie Bollman**
Maumee, OH

*Makes 6 1-cup servings*

32-oz. bottle cranberry
  juice
2 sticks cinnamon
6-oz. can frozen lemonade
12-oz. can frozen orange
  juice

1. Mix together all ingredients in slow cooker.
2. Cook on High 3-4 hours.

# Spiced Wassail

**Dorothy Horst**
Tiskilwa, IL

*Makes 10-11 1-cup servings*

2 32-oz. jars cranberry
  juice
2 cups water
6-oz. can frozen orange
  juice concentrate
3 3-inch cinnamon sticks
3 whole cloves

1. Combine all ingredients in 5-quart slow cooker.
2. Cover and cook on Low 2-8 hours.

**Variation:**
Use small candy canes as stir sticks in individual cups during the holiday season.

**Note:**
This is a refreshing cold drink to serve over ice on a hot day.

# Hot Cranberry Punch

**Marianne Troyer**
Millersburg, OH

*Makes 13-14 1-cup servings*

2 qts. hot water
1½ cups sugar
1 qt. cranberry juice
¾ cup orange juice
¼ cup lemon juice
12 whole cloves, optional
½ cup red hot candies

1. Combine water, sugar, and juices. Stir until sugar is dissolved.
2. Place cloves in double thickness of cheesecloth and tie with string. Add to slow cooker.
3. Add cinnamon candies.
4. Cover and Cook on Low 2-3 hours, or until heated thoroughly.
5. Remove spice bag before serving.

# Hot Spicy Lemonade Punch

**Mary E. Herr**
**The Hermitage**
Three Rivers, MI

*Makes 9-10 1-cup servings*

4 cups cranberry juice
⅓-⅔ cup sugar
12-oz. can lemonade concentrate, thawed
4 cups water
1-2 Tbsp. honey
6 whole cloves
2 cinnamon sticks, broken
1 lemon, sliced

1. Combine juice, sugar, lemonade, water, and honey in slow cooker.
2. Tie cloves and cinnamon in small cheesecloth square. Add spice bag and lemon slices to slow cooker.
3. Cover and cook on Low 3-4 hours. Remove spice bag. Keep hot in slow cooker until ready to serve.

# Hot Fruit Punch

**Karen Stoltzfus**
Alto, MI

*Makes 10 1-cup servings*

1 qt. cranberry juice
3 cups water
6-oz. can frozen orange juice concentrate, thawed
10-oz. pkg. frozen red raspberries, thawed
2 oranges, sliced
6 sticks cinnamon
12 whole allspice

1. Combine all ingredients in slow cooker.
2. Heat on High 1 hour, or until hot. Turn to Low while serving.

# Punch

**Kathy Hertzler**
Lancaster, PA

*Makes 12 1-cup servings*

1 tsp. whole cloves
5 cups pineapple juice
5 cups cranberry juice
2¼ cups water
½ cup brown sugar
2 cinnamon sticks
¼ tsp. salt

1. Place cloves in small cheesecloth bag or tea ball.
2. Mix together all ingredients in slow cooker.
3. Cook on Low 6 hours. Remove cloves. Serve hot.

# Wine-Cranberry Punch

**C. J. Slagle**
Roann, IN

*Makes 8 1-cup servings*

1 pint cranberry juice
   cocktail
1 cup water
¾ cup sugar
2 sticks cinnamon
6 whole cloves
4/5 qt. burgundy wine
1 lemon, sliced thin

1. Combine ingredients in slow cooker.

2. Heat on Low 1-2 hours. Strain and serve hot.
3. Keep hot and serve from slow cooker set on lowest setting.

# Hot Cranberry Punch

**Barbara Aston**
Ashdown, AR

*Makes 10 1-cup servings*

2 16-oz. cans jellied
   cranberry sauce
2 qts. water
2 cups frozen orange juice
   concentrate
1 qt. pineapple juice,
   optional
half a stick of butter
¾ cup firmly packed
   brown sugar
½ tsp. ground cinnamon
½ tsp. ground allspice
¼ tsp. ground cloves
¼ tsp. ground nutmeg
¼ tsp. salt

1. Mix together all ingredients.
2. Heat on High until boiling, then reduce to Low for 4 hours. Serve hot.

# Kate's Mulled Cider / Wine

**Mitzi McGlynchey**
Downingtown, PA

*Makes 8-10 1-cup servings*

½ tsp. whole cloves
½ tsp. whole allspice
½ gallon apple cider, *or*
   red burgundy wine
2 3-inch cinnamon sticks
1 tsp. ground nutmeg
orange slices, optional
cinnamon sticks, optional

1. Place cloves and allspice in cheesecloth bag or tea ball.
2. Combine spices, apple cider or wine, 2 cinnamon sticks, and nutmeg in slow cooker.
3. Cook on High 1 hour. Reduce heat, and simmer 2-3 hours.
4. Garnish individual servings with orange slices or cinnamon sticks.

# Mulled Wine

**Julie McKenzie**
Punxsutawney, PA

---

*Makes 8 1-cup servings*

1/2 cup sugar
1 1/2 cups boiling water
half a lemon, sliced thin
3 cinnamon sticks
3 whole cloves
1 bottle red dinner wine
    (burgundy *or* claret)

1. Dissolve sugar in boiling water in saucepan.
2. Add remaining ingredients.
3. Pour into slow cooker. Heat on Low for at least 1 hour, until wine is hot. Do not boil.
4. Serve from cooker into mugs.

# Almond Tea

**Frances Schrag**
Newton, KS

---

*Makes 12 1-cup servings*

10 cups boiling water
1 Tbsp. instant tea
2/3 cup lemon juice
1 cup sugar
1 tsp. vanilla
1 tsp. almond extract

1. Mix together all ingredients in slow cooker.

2. Turn to High and heat thoroughly (about 1 hour). Turn to Low while serving.

# Carolers Hot Chocolate

**Pat Unternahrer**
Wayland, IA

---

*Makes 12-14 1-cup servings*

10 cups milk
3/4 cup sugar
3/4 cup cocoa, *or* hot chocolate mix
1/2 tsp. salt
2 cups hot water
marshmallows

1. Measure milk into slow cooker. Turn on High.
2. Mix together sugar, salt, and cocoa in heavy pan. Add hot water. Stir and boil 3 minutes, stirring often.
3. Pour into milk. Cook on High 2-2 1/2 hours.

# Home-Style Tomato Juice

**Jean Butzer**
Batavia, NY

---

*Makes 4-5 1-cup servings*

10-12 large tomatoes
1 tsp. salt
1 tsp. seasoned salt
1/4 tsp. pepper
1 Tbsp. sugar

1. Wash and drain tomatoes. Remove cores and blossom ends. Place in slow cooker.
2. Cover and cook on Low 4-6 hours, or until tomatoes are soft.
3. Press through sieve or food mill.
4. Stir in seasonings. Chill.

# Index

# Index

# Index

# About the Authors

Dawn J. Ranck has been a convinced slow-cooker user for years. She, along with her many friends, have been lining up their various-sized cookers on their kitchen counters before they set off each morning—and coming home to richly flavored full dinners.

Ranck , who lives in Harrisonburg, Virginia, is the co-author of *A Quilter's Christmas Cookbook* and *Favorite Recipes with Herbs*.

Phyllis Pellman Good has been part of many cookbook projects, authoring **The Best of Amish Cooking** and **The Festival Cookbook**, and co-authoring **Recipes from Central Market, Favorite Recipes with Herbs, The Best of Mennonite Fellowship Meals,** and **From Amish and Mennonite Kitchens.**

Good and her husband, Merle, live in Lancaster, Pennsylvania, and are co-directors of The People's Place, a heritage interpretation center in the Lancaster County village of Intercourse, Pennsylvania.